Administrations
of Lunacy

Administrations of Lunacy

Racism and the Haunting of
American Psychiatry at
the Milledgeville Asylum

MAB SEGREST

THE
NEW
PRESS

NEW YORK
LONDON

Requests for permission to reproduce selections from this book should be made through our
website: https://thenewpress.com/contact.

Published in the United States by The New Press, New York, 2020
Distributed by Two Rivers Distribution

ISBN 978-1-62097-298-4 (ebook)

LIBRARY OF CONGRESS CATALOGING-IN-PUBLICATION DATA

Names: Segrest, Mab, 1949- author.
Title: Administrations of lunacy : racism and the haunting of American psychiatry
at the Milledgeville Asylum / Mab Segrest.
Description: New York : The New Press, 2020. | Includes bibliographical references and
index. | Summary: "A look at the racist origins of psychiatry, through the story of the
largest mental institution in the world"—Provided by publisher.
Identifiers: LCCN 2019048361 | ISBN 9781620972977 (hardback)
Subjects: LCSH: Central State Hospital (Milledgeville, Ga.)—History. | Psychiatric
hospitals—Georgia—Milledgeville—History. | Psychiatry and racism—Georgia—
Milledgeville—History. | Racism—Georgia—Milledgeville—History.
Classification: LCC RA982.M552 C467 2020 | DDC 362.2/109758573—dc23
LC record available at https://lccn.loc.gov/2019048361

The New Press publishes books that promote and enrich public discussion and understanding
of the issues vital to our democracy and to a more equitable world. These books are
made possible by the enthusiasm of our readers; the support of a committed group of
donors, large and small; the collaboration of our many partners in the independent media
and the not-for-profit sector; booksellers, who often hand-sell New Press books;
librarians; and above all by our authors.

www.thenewpress.com

Composition by Westchester Publishing Services
This book was set in Adobe Caslon Pro

Printed in the United States of America

2 4 6 8 10 9 7 5 3 1

For
Annie Elizabeth Culbertson-Jolly Segrest

In one particular alone does lunacy administration in the South differ from the same problem elsewhere in the country. What the race problem is to our whole section, so is the question of the colored insane to our speciality [*sic*].

—Superintendent T.O. Powell, Georgia Lunatic Asylum, 1898[1]

Rows upon rows of numbered, small, rusted markers as far as you can see. . . . It must be the most gruesome sight in Georgia. Unknown humans, shunned when living, deprived of their very names in death—and literally known only to God. They were the unwanted of society, the throwaways. Nobody cared if they had markers. We knew that they could have been us. It was devastating.

—Joe Ingram, 1940s hospital staff[2]

Slavery broke the world in half, it broke it in every way. It broke Europe. They had to dehumanize, not just the slaves but themselves. They have had to reconstruct everything in order to make the system appear true. It made them into something else, it made them slave masters, it made them crazy.

—Toni Morrison, "Living Memory"[3]

No pseudo-rational mystification finds grace when up against the demand to think.

—Frantz Fanon, "Letter to the Resident Ministry"[4]

A patient who could get well here could get well as easily in the Okefenokee Swamp.

—patient observation about Milledgeville State Hospital, 1940s

Contents

Georgia on My Mind

My mother joined me up long ago in the United Daughters of the Confederacy, and I have spent my entire adult life dis-uniting. A quarter of a century ago, I published *Memoir of a Race Traitor*, which I explained in its foreword was a "treatise on the souls of white folks." In it I used my reflections on my own white southern family and the documentation that I helped to amass while fighting the Klan and neo-Nazi movements in North Carolina that were, in the 1980s, the worst in the United States. "What therapist would tell us to read history?" I pondered, writing across the gaps of "the intimate and the historic, action and reflection," and the gaps between my distant cousin Marvin Segrest and Sammy Younge, the civil rights worker he shot to death in my hometown of Tuskegee.[1] Twenty-five years later, *Memoir of a Race Traitor* emerges in a new edition, along with this book. Here also I am reading history in order to understand again the relationship between the "intimate and the historic, action and reflection"—this time through the story of an infamous southern state mental hospital, the Georgia State Lunatic, Idiot, and Epileptic Asylum—subsequently called the Georgia Sanitarium, Milledgeville State Hospital, and, most recently, Central State Hospital.

As a longtime scholar and a social justice activist on issues of gender, race, and class in the U.S. South, I found the questions of "southern insanity" embedded in the Milledgeville archives compelling. Given the variety of white southern family dysfunctions and what I had come to understand about the profound illogic of slavery and racism, "southern insanity" seemed redundant. Over a decade ago, as I was drawn into the Georgia archives, I asked myself a generative question: How does a state that conquered native peoples, innovated and administered the system of chattel slavery for Africans, encouraged or refused to stop the atrocities of lynching, and developed Jim Crow—how could *that* state (be it Georgia or the United

States) decide who was and was not sane? And how did national policies hold that southern system in place? Not the *why* of it, which might be easily answered with words like "greed" and "social control" and "power"— but *how*?

This book works to capture how those larger historical forces shaped what Michel Servan termed the "soft fibers of our brains" on which empires are founded" in these state institutions that determined who was sane, normal, healthy, and free.[2] We struggle with these questions today, and in many cases we do so in the same terms as we have for centuries. How can we break that hold?

Another reason for my commitment to Milledgeville is that when I was in my thirties my Aunt May Segrest revealed to me the family secret that in 1902 my great-grandfather Charles Bosch Segrest died in Alabama's Bryce State Hospital. May said he began seeing people shooting at him from the trees and started shooting back. Charles Segrest died of a cellulitis infection on his face within six months of entering Bryce. These events, my Aunt May informed me, explained *all* of our Segrest family "issues" because of the shame that she and my father carried as children of a family member declared crazy and committed to a "loony bin." She speculated that her grandfather's hallucinations were caused by PTSD resulting from his experience as a foot soldier in Gen. Robert E. Lee's Army of Northern Virginia during the Civil War, where the rivers ran red with soldiers' blood, and then from his long walk back home to Macon County and Alabama's "Big Hungry," what my aunt called the period of starvation after the Civil War ended. Or perhaps, she speculated, Charles Segrest's actions in response to actors unseen by his family were caused by pellagra, a new scourge sweeping the South in the early twentieth century. In other words, Aunt May understood that our most intimate family legacies were shaped by Alabama's state mental hospital. So, my Aunt May Segrest and Confederate veteran Charles Segrest walk these pages.

As an ardent lover of modern southern literature, I soon found the asylum popping up across a range of literary landscapes, where it had been hidden in plain sight. For example, it was all over Tennessee Williams. "I have always depended on the kindness of [psychiatric] strangers," is Blanche DuBois' elegiac last sentence in Williams' *A Streetcar Named Desire*, published in 1947. She speaks the line to the doctor in the white coat who comes to take her to the state asylum, to which her sister, Stella, and brother-in-law, Stanley, commit her after Stanley rapes her. "Cut that story out of her brain!" Violet Venable exclaims in *Suddenly Last Summer* about how a lobotomy might keep her niece from spilling family secrets. The play opened on Broadway in 1958, three years before Michel Foucault's 1961 *Folie et Déraison* was published in France, then three years later in English as *Madness and Civilization*. Ken Kesey's *One Flew Over the Cuckoo's Nest* was published as a book, then later made into a film, in the early 1960s as well. The creative chorus to the discredited asylum was by then full-throated. But the anti-asylum critique had not started with Kesey or Foucault. It was there in southerners' writing, like seismographs from the region's tectonic shifts.

Consider other examples. William Faulkner's adolescent character Vardamon Bundren muses at the end of *As I Lay Dying*, "Jackson is farther than crazy," after his father commits his brother Darl to Jackson, the location of Mississippi's state hospital. Darl had burned down a farmer's barn to cremate his mother, whose ripening corpse, to Darl, had become a desecration. Also, Faulkner's *The Sound and the Fury* is haunted by the specter of the "idiot" brother Benjy Compson, who was sent to Jackson in spite of the care labor of both the African Americans living on Compson land and Benjy's siblings, Caddy and Quentin Compson. The novel's opening monologue from Benjy's consciousness begins the modern American novel.

For Harper Lee in Alabama, Boo Radley's ghost-like presence in *To Kill a Mockingbird* also haunts the siblings, Scout and Jem. Boo's father had kept him locked at home so as to not suffer the stigma (as the Segrest family did) of having a family member marked by institutionalization or the family degeneracy it implied—until Boo emerges from his haunted house to rescue the two siblings from the clutches of a white rapist. Because of Atticus Finch, *Mockingbird* became America's favorite book. But for me, Boo Radley was its real hero.

In the works of my favorite Georgia writers—Lillian Smith, Carson McCullers, Alice Walker, and Flannery O'Connor—the possibility and consequences of "being dragged off to Milledgeville" were written very large. McCullers' threat, put into the mouth of Berenice Sadie Brown to her young white charge Frankie Addams, resonated throughout my childhood; those blue police might "come round here, tie you up, and drag you off to Milledgeville" (or Bryce, or Jackson, or fill in your state's asylum town).[3] Flannery O'Connor found herself in Milledgeville in the 1950s, an invalid with lupus stuck with her mother, Regina, and writing at the ground zero of southern psychiatry as she helped to shape the literary version of the southern grotesque. All of these books are also steeped in what Lillian Smith called "the dream, and the killers of the dream": the legacies of slavery and racism in the United States that still haunt the landscapes.

I myself have never been committed to a psychiatric institution or diagnosed with a category from the American Psychiatric Association's *Diagnostic and Statistical Manual (DSM)*. This work does not arise out of that lived experience. Yet when I read these authors, the threat of being "dragged off" to a state asylum, whatever its locale, resonated for me as an adolescent. In the 1950s, children growing up in apartheid Alabama would threaten each other with Bryce, Alabama's state hospital, half as a joke, none of it funny. (It turned out to be the same institution in which my great-grandfather died.) In the 1970s, I came to realize that as a lesbian I was diagnosable under DSM, a felon under North Carolina sodomy laws, and a sinner under most Christian denominations. Almost half a century later, I've beaten the rap on at least two out of three of these homophobic strictures, for the time anyway. But not everyone has escaped these charges. And I have learned repeatedly how these libels against homosexuals are always underwritten by older codes and practices of white supremacy, misogyny, and slavery.

A Note About Language

My subject in *Administrations of Lunacy* is the institution whose original name was the Georgia State Lunatic, Idiot, and Epileptic Asylum. Today, two out of three of those designations are odious labels for the forms of perceived difference that landed certain Georgians in Milledgeville. The issue of nomenclature resonates as well across the racial categories by which white supremacy and U.S. racism were shaped, as enslaved Africans and various Indigenous tribes were named by white settlers in ways that positioned them for slavery and attempts at extinction, respectively.

Take, for example, the term "Creek Indians." That name itself, as chapter 3 examines, emerged at a convergence of Indigenous, colonial, and imperial narratives. In the early eighteenth century, as historian Joel W. Martin explains, South Carolina traders were calling Indians living on Ochese Creek near Macon, Georgia, by the shorthand of "Creeks" because they lived along rivers and streams. White traders spread the name gradually and applied it to all of the ten thousand Indigenous people across the Southeast. Martin explains, it was "not simply a name of English origin but an English synecdoche, a figure of speech in which a part stands for the whole." In other words, the stream on which one or more tribes lived came to stand in for any Indigenous person in the Southeast. Synecdoche commonly occurs in situations of cultural contact, as Martin explains. But in this instance, it had lethal results because in the settler mind the geographical term "Creek" made all the native people it referenced a unified "nation," any member of which could be held accountable for any individual acts carried out by others living along creeks, providing convenient reasons for their removal or extinction—whichever was required to get their land. These various southeastern tribes at times called their alliance "Muscogee," from the most frequently used language. That is the name most often used by contemporary historians respectful of Indigenous cultures to name the people and their land base, which stretched across what became the states of Alabama and Georgia.[4] United States poet laureate Joy Harjo's recent poetry volume *American Sunrise* narrates her return from Oklahoma to her people's territory in Alabama/Georgia; Harjo, spells the term "Mvskoke" in a book immersed in the knowledge (as this one is) that history will always "wrap you in its arms."[5]

Official designations of "negro," "colored," and "mulatto" in archival sources of U.S. census records let us know the official or personal mind-set of the user of a particular historical period. When official sources used "negro," African Americans of the period insist on its capitalization, "Negro." In this text, contemporary self-designations of African American and Black circulate with designations from earlier periods when they denote the attitudes of the times. I choose to capitalize Black, and leave white in lower case.

The fate of Georgians diagnosed as "idiots" is examined in chapter 4 (Nancy Malone) and chapter 16 (Dora Williams and Carrie Buck). From the institution's founding through Dora Williams admission in the 1910s, "idiot" was the term used for what we now call cognitive, intellectual, or developmental disability. In the 1910s, the development of IQ tests distributed these differences across levels of measured intelligence, with "feeble-minded" encompassing "idiots," "morons," and "imbeciles." These terms were the inventions of the eugenics movement and its vanguard at its Cold Spring Harbor headquarters on New York's Long Island. Such tests and terminology, devised by academics in the nation's premier universities, helped to prepare the U.S. population for the policies of sterilization that were instituted in America's sanitariums and state mental hospitals and its new institutions for the "feeble-minded, such as Gracewood in Georgia. They also contributed to the mass extermination of disabled people in Nazi Germany in the Aktion T-4 Program in 1939, traced in the epilogue.

These terms (moron, imbecile, idiot) were used as epithets and eventually gained enough opprobrium for professionals to devise new terms, such as "mental defective," "feeble-minded," and "handicapped." In 1914, "mental retardation" entered the lexicon. In 1975, under pressure from a new disability movement, "developmental disability" became standard. Now cognitive, intellectual, and developmental disability are used interchangeably. Today, people who were once labeled "idiot" or "feeble-minded" might include someone with Down syndrome, autism, ADHD, traumatic brain injury, or any number of learning disabilities. Or, they are part of the "neurotribes," with a range of cognitive abilities beyond the insults, the injuries, and the lies that uphold them.

But, as disability historian James Trent says, behind these evolving terms, "the gaze we turn on those we label mentally retarded continues to be informed by the long history of condescension, suspicion, and exclusion. That history is unavoidably manifest in the words we now find offensive."[6] That is why Trent chooses to use the words that we now find offensive, as appropriate to the historical context—a practice this book follows—but I use a mixed vernacular in a sentence or paragraph when a more contemporary and self-chosen term illuminates the limits of historical categories.

"Lunatic," one-third of the original triumvirate at the Georgia Asylum, represented categories for what we now call "mental illness," with a plethora of hurtful colloquialisms that we still hear today; the antonym, or opposite, of all of them is "sane," which I intend to keep in circulation as an antidote and an anchor for best practices or ecologies.[7] As I trace in this book's last part, "Jim Crowed Psychiatric Modernity," a new set of diagnostic categories compiled in Germany by Emil Kraepelin began to be applied in Milledgeville in 1910. It displaced a former list of "causes of insanity" that mixed willy-nilly presenting symptoms, underlying causes, and categorized individuals. In the late nineteenth century, the new diagnostics gave a modern, scientific patina to descriptions of human behavior that the state and people in families, counties, and communities found to be destructive to self and to others, and/or outside the norms. This set of characteristics became the basis of the American Psychiatric Association's *Diagnostic and Statistical Manual*, begun in 1952 and now in its fifth edition. More recently, the shift from "mental health and substance abuse" to "behavioral health" signals new tectonic shifts in a highly mobile field. DSM-5's arrival in 2013 marked the collapse of "neo-Kraepelian" diagnostics (which is to say, those categories systematized by Emil Kraepelin at the turn of the century) when the method was repudiated by the National Institute for Mental Health as being insufficiently scientific to serve as a basis for its research.

Nor have I found among disability activists the tolerance for words like "crazy" that people in sexual and gender minority communities have established for "queer." I generally avoid it but do quote literary authors whose vernacular use of the term brings insight—such as W.B. Yeats' "Crazy Jane and the Bishop," or Toni Morrison's vernacular use when she explains how "racism made us crazy."

This range of terms that replace the asylum's designation of "Lunatic" is part of historic processes in what we have come to call the social construction of insanity, a context in which our Superintendent Powell noted in 1888 as the "shifting boundary lines of sanity." In this book, shifting boundary lines of social constructs play with and against the biological causes of human behavior and emotion. These ideological struggles over heredity and environment fill these pages and reach across centuries. Here neither predominates or eliminates the other. In these pages, mental illness is real and its causes are complex. This book is neither anti-psychiatric nor against psychiatric medications. It does explore deep historical contradictions in both psychiatry and the broader field of medicine in order to distinguish worst and best practices and treatments.

Today, as historian of medicine Anne Harrington details, medical research on the placebo effect of psychiatric drugs led in 2013 to the National Institute of Mental Health's repudiation of DSM-5.[8] This and the "Decade of the Brain" research in the 1990s signaled a major shift away from the "Second Biological Revolution" in the field of psychiatry, a juncture whose dangers and opportunities we will explore. My eventual formulation of "ecologies of sanity" and "afterlives of slavery" is my attempt to name the contemporary effects of white supremacy and to provide a framework with which to get underneath the binary oppositions of heredity and environment so as to think clearly about the fates of mindbodies always in the world.

INTRODUCTION

Administrations of Lunacy

Administrations of Lunacy: Racism and the Haunting of American Psychiatry at the Milledgeville Asylum is based on the 170-year arc of Georgia's infamous state mental hospital that in 1842 opened its doors in the town of Milledgeville. In the 1940s and 1950s, at its apogee, it was the largest state hospital in the world, with the largest graveyard of disabled people—25,000 numbered grave markers reaching into the woods. In 1948, journalist Albert Deutsch in his exposé on state mental hospitals proclaimed it one of the most shameful of such institutions in the nation. In 1949, *Ebony* declared it the equivalent of a Nazi concentration camp or "the lower levels of Dante's Inferno" for African Americans. And historian Edward Shorter considered it "American [asylum] psychiatry writ large."[1] Such a reputation had been a long time coming. And it had lasting effects.

Today, a decade after Central State Hospital closed its doors, the largest mental institution in Baldwin County is the Baldwin County Jail, the largest mental institution in Georgia is the Fulton County Jail, and the largest mental institution in the United States is Chicago's Cook County Jail. In fact, in 2014 the National Sheriffs' Association lamented as "incomprehensible" how the vast proportion of psychiatric beds today have migrated into jails and prisons. How, indeed, could that be? This book explores the origins of such a grotesque contemporary fact and its implications.

Georgia's asylum was not London's Royal Bethlehem Hospital, founded in 1247 and from which the term "bedlam" originated. But at times it might as well have been. The dictionary definition of "bedlam" instructs us in how the uproar, pandemonium, commotion, mayhem, disorders, and lawlessness of London's hospital came to be synonymous with "institutions for the care of mentally ill people."[2] In Georgia, the bedlam was just as often found outside in the wider culture as it was inside the asylum. This book reconstructs psychiatric history within the cauldron of U.S. and southern history to restore a version of the official lawlessness, disorder, and mayhem that is so often denied by official records and processes and that shaped occurrences of and responses to severe mental illness.

My intent is not to vilify this one institution. Albert Deutsch's position on the Georgia hospital is in fact the same as my own. He wrote in 1948 in *The Shame of the States*: "If I found shameful conditions at Milledgeville, they differed only in degree, not in kind, from those found in most American mental hospitals. The shame is not Georgia's alone, or the South's alone, but the nation's." He echoed my own conviction that often the worst and the best practices happen in the same places because they arise from the same conditions when conscious people step up to take the worst on: "Physically, the best I saw at Milledgeville ranked with the best I've seen anywhere; the worst was the worst I had ever seen." But Deutsch also asserted: "From the medical viewpoint the institution ranks with the lowest of the 190 state mental hospitals in the United States." As one attendant's affidavit read, "A patient who could get well here could get well just as easy if he were lost out in the Okefenokee Swamp."[3]

That Georgia's worst became a national paradigm testifies to how the attempted genocide of Indigenous people and the enslavement of African Americans continue to shape U.S. history. I take this book's title from a remark made by the Georgia hospital's most iconic superintendent in his Presidential Address to the institutional precursor to the American Psychiatric Association. In 1897 in Baltimore, Maryland, Supt. T.O. Powell explained to his professional peers about "Psychiatry in the Southern States" that "in one particular alone does lunacy administration in the South differ from the same problem elsewhere in the country. What the race problem is to our whole section, so is the question of the colored insane to our speciality [*sic*]." Today, Georgians' access to psychiatric care is forty-seventh among the fifty states—a legacy of the story told here and the latest embodiments of the "southern specialities" of its "lunacy administrators."[4]

This book is a study of how all that happened. Even deeper, this book explores how what African American scholar Saidiya Hartman has called "the afterlife of slavery" has shaped America intimately and historically.[5] I trace these afterlives through the post-Confederacy's fiction of its "Lost Cause," so named even as post-Confederate elites moved rapidly in the years following surrender to reclaim the South by brute and sadistic violence. What we explore here is how the southern states' asylum system helped to undergird and create these haunting afterlives nationally—and to establish carceral ideologies of mental health care and treatment that continue to persist today.

To uncover the psychiatric version of these histories, I have, as Ray Charles croons, had Georgia on my mind.

This study joins a constellation of recent books on the current state of the U.S. mental health system.[6] The titles read like a professional obituary—for example, *Toxic Psychiatry* or *Insane Consequences* or *No One Cares About Crazy People*. The subtitles fill out a story of "bad science, bad medicine, and the enduring mistreatment of the mentally ill . . . the chaos and heartbreak of mental health in America . . . how the mental health industry fails the mentally ill." When these writers use the word "insane," they are talking not about their patients, but rather about a system that relies on institutionalization and medication in the context of the lack of community support and adequate access to psychiatric care available to the most severely afflicted people. There is a growing consensus that our contemporary mental health care system is deeply broken, a consensus that has deepened even as I have worked to finish this book.

In fact, some of the first warnings of this new crisis in psychiatry came from professionals in the field. The National Sheriffs' Association admonished in 2014 the fact that prisons contain ten times the number of those with mental illness as state psychiatric hospitals do, stating that "prison and jail officials are being asked to assume responsibility for the nation's most seriously mentally ill individuals, despite the fact that the officials did not sign up to do this job; are not trained to do it; face severe legal restrictions in their ability to provide treatment for such individuals; and yet are held responsible when things go wrong, as they inevitably do under such circumstances. This misguided public policy has no equal in the United States."[7]

The same year, a broad coalition of psychologists and psychiatrists published a letter against the latest (fifth) edition of the *Diagnostic and Statistical Manual*, released in 2013. They lamented its over-diagnoses, which lead to false epidemics that target the most socially marginal, and its return to assertions of deviancy. In response, they called for diagnoses to move beyond what they call neo-Kraepelian psychiatric categories (named after Emil Kraepelin) and for "psychology and psychiatry collaboratively to explore the possibility of developing an alternative approach to the conceptualization of emotional distress."[8] These diagnostic maladies have deep historical roots.

In 2015, three ethicists argued in the *Journal of the American Medical Association* that given the failures of deinstitutionalization and the criminalization of the mentally ill, "the way forward includes a return to psychiatric asylums." This is a dangerously anachronistic phrasing for the need for longer-term psychiatric care as one in a range of tools.[9] This is a terrible idea, the reasons for which constitute this book. It would be a return to a lunacy of administration, in an era of political bedlam.

Before we begin the deep dive into the Georgia State Lunatic, Idiot, and Epileptic Asylum, we should briefly visit the campus of what is now called Central State Hospital (CSH), the Georgia Asylum's latest haunted incarnation, its psychiatric ruin. In the 1940s, African American staff person Joe Ingram described the asylum most succinctly from the view of its cemeteries: "Rows upon rows of numbered, small, rusted markers as far as you can see. No names, just numbers. It must be the most gruesome sight in Georgia. Unknown humans, shunned when living, deprived of their very names in death—and literally known only to God."[10]

Today, abandoned asylum properties attract adventure-seeking college students or camera-wielding ghostbusters with their derelict buildings backlit beneath rumbling skies. This new genre of the cyber-Gothic prefers asylum buildings surrounded by low-hanging clouds, perhaps darkened broodingly with Photoshop's special effects. Two such structures from Central State Hospital take their place in Jim Miles' *Weird Georgia* along with tales of werewolves, Elephant Man, Hogzilla, Indian ruins, and plenty of hauntings of the cheaper variety. Apparitions in a window, footprints in sawdust, or sudden drops in temperature supposedly signal the unquiet dead. There are also the legends of those still living deep in the bowels of the buildings: *Weird Georgia* advertises "homeless weirdos and freaked-out former inmates" or prisoners gone missing.[11] Richard Nickel Jr., "urban guerilla" photographer, braved trespass laws and slipped into the Walker Building, dodging a coyote on the third floor, to add representations of its exquisitely pastel decay, algae a kinder shade of institutional green, to his online website of "guerilla preservation and urban archaeology." What he encountered was an asylum being reclaimed by Georgia's teeming natural world. There, "the heat and humidity of central Georgia have taken their toll" in the collapsed ceilings, its walls "a tapestry of peeling paint, algae, mold, and disintegrating plaster." Foliage spreads over the outsides of the building and finds crevices via which to invade its interior spaces, where insects, mammals, snakes, and that large coyote make their home. "Yet through all this, some aspects of grandeur remain in this venerable building, used for almost a century," Nickel muses.[12]

Our tour guide for this readers' trip, as she was in previous actual visits, is public relations director Kari Brown. She first takes us out to Carl Vinson Highway, where we pass five buildings now used as hospitals by the Georgia Department of Veterans' Services. Kari also points out a building that houses the developmentally disabled, and down another driveway the swimming pool and the building for occupational and recreational therapy, where the few remaining patients can work for wages. We still have in mind the shock boxes, straightjackets, and lobotomy tools we'd seen earlier in the little train station–turned–museum. The disconcerting mixture of the restorative and the punitive goes down past grass and loam into red clay: institutional bedrock.

With a few more turns we pass several of the maximum-security prisons on the east side, visible through massive silver coils of razor-sharp wire. By the 1990s, ten hospital buildings had been converted into five prisons. Patient rooms became cells for inmates, and CSH employees became prison guards as the behemoth mental hospital emptied. This transition occurred at the same time that the U.S. prison population ballooned from three hundred thousand to 2.3 million, its residents disproportionately Black and brown. In early visits at the turn of the twenty-first century, I saw Black men in orange jumpsuits ranging inside the wire and encountered guards and State Patrol officers ready to be on hand in a split second should a visitor stray from the state's curative to its penal acreage. These prisons themselves now have emptied out to newer facilities in other counties and new forms of incarceration closer to home. In fact, Baldwin County in 2010 had an unemployment rate of 15 percent, with 2,700 jobs lost in the previous four years from the deinstitutionalization process.[13]

Lobotomy tools displayed in the Central State Hospital Museum, Milledgeville, Georgia *(Photograph taken by the author)*

We roll past the Ingram Building (named after Joe Ingram, known as "the Black superintendent"). There, Blind Willie McTell, Georgia's premier bluesman, died of a cerebral hemorrhage, but not because anyone considered him mentally ill. He was there because Central State Hospital was willing to give a Black man free medical care when other hospitals in the region were not, as long as he was admitted to CSH via the Commission of Lunacy in his county.[14] Blind Willie's Milledgeville experience reminds me again that this story is too rich and complex to collapse into its most negative and sensational elements. Now the building, which had become part of Scott Prison, stands strangely empty. Blind Willie's blues join this journey's playlist in laments such as "Death Cell Blues" and "Dark Night Blues," also cited in the epigraphs.

We arrive at Cedar Lane, one of six cemeteries that over the years buried up to twenty-five thousand unclaimed bodies. Now, two thousand ancient metal stakes are laid out in a geometrical pattern near the road. The numbers stamped in the rusting iron mark the algebra of the largest graveyard of disabled people in the world. If we walked through the pines,

"Angel Reaching," Cedar Lane Cemetery, grounds of Central State Hospital, Milledgeville, Georgia *(Photograph taken by the author)*

Cedar Lane would bring us to the statue of the androgynous angel that looks out over the pine woods and over the thousands of still-unmarked graves, its pronoun "they." This memorial, the pattern of stakes and the angel near the edge of the trees, was a project of the Georgia Consumer Council. After a wrenching 1997 visit, Consumer Council members (which is to say, users and survivors of the state's mental health system) worked with CSH staff to establish the memorial. There, they gather annually to remember the hospital's dead. At those gatherings, the elderly Black women among them also slip up the hill near the Rivers Building to what was the African American burial ground, where lines of the metal stakes run downhill in all directions and into the bushes. It is here they pay their respects to the hospital's African American ancestors.

On two different visits I joined Consumer Council members meeting in the chapel with former patients and Consumer Council director Larry Fricks. On the second visit, one of them told me that if I was "crazy enough to come back voluntarily a second time," I belonged with them. I took it as a point of honor.

On the day of our tour, the shimmering geometric pattern of stakes, modeled after the graves at Arlington, gives some semblance of order and grace at Cedar Lane although the barbed wire visible across the highway at the prison that was once the Holly Building for Negro Patients distracts. So does the tour guide's comment that bodies are buried in the woods "as far as the eye can see"—which is quite far. On a prior visit before the hospital closed, an employee told one of my traveling companions that the state had stopped digging in these woods because construction, or the roots of giant trees toppled in a thunderstorm, brought up human bones, this land being charnel grounds for the disabled. On even our sunny spring day, with fruit trees an insurrection of pink and dogwoods blazing, the spectral image brings a sudden chill. Although the Consumers had probably not planned it when they chose this site, Cedar Lane also memorializes the prisons on the other side of the road.

The newest CSH structure, the Cook Building, which we had passed back on Carl Vinson Highway, is a fortress-like forensic hospital the color of Georgia clay. It sits there like a spaceship from a highly penal planet. Down another road stands a new private prison run by Geo, one of the largest private prison corporations in the world. The prison operates on a thirty-year state contract that guarantees Geo the state will fill 90 percent of its beds. Both buildings are an ominous sign of our present condition, in which, once again, "with minimal exception, incarceration has replaced hospitalization for thousands of individuals in every single state."[15]

We climb back on the bus to head back to our cars. As the bus careens around yet another corner, we are buffeted by the energies of these layered spaces where southern geography and southern psyche collapsed in one another's arms.

The asylum that opened in 1842 and the penitentiary built in 1817 across from the lot on which the governor's mansion rose in antebellum Milledgeville were disciplinary institutions for white people, while the antebellum plantation kept slave labor in line under circumstances that could make the strongest enslaved person insane but mostly did not. This triumvirate was the root of what contemporary prison activists/abolitionists term the "prison–industrial complex" and what Michelle Alexander has called "the New Jim Crow," neither of which could have happened if the South's elite had not won its Lost Cause again and again in subsequent eras, another thread of *Administrations of Lunacy*'s story.[16] Joe Ingram was right: Milledgeville is a mirror of a culture (not only Georgian) that throws people away, of the state that structures such dumping, of the desperation, greed, or denial that holds it in place, and of the range of motives and behaviors (from deeply humanitarian to sadistic) of the hundreds of employees who worked there. It is also a classroom for us today to understand the abiding effect of white settler colonialism and the legacies of slavery on contemporary psychiatry and our own struggles to be sane, so as to understand ourselves and our national choices more clearly. This is a history not only of the New Jim Crow, but also of the first Jim Crow, and before that of chattel slavery itself and the genocides of Indigenous people, and the still-fighting Confederacy, all of whose afterlives we have yet to vanquish.

History itself and what the dead have to teach us about the troubled relationship between insanity, disability, and racism in both the South and the nation is considerably more complex than either Gothic fantasies or Chamber of Commerce public relations on a hospital campus that now seems more like a time warp or a movie set. This book will serve as a lesson in what that haunted history really is, and what our exorcisms of that history might look like and the depths we have to fall as a culture and a nation should we regress.

This book is neither anti-psychiatric nor anti-science, but it is anti-racist. Writers like Ron Powers and D.J. Jaffey have lowered themselves into the histories of the treatment of the insane. It is past time to join or challenge those accounts with the brilliant historians of slavery, racism, and gendered white supremacy. W.E.B. Du Bois saw from Georgia how the global color line shaped the twentieth century, and here we remember that it is always already gendered, classed, and deeply informed by power's response to human sexuality. The brilliant anti-colonial psychiatrist Frantz Fanon, working in the mental hospitals of Algeria in the 1940s and 1950s, saw that there could not be a post-colonial psychology that did not account for the import of history. He named its requirement as the "demand to think" in the face of "pseudo-national mystification."[17]

While I was doing this work in Georgia, others were pursuing a similar intent to retrieve and document the history of racism in psychiatric institutions. Professor King Davis has spent a decade digitizing over eight hundred thousand documents from African American asylums in Virginia, particularly that state's Central State Hospital. In 2019, Wendy Gonaver's *The Peculiar Institution and the Making of Modern Psychiatry* drew on Virginia archives through her study of the Eastern Lunatic Asylum in Williamsburg and the Central Lunatic Asylum in Petersburg, the first asylum created for African Americans. Also, Martin Summers' *Madness in the City of Magnificent Institutions: A History of Race and Mental Illness in the Nation's Capital*, published in 2019, drew on archives from St Elizabeth's, the only federal asylum and one that admitted Black patients.[18] Unlike Virginia, Georgia moved emancipated African Americans into the Georgia Asylum rather than build a separate institution, because it was cheaper. St. Elizabeth's also took in both Black and white patients, including Civil War veterans from the Union Army. Together, these new books and archives help to move discussions of race into a more central place in U.S. psychiatric history.

These chapters in *Administrations of Lunacy* map the South's revolutions and counter-revolutions onto a succession of medical paradigms (e.g., bodily humors, germ theory, public health, behavioral medicine) that shaped asylum-sanitarium-hospital psychiatry, drawing on familiar figures such as Dorothea Dix, General William Tecumseh Sherman, W.E.B. Du Bois, and Jimmy and Rosalynn Carter. But it is the unknown patients and their families, the nurses, orderlies, doctors, and trustees, who take us to the complex heart of this protean story that is at once both Georgian and American. This narrative emerges from a Milledgeville way of reading patient narratives through and against hospital records, newspaper accounts, literary texts, geographical journeys, and oral histories. It is a reading grid that exposes one hospital's psychiatric history to the dense historical contexts that shaped its patients.

U.S. psychiatry extracted history from its sufferers every bit as much as colonialism extracted African labor, indigenous land, and silver, gold, forests, and uranium, for the sake of profits elsewhere. I intend this book as an act of restorative history to its Georgia patients, from whose experiences and our own we can continue to understand slavery's afterlives and shape ecologies of sanity in these also turbulent times.

PART I

The Asylum's Antebellum Origins

No other disease, probably, is increasing faster in our country than insanity, and from investigations recently made in several of the northern states, there is reason to fear that it already prevails here to a greater extent than in any other country. This, however, is not strange, for insanity is a disease that always prevails most in countries where the people enjoy civil and religious freedom, and where all are induced, or at liberty to engage in the strife for wealth, and for the highest honors and distinctions of society. We need therefore to be exceedingly careful not to add other causes to those already existing, of this most deplorable disease.

—Amariah Brigham, *Observations on the Influence of Religion Upon the Health and Physical Welfare of Mankind*, 1835[1]

The unshakeable basis of the most solid empires is founded on the soft fibers of the brain.

—Joseph Michel Antoine Servan, *Discours sur l'administration de la justice criminelle*[2]

1

"Demonic and Legionized, They Entered": Samuel Henderson, Supt. Cooper, and the *American Journal of Insanity*

Samuel Henderson had been in chains a long time for a white man. That March of 1844, as he stood upright in the groaning wagon and strained against the iron around his wrists, he must have heard the voice of God somewhere along the road from Cobb County to Milledgeville.

"If thy eye offend thee, pluck it out!"

Perhaps God spoke to Samuel not so far from where the drivers sought shelter in a sudden storm. In the slash of thunder, searing light turned to *crack!* then *boom!* as it hit a massive oak; or it crashed then corkscrewed down a nearby pine, first stripping bark, then blowing it two feet out, the surge following trunk to root and then to ground. Perhaps Samuel then began to pull and rattle in his chains until he felt the fury that started like the lightning but running *up* his body until all he heard was his own roaring sound.

By his journey's end Samuel *had* plucked out the offending organ. He arrived at the doors of the Georgia State Lunatic, Idiot, and Epileptic Asylum with his eyeball hanging from its socket. "Paroxysms," the superintendent would note, one of two Samuel suffered getting to the doctor's door.[3] The Georgia Asylum had opened eighteen months before his arrival, financed with money that white settlers paid at bargain prices for native land. The road Samuel traveled that March, driven in the wagon by two white men from home, covered the 150 miles or more to Milledgeville.

Over the next seventeen decades, thousands of patients like Samuel Henderson would make the journey to Milledgeville and cross the Center

Building's portal in steps that would become the most portentous of their lives.

Perhaps when his mind had cleared from sleep or exhaustion, Samuel wondered what he had done to deserve his condition. The drivers carried a letter from his brothers to Superintendent David Cooper about his family's decade of difficulties. "For many years," Cooper noted in his records, "this subject had been a devout member of the Presbyterian Church, filling the station of delegate to conventions, Presbyteries, etc.," and he had "enjoyed the utmost confidence of his brethren, sustaining all social relations characteristic of a kind neighbor, an affectionate husband and father." The only ostensible cause of derangement, the brothers' letter speculated, was his enthusiasm for God.[4] Of a literary turn of mind, Cooper would have known that case studies of extreme mental states were as old as Galen, and biographic sketches describing someone's life as the context for illness were becoming increasingly popular.

Samuel's brothers had probably not shown him the letter, but in his clearer moments he knew its contents. He had lived with his brothers' story about him for the past decade, after what his family called his "attack." Samuel's family thought that he was abandoning them, and certainly abandoning his role as an upstanding citizen in the county and the expanding state. They noted an "apparent indifference" to family interests and "acts of devotion . . . attended with a want of solemnity, or too much facetiousness," and prayers that "savored of irony." These are probably Cooper's words. He also judged the family to be "not over discriminating and intelligent," so probably not attuned to the ironic. Cooper interprets the brothers' letter to mean that Samuel's conversation and actions "exhibited so much incoherence as to demonstrate incipient insanity." They increasingly tried to restrain him from "devotion, family prayer, fireside lecturing, etc. and attending religious meetings." Samuel fought back, exhorting them: "God's authority is above all others." The brothers reported that he "threatened them, exhibited evidence of indications of violence and homicidal impulses, became furious and ferocious requiring restraint." Whatever else his conditions (homicidal, furious, ferocious), his family outnumbered him, and his fury and ferocity just as likely came from their treatment of him. But in the power dynamics, he was outnumbered as well. It was not hard to find chains in Georgia.

So his brothers put chains on his legs and iron handcuffs around his wrists, by which Samuel was constrained "for nearly 9 years to one spot . . . most of the time." No doubt he lost track of the time. In the asylum, Cooper would note Samuel's "stupor." Probably his fury at their power over him also grew during these years. When the new Georgia asylum opened in 1842, the fifth one in the South, the fourteenth in the country, the Hendersons decided to send Samuel. The seven white men convened by the Cobb County Ordinary (or probate judge) to determine if Samuel was dangerous to the community decided that he was. So they transferred the chains that had fixed him in a cellar or in a wooden hut or house out back to the floor of the cart for his trip to the Georgia Lunatic Asylum in Milledgeville.

Perhaps the move to the cart came as a relief, with so much open sky and air, trees to watch, so many birds whose names he perhaps knew and spotted along the roads or in the ponds and rivers along the way: the lapwings and plovers, jays and larks, chickadees, thrush, wood warblers and roseate spoonbills, coots and rails; even just their names were lovely, as he also marked their sharp or lilting sounds, a place to rest his mind. Perhaps these soothed him even though the roads were dreadful, muddy in the rains, ruts so vast they had to lean to left or right to keep the wagon from falling in.[5] Perhaps spending more than a week sleeping under the March sky also calmed Samuel, gave him clear nights, with leaves not yet on the trees, so that stars wheeled around in the branches, pinned to the heavens by the pole star. He could lie calm in those moments, and sleep came as an answer to prayers.

Other times, he must have had a head of chatter. *If thy eye offend thee. If thy eye offend.* He had offended his family. And they had plucked him out. Maybe then the energy, the lightning, took him, "furious and ferocious." Maybe in that last paroxysm he obeyed the voice he heard as God, so different from the coots' calls and the chickadees'.

The "Moral Therapy" and Heroic Medicine

Perhaps Supt. David Cooper stood at the asylum's window on its fourth-floor promenade, watching Samuel's wagon approach up the slight incline from town. The three men would have rolled through the town, raucous after the country's quiet, and out the other side, crossing the wooden bridge at Fishing Creek—*Thlock-loosa* to the long-absent Muscogee. Then the asylum's only building would have loomed on the hill above them.

At the time of Henderson's arrival in the spring of 1844, Supt. Cooper had received seventeen patients over the previous fifteen months. Cooper would have stood at the north end of what was in 1844 the asylum's only building, which was the first wing of what would become in the next decade a U-shaped structure. Its basement and three upper floors ran north to south, and the architect's design projected a second wing to the west and a structure that would join them. Cooper would have been waiting at what would become the Center Building's closed end. Samuel must have been one of the most dramatic arrivals, with cuffs and chains, his feet swollen, probably dust-covered from the long road. Then Cooper would have seen Samuel's face. *If thy eye offend thee, pluck it out.* "This disfiguration," Cooper would write, "remains a reminder of the demoniac and legionized state into which the mind might be thrown by excess, though the generation of that excess are the impulses of inspiration and religion; thus situated, he entered our asylum."

David Cooper was the first superintendent of the Georgia Asylum, and at the time of Samuel Henderson's arrival he was in the process of establishing himself as an eccentric humanitarian. He set a high standard for the asylum's first employees: "Duty, a desire to increase the happiness and diminish the sufferings of each and every inmate in the Institution, should be the governing motive of our daily exertion." Such a duty should protect the patients against neglect, unkind language, taunts and recriminations, and outright violence. He regarded his "maniac" patients as existing along a human continuum, with "the same desire to be active and useful that is found in other men."[6] There is little else but his first annual report in the archives to contextualize Dr. Cooper. In fact, it was his ardent efforts to immortalize himself by writing too frankly about the asylum that after three years would result in his being fired, after which event David Cooper disappeared from sight and into the ether.

We can imagine that Samuel was grateful for Supt. Cooper's welcome. "We gave him a comfortable room, bedding, etc.," Cooper noted. At Henderson's own urging, Cooper records, they chained him again to the floor of his new room, as "this confinement he expostulated with us to resort to, as protection to ourselves and to him." Cooper must have noted a welcome rationality in his new patient's advice, what doctors termed "insight": that patients suffering lunacy, as Cooper would have termed it, recognized the situation they were in. Within six hours, Henderson was "furious as a tiger and roaring like a lion . . . cursing, stamping, clanking in his chains," then passing into a "silent or dumb" stupor, a "deeply meditative state in which his eye was fixed upon an object steadfastly for half hour." Between these two extremes, Samuel was "mild, sociable and affable, conversing freely on different subjects," from crops and cotton prices to news and politics. These furious or stuporous states began to subside from daily to weekly, then "much more seldom." By September, Cooper reported that he had freed Samuel Henderson from his chains.

Psychiatry itself began in European asylums with the idea that formerly custodial institutions could cure their inhabitants through a "moral therapy" that combined orderly routines and settings of natural beauty with an attentive doctor–patient relationship. David Cooper's proud account of this remarkable success exhibited, in historian Edward Shorter's terms, the "new therapeutic optimism [that] engulfed the world of medicine in the second half of the eighteenth century," such that a new generation of asylum doctors grew up "filled with confidence in their ability to heal." As he unchained Henderson, perhaps Supt. Cooper was chasing the fame that Philippe Pinel at Paris' Bicêtre hospital had guaranteed himself when he had removed his patients' chains. Pinel had acted in the midst of the French Revolution, one decade before the newly built city of Milledgeville became an expanding Georgia's capital.[7] By 1808 in Europe, "psychiatrie" became the name of the new discipline that Cooper was performing in Georgia less than four decades later.[8] Cooper knew his lineage. He wrote, "The work of Pinel on liberating the maniac from his chains was in 1792, and his published writings which will 'eternize' [Cooper's own term] his fame, appeared some time after."[9] Supt. Cooper anticipated that he could lift Samuel from his "squallid wretchedness and filth" by a "high scale of civilization, expansive philanthropy, elevated mental and moral culture."[10]

Belief in science was replacing older understandings of insane people as "demonic and legionized," the biblical language with which Cooper had earlier described Samuel. Medical historian Roy Porter observes that "madness may be as old as mankind," citing skulls unearthed from 5,000 BCE with small holes bored into them, probably to free the person of devil possession. "Wild disturbances of mood, speech, and behavior were generally imputed to supernatural powers," Porter wrote.[11] Samuel would have known Cooper's reference as being from a passage in the Bible, in which a man with unclean spirits approached Jesus from his home in the tombs and Jesus cast the spirits into a herd of swine that then plunged into the sea. When Jesus asked the man's name, he replied: "My name is Legion, for we are many."

But after Samuel Henderson arrived, Cooper also noted him as "sanguine" in the ledger where he entered each new patient's name, county, age, marital status, sex, occupation, and cause and duration of insanity.[12] Samuel's sanguine temperament would have tipped him toward the more boisterous and cheerful. His history decidedly did not, nor would his treatments.

"Sanguine" was a reference to a system of medicine that was by Samuel's day already two thousand years old. It referred to what was called "humoral medicine," built around the concept of four bodily humors (sanguine, choleric, melancholic, and phlegmatic) that since the time of ancient Hellenic medicine were thought to determine individual temperament, health, and bodily features. Ideally, a person's constitution balanced all four humors. If not, the restoration of the body's balance involved drastic interventions. The humoral approach to medicine brought into the asylum its own medical regimes, called "heroic medicine" because of the extremities of their effects. Benjamin Rush, considered the father of American psychiatry and a mentor of both Supt. Cooper and prominent local physician Tomlinson Fort, was a proponent of heroic medicine. He taught the use of bleeding (*venesection*, or opening a vein; *scarification*, or making small cuts with a machine; *blistering* through hot plasters; and *cupping*, or drawing out blood from the vacuum created by a hot cup). Rush also taught the "heroic" use of purgatives, such as laxatives for diarrhea and emetics for vomiting, and medicines that included mercury and lead. *The Cambridge History of Medicine* explains how heroic treatments "amounted to making patients anaemic through bloodletting, depleting them of fluids and valuable electrolytes via the stool, and poisoning them with compounds of such heavy metals as mercury and lead."[13]

Heroic medicine and the moral therapy, then, were different systems: heroic medicine referred to extreme medical techniques that resulted from the millennia-old belief in bodily humors, and moral therapy arose from an eighteenth-century (Enlightenment) conviction that institutions that housed lunatics could become themselves curative. This shift in attitude toward the institutions that housed lunatics provided the basis for psychiatry. But people often stayed in these institutions for decades and thus developed a range of diseases and symptoms. There, the superintendent and doctors treated them according to the medical regimes of the times. But the practices from the underlying medical philosophy of heroic medicine worked against the psychiatric philosophy of moral therapy with its healing environment.

Patients, some of whom stayed in the Georgia Asylum for decades, had little choice in these treatments. Plenty of patients, asylum records show, resisted them as best they could.

Cooper explained heroic measures as being key to his success with Samuel: "The medical treatment in this case has admitted of, or required, but little variation . . . and comprised the nauseant, aperient [having a laxative effect] and shower bath course with occasional anodynes [painkillers], and our uniform, mild, soothing and conciliatory conduct and conversation." The superintendent also would have bled Samuel. Simultaneous violent nausea, diarrhea, opiates, and bleeding would certainly calm a person down, as would the "muffs, mittens, wristbands, body belts, and arms straps, strait-jackets and . . . tranquilizing chair" listed among his asylum's "soothing moral appliances . . . never to be put on unless by order of the officers."[14]

Cooper also believed in the healing power of the town of Milledgeville, then the capital of Georgia. Writing in his only annual report as superintendent in a remarkable prose style that would doom his efforts to "eternize" himself, he showed his readers the nearby village of Midway, "ornamented" with a female academy, preparatory school, female literary institute, and the white male Oglethorpe University, from which "radiate in her alumni, perennial streams of literature, science, moral worth and piety." He then directed the eye north to Milledgeville—with a vocabulary incomprehensible both then and now—in its "amphitheatrical variegation, its tululous mausoles," and its churches, from which a thick enough cloud of incense rose to "expiate all the turpitude, crime and guilt of its citizens." Then he revealed the capitol building, "its elevated dome, proud cupola and cloud capped," nearby the government arsenal, "stored with the attractive metal of fire arms and the inflammable deposit of gun powder." The governor's mansion, the courthouse, the Masonic Hall, the county prison, and the "elevated octagon dome" of the state penitentiary stretched out before the asylum patients' view, from which Cooper showed his readers the "innumerable murmuring rills, splashing currents and swelling torrents" of the Oconee River.[15] In the view from the top floor, the state and nature conspired with Cooper to bring the lunatic to sanity, with the help of Cooper's anodynes (painkillers) and soothing moral appliances. This landscape will become increasingly familiar to us in these pages.

A century later, historian James Bonner painted a different picture of the frontier capital in the 1840s. The pungent odors of the night depositories into which domestic slaves emptied chamber pots were their own kind of incense, and the grunt and rooting of hogs in the streets and of boisterous patrons of the capital's taverns was a different choir. In November and December, legislators filled the inns, sleeping two to three men to a bed, away from home and drinking liberally of the town's wines and spirits, some of them taking advantage of the prostitutes on Franklin Street, not far from the capitol. The often muddy streets of Milledgeville jostled with people, wagons, animals, commerce, and governing. The town's orderly grid, laid out on Savannah's model, had not taken into account the natural terrain, so that gullies intersected the streets. The ravine at Wayne and Hancock ran northward down Tanyard Branch, a "gorge so deep the stagecoach disappeared from view when it crossed."[16]

Disputes in Milledgeville took political turns as factions argued in the state house, planter interests versus farmers and frontiersmen, then took the fight outside with pistols. On an 1831 visit, noted author Mrs. Anne Royal described Milledgeville as "the refuse of all nations, runaway convicts from other states, wooden nutmeg Yankees," and stated that in the statehouse and government offices there was as "vulgar a set of men as ever disgraced a seat of government."[17]

The Walls of the Asylum

From his room, the chained Samuel Henderson had probably already pieced together what he could of the building's daily functioning and the movements and energies of its people. In terms of its layout, Samuel was located on one of the two male floors of the four-story structure, which included a basement. Probably, Supt. Cooper put him in an upper story and a room with a view in one of twenty single rooms that stretched out ten to a side along the hall. The dining hall was on the north end, where in the next decade the Center Building's front would connect two wings. There was also a water closet, shower, and bath on each floor, probably at the other end from the dining hall. The building's four stories could accommodate twenty patients each, or eighty in all. At this point, staff lived off site. Samuel was the thirteenth patient, eight of whom were men. The new asylum's rooms were filling slowly as word filtered out to Georgia counties that families or sheriffs could send people to Milledgeville.

This first Georgia Asylum building was not laid out on the "Kirkbride Plan" famous to the nineteenth century that was adopted in the late 1840s and named after Thomas Kirkbride, superintendent of the Pennsylvania Hospital for the Insane. Over the coming decades, Kirkbride would work to bring asylum architecture more fully into line with the moral treatment's and superintendents' needs. Like his Enlightenment predecessors, Kirkbride conceived the hospitals "as ideal sanctuaries for the mentally ill and as an active participant in their recovery," so that he gave "careful attention . . . to every detail of their design to promote a healthy environment and convey a sense of respectable decorum." Described as "linear," the Kirkbride hospital was actually built with *echelons*, or groups of rooms stepped back on either side, with connecting rooms and halls. In this way, "air circulated more freely and patients were not observable from other wards." These windows wafted out the miasmas and fetid airs believed to carry disease in the era before the germ theory would take hold.[18]

In the early 1840s, Georgia's architectural emissaries had visited Worcester, Massachusetts, and the McLean Asylum in Charlestown, near Boston, to investigate asylum structure and design.[19] Historian Carla Yanni observes of Worcester's original U-shaped building: "Economy was the primary concern at the pauper hospital at Worcester . . . [It] was built quickly; critics abhorred its shoddy construction. It did not spawn many followers."[20] Georgia would follow the cheaper Worcester, not McLean's elite model for the "gracefully insane." The Georgia Asylum lacked those echelons that moved agitated patients inward to more spacious and illuminated wards from the farther-out lockdown cells. So

Supt. Cooper's staff must have used the series of rooms on a hall to separate out the most violent disruptions from the "liberty patients," those
who occupied themselves calmly with newspaper reading and chitchat.

Samuel had learned over the summer that plumbing was key. Many
asylums had the latest devices, a water closet Cooper described as being "for necessary purposes; and capable of being washed and rinsed
with water from the shower bath, contents carried off by tubes or pipes."[21]
The water closet, shower, and bath on each floor were kept quite busy
by the more forceful therapies of the heroic treatment. The human digestive system was designed to move food downward from mouth to
esophagus to stomach to small and large intestines and out the rectum at
the anus. Doctors' heroic treatments could forcefully reverse that movement with emetics, or speed it up considerably with purgatives, as Samuel
had learned.

Out his window, if Samuel was on the west side and the ground floor,
he could have seen the more reformed women and men, the liberty patients, walking in the yard below with what must have seemed remarkable freedom, or working in the garden in "botanical" therapy, or in the
courtyard that provided the only time that male and female patients
mixed. From a western-side room, he would have seen the clearing and,
over the top of the wooden fence, a swipe of road and the far pines, the
boundaries of the world beyond which might have meant freedom or terror on any particular day.[22]

Along with the smells, it was the sounds of the Georgia "bedlam" that
told Henderson the most. His first days and weeks had tutored him in
furies other than his own with the hallowing, singing, cursing, praying, crying; footsteps running past his door and the crash of broken glass
in the window's first sash, or furniture being slammed against a wall.
During the moments and days when those sounds were not his own, he
could contemplate his own arrival in Georgia's Bedlam. He recognized
first the inmate down the hall from the old seaman's curses delivered in
full Irish brogue amidst bouts of kicking, butting, and spitting at whatever staff member ventured through his door. When the fight subsided,
the sailor, John Smith, perhaps began hailing and hallowing God like a
whale that Smith had spotted breeching out to sea or that he imagined
swallowing Jonah down its dark, slick gullet along with brine and other
slithering fish and seaweed, only for Jonah to finally land in the sloshing

belly of the beast—perhaps not so unlike Smith, or Henderson himself swallowed up by the asylum. Henderson also heard Smith cursing in languages the sailor must have learned on his voyages across the Atlantic or out of Savannah on runs down to Jamaica carrying supplies or slaves or rum, or perhaps even around the horn into the sudden Pacific.[23]

The ladies hardly fared better, as Henderson deduced from the glass shattering on the floor above him. Mrs. Mary Riley was readmitted on March 31, eight days after Samuel, with furies that put his to shame: each pane shattered, bed destroyed two nights straight, ripped apart (with her teeth? There was nothing else there!), then shredded. The matron's voice out the window, "Put them back on, Mrs. Riley, put your clothes on!" That image of her naked body may have stirred Samuel, filling mind and loins with terrible admiration. It took many heroics to calm her: douche, cold shower, straitjacket, nausea several times in the day, though she resisted bleeding, but got the "auxilium of soothing moral appliances." Later again they gave her the bath and jackets and nauseates, to which she "sooner yielded" and got on Cooper's program, sewing, quilting, knitting, carding, spinning, washing, and reading her Bible.[24]

Henderson could also see and hear Nancy Malone, whom Cooper revealed was fifty years old, single, an "idiot" for twenty years, and who came on July 19 of Samuel's same year. We will travel with Nancy later in this story.

On his hall, up the other way from Smith, Samuel recognized a younger man's voice, whom he later met as John Nelson of Macon: its timbre closer to home, not prayers but demands for his rights and his ownership in property, his mind's break "at the closed store door" of his business. "What crime did I commit to land me here?" he yelled. "Tell me what crime!" Then steps, the door opened and shut, Cooper's voice on a lower register, calm but insistent, reading him his court documents and pamphlets on lunacy to persuade him of the reasonableness of his commitment, and entreating him to write home to his family and friends. Then a crash again, ink pot against the wall, and rising fury. Nelson, like other patients, found the laxatives and emetics objectionable, so they were given to him by coercion or slipped into his food.[25]

In September of that year, Samuel Henderson was unchained. Probably with Supt. Cooper by his side, he walked gingerly out of his room into the hall of the first floor of the Georgia Lunatic Asylum, his gait unsteady and his feet and legs weirdly light. Free of shackles for the first time in ten years, he walked the hall's 129 feet to the front window to look out on the road that had brought him to the building six months before. The sweltering summer was behind him, much of his recollection a blur or a blank to him, but memorable to Cooper were those "countenance and gestures, those fits [that] do not admit of description." Over the summer months, Samuel's paroxysms had diminished gradually from daily to weekly and recently "much more seldom," with the "rational, mild, sociable states" occurring much more frequently.[26] And now here he was, walking toward the dining room at the north end of his hall, where he could eat his meals at a table, not on the metal tray brought to his room by slaves or white attendants. From the dining area he could see more of the world than had been available through his cell's double-sashed window, the inner sash wood and glass, the outer cast iron and fixed, its double structure of patient/inmate, hospital/prison.

Perhaps Samuel was relieved that he would now be free to "read the newspapers and other miscellaneous works, sometimes the Bible and Hymn book." Cooper would also note that after his release Samuel Henderson "sleeps well and his dreams are pleasant, tho' very different when he came in, talks of his family with affection, reads their letters with pleasure, tho' he says he used to wish to kill them, particularly his infant."[27]

George Maxwell, who had been seemingly frozen in a stupor in the hall, would escape from the asylum a year later to be "heard from two months afterward in Savannah."[28]

Amariah Brigham and the American Journal of Insanity

In 1845, David Cooper must have been a happy man as he penned his first and only annual report, dipping pen in ink to write sentence after florid sentence, perhaps waving the pages to let the ink dry and stacking them neatly to the side as they accumulated. Then, electrified by his own prose, Cooper sent it across town to Georgia's governor George W. Crawford and the legislature, then to the new *American Journal of Insanity* for review. Determined that "it may be published in pamphlet form, and distributed through the Post Office, in this, and other States not yet favored with like Institutions," he put it on the mail coach, which took the slender volume up the muddy roads through north Georgia, past York, South Carolina, with the Blue Ridge mountains on its left, into North Carolina at Charlotte, then east to Washington before turning northward.[29] At the Utica Asylum in upstate New York, Dr. Amariah Brigham received Dr. Cooper's annual report in his capacity as founding editor of the new professional journal. Brigham had recently arrived at Utica, hired out of the exclusive Connecticut asylum the Hartford Retreat to lead New York's first public asylum. Georgia's entry into his journal's pages would prove inauspicious for Georgia and disastrous for Cooper.

Amariah Brigham ranked among the foremost U.S. psychiatrists, and he was ambitious for himself and for the field of psychiatry. Portraits show him to be a thin, intense man, bushy brows overhanging an intelligent face that narrowed to his chin. "For sheer brilliance, few rivaled Brigham's intellect and talent for medicine," Lawrence B. Goodheart summarized in his compelling portrait of the doctor in his book *Mad Yankees*. Brigham was a Democrat in the age of Andrew Jackson's party of outsider white men, a "Unitarian apostate from Calvinist pessimism," a self-taught man who rose to prominence on merit rather than "the Standing Order of Federalist politics, Congressional religion and Yale education."[30] After graduating from medical college in 1828, Brigham set sail for Europe, one of more than seven hundred of the best U.S. physicians who did so between 1820 and 1860. He spent a year touring hospitals and insane asylums from Manchester to Ireland and Scotland, then back to London. In Paris, he attended lectures at the Sorbonne and explored the Bicêtre and Salpetrière asylums, then headed to Geneva and Genoa, studying with the continent's pre-eminent doctors.[31] A year later, Brigham returned to the States convinced that "the brain is the organ of the mind" and "the course of insanity will be looked for in the brain." He went on to publish avant-garde psychiatric works that explained for the New World the new understandings in Europe of the brain's workings.[32] He soon joined the staff of the Hartford Retreat, where Superintendent Eli Todd tutored him in a moral treatment with more kindness and less of Benjamin Rush's heroic medicine. He became superintendent upon Todd's death in 1840, then moved to Utica in 1842, the same year the Georgia State Lunatic, Idiot, and Epileptic Asylum opened farther down south in Milledgeville.

In 1842, U.S. asylum medicine was in a period of professional consolidation, with Dr. Brigham at the lead, having already set out to reshape the psychiatric landscape. In 1844, he founded the *American Journal of Insanity* to be the professional organ of the Association of Medical Superintendents of American Institutes of the Insane (AMSAII), which Brigham was also instrumental in forming in that same year. In the twentieth century, these institutions would become the *American Journal of Psychiatry* and the American Psychiatric Association. Brigham would edit the journal's first five volumes, "bringing the subject of insanity . . . more fully before the public than in any other way would have been possible."[33]

In 1844, the year of Samuel's journey to Milledgeville, the association's first meeting was held in Philadelphia, with thirteen asylums represented. Those attending included many of the major figures in American psychiatry at the time: Brigham from Utica; Luther Bell of McLean Asylum in Somerville, Massachusetts; Pliney Earle of the Bloomingdale Asylum in New York; Thomas Kirkbride of the Pennsylvania Hospital for the Insane in Philadelphia; John Galt of the Eastern Asylum of Virginia at Williamsburg; and Francis Stribling of the Western Asylum of Virginia at Staunton. Brigham would include the published proceedings of the Association of Medical Superintendents' annual meetings in the *American Journal of Insanity.*

Amariah Brigham was the standard against which David Cooper would be measured, and he was the measurer. So our Supt. Cooper's own ambitions traveled north with the mail coach. It's easy to imagine Brigham with his intense blue eyes reading through raised brows. Perhaps farther south Cooper felt a shiver down his spine. After reading Cooper's magnum opus, editor Brigham wrote in his review of asylum reports for 1845 that he "still had doubts respecting an Asylum for the Insane in Georgia. . . . We could scarce believe this report to be genuine." How, he wondered, could any board of trustees, together with the governor of the state to whom it was addressed, ever have sanctioned the publication of "such a confused medley of facts, and reasoning, and unusual words, that we find it difficult to learn much of the actual condition of the Asylum?" Brigham offered his own sample of Cooper's prose, in which the Georgia superintendent labored to describe the financial benefits of his institution to taxpayers and county governments, passages in which Cooper described his "few prolegomenous deductions and the aid of a few arithmetical prolepsis." As Cooper went on to explain, "in a pecuniary and politico economical point of view, it will be to our financial interests, the

Archmedian lever to oscillate the incubus beam of deranged, and depressed fiscal oppression which has shed its blighting effects upon the monetary affairs."[34] Brigham was aghast.

Brigham admonished his colleagues farther south, his own pen scratching across the page, that the extensive case histories (such as Samuel Henderson's), published almost verbatim by Cooper, brought "nothing but disgrace to the writer and the Institution he conducts, and in fact to all similar Institutions in our country." Brigham, in "all kindness," warned Cooper "never to publish another Report of this kind."[35] David Cooper must have been crushed. The asylum's trustees dismissed David Cooper after Brigham's professional chastisement, and Cooper's tracks in the records vanish.

Brigham was harsh, even humiliating, to Cooper, but he was not wrong in his assessment of Cooper's peculiar prose or of the dangers to asylum medicine's reputation caused by such frank disclosures of patients' symptoms and histories. He was also exercising his editorial power in policing the emerging asylum movement.

But Cooper's humiliation is to our benefit, and not only because his baroque language bemuses us. The asylum door that closed on him opens for us. Surely that was part of the reason for Brigham's warning—the injudicious hodgepodge of asylum life that Cooper revealed included detailed case histories and descriptions of actual treatments that today would be legally confidential. In his enthusiasm, Cooper gave us a view into the workings of America's bedlam that most superintendents had too much judgment or too little nerve or ego to publicly memorialize. At the end of the twentieth century, employees of what was by then Central State Hospital often repeated the mantra of their superiors: "What happens here, stays here." Supt. Cooper sent what happened in the Georgia Asylum to the editor of the *American Journal of Insanity*.

2

Asylum Psychiatry and Slavery: Fellow Travelers

Understanding something of what it felt like to suffer, and what it cost to endure that suffering, is crucial to understanding the course of U.S. history.

—Edward Baptist, *The Half Has Never Been Told* [1]

For moral therapists such as Superintendent David Cooper, unchaining a lunatic such as Samuel Henderson was a liberating act, harkening back to Philippe Pinel and the French Revolution's cry for "liberté, égalité, fraternité!" But enslaved smithies had forged the very chains that the Georgia superintendent unlocked. Perhaps this contradiction of American slavery and French liberty savored of an irony too dangerous for Cooper to acknowledge. After all, he had noted that when Samuel's prayers "savored of too much irony" his brothers had chained him to the floor. Yet the slave system and its economies spread out all around them and reconfigured the liberating impulses of Cooper's gesture.

Political Economies of Lunacy Administration

As the South's lunacy administrators bragged, the slave system gave them the cheap labor that meant rock-bottom costs. This was the real meaning of Cooper's gibberish about his "few prolegominous deductions and the aid of a few arithmetical prolepsis," whose obfuscations the editor Amariah Brigham so scathingly derided. Cooper was writing about the asylum's financial statements, and as is often the case, the balance sheet of the institution reveals something about its true functioning. If we bear with Cooper, we can detect disastrous tendencies that would play out over the following seventeen decades. "We hire our attendants, servants and domestics for half of what they [other institutions, mostly non-southern] report to pay them," Cooper explained.[2] His treasurer's report on labor costs contains references to "Benj. Brewer (Negro) Sunday wages $5.00"; "JB Davis, Negro hire as per voucher, 5.00" (twice); "J.D. Owen contingent funds for negro hire." These annotations were among $100 worth of expenses for "clothing, groceries &c. &c." And on November 1, 1844, he noted a "Negro hire for the year averaging 3 nearly" at $188.00, which would mean $62.67 per year per enslaved worker. These hired-out enslaved people worked, we can assume, at the asylum's most menial and unpleasant tasks—those water closets, those walls smeared with excrement.[3] Subsidized by enslaved people's labor, Cooper boasted that Georgia's asylum would be "cheaper than any other Institution in the United States, or in the civilized world."[4]

With his arithmetical prolepses, Cooper was trying to explain to his bosses in the legislature the financial benefits to Georgia counties of transferring indigent care to a state institution. First, he conservatively estimated the total lunatic/epileptic/idiot patient base in Georgia as five hundred people. With $100 as a per capita annual cost for five hundred people, he calculated $50,000 per year all told that the counties could save after the state assumed all of the cost for county patients. By assuming this responsibility, the state consolidated its authority. The estimated cost to the state was $1.918 per week per patient. This figure beat the lowest costs at that time of Vermont and New Hampshire, with each of these lowest-spending states averaging $2 per patient per week. Thus, Georgia firmly established its place near the bottom in outlays for patient care, where it would stay. Patients' labor also helped his bottom line and his moral therapy. Dr. Cooper, like other southern men of his class, had a firm belief in the benefits of other people's labor. For the legislators, Cooper calculated the benefits of patients' work that literally freed their hands from chains; over the year, the hours of all the female patients added up to 5.71 full-time female workers out of a total of twelve women who worked in the first cohort of thirty-four patients. The savings that these composite "5.71 females" produced was only $56.81, but their piecework was substantial. Over one year, they produced by hand six quilts, thirteen night comforters, twenty-three dresses, seventeen shirts, eight pairs of stockings, eight capes, six caps, four handkerchiefs, two quilts of smaller pieces, ten days of occasional washing of finer articles, spinning and twisting thread for various purposes, two pants and shirts, seven aprons, and six hand towels. The industry of 8.23 full-time male patients that year saved the institution $108.26. It included "getting wood, gardening, &c., viz" to produce 12 bushels of corn; 120 pounds of fodder; 75 bushels of sweet potatoes; 30 bushels of Irish potatoes, cabbages, and cucumbers; 180 gallons of milk; and 15 pounds of butter.[5] When the 5.71 full-time workers is divided by twelve women, it comes out to each woman working 47.6 percent of full time. For men, their 8.23 full-time composite divided by twenty-two men comes to 39 percent of full time. The women, then, worked more than the men did—not an unusual circumstance. These accounts of produce grow exponentially over decades of annual reports.

All this was an immense amount of work for 13.94 "full-time" male and female patients, given all of the cathartics, purgatives, and various debilitating symptoms, as well as the walks on the promenade, trips into town, and picking of melons and fruits Cooper uplifted in other portions of the report. The justification of "moral therapy" was, in Cooper's words, a tradeoff between "abolishing restraints and confinement, and introducing labor in their stead." In this way, "in the work shop, the garden, the field of labor," the patient finds the "pleasure, happiness, and contentment" that replace "hallucinations, delusions and derangement." All of this work was probably preferable for the patients to laxatives and emetics and trips to the water closet or the chamber pot or the cuffs and restraining chairs and straitjackets. Whether it provided "pleasure and happiness" in exchange for hallucinations and delusions is much less clear. But for administrators, patient labor was its own reward, and in this regard American institutions led the world. Cooper bragged about the work requirements thusly: "Our progress in America in this laudable enterprize within the last dozen years has surpassed any other three nations upon the Globe."[6] And that was only white workers. In 1867, when freedpeople entered the picture, the distribution of patient labor would shift, dramatically.

And what of the enslaved African American workers? Surely all six of them knew white people could be crazy. There is evidence enough of this opinion that emerged in former slaves' narratives, like that of Frederick Douglass, published in 1845—the year after Samuel's arrival. Power corrupts white slave owners, makes them cruel, these formerly enslaved narrators asserted as they rattled their former chains, determined to bring down slavery. Thomas Jefferson made a similar argument in *Notes on the State of Virginia*, as he struggled with his conflicting desires for justice and for Sally Hemings, the enslaved woman who bore his children. Jefferson wrote, "The whole commerce between master and slave is a perpetual exercise of the most boisterous passions, the most unremitting despotism on the one part, and degrading subjugation on the other. Our children see this, and learn to imitate it: for man is an imitative animal."[7]

From Reasons Not Necessary Here to Allude . . .

Supt. Cooper avoided acknowledging slavery's dreadful realities, but Amariah Brigham did too. He steered his new journal away from the turbulent debates over slavery taking place in the mid-1840s, perhaps out of concern about the mental excitement they generated. Rather than joining these debates, the early volumes of the *American Journal of Insanity* (AJI) reveal the editor's and contributors' strategic use of omissions, euphemisms, and indirections concerning the controversies about slavery roiling the nation at the time. For example, in the mid-1840s Superintendents John Galt and Francis Stribling of Virginia and William Awl of the Ohio Lunatic Asylum manned the Association of Medical Superintendents of American Institutions for the Insane (AMSAII) committee "On Asylums for Colored Persons." In AJI volume II, reports from both Virginia and South Carolina "*allude* to the importance of some provision being made for the proper care and treatment of insane colored persons." The South Carolina report summarized how their work proceeded "from reasons *to which it is not necessary here to allude*, the white and colored subjects can not be associated, and any provision for this latter class will necessarily involve the erection of another building" (both emphases mine).[8] Such euphemisms and marked indirection characterized most of the journal's subsequent antebellum discussions about slavery and African Americans.

   This lack of debate over the ethics of slavery and race within psychiatry's preeminent professional journal, even when slavery was being vehemently debated in the wider culture, ensured that these ideas entered national psychiatric discourse in a more subterranean form. In the AJI, instead of essays on race, there are articles on pyromania, witchcraft, money-making mania, suicides, escapes, numerous female mental disorders, reports on asylum organization and architecture, inebriety, effects of religious excitement, and tubercule of the brain.

Editor Brigham asserted that "no other disease, probably, is increasing faster in our country than insanity, and from investigations recently made in several of the northern states, there is reason to fear that it already prevails here to a greater extent than in any other country." Brigham speculated that insanity prevails most in countries where the people enjoy "civil and religious freedom" and are "induced, or at liberty to engage in the strife for wealth, and for the highest honors and distinctions of society." Here, Brigham wedded the virtues of American freedoms with the highly competitive capitalist economy in which all Americans were "induced, or at liberty to engage" in the strife for wealth, recognition, and high distinction.[9] Nor did he note the difference in being "at liberty" and being "induced" when such incentives included whips and chains.

Those psychiatrists who agreed with Brigham on the vulnerabilities arising from these rapid changes in America never considered that one culprit might also be the violence that accompanied the "strife for wealth" over such huge fortunes to be made from Indian land and labor and the race to position oneself for the "highest honors and distinctions of society" in settler colonies, then states. Once we consider this possibility, it seems almost peculiar that they did not.

Brigham was "not a social leveler or racial egalitarian," according to his biographer Lawrence Goodheart, but rather a person who believed that, in his own words, "no improvement equal to what the white races have made or are capable of making is to be expected, from the dark colored races, unless their physical organization is improved." So, with all of his professional credentials and accomplishments, Supt. Brigham was not so different in this regard from his colleagues farther south, who found Blacks and Indians, in Brigham's words, "inferior to white men in cerebral capacity for abstract thought, the engine of civilization."[10]

Likewise, Brigham's opinions on whites' vulnerabilities to insanity were hardly unique. "Before the Civil War," writes historian David Rothman, "practically no one in the United States protested the simple connection between insanity and civilization," particularly civilization increasingly shaped by urban and industrial forces. Rothman notes that most American psychiatrists believed that slaves were particularly insulated from insanity, as John Galt of Eastern State Hospital explained, "perhaps owing not only to less degree of mental cultivation, but also to the absence of all cares for the future, the great depressing influence with whites," an opinion remarkable for its willed ignorance of the brutalities of slavery. Historian of asylums Gerald Grob identifies this thinking as a variant of the agrarian myth: "The idea that virtue could exist only in a simple, rural and agrarian society untouched by the ravages of industrialism and urbanism." He quotes the trustees of the Worcester, Massachusetts, hospital in its 1845 report: "Insanity is rare in a savage state of society."[11] African American scholar Martha Diana Louis terms the result of such thinking "proslavery psychiatry."[12]

Rothman also shows that Europeans were more cautious in accepting this premise about high rates of U.S. insanity that Americans accepted "without qualification" in spite of the "tenuous quality" of the evidence. For England's Samuel Tuke, Quaker head of the York Retreat, the evidence was "deficient, to an extent which . . . does not warrant us to decide." His colleague and fellow British psychiatrist Henry Maudsley pointed out that European travelers reporting on "primitive" people were, in Rothman's words, "neither competent nor learned enough to reach valid conclusions." In Germany, Wilhelm Griesinger argued that higher rates of insanity might reflect better treatments that made symptoms more public, and that civilization brought higher living standards that "ought to compensate, at least to a certain extent, for any injurious influence of the spread of civilization."[13] We do not have to accept the U.S. assessment of national insanity to note its ideological function. White insanity equaled white mental superiority. However, those sufferers committed to Georgia's asylum did not feel their positions as superior, nor were they treated as such.

Exemptions from Insanity?

In spite of Brigham, history inevitably showed up in his journal's pages, if between the lines and at times in remarkable ways. For example, a brief article in the second volume (1845) of the *American Journal of Insanity*,

"Exemption of the Cherokee Indians and Africans from Insanity," provided three perspectives on settler-colonial psychiatry, two of which were from Georgia. Testimony from all three informants purported to demonstrate the superiority of white people's tendencies toward going insane in comparison to more primitive mental types. First, the article conveyed the report of Dr. Charles Lillybridge, Government Medical Officer, who "superintend[ed] the removal of the Cherokee Indians, in 1837–8 and 9, and who saw more than twenty thousand Indians, and inquired much about their diseases" on their forced journeys west. It concluded that Lillybridge "never saw or heard of a case of insanity among them." Second, Dr. Elizur Butler, for twenty-five years a "devoted Missionary and Physician among the Cherokees," reported that an intelligent chief who had toured the asylum in Philadelphia, "a man now 80 years old, told him that 'he had never known a case of insanity among his people, such as he had seen [there].'" Third, Cinqué of "the *Amistad* Negroes" had "visited the retreat for the Insane at Hartford, CT and saw many of the patients there." He reported that the sight was "very rare" in African countries.[14]

Seemingly unknown to Brigham, the article provided a covert glimpse into the settler-colonial history, whose lessons the AJI so avoided, with two informants from the infamous Trail of Tears, on which Cherokees were forced west, and the third from the most famous slave uprising and trial of the antebellum period, that of Cinqué of the *Amistad*. We will hear from Reverend Butler later to appreciate the contradictions.

No Sense of Urgency Outside the South

As noted historian of U.S. asylums Gerald Grob notes, asylum psychiatrists were remarkably absent from the debates over race occurring in the scientific community of the nineteenth century, rarely engaging in discussions in such theoretical terms. "Outside of the South the issue of mental illness among Blacks did not arouse any sense of urgency among hospital or welfare officials, if only because the proportion of Blacks in the general population was low," Grob explains.[15] Before the Civil War, Grob documents, the slave states had a variety of policies and practices toward

African Americans. Maryland did not segregate patients. Western Kentucky Lunatic Asylum admitted slaves paid for by owners but separated them from whites. Eastern Kentucky Lunatic Asylum refused to accept slaves. Georgia, Tennessee, and Mississippi made no provision. Louisiana accepted free Blacks and some slaves. South Carolina after 1848 authorized acceptance of Black patients in separate facilities, but by 1860 accepted only Black females. At Williamsburg, John Galt accepted enslaved people as patients beginning in the mid-1800s, with Black females housed in separate structures and Black males in integrated wards with whites, until 1856, when the asylum no longer accepted slaves. At Virginia's Western Lunatic Asylum, Superintendent Francis Stribling insisted on separate and distinct institutions.[16]

One factor in the lack of acrimony over slavery among antebellum psychiatrists was, as Grob explains, that asylums outside of the antebellum South had similar policies to southern ones: Black people were at the bottom, either denied admission or segregated within an existing institution with inferior care. The Massachusetts General Hospital in 1836 rejected Black applicants. The hospital at Worcester, Massachusetts, in 1833 built separate lodgings (in the brick shop), as did the Government Hospital for the Insane in Washington, DC, in 1855. In Indiana in 1854, the state hospital rejected Black applicants. The New York City Almshouse in 1837 provided a separate building for Black patients, described as "a scene of neglect, and filth, and putrefaction, and vermin . . . a scene the recollection of which are too sickening to describe."[17]

These antebellum superintendents' approach to questions of African Americans and of slavery was not so different from that of noted reformer Dorothea Dix, who began advocating for the mentally ill in 1841 in Massachusetts, documenting the conditions of the mentally ill incarcerated in prisons. She went on to document and advocate across the states, becoming a "voice for the mad." After 1845 she worked for fifteen years mainly with southern legislators because they welcomed her position that the condition of the insane was worse than that of slaves. Comments her biographer David Gollaher, "She turned her back on the prejudice, hate, and violence of the slave system. . . . For her, the slaves seem barely to have existed."[18]

The 1840 Census, John C. Calhoun, and Slavery's Hygienic Effects

Such assertions of African American and native people's lack of intelligence and emotional capacity flew in the face of observers' accounts of their actual experiences on forced migrations or in cotton and sugar fields or on the block for sale in slave markets.

In 1840, as the debate around abolition heated up, the U.S. census became an ideological driver when for the first time it listed "insane" and "idiot" as categories. The highly controversial interpretation of the resulting data pitted firebrand secretary of state John C. Calhoun against two foremost experts in the emerging field of statistics, one a Black man, the other white. That these two proved the data's interpretation to be impossible did little to blunt its ideological force. Today we might call it "alternative facts."

According to the official interpretation, the 1840 census's results showed greater numbers of those in the "insane" and "idiot" categories among free Black people outside the South than it did among enslaved Blacks within it. As journalist and scholar on issues of medical ethics Harriet Washington observes in *Medical Apartheid: The Dark History of Medical Experimentation on African Americans*: "Printed in 1841 under the aegis of the U.S. Department of State, the document seemed the very model of objectivity, offering dense orderly rows and columns of numbers collected by census takers without salient bias." It recorded a ratio of 1:1558 "idiot or insane" Blacks to "normal" ones in the South and 1:144 in the North. The data fed such firebrand architects of the new form of slavery that was unfolding across the Deep South in states such as Georgia as Secretary of State John C. Calhoun, who argued from its results that slavery had beneficial effects.[19] Two eminent statisticians soon contradicted the census data and its conclusions. Edward Jarvis from Massachusetts, a white physician and recent founder of the American Statistical Association, analyzed the northern data to show the census to be a "fallacious and self-condemning document." Dr. James McCune Smith, an African American doctor at Harvard and also a member of the new American Statistical Association, analyzed data across regions and presented his own critical assessment to the Senate in 1844. Armed with their analysis, John Quincy Adams (who soon would defend Cinqué of the *Amistad*) sought to get a resolution through the U.S. House of Representatives repudiating its conclusions, but Secretary of State Calhoun blocked his efforts.[20] One AJI article from 1851 does reference the 1840 census data as fact: "Who would believe without the fact, in black and white, before his eyes, that every fourteenth colored person in the State of Maine is an idiot or a lunatic?"[21] Black and white, indeed.

For Samuel Henderson, his residency at the Georgia Asylum could not have felt like a badge of white superiority. His experience was the retching, puking, shitting, the struggles against humans and restraints, the nausea-inducing drops slipped in coffee or drinks, then the hot calm, the views of men and women inmates walking together in the yard or botanizing. Limning his own cycles, he perhaps learned to read and predict these wild waves of ferocious energy and successive calms that at times coincided with a swelling moon or changes in atmosphere, storms coming in or passing through the rustling, bending trees and minds.[22]

Soon enough, Samuel would join Crazy Nancy, rolling John Smith, and a clothed Mary Riley in the yard, and the white men in the fields. Henderson would get to know the staff and other inmates at the Georgia Asylum quite well over the next decade. He would die there in 1855, an early inhabitant of the grounds' cemeteries, eventually to be the largest burial place of disabled people in the world. Henderson had learned the hard way the dangers of irony in a culture so committed to its deceptions, to those obvious lies that held together its violent rationales. Supt. Cooper avoided his profession's contradictions and, even if he had tried to explain them, his prose was incomprehensible.

3

"Stark Mad After Negroes!":
The Asylum's Georgia Backstory

History will always find you, and wrap you
In its thousand arms.

—Joy Harjo, *American Sunrise*[1]

The hundreds of acres that would house the state's asylum two miles outside of what became the Georgia capital of Milledgeville carried the land's stories. They start for us with the Muscogee, with their culture of reciprocity, gift giving, and mediation that helped to preserve the peace.[2] For centuries these Muscogee peoples knew an Upper World of sun and moon and thunder, marking time, releasing powers of perfection, order, and clarity. They also knew a Lower World of madness, creation, upset, and chaos. The great antlered snake, the Tie-Snake, lurked in the river bottoms, making humans sick or mad. Its scales shone like mirrors; its head was a crystal. In the Lower World traveled restless ghosts who could also bring sickness or trouble, haunting homes until their deaths were avenged. These ghosts in their changing forms (man, woman, owl, or bear) consumed human souls. *Sti:kinni*, as the Muscogee called them, might come upon the hunter or herb gatherer alone in the forest, or on the aged or the newborn. Holding these worlds together and restoring balance was the Creator, *Hesákádum Esée*, the Holder of Breath.[3] For them, land was sacred to all the people and creatures and could not be owned.

A Colony Late to the Game But Fast Catching Up

The Georgia Asylum was built on Muscogee land along the Oconee River. As if he owned it, in 1732 England's King George II created the colony of Georgia and gave the colony's trustees, under the direction of James Oglethorpe, all the land between the Savannah and Altamaha Rivers north to their headwaters and extending in a narrow strip of land along parallel latitudes across the entire continent to the "South Seas," or the Pacific Ocean. That strip was approximately 2,700 miles long. Subsequent wars and their treaties whittled down this grandiose reach into contested lands claimed variously by French, Spanish, and English as their "right of discovery" and "right of conquest."

In 1732, Oglethorpe landed with his contingent of 114 skilled and "worthy poor" English immigrants at Yamacraw Bluff beneath what would become the city of Savannah. They were met by the Muscogee chief Tomochichi, the representative of indigenous survivors of other European arrivals on the coast, which was already a "shatter zone" of less than one thousand native people. Writes historian Paul Pressley, "The depopulated strip of land from the Savannah to the St. Marys River served as mute testimony to the far-reaching effect on this latter day version of the 'Columbia cataclysm.'"[4] Oglethorpe set up Savannah as the civilian seat of the new colony, premised on the success of yeoman farmers; Fort Frederica on St. Simons Island as the British military command along the coast; and the frontier trading post at Augusta, where the trading paths into Muscogee territory came together as its commercial center.[5]

As the southernmost of the thirteen British colonies, Georgia came relatively late to the colonial game. In the beginning, Georgia's utopian-minded founders outlawed both rum and slaves. They intended for Georgia to be more radically egalitarian than the South Carolina plantations that loomed to the north and were based on the gulag-like Caribbean system of sugar production that dominated the first three centuries of slavery in the Americas. South Carolina had adopted the 1661 Slave Code of the island of Barbados: its tenets included characterization of slaves as "brutish" and "heathen," a brutal reliance on the whip, and establishing policing as the heart of the system. Georgia's founding idealism lasted two decades, proving economically unviable in the slave- and profit-driven economies of the New World. In 1750, Georgia trustees voted for slavery and rum even as they called on Georgians to elect their first representative assembly and turned the colony's governance over to it and them.

"My Lord they are stark Mad after Negroes," an antislavery Georgia school master commented in 1746.[6] Between 1751 and 1754 along the

Georgia coast, the new dispensation put in place the type of brutal plantation economy that South Carolina had taken eighty years to construct. In this process, a small Savannah elite made awards of up to five hundred acres of land to themselves and to settlers and planters from the West Indies and South Carolina, who brought with them their enslaved people already "seasoned" by the whip.[7] By 1770, Georgia had followed South Carolina's lead in adopting the Barbados system. In all, slave traders through the (First) Middle Passage would forcibly land 388,000 Africans in North America, and 56 percent of them would arrive through the low country of coastal Georgia and South Carolina.[8]

"These oligarchs' rise to power was as rapid as it was astonishing," Pressley observed in *On the Rim of the Caribbean*.[9] Georgia's slave economy entered international markets at a fortuitous time during both the "appalling height of the entire slave trade" and a peak in the price for Carolina rice. Pressley writes that by the mid-1760s "Georgia represented the imperial dream at its best." For enslaved Africans, of course, it was a different story. "No region in the United States had a harsher form of slavery than the lowcountry," Pressley explains. The tidewater rice plantation that drove the economy was a "huge hydraulic machine," a "feat of modern social engineering, making enormous demands of its labor force."[10] By the Revolution, sixty planters owned half of the slaves in Georgia.[11]

White settlers would remain stark mad for Negroes as long as the Negroes were their slaves. After 1763, the colony's pincer movements to obtain native land and acquire African workers accelerated when the British won the French and Indian War (in Europe called the Seven Years' War) against both French and Spanish to achieve British control of the southeast. This war was settled by the 1763 Treaty of Paris.

British into Muscogee Heartlands

This victory had multiple negative consequences for the Muscogee because it brought the interior land and its people into direct contact with the British for the first time. By 1763, the Muscogee were one of the few southeastern native peoples whose population was growing, with a fifty-town confederacy that had absorbed refugees from many other tribes already decimated and displaced by settler incursion. In 1760, the Muscogee had 3,655 fighting men and a total population of 13,000, compared with 6,000 white Georgians and 3,550 Blacks. The 1763 treaty ended their autonomy.[12]

There were other consequences of British victory. The Muscogee were no longer able to play English, French, and Spanish against one another to their advantage. Also, they entered into direct contact with Georgia traders for access to global markets—for guns, powder, balls, cloth from India, beads from Vienna, vermillion from Venice for war paint, and rum. Savannah merchants began to compete with Charleston in the deerskin trade. In another of the cascade of consequences, a collapse of regulations for commerce brought unprecedented levels of Caribbean rum into these commodity circuits. From 1868 to 1872, 99,000 gallons of rum flowed into Georgia, one-third of it into the native market for the Muscogee, who had no cultural prohibitions against alcohol overconsumption. The resulting trade deficit with the Georgians led to the overhunting of deer to pay for a rum habit that cost them 670,000 skins per year. The Muscogee surrendered 2.3 million acres east of the Ogeechee River in the 1863 Treaty of Augusta in return for debt "forgiveness" and a guaranteed boundary that Georgia settlers were determined to violate. In treaty after treaty, the Muscogee traded their land to pay off these debts, many of them for the rum that undermined their cultural forms.[13] Thus, alcohol's ability to shatter cultures opened up the Georgia interior where its asylum would stand, and white settlers would not be immune to the "whiskey frolics" that the alcohol trade brought, as we will see.

In Georgia, the new deer trade opened up multiple schisms between interior and coast: trade versus agriculture, deer versus rice, small towns and small farmers versus planters, few Africans in the interior versus the vast majority of them along the coasts, linguistic diversity versus English-only in Savannah. All of these tensions are recognizable to us today. The American Revolution resolved these underlying tensions between British Empire and American nation-state, after which Georgia shifted into an aggressive white-settler society.[14] After the Revolution, upcountry whites displaced the pro-British Savannah elite, and Savannah gave up its place as state capital.[15]

An Aggressive White-Settler State

Upcountry dominance would be fed by a powerful new commodity—short-leaf cotton, whose fibers could be harvested by the new cotton gin. In 1793, on a Georgia plantation, Eli Whitney invented the gin for short-leaf cotton.[16] The machine's combing device separated fibers from the sticky seeds within them. It broke the bottleneck in short-leaf cotton production and opened up the Cotton Kingdom across the Deep South, the numbers of bales of cotton burgeoning in tandem with the numbers of enslaved Africans.

The southernmost of the Thirteen Colonies, Georgia became the easternmost state of the Cotton Kingdom and played a pivotal role in the growth of slavery in the Deep South. From 1783 to 1861, the number of U.S. slaves would multiply five times over, producing two billion pounds of cotton in 1861.[17] The labor of enslaved African Americans over the next half century would make the southern states dominant in global cotton markets. Southern plantations made cotton the most widely traded global commodity. King Cotton was the key raw material in the textile industry, and textiles were the first to mechanize in the newly emerging factory system of the Industrial Revolution in both Europe and the United States. Historian Edward Baptist summarizes the massive and rapid changes under way thusly: "In the space of a single lifetime after the 1780s, the South grew from a narrow coastal strip of worn-out plantations to a sub-continental empire." Thus, the cotton monopoly modernized the U.S. economy, making the United States the second nation after England to industrialize on a large scale. "In fact," Baptist argues, "slavery's expansion shaped every crucial aspect of the economy and politics of the new nation" including the understanding of "what it felt to suffer."[18]

The new capital of Milledgeville would be built on the frontier between whites and natives, its purpose to direct the aggressive white-settler society. Administered from the new capital, the income from the conquest and theft of native land would multiply in astounding ways in the new state's coffers. This process would enrich white settlers, who moved into "ceded" territory, and the distribution of stolen native land became the most important function of the state in the first third of the nineteenth century.[19]

Ensnaring the Muscogee in debt opened the way for settlement into a previously Muscogee region. In 1787, on the West bank of the Oconee River, the United States built Fort Wilkinson as a federal trading post to lure the Muscogee into debt by trading for deer pelts or by extending credit for iron cook pots, winter hunting supplies, cloth clothing, cotton leggings, hats, buttons, combs, rifles, lead, tobacco, fish hooks, and beaver traps. In 1802, the Treaty of Fort Wilkinson excused $23,000 of debt that the Muscogee subsequently amassed in trading, in exchange for their hunting lands. On this former hunting land, the new County of Baldwin was founded in 1803, and in 1804 the state capital of Milledgeville was built upstream from Fort Wilkinson. In 1843, the Georgia Asylum would open up the hill from the trading post on the Oconee. The new capital would provide its own pivot point into the interior for the final removal of the Muscogee and the Cherokee and the expansion of slavery into the Kingdom of Cotton.

In 1802, Georgia signed the Articles of Agreement and Cession with the federal government to fix Georgia's boundaries roughly into its current shape. It moved the western boundary to the Chattahoochee River that then would divide Georgia from the new territory-cum-state of Alabama. Georgia gave up its claims to land beyond the Chattahoochee in exchange for $1.25 million that would be paid as the land was sold. The federal government also agreed to extinguish native tribes' claims to lands within the state of Georgia. Georgia became the last state to sell its land claims to the United States and the only state to get a substantial cash settlement for them. Congress awarded the money so as to allow Georgia to pay off shady investors. These included many members of Congress who had invested in the scandalous Yazoo land scheme to control the territory that was to become Alabama and Mississippi. Those congressmen made sure they were repaid for their bad gamble.

The 1802 cession agreement and the 1803 Louisiana Purchase guaranteed Indian removal, which would take thirty more years, first of the Muscogee, then of the Cherokee.[20] In the words of Thomas Jefferson, the Louisiana Purchase "put in our power the means of inducing the Indians to transplant themselves to the other side of the Mississippi before many years get about."[21]

Free Land for 100,000 White Settlers

In 1803, the Georgia assembly passed a law providing for distribution of ceded land by lottery, a process that only Georgia used for land distribution. Registered white males, widows, and orphans put their names in one drum, with property-lot numbers in the other to be matched until all lots were distributed. Between 1805 and 1833, Georgia conducted eight such land lotteries, seven of which were organized out of the new capital of Milledgeville, its statehouse built over a Muscogee burial ground and opened for business by 1807. Winning this lottery meant that Georgia heads of household could get two hundred acres, or double that, for four to seven cents an acre. In this manner, over the next quarter century "Georgia sold approximately three-quarters of the state to about 100,000 families and individuals for miniscule amounts of money."[22] With the backing of the U.S. army and Georgia militias, over those three decades the State of Georgia pushed native tribes out, as white families moved into farms, woods, mountains, and valleys that native inhabitants fought to defend. Such dispossession was by its nature violent, and it left its mark on both the land and its new white settlers.

By the 1810s, Georgia began to net large sums from the state's land lotteries. In 1817 and 1818, the final federal payment of $756,000 to Georgia from the 1802 agreement went to building up the state's infrastructure of roads, railroads, canals, passable rivers, and "poor schools" without requiring taxes to do so. The payout was also used to build the Georgia Penitentiary in Milledgeville to consolidate state authority over counties that previously kept their criminals in county jails.[23] It was the beginning of Baldwin County's carceral history. The penitentiary policed and punished white people, while the plantation system mostly policed its enslaved African Americans. The fate of antebellum appropriations rose and fell with cash infusions into the treasury from the sale of stolen native lands and the booms and busts of the increasingly frenzied trade in cotton and slaves. In 1828, chronic surpluses led the general assembly to create the Central Bank of Georgia to channel public funds into long-term loans to select citizens so that the state could directly profit.[24] The income from state banking compensated for the decline in land sales after Georgia's last lottery of Cherokee land in 1832.[25]

The Trail Where They Cried

In the 1820s, the Cherokee were in the last bitter part of their epic struggle for their homelands. Over sixty tribes, mostly from the Southeast, would end up in Oklahoma by the century's end, only 10 percent of which were Cherokee. But historians Theda Perdue and Michael D. Green explain that the Cherokee's story of *Nu No Du Na Tlo Hi Lu*, "The Trail Where They Cried," has been used to tell the overall story of Indian removal.[26] It was the Cherokee, at their capital of New Echota, Georgia, in the 1820s and 1830s, who most fulfilled the "civilization strategy" of Presidents Washington, Jefferson, Madison, and John Quincy Adams, which sought to force Indians to assimilate into white ways as a step toward privatizing their land. The Cherokee were, Perdue and Green explain, "uniquely well educated and extraordinarily articulate in both spoken and written English . . . [In] countless public speeches and written statements, they produced a trove of documents that dwarfs the records of other Native nations."[27] The *Cherokee Phoenix*, published in English from 1828 to 1834, was only the latest result of the Cherokee strategy over the previous two decades to assimilate selectively into white culture, but never to relinquish collective land ownership.

In 1824, Governor George Troup explained, "The utmost of rights and privileges which public opinion would concede to Indians would fix them in a middle station, between the negro and white man [so that the Indian would] gradually sink to the condition of the former, a point of degeneracy below which they could not fall."[28]

The willing sale of individual parcels of native land was exactly the result that the "civilization strategy" proponents most expected from the Cherokee. Such would-be civilizers thought that because the Cherokee had developed an alphabet, learned English, wore pants (the men) and skirts (the women), and had their own constitution—that they had also been newly civilized into "love for exclusive property" and so would willingly sell their land for money. But instead, by 1822 the increasingly centralized Cherokee Nation, which perfectly understood the logic of the colonials (including their ideas of private property), had refused to cede another acre, and by 1827 rewrote their constitution to assert their sovereignty over their territory. In response, Georgia's governor, legislators, and land-hungry whites embraced the logic of expulsion that Perdue and Green compare to ethnic cleansing. They annexed Cherokee land, abolished their government, and established a process for seizing and distributing millions of acres to whites. In 1828, Old Hickory's election sealed the Cherokee's fate. Representatives from Georgia and other southern states pushed through the Indian Relocation Act (1830), which gave President Andrew Jackson the authority he sought to negotiate or demand removal.

At this juncture, Jackson encountered again that white missionary friend of the Cherokee Elizur Butler. Reverend Butler was one of the three informants in the *American Journal of Insanity* piece on Africans' and Cherokees' being "exempt from insanity." He was one of the ministers who supported the Cherokee and sued the U.S. government. This larger context of his story illuminates how much history the *American Journal of Insanity* obscured. New settlers poured into Cherokee land, and Cherokee leadership fought back through the courts. The Georgia legislature passed a law forbidding whites to live within the Cherokee Nation without the state's permission. Working with Cherokee leaders and lawyers, Elizur Butler, along with several other white missionaries, decided to challenge the law. After a series of arrests and releases, in September of 1831 the missionaries were convicted and sentenced to four years of hard labor in the state penitentiary at Milledgeville. Represented by Cherokee Nation lawyers, the white missionaries appealed to the U.S. Supreme Court. In 1832 Chief Justice John Marshall's decision in *Worcester v. Georgia* struck down the Georgia laws, as Marshall wrote, finding Indian nations "distinct, independent, political communities retaining their original rights," a landmark decision for Native American sovereignty. But President Jackson refused to enforce the high court's decision. Marshall and the Supreme Court be damned, U.S. soldiers began the Cherokees' forced marches westward.

By the late summer of 1838, General Winfield Scott and seven thousand U.S. soldiers and Georgia militias burst into homes, woods, and fields to round up thousands of Cherokee, leaving corn in the furrows, venison on the table, children or mates behind in the woods. From the missions that dotted the landscape of the remaining Cherokee land, white missionaries watched their friends be taken away. General Scott's forces herded over ten thousand Cherokee into thirty-one recently built forts, then soon relocated their prisoners to eleven internment camps "like droves of hogs . . . hastening to a premature grave," Butler's missionary friend Reverend Daniel Butrick would write. The forts and camps were abysmal, with the whiskey hawked by whites for the Indians' last U.S. dollars the only thing in ample supply, along with the sexual abuse of women, as Rev. Butrick described, "debauched through terror."[29]

Chief Ross had led the Cherokee in a brilliant campaign of resistance up to the Supreme Court. When a faction of Cherokee signed a treaty of voluntary removal in 1836, Chief Ross and the majority of the Cherokee opposed the "treaty tribe." "Our hearts are sickened," Chief Ross wrote from the Red Clay Council Ground in 1836 to the Senate and House of Representatives in a final but futile effort to change white elite minds. "We are overwhelmed! . . . For assuredly, we are not ignorant of our condition; we are not insensible to our suffering. We feel them! We groan under their pressure! An anticipation crowds our breasts with sorrows yet to come."[30] The senators' and congressmen's hearts were insensible to Cherokee suffering. By August of 1838, Ross knew the battle was lost.

These Cherokee sorrows so piercingly expressed in the English language put the lie to whatever the *American Journal of Insanity* might opine about the inability of "primitive" people to feel and therefore about their "exemption" from insanity given whatever the white-settler state might do to them.

Going Away to Georgia, Oh, Heave O!

In the 1830s, while the Cherokee in Georgia made their last stand, a new kind of slavery was in the making, captured in a Chesapeake watermen's chant, "Going away to Georgia, oh, heave, O! / Massa sell poor negro, ho, heave, O! / Leave poor wife and children, ho, heave, O!"[31] These shackled slaves were the leading edge in another wave of forced migrations, a Second Middle Passage, this one not over the oceans as the First Middle Passage had been, but over land. Historian Edward Baptist calculated "another 1 million walkers' 1.5 trillion steps [that] would shape seven decades of slavery's expansion in the new United States."[32] Enslaved people walked south, then west, in coffles, "twenty pounds of chains that draped from neck to neck, wrist to wrist, binding them all together" in lock step as they came down the road "like a giant machine."[33] Because of this shift of slavery south and west, Baptist calls this period from 1829 to 1837 the "hinge" of U.S. history, with Georgia forming the hinge on which slavery swung from the tobacco, rice, and indigo plantations of the Carolinas to the cotton and sugar plantations of the Deep South.[34]

In 1837, Georgia, along with other states, received a payment from recent federal sales of western land stolen from its native people. Georgia's slice was $1,051,422, deposited into the Central Bank of Georgia. From 1835 to 1840, riding this wave of largesse, Georgia charged its citizens no taxes, as the U.S. army forced more Cherokees westward so that white settlers had more land. The Georgia General Assembly used the federal payment to allocate the initial $44,000 from 1837 to 1841 to build the first building of the Georgia State Lunatic, Idiot, and Epileptic Asylum and to hire Superintendent David Cooper as its leader.[35]

The same generation of white men who from the Milledgeville capital developed even newer ways to expel the Cherokee people and to develop newer and more brutally profitable forms of slavery—these same men also built and oversaw the Georgia Lunatic Asylum. For example, asylum founder and trustee Dr. Tomlinson Fort, whom Benjamin Rush (the "father of American psychiatry") had taught medicine in Philadelphia, served as president of the Central Bank of Georgia from 1832 to 1844.[36]

Then in 1838 the cotton bubble burst when the price of cotton finally dropped on global markets, and the price of land and slaves plummeted along with it. It also caused a massive sell-off in enslaved people because they were the collateral for planters' loans, bundled together at $500 per human to sell on global markets. All the promised additional money to the states from federal sales of conquered and stolen native lands evaporated. The bubbles and bursts of this rapacious new capitalism would carry white settlers as well as native and African peoples in its tumults.

The Georgia Asylum Opens

So by 1842 when the Georgia Asylum opened, the Muscogee were long gone. But its buildings rose on the land that Muscogee bands had inhabited. And the Tie-Snake perhaps still lurked in the Oconee River's shallows and edged its crystal-mirror head along its muddy flows. The asylum's patients and its staff left no sign that only sixty years before Muscogee families might have danced and cooked and played on the land outside their windows, underneath their feet, and that English traders sold them beads and guns and rum from the trading post at Fort Wilkinson just down the hill by the river before Treaty of Fort Wilkinson grabbed 2.3 million acres of Muscogee land.

Similar funds from confiscated Indian land caused a nationwide surge in asylums and encouraged the consolidation of U.S. psychiatry as an asylum-based profession. For example, the New York State Legislature also made appropriations for state asylums in 1836–37, in part from recent money from sold-off Indian lands, and opened its asylum at Utica within a year of the asylum's opening in Milledgeville.[37] It was from these funds that Dr. Amariah Brigham was hired to run the Utica Asylum, from which he published the *American Journal of Insanity* that brought about the downfall of Supt. Cooper.

When Nancy Malone entered the Georgia Asylum in 1844, she carried part of this history with her in the vigorous chattering that had gotten her committed as an idiot. In her own way, she was a griot, a historian whose "mad farragoes" were a mix-tape, a mash-up of this Georgia "stark mad" for Negroes and for Indigenous land.

PART II

The Settler-Colonial Mind

No phenomenon better captures the fundamental race bias of public policy in Georgia than the most important undertaking of state government during its first half-century under the U.S. Constitution: the transfer of land from Indians to whites, land that was in turn, much of it, worked by slaves.

—Peter Wallenstein, *From Slave South to New South: Public Policy in Nineteenth-Century Georgia*[1]

"Fair and foul are near of kin,
And fair needs foul," I cried.
"My friends are gone, but that's a truth
Nor grave nor bed denied.
Learned in bodily lowliness
And in the heart's pride."

—William Butler Yeats, "Crazy Jane Talks with the Bishop"[2]

4

"Confused Farragoes" and "Mesmerized" Alcoholics: Nancy Malone, John Wade, Cherokee Removal, and Slavery

For nothing can be sole or whole
That has not been rent.
      —"Crazy Jane Talks with the Bishop," William Butler Yeats[3]

Mary Moore, matron of the Georgia Lunatic Asylum, first laid eyes on Nancy Malone on July 19, 1844, when Superintendent David Cooper or his steward William B. Moore received her and signed her in. One of them noted that Nancy was fifty years old, single, a pauper, and had been an idiot for twenty years, most recently supported by Pike County at the tune of $150 per year for food, clothing, and care. Nancy was the tenth woman admitted, seven before her still present on the asylum's female floor, only two yet returned as cured. She was the twenty-eighth patient, counting the eighteen males, one of whom had died and four others of whom had been discharged as improved or removed by friends. There were twenty-one patients at the asylum, then, when Nancy arrived. Supt. Cooper's injudicious 1845 annual report brings Nancy to us in vivid detail.

Nancy was loquacious, querulous, ranting, and profane; "frequently imagining wars, battles, murders, camp-meetings, Indian invasions and massacres, going on in rapid progression and retrogression, in her confused farrago of delusive mental perceptions and aberrations," with their "appalling apprehensions of defeat or exhilarating anticipations of success by the belligerent combatant." Then Nancy, "assaulted tho innocent, holding religion and scripture, &c. in derision and contempt; almost incessantly talking to herself, and supposed persons." She was "Crazy Nancy," channeling the energies of Georgia's settler history.[4]

Nancy, in her own way, was every bit as much a sight on arrival as Samuel Henderson had been. A wanderer and beggar, Nancy was unkempt, her clothes and person "disheviled." But most notable was her hair: so "long, glued and matted together that it could not be combed," the ledger noted as Nancy was handed over to "the Matron, and her servants"— Mrs. Mary Moore, William's wife, and unnamed slaves for cleaning up. We will assume that it was these enslaved women who first tackled Nancy's hair. The snip of scissors might have started at the back of her head, matted hair beginning to cover the ground around her or a fill a bucket. Closer to the skull her attendants discovered, as Cooper described later, "not only the ordinary vermin of more than ordinary size, and of unusual corpulence, ensconced in countless numbers," but also "the hairy worm and skipper, which are found in old bacon."[5] These creatures, too, dropped into the bucket as Nancy's hair bristled short, and her scarred and scabbed scalp breathed, and the bucket was hurried away, its contents to be burned with her flea-ridden and tattered clothing. Next would have come a hard scrubbing for layers of accumulated dirt and grime, and then simple but clean new clothes and a room of her own. She must have felt like a new woman.

Supt. Cooper did not "find it necessary to confine her," but "permit[ted] her daily to go out at will about the yards, kitchen, grove, &c., in sight of the building." He further reported: "She enjoys good health, eats and sleeps well, smokes her pipe, is often pleasant, facetious and jocular and taunting in some of her replies to jokes, and probably will live long and (in her capacity) see many happy days." She has "required only occasional a little aperient medicine when costive" (e.g., laxative when constipated).

The moral treatment seemed to be working for Nancy Malone.

Perhaps Nancy can help us to understand Supt. Amariah Brigham's assertion that U.S. insanity was increasing faster than in any other country. What might it mean to add Nancy's list of New World disturbances ("wars, massacres, &c.") to Amariah's speculations that insanity prevails most in countries where the people strive for honors, distinction, and wealth![6] It is the energies of this settler-colonial process to which Nancy was particularly attuned. And what did it mean for the editor Brigham to be so oblivious to the history of Cherokee removal that a figure like Rev. Elizur Butler (whom we will soon meet) evoked?

Folks back in Pike County had pegged Nancy as an "idiot" for the previous twenty years, and the asylum ledger concurred. Idiocy was one of the triumvirate of afflictions that made Georgia's asylum rare in its "towering munificence" (again David Cooper to his legislative bosses).[7] Today we are conditioned to read "idiot" back through the meanings that emerged in the early twentieth century. As we will later learn, the Binet-Simon scale and the Stanford-Binet test derived an "intelligence quotient" or IQ that declared "idiots" to be those below 20 IQ with less than three years' mental capacity. But no three-year-old in Georgia was capable of Nancy's "farragoes" or her probably informed "derision" of scripture; no three-year-old could have matched the suggested syntax and vocabulary of her constant conversation.

For Nancy and her keepers, what did this label mean? When the Georgia legislature founded its asylum, the law specified that it should accept "lunatics, epileptics, and idiots." The last category always contained the youngest and most vulnerable of the patients. Between 1842 and 1850, 21 of the 244 entries were described as "idiot," and by the end of the first volume of ledgers there are twenty-five entries noting idiocy. Lumped together under the term, these patients came from a range of circumstances and causes. "Idiocy was congenital" for some, indicating the condition was there from birth. To congenital in a few cases is added "deformity." Two entries noted fevers, one person who was "attacked by fever" at three years old and did not speak for three years. Another young woman who entered with an "illegitimate" baby had "sufficient mind to take care of herself" and was sent home. Others had epilepsy in addition to idiocy. Others came with other congenital conditions such as blindness.[8]

Cherokee County in 1846 sent eighteen-year-old and sixteen-year-old siblings, at least one of whom lived in the institution until 1909. In 1847, Paulding County sent four people, three from the same family, ages twenty-six, eighteen, and eight, two of these labeled "congenital." In February 1848, two sisters were brought from Houston County, twenty-one and twenty-three years old. In the earliest antebellum years, the youngest patients in the asylum were admitted for idiocy: a five-year-old from Paulding County, who soon "died in convulsions," and a seven-year-old from Lee County, who soon died of dysentery. Like Nancy, the term "idiot" covered a lot of territory.[9]

Coming into Middle English from Greek and Latin, *idiota* was a "private person, lacking skills or expertise," as opposed to "an educated citizen." "Idiot" attached to "dunce" (no learning), "fool" (no wisdom), and "ignoramus" (no education). It seems not so much Nancy's lack of intelligence as what she did with it that got her put away. Cooper described Nancy's mental state in terms of her "delusive mental perceptions and aberrations" and her energetic and constant delivery of them: "almost incessantly talking to herself, and supposed persons." Nancy was also a "wanderer," probably a beggar, who seems to have passed through enough places that they blurred in her mind, and she was "unable to tell what state or country [she was] born and raised in, the names of any villages, towns, or cities, with any certainty, or any rivers, but by accident."

Nancy had no formal education, but she had seen a lot in her wandering, and she was an open channel, a tabula rasa and town crier for half a century's settler history, which she talked about incessantly to herself, to the air, to the people around her, and to her more invisible interlocutors, conveying to all not only its content but also its emotional energies. Cooper summarized her patter as "frequently imagining wars, battles, murders, camp-meetings, Indian invasions and massacres," with Nancy stuck in a loop running constantly backward and forward in "rapid progression and retrogression." Her "highly excited" ups and downs coincided "with appalling apprehensions of defeat or exhilarating anticipations of success by belligerent combatants, and as often exulting in the success of the aggressors as the aggressed." The extreme alterations of her mental energies seem synched to those of her culture, her inner battles shaped by and replaying its outer wars and the booms and busts of its slave profit–driven capitalism.

A day or two into her stay at the Georgia Asylum, Nancy Malone probably decided to steer away from the other women on her floor in whose agonies sounded the domestic and female difficulties she had fled two decades before. There was Mrs. Joel, in her nineties, sent by daughter and friends with "advanced senectitude of a chaos of all those facilities of the mind," who kept mostly to her room as Supt. Cooper eagerly anticipated her departure for heaven. Juliana Mayer, in her early twenties, had "pecuniary misfortunes, disappointed affection, and physical disease pe-

culiar to her sex" that had sent her into seizures and paroxysms and resulted in her trip to the asylum. Now Supt. Cooper viewed her with
"weeping sympathy," and Nancy no doubt avoided the lachrymose pair.
By then Mrs. Mary Riley had calmed down from her naked furies and
was quilting away, reading the Bible, and chatting pleasantly with Matron Moore. Perhaps Nancy did sympathize with Mrs. Bridget LaRoux,
age twenty-five, who was admitted with her child but not before her husband had threatened to take it with him to France when he left her. Bridget
rejected Cooper's heroic treatments, protested she "wanted no medicine,
the Doctors gave me enough in the hospital to kill a horse, forty horses!"
Bridget periodically emerged into "more rationality, sociability, and . . .
pleasant affability," a "crude Irish woman" whom Nancy might have pre-
ferred. In her calm periods, Bridget too was allowed outside, and she and
Nancy perhaps searched together for fruits and melons farther afield, enjoying a sense of freedom and space, Bridget's child beside her and Nancy
chattering away.[10]

If Nancy Malone could head for the territory or the woods, Mary
Moore's job was the women left on the floor.[11] Mary's recent experience
as a wife, mother, and, most recently, a widow (her husband, steward
William B. Moore, died in 1844) might have given her sympathy for their
female plights. As matron, she directed the attendants to be sure that their
rooms were warm and clean, the helpless patients "dressed, washed, and
combed," and all fed. In her interactions with patients she was to "incite
to and superintend their voluntary acts of industry and amusements; enter into social conversations with them, solicit them to exercise by walks
and promenades; and above all, when melancholic, dejected and despond-
ing, cheer them by solacing recitals of God's overflowing mercies on
them."[12]

Probably to the staff's great relief, the most Nancy needed was tobacco
for her pipe. Like William Butler Yeats' Crazy Jane, Nancy Malone had
had enough of scripture.

Elizur Butler, Enemy of the State

Reverend Elizur Butler, of course, was a believer in scripture, at least in
the most important ones. But as dissimilar as Nancy and Elizur might

seem, they were fellow travelers and perhaps as such fellow enemies of the state. Both of them made consequential journeys to Milledgeville: Butler to its penitentiary, Malone to its asylum. The Latin sources of "idiot," if we recall, put people without learning in opposition to educated citizens, a kind of non-citizen status. Butler's jailers would pronounce him an enemy of the state.

So, let's return to 1826, when the American Board of Commissioners for Foreign Missions sent Rev. Butler and his wife, Esther, to Haweis Mission near Rome, in northwest Georgia. Living near the Cherokee capital of New Echota, the Butlers soon met Cherokee leaders, along with Rev. Samuel Worcester and other white missionaries who were the Cherokee's staunch allies. It was through this association that Elizur Butler had joined Worcester in suing the State of Georgia when it tried to evict white people from Cherokee land. In the meantime, the missionaries stayed put in violation of the Georgia law. After a series of arrests and releases, the missionaries in September of 1831 were convicted and sentenced to four years of hard labor in the state penitentiary at Milledgeville.

The Georgia militia arrested Elizur Butler at his mission. They chained him by the neck to a soldier's horse, and they journeyed into the night. Next to the horse, Elizur stumbled through the roots and darkness, terrified of falling and being dragged. His friend Rev. Worcester would later describe what happened. They finally let him ride behind the soldier's saddle, but the tight neck chain bound them both. "In this situation the horse fell, both his riders fell under him and neither the horse nor either of the men could rise till others could come and, after ascertaining their situation by the sense of feeling, roll the horse over. Dr. Butler was considerably hurt." They finally arrived in Milledgeville, where Butler was "marched into camp under the sound of fife and drum." The penitentiary's jailer proclaimed on his entrance into the missionaries' cell: "Here is w[h]ere all the enemies of Georgia have to land—Here and in Hell."[13]

Despite the missionaries' victory in the U.S. Supreme Court with the *Worcester v. Georgia* decision, U.S. soldiers soon began herding the Cherokees west at the direction of Andrew Jackson. The Supreme Court under Chief Justice John Marshall upheld the Cherokee claims, but President Andrew Jackson refused to be deterred and the U.S. army began to move the Cherokees out. By the end of August 1838, the wagon train carrying the provisions for the journey stretched along the road out of New Echota: thirty-plus wagons loaded by Chief Ross with provisions; families lined up with horses and mules and dogs, most walking with supplies and belongings strapped to their backs, or for the women, their young children. Elizur Butler, by now a free man, accompanied them as the band's doctor and friend. People were saying goodbyes, all their faces etched with grief and "in all the bustle of preparation . . . a silence and stillness of the voice that betrayed sadness of the heart." When Chief Going Snake finally gave the word to *move* and led on horseback with his young braves, thunder rumbled in the distance in spite of the strikingly blue sky. Cherokee leader William Sorey Coodey later wrote to a friend: "I almost fancied a voice of divine indignation for the wrongs of my poor and unhappy countrymen, driven by brutal power from all they loved and cherished in the land of their fathers, to gratify the cravings of avarice."[14]

Given the droughts encountered by previous detachments' boats that had made rivers impassable, Chief Ross's thirteen parties of one thousand or so each would walk the 820-plus miles over land. This first detachment's late-August departure would soon be delayed for more weeks by lack of rain, before it finally rolled out again in October. Then they suffered torrential rains, with roads sloshing and hardly passable. After that the cold came, driving snow and ice, with blankets, clothes, and moccasins tattered. Braves could supplement their supplies of dried corn and salted meat by hunting along the roadside, but the land would be increasingly depleted of game for the people coming behind them.

Their party of 710 people would have fifty-seven deaths, nine births, and twenty-four desertions before arriving in Oklahoma in early January 1839. Butler either stopped in Arkansas on the way to Oklahoma or returned there to live and work until his death in 1847.[15] At some point before his death, Butler and one of the elderly chiefs apparently visited the Philadelphia asylum, or Butler met later with the chief who did visit.

What a visit that must have been when Butler's friend the eighty-plus-year-old "intelligent chief" toured the Pennsylvania Hospital for the Insane in Philadelphia with Supt. Thomas Kirkbride, of the famous architectural Kirkbride Plan. I would guess that this intelligent chief was Cherokee chief John Ross. The year is not given, but it would have been before the 1845 publication of the brief piece in the *American Journal of Insanity*. Ross would have been a craggy man, no doubt in Philadelphia dressed in European garb that befit both his mixed-raced heritage and his record of strategic assimilation to white norms. By the *American Journal of Insanity* account, the chief told Butler of the visit, and he passed the information on to the anonymous *American Journal of Insanity* author. The chief's reply was surely not intended to buttress any argument about superior white intelligence. And if any white man in the United States knew that Brigham's arguments that "darker races" lacked the capacity for "civilization" were spurious, it would have been Rev. Elizur Butler. The Cherokee were the nation that had done the most to assimilate to white norms of dress, language, political organization, and work—everything but make the land that the Spirit provided as their home into private plots to be pilfered by whites. It would have given the old chief and Elizur Butler some good laughs on the train or coach ride home, if indeed they made the journey together—or when they next met.

Dr. Butler and Chief Ross knew that Georgia's society was anything but the simple, untouched, agrarian myth of white enslavers. That white modernity's violent incursions in urban *and* rural areas were savage would never really compute to antebellum asylum superintendents. Yet their institutions would be paid for by the massive infusion of money into state coffers from the sale of stolen native land to white settlers at bargain prices. All the while states battled native tribes, the federal government displaced the survivors to the Midwest, and coffles of enslaved Africans shuffled wretchedly south to work plantations sprouting up on what had been Indigenous land.

This was the history that Georgia's people brought with them into its lunatic asylum. For Nancy Malone, its farragoes, its "appalling apprehensions of defeat or exhilarating anticipations of success by the belligerent combatant," set the tempo of their minds to the tempo of their times.

John Wade's whiskey frolics would do the same.

John Wade's Aberrant Fears of Insurrection

As Nancy Malone traveled west, she obsessed about Indian wars. It was insurrections that terrified John Wade. Again, we are indebted to Supt. Cooper for these descriptions. "The first aberrant impressions were (without any evident cause) an alarm in 1840 of an approaching insurrection,"

David Cooper read the Savannah court's report of John Wade, admitted to the Georgia Asylum on April 11, 1844, three months before Nancy Malone entered from Pike County and a month after Samuel Henderson. Wade was thirty-four and a pauper. Supt. Cooper noted that he was of sanguine bilious temperament and melancholic. Wade was an Englishman by "birth, education and raising" and an engineer and a millwright by profession. These fears of slave insurrection "grew upon his mind until it ripened into a firm belief that his own female servant had poisoned him to effect her part of the project," Supt. Cooper described Wade's case.

John Wade was born around 1811 in England. Probably in the 1830s, Wade migrated to Georgia after being trained in skills valuable in building the machinery of the young nation. He left his mother behind and established a family in Savannah. Then he became terrified of the slaves he found all around him and what he perceived as a smoldering anger at their treatment. Like Nancy, on some level he was paying attention to history.

To protect himself, Wade sold the enslaved woman (we do not know who she was or to whom or to where she was sold) and set off to England to visit friends and his mother, thinking he might move back there, "thereby avert[ing] the threatening desolation awaiting himself and his family." In the meantime, he left his wife and two children behind, "in the care of her mother in his absence."[16] Mrs. John Wade must have noticed that his concern to get himself to safety did not extend to her and her children. We will soon see how her greatest danger lay in her husband himself.

By 1844, John Wade's "aberrant impressions . . . of an approaching insurrection" were hardly anomalous in Milledgeville, nor across Georgia, although the personal lengths to which he went to assuage them perhaps were. White and African American populations had grown in tandem in Milledgeville in the decades since the capital's founding. Almost immediately upon moving in, the town fathers had instituted legal controls over both enslaved and free persons of color and added to and modified the resulting "codes" until the Civil War ended. They legislated that slaves must live on the same premises as masters, could not assemble or own property, or wash in or "abuse" a spring, or cut trees (thirty lashes or $20 fine), or smoke cigars on the streets or sidewalk, or build their own churches on city lands, or meet in Methodist and Baptist (white) churches without supervision of a white pastor or other acceptable white person, or practice music later than 10 p.m., or dance socially except for balls at Christmas. After the nine o'clock curfew, white men assembled at the Market House for patrols on secret schedules until four in the morning, riding the streets and county roads to be sure no crimes, freedoms, or insurrections were about.[17] Such laws, which Savannah shared with the Milledgeville capital, helped to shape John Wade's fears, just as such white fears created the laws.

In 1831, a new wave of fear swept through white southerners after Nat Turner led a rebellion in Southampton County, Virginia, that killed sixty-five white people before a massive turnout of white forces arrested and executed Turner and over seventy enslaved and freed Black people who had joined him. Like Southampton County, Baldwin County was majority Black. By 1830, the slave and white populations in the town of Milledgeville each stood at 1,048. In Baldwin County, slaves were 56 percent of the 7,250 total population.[18] After Nat Turner's uprising, white state and local governments put in place even more stringent measures of control.

As he read Wade's reports and settled him in, perhaps Supt. Cooper remembered the uproar in Milledgeville after news of the Turner rebellion brought rumors of a slave uprising in nearby Jones County. A volunteer guard was created in the command of *Southern Recorder* editor John A. Cuthbert, a Unionist and the "Military Commander of Milledgeville." As his rival, *States Rights* editor Seaton Grantland, reported: "Cuthbert did run, halloo, and sever the air with his sword for a great distance through the town of Milledgeville, more like a maniac than a man of cool, deliberate courage, crying out as he thus ran and flourished his weapons, 'To your Arms!'" Cuthbert fired back that locals had spotted Grantland "fleeing the town in the direction of his plantation," as historian James Bonner reports, where "his aged mother and children were living . . . with fifty slaves and without the supervision of an overseer." Grantland soon hurried to Cuthbert's office and hit him in the face with a stick. Grantland drew his pistol, Cuthbert flourished his knife, and legislators and the governor intervened before either was hurt, taking both into temporary custody.[19]

Apparently the fears of Cuthbert, Grantland, and their neighbors were "aberrant impressions (without any evident cause)," as Cooper had described John Wade: no slave uprising materialized. But Wade's fears about slaves were part and parcel of Georgia's white culture in which slavery grew with a brutal ferocity, and for Grantland the "like a maniac" simile was already close to hand—and within the decade would be quite closer as lunatic patients rolled in.

John Wade's Whiskey Frolics

Once back in England, John Wade seemed helped by visiting his mother, by escaping Georgia's dangers, and by renewing memories of "puerile gambols, juvenile sports and adolescent amusements," as Supt. Cooper explained. (Freud might later call it "regression" or "decompensating.") Feeling better, he changed his mind about moving his family. On the voyage home, however, he became terrified of "capture and murder by pirates." The good effects of his visit to his mother soon dissipated back in Georgia as his "reason was again oscillated" with hallucinations rising from his "actuated susceptibilities of his vivid imagination" into "more aberrant flights and erratic perceptions," although they did not as yet lead him, Cooper wrote, into "any violations of decorum, [or] ostensible inconsistencies or demonstrations of hostility towards any one." The main "strange idea" now harassing his mind was an economic one: that of "friends and neighbors wishing to get his money without a return for it," an obsession with leveraging capital endemic to the age. Such crippling obsessions with money and business disrupted many Georgians who entered its antebellum asylum, as we will continue to see.

Wade was soon drinking freely to help his stomach and his mind. He developed "hepatic derangement," or obstruction of the liver, no doubt from the "intemperance and crapulence and frequent devotions at the shrine of cotyttes" (*crapulence* being drunkenness, *Cotyttes* being the Greek goddess of sex). He soon fell in with bad company and lost money by gambling, and then his domestic and business life unraveled. First, his associates "began to reproach him as crazy, his business declined, employ became scarce . . . and he could not make mathematical calculations," a dire development for a businessman and a gambler. Not surprisingly, "he was harassed with bad feelings about the stomach, heart burn, became costive, felt lifeless and dull, unpleasant and light feelings in his head." Persuaded to set up a store, he "found he could not attend to it."

Then he turned violent, first at his long-suffering wife; "finding fault with [her], [he] threatened and struck her without cause." She fled the house, and he followed, stabbing a friend almost mortally who tried to intervene. All this activity produced enough alarm that he was arrested, imprisoned, and, on March 9, 1844, "tried for insanity, convicted by the Court and Jury, remanded to prison and on the 11th of April received into our institution as a pauper Lunatic," which was by then open to receive him.[20] Early on, as Wade's case shows, local courts began to make distinctions in terms of dealing with a county's violent white citizens about whether jail, the penitentiary, or the asylum was most appropriate. By the next decade, many Georgians guilty of attacks on white family members were sent to Milledgeville. As to his alcoholism, all of the liquor that had flooded Georgia, from the deerskin trade to the "triangle trade" in rum, was coming home to roost.

"I am Mesmerized, . . . an African!"

The economic devastation of 1837 unsettled John Wade, whose business had collapsed along with his sanity. In 1844, once in the Georgia Asylum, John Wade's bad behaviors soon resumed, as did his terror of slaves, and Cooper gave him the full heroic treatment: mercurial cathartic, restraint in his room, cold bath, digitalis. Wade created a predictable uproar from three to six o'clock in the afternoon and from nine to twelve in the evening: "his imagination . . . when awake haunting him with apparitions and indications and menaces of suicide, alarmed at the prospects of being poisoned by the cook and servants to effect insurrectionary purposes." Down the hall and out the window came his increasingly frantic cries: "I am poisoned! I am mesmerized! I am an African!" he would cry. "Look at the blackness of my hands! My face!"—his fear of poisoning by Africans morphed into a hallucination of being one, the Other as doppelganger Self.

There were lucid intervals, during which Cooper switched from heroic to moral therapies and Wade visited in the neighborhood, picked the abundant fruits and melons, went into town, then to Macon and back alone, then to Savannah and back alone. No doubt he pitched in as well in the gathering of wood and growing all those bushels, pounds, gallons

of fodder, corn, sweet potatoes, cabbages and cucumbers, milk and butter. "And on the 4th of July, 1844, [he] was discharged as sufficiently
convalescent to visit Tennessee on business."[21] The ledger reports that he
was returned August 26 to December 16, 1845, but the asylum had "no
legal right to hold him," and he was "last heard of at work in machine
shop [in Savannah] badly insane."[22] Then he drops from the records.

5

"Beat Her with a Wagon Whip": Frances Edwards, Mary Cobb Howell, and White Wives' Miseries

On the morning of October 6, 1856, Frances M. Edwards, a thirty-four-year-old white pay patient from Cherokee County, walked up the steps, past the white-columned portico, and through the heavy doors of the recently finished Center Building, wondering if she would see the red splash of leaves outside its walls again. Frances was perhaps more relieved about what she was leaving behind than apprehensive about what lay ahead. The entry that Superintendent T.F. Green (who had taken the deposed Supt. Cooper's place) or his assistant wrote in the Georgia Asylum's hefty ledger book was murky about the sequence of events that triggered her commitment:

> [She] has attempted violence towards her husband, for the first year appeared inordinately fond of her husband, since that time just the reverse and has grown constantly worse in that particular, about a year after the first manifestation of insanity her husband whipped her with a wagon whip she seems presently to be in good health.[1]

Frances' husband, Benson Edwards, who probably provided this narrative, was a merchant.[2] Perhaps his store was in the county seat of Canton, named after the city in China in a period of brief hope that Georgians could raise silkworms. Their home county of Cherokee was named after the indigenous people from whom it had been stolen, their final forced march westward now almost two decades in the past.

Frances was met by Supt. Thomas Fitzgerald Green, by all accounts a genuinely kind man, who was a decade into what would be a thirty-three-year tenure as superintendent of the Georgia Asylum, having been persuaded to take over when the trustees fired Supt. David Cooper in 1845 for his literary indiscretions. Over the next three decades, Supt. Green would bring stability and good repute to the asylum, pulling it through some of its most turbulent years. Green was an apt foil for Benson Edwards, the whip-wielding husband. Mr. Edwards represented the worst of heterosexual marriage (then a redundancy) and southern patriarchy. Green ran a lunatic asylum for which he was the best incarnation of patriarchal order. The institution was to be run like a family. That his own family lived with him in the Center Building certainly reinforced that role and duty.

In theory, the superintendent was responsible for providing moral leadership in the moral therapy—a huge and totally consuming expectation. Such influence, as the French asylum doctor F.E. Fodéré explained in 1817, required a "noble and manly physique . . . especially indispensable for impressing the mad." Its particulars should include "dark hair, or whitened by age, lively eyes, a proud bearing, limbs and chest announcing strength and health, prominent features, and a strong and expressive voice."[3] Green was a short, stout man, of "humane countenance in his youth, and in his old age handsome," as T.O. Powell, his successor, would eulogize.[4] But perhaps Fodéré would have counted his height and weight against the declared need for an asylum doctor's "manly physique." Clearly, Green would have had to rely on something other than physique in his work. In 1847, Green hired the institution's first assistant physician, tasked with keeping "a constant vigilance of the conduct and management of every sub-officer, attendant, and servant . . . in preserving that rigid system of personal responsibility for every deviation."[5]

It was not Mrs. Frances Edwards' husband, Benson, whom Supt. Green had to impress, although Benson probably should have been the person committed given his handiness with the whip. It was Frances herself. But it is striking how the ledger entry's scribe listed the wagon whip almost casually alongside other details of her life. There is not a note, nor comment, nor even a period or a comma about such evidence of domestic brutality as a possible "cause of insanity" or crime. There is no glimpse of the notion that the wagon whip might be the source of Frances's sudden alienation from her husband. The disjunctions in Frances's ledger entry provide food for thought on how Georgia's violent antebellum slave culture shaped white domestic relations, even as its proceeds paid for the Georgia Asylum's infrastructure. Slavery and the asylum continued to walk hand in hand, and Papa Green was in charge.

Philippe Pinel explained from the Bicêtre asylum in Paris that the key consequence of the supervisor's "physical and moral leadership" was "maintaining calm and order," which could allow him to provide an "exact observation" that would achieve a "permanent cure," along with the administration of "highly praised medicaments"—usually those of the heroic/humoral medicine. Pinel wrote:

> One should not be greatly surprised at the great importance I attach to maintaining calm and order in a house for the insane and to the physical and moral qualities that such supervision requires, since this is one of the fundamental bases of the treatment of mania, and without it we will obtain neither exact observations nor a permanent cure, however we insist on the most highly praised medicaments.[6]

French philosopher Michel Foucault would shape an influential theory of "psychiatric power" that assumed the ability of asylums to maintain this calm and ordered control. Foucault used the above passages from Fodéré and Pinel to explain asylum psychiatry as

> a never ending, permanent regulation of time, activities, and actions; an order which surrounds, penetrates, and works on bodies, applies itself to their surfaces, but which equally imprints itself on the nerves and what [Servan] called "the soft fibers of the brain."[7]

Those were extraordinarily high expectations from both Pinel and Foucault, which few U.S. superintendents would be able to meet over the following decades. Nor would the rough and tumble of asylums such as Georgia's allow such a level of "never ending" and "permanent" regulation, particularly with war and its aftermath soon arriving on their doorstep and over the lintel. These American institutions' power would come from other sources: the ability to involuntarily commit people to an institution from which they could not voluntarily leave, whatever its conditions, was a huge source of power, however regulated or not that institution might be. Later on, racial segregation and penurious legislators will be added to the mix of destabilizing influence on calm and order.

Husbands with Whips

Frances Edwards was not the only white antebellum wife whose husband beat her with a whip. Legal historian Loren Schweninger writes in *Families in Crisis in the Old South*: "Wives suing for divorce claimed that their husbands also used 'cowhide or horse whip' as a means of punishment, in much the same manner as they punished their slaves." He cites Mary Davis, who testified that her husband of eighteen years beat her with his "hands feet rods and wagon whips," and South Carolina husband Leroy Mattison, who "whipped [his wife] and he thought it was his duty—it was his God's duty—it was the best thing he ever did for her."[8] Fortunately for these women—though fortune is relative here—their stories of abuse emerged in their efforts at divorce and separation from their abusive husbands. Schweninger concludes that abuse was the predominant complaint in the divorce proceedings of two-thirds of the white southern women in his study. Only a small number of their husbands would be committed to southern asylums in the process.[9]

Schweninger summarizes the influence of slavery on white southern families as follows: "The legal ownership of human property and the social and cultural acceptance of its consequences created an environment where it was understood that the need [existed] to exert power and authority over slaves as well as family members." This system "sometimes prompted some men to do strange things."[10] The Georgia Asylum's ledgers are filled with accounts of these "strange things." Seemingly, a husband's brutal behavior should be the psychiatric issue. But far more often, the abused women were institutionalized, with a range of ways to name their predicaments. Later, their suffering would be standardized into modern diagnostic categories that did not take factors such as domestic violence into consideration.

In the 1850s, the Georgia Asylum's ledgers began to show more clearly the often violent familial conflicts that landed women and men on the wards. Paul Graham's index to *Admission Register of Central State*

Hospital Milledgeville Georgia 1842–1861 lists the following range of "causes":

- abuse, from husband (3 cases)
- conduct bad, of her husband (1 case)
- disturbance, domestic (1 case)
- divorce (1 case)
- temper, ungovernable, violent (2 cases)
- ill treatment (1 case) by father (1 case), husband (3 cases), brother (1 case), of her husband (1 case), on part of her husband (1 case)
- trouble, domestic (12 cases)
- troubles, domestic (1 case)
- unhappiness, domestic (3 cases)

Violence against white wives and daughters was habitual, as these ledgers and Schweninger's research point out. The same asylum ledgers show that for many of the women, commitment was a life sentence, whether their deaths on the wards came within months from typhoid or dysentery or within decades from old age. For others, the Georgia Asylum might have lived up to its name as a refuge from white men's continuing sadistic domestic abuse.

Homicidal and Suicidal Impulses Afoot

By laying bare the violence that often brought women to the asylum, the 1850s entries reveal the range of homicidal and suicidal impulses afoot in 1850s Georgia's settler-colonial culture—the accounts of stabbings, shootings, and suicide attempts by hanging or drowning or throwing oneself down a well. These suicidal entries also make clear the despair embedded in the colonizing process and in antebellum patriarchal marriage arrangements for white women. These early entries overall show that whatever the range of reasons for commitment or "causes of insanity" listed, there was what I have come to think of as a "tripwire back home." A family or community member's violent behaviors, cognitive differences, recent or worsening illnesses, peculiar or "irreverent" actions, or other suddenly excessive needs could cause them to stumble over this tripwire and end up getting them committed. "Insanity" in antebellum Georgia was the compendium of all these tripwire events.

Frances Edwards' Alienations

So, what happened to Frances Edwards? Her entry noted insanity that began in January 1854, when she developed mumps. In the months following, her behaviors began to draw suspicion from "unnamed but hostile and influential observers," the ledger reads, who might have been ministers or local authorities, including doctors. This surveillance suggests that the presence of the asylum encouraged Georgians to keep a watchful eye for signs of lunacy as white citizens internalized the institution's psychiatric standards. Frances' husband soon began to note suspicious behaviors as well: "From that time, certain persons alleged that they discovered something unusual in her deportment but nothing of the kind was noticed by her husband until a month later," her ledger entry read. Benson Edwards saw, in retrospect, "the earliest indications of insanity [as] delusions in reference to departure from religious duties (she being a professor of religion and member of the Methodist church)." This sequence of her departure from expected religious practices echoes Samuel Henderson's story. These departures from religious duties were accompanied by "declarations [by some still unspecified watcher] that she had been bewitched and was worshipping the Devil." At the time of this heightened surveillance, Frances was eight months pregnant and had given up tobacco.

Next, it seems, came attempted "heroic" medical interventions on the pregnant woman, who "has never been treated for insanity, has never been bled but once since in this condition, has never been subjected to mechanical restraint, [though] it has been unsuccessfully attempted, has attempted violence towards her husband." If Green or whoever else made the entry did not note the relationships between these events, we should: Frances Edwards was pregnant, highly surveilled, bled, and then someone(s) tried to force her pregnant body into a straitjacket or other "mechanical restraint." At this point, it seems, she "attempted violence towards her husband," for which she was blamed. Within a year of her mumps (February 1855), at some unnamed juncture in these events, Benson Edwards beat Frances with a wagon whip. Surely at this point her "inordinate fondness" for her husband had turned to "just the reverse," and the causes of her alienation should not have seemed so mysterious. By October 1856, she was brought to Milledgeville, with the assurance "she seems presently in good health."

As Frances settled into her room and her new routine on the female wing of the Center Building, tired as she was from the journey, she probably took stock of the bumping and crying ward. It is fair to imagine her there. If she looked down at her hands, she would have seen callouses and the corded muscles on her arm from carrying her babies and firewood and lifting bags of rice or coffee beans or bolts of cloth at Benson's store. She missed all seven of her children, but especially six-month-old Lutha. Her arms felt weirdly light and empty, and her breasts ached and leaked Lutha's milk, the stain spreading on her dress front, perhaps making her both proud and ashamed.[11]

Meanwhile, when some unnamed person from a nearby plantation had dropped an enslaved child on the asylum grounds, Supt. Green did not send her back, but put her in the care of a Black washerwoman who did laundry for the asylum, who took her home, where she was likely helped by her community of enslaved people to keep an eye on the child and share in her care.[12]

Isaac Rawdon, His Son a Sacrifice

Frances Edwards was a white southern woman sent away to the asylum for her husband's abuse. Isaac Rawdon was sent from Alabama because he obeyed a biblical injunction to sacrifice his disabled son. Rarely did asylum records show men sent for reasons of domestic abuse. Rawdon, who entered the Georgia Lunatic Asylum in 1848, shows how misleading men's records on this account could be. Rawdon's is also a tragic story about what could happen to cognitively disabled people in that time and place.[13]

Isaac Rawdon was an Alabama planter with a history of "unpredictable and violent behavior." Court records would later show that Rawdon had twenty-eight years of "mental aberrations"—mood swings, mumblings and chanting, rage "about the subject of religion." After one incident, he whipped his slaves unmercifully. The morning of the tragedy, he was just home from several months in the Talladega County Jail because of one such fit.

That morning, he sat at the breakfast table with his wife, Lydia, and their adult son, who, court records would describe, was "not endowed by nature with a Strong mind." Lydia was nervous and fearful, and for good reason. Soon Isaac rose and took the young man by the hand out the door, a kitchen knife in his other hand. Lydia pursued them into the yard, but before she could stop him, Isaac cut their son's throat. Lydia and the enslaved people there witnessed the attack and ran terrified toward Lydia's brother-in-law's plantation. She returned with help to face more horror: Isaac had knocked a fence down with a sledgehammer, made a scaffold from it, and laid a fire, then "offered his son [as] a sacrifice to God, as Abraham had offered his son Isaac."[14] It was not a scene likely to fade from memory.

Lydia had her husband declared insane. She sent him to faraway Milledgeville because Isaac threatened revenge on her and his brother.

He was admitted to the Georgia Lunatic Asylum on December 7, 1848. Apparently, Lydia would give up on his recovery; in June of 1854, she filed for divorce, division of property, alimony, and a guardian for her husband's holdings.[15] But the Georgia Lunatic Asylum ledger's record of her husband was brief: "Isaac Rowdon, lunatic from Talladega County, Alabama, pay patient, Age 55, married, farmer, cause religious study, duration 26 years, Admitted 7th December 1848, died July 23, 1873."[16] It was a remarkably insufficient description of the brutality of Rawdon's act back in Alabama. It might have left asylum staff unprepared for any reappearances of such homicidal impulses from Rawdon toward, for example, the cognitively disabled young people mixed among the white male patients.

Isaac Rawdon and Frances Edwards shared the asylum for the eleven months of Frances' commitment. Perhaps she and other women with violent husbands spotted Isaac in the yard, mumbling or chanting, and shuddered or steered clear. Perhaps his mind still turned to his son and the biblical Isaac for whom he himself had been named. *The fire and wood are here,* he might say again or mumble as he walked Supt. Green's wall. *But where is the lamb? Where, lamb?* Or the other verse he had forgotten in that blazing morning: *Do not lay a hand on the boy. Do not do anything to him. You have not withheld from me your son, your only son.* Or perhaps doses of opium, calomel, arsenic, and laxatives contained him, his violence or his anguish.

The story of Lydia Rawdon, who brought her violent husband to account, was not the story of Frances Edwards, or of many of the white women with her on the Georgia Asylum's wards. By the scant accounts we have of her, Frances had a "composed mind"—not given to mania or melancholia, no huge mood shifts up and down; she was neither epileptic nor "idiot." So it is reasonable to assume that she could cast a cold eye on her surroundings and that she would look for allies among the other women patients and staff who might find ways to help one another and the more helpless of their fellow inmates. It was a caring practice that must have provided some psychic balance among the inmate-patients.

If so, and if Frances was fortunate, perhaps she met Patsy Oliver in the sewing circles or gardening, both of which were considered therapeutic for the inmates and efficient for the asylum. These work details surely also gave them a context to form alliances. Patsy was admitted on March 29, 1856, six to seven months before Frances, so she would have been conditioned to the institution's female routines. Her ledger entry describes her as forty-five, a widow with no children, "at present in tolerable health, generally peaceably disposed and industrious, supposed cause of insanity loss of property, duration five years."[17] She had no children at home to grieve. Her husband was dead, and her "loss of property" was the only cause of insanity given. Perhaps she had been hit by the tail of a swinging slave economy. Perhaps there was no one left back in Talbot County willing to take care of her. In the nine women who came between her arrival and Frances', Patsy may have kept her eyes peeled for a friend. Mrs. Pamelia Holt, aged thirty-five, a widow with four children whose insanity coincided with the death of her husband, had no listed symptoms, and her health "appears tolerably good."

So perhaps Patsy and Frances and Pamelia stitched and weeded together and maybe took meals in the dining room, as they slowly built trust, swapped stories, and kept their eyes out for the other women, helping when they could, encouraging each other and coaching in the behaviors that made them less susceptible to the institution's depleting cures. Whatever else sanity was at the institution over the decades and centuries, it was also a performance, as patients learned rapidly.[18]

Frances Edwards' husband, Benson, came to retrieve her eleven months later, on September 16, 1857, when she was "discharged cured." Whether Benson had also been cured is not noted. Pamelia and Patsy perhaps took sharp note of him and watched the couple disappear in the receding wagon's dust. Asylum records show that after reaching home, Frances "relapsed in a few weeks and after having another child was readmitted on February 14, 1959."[19] We cannot know what influence Benson's wagon whip had on her relapse, or how voluntary the intercourse with him was preceding the new pregnancy. Census records locate Benson Edwards in 1860 in Hamilton County, Tennessee, with Frances' children, including Delia, Priscilla, Thomas, David, Noah, Temperance, and Lutha.[20]

Frances drops from the archives, and we can only speculate that she never saw her children again after Benson dropped her off in Milledgeville and headed West.

The Havoc It Wreaked

Across the southern slaveholding states many white women took care of severely mentally ill family members, including slave-owning husbands whose behavior was described in divorce proceedings as "volatile, mercurial, erratic and at times sadistic." These men were also "unpredictable, displayed obsessive and paranoid jealousies, failed to comprehend financial matters, and sometimes disciplined members of their families and slaves with wonton cruelties." It was generally only when the wives' situations veered extremely out of control, such as with Isaac's murder of his son, that some white women took action. Schweninger observes that only recently have historians provided more than glimpses into the "havoc it [slavery] wreaked on [white] southern families."[21]

The status of "wife," with its legal resources, was available only to white women, and many of these women abused their slaves or found themselves in grotesque situations of jealousy given their husbands' predatory access to enslaved women and girls. At other times, court action went against the wife or precipitated new rounds of family struggles, lawsuits, and countersuits.

Schweninger argues: "Many of the cases reveal that there was much more conflict within southern families than has been portrayed by scholars, who argue that white women could rely on family and kinship networks in times of crisis," concluding that "neither the pervasiveness nor the brutality of abuse within southern households has received the attention it deserves." He finds it ironic that the evidence of these behaviors is found in divorce proceedings, not in criminal prosecutions, most of which could exacerbate wives' dangers. They are also found in psychiatric records.

A First Lady's Milledgeville Meltdown

Three years before Frances Edwards entered the Georgia Asylum, two miles north, Georgia's first lady, Mary Ann Lamar Cobb, released her misery in screams and howls. By the autumn of 1852 and a year into her husband Howell Cobb's two-year term as governor, her wails floated out the third-floor windows of the governor's mansion, whose green shutters slowed them not at all, startling passersby and the criminals at the penitentiary across Hancock Street hard at work making railway cars for Georgia's expanding rail system. Surely at least one or two penitents scratched liced heads at the misery of this woman who was living in such a mansion, from such a wealthy family, wife of the governor.

Locals knew that her father, Zachariah Lamar, was one of the richest planters in the state, having settled in 1810 on Little River ten miles north of the capital. His tax returns at his death twenty-two years later listed 220 slaves, 15,000 acres across Baldwin and other counties, and hundreds of pigs, cows, and other livestock. Mary Ann and her brother, John Basil, were Zachariah's only surviving children, and Mary Ann inherited the bulk of her father's estate.[22] She fell in love with Howell Cobb when John Basil brought his ambitious young friend home from the University of Georgia. Howell fell in love with John's sister *and* her fortune, and they married in 1835. The union gave the ostentatious Howell Cobb almost unlimited access to his wife's money, unless John Basil stepped in to moderate his excesses even as he exercised his own. In 1850, Hurricane Plantation, a few miles north of the capital, with 150 slaves growing cotton and raising livestock, provided considerable comfort for the Cobbs. By 1860, with the benefits of the Lamar wealth and good management, Cobb was one of Georgia's largest slaveholders.[23] Historian of Milledgeville John Bonner would observe, "No family who occupied the [Milledgeville] Mansion ever matched the ostentatious glitter of the Howell Cobbs."[24]

But that was not Mary Ann's doing. The year before, she watched Howell's extravagances for the Inaugural Ball of 1851 march past her on the mansion's walks, in its kitchens and halls, all paid for by Lamar money: pyramids of spun candies, fruits and jellies, oysters and ice brought in from Savannah; the fifty-pound cake at the table's center; the gallons of ice cream.[25] By the time it was ready to serve, she either could not or would not stand beside her husband in the receiving line. Then, she had quietly slipped upstairs to read the *Congressional Globe,* the *Macon Telegraph, Washington Union,* the *Atlanta Intelligencer,* and her Bible. But now, the howls came out of her, and if she was hallucinating, as they suggested, perhaps it was visions of piles, pounds, platters of cakes and oysters, all dancing.

Some historians would later laud Mary Ann Cobb as the antebellum South's ideal lady—with the "cardinal virtues necessary in a true companion, [to] be pleasing personally, sit and walk gracefully, be soft and retiring, yet dignified, her temper equable and affectionate, really anxious to make others around her happy."[26] Bonner would call her "one of the most tragic women who ever filled the role of mistress at the mansion."[27]

Women two miles south in the Georgia Asylum might not have understood Mary Ann's wealth, but they knew of female misery, of cheating and absentee husbands, of children's deaths measured by the decades: Zach, Basil, and Henry, and most recently her baby Laura, who died that October. "Your sister sustains this calamity much better than any member of the family could have imagined," a friend wrote to her brother after Laura's death. "Mr. Jackson describes her as very composed and tranquil and does not apprehend any attack of sickness in consequence of the child's death as was at first feared. You know how subject she is to nervous attacks."[28]

But soon Mary Ann wrote to a friend that she "needed to cry from morning to night." Governor Cobb took the situation in hand and sent his wife north to a New York specialist for several months. When she returned in the spring, she had quieted. She spent hours in the rose garden on the Greene Street side of the mansion, pruning and clipping, weeding and cutting roses white, red, pink, yellow, variegated, long- and short-stemmed to bring them inside to arrange in porcelain vases. When outside in the garden, she kept a sharp eye on her son and his pony. By July she took the children to Saratoga Springs with Lavinia Flagg, an African American freedwoman and wife of Wilkes Flagg.[29] Wilkes' position as minister of a local Black congregation and as butler and waiter in the governor's mansion gave him an unusually privileged status in Milledgeville.

Tellingly, Governor Cobb did not consider Georgia's new lunatic asylum as a place of treatment for his wife. Sending her out of state kept news of her situation more contained and avoided stigma. Lavinia must have provided Mary Ann the discretion that the town's elites had come to expect of the Flagg family. And as she was a freedwoman of color, Cobb probably calculated that Lavinia Flagg did not have the motive to escape as she accompanied Mary Ann to Saratoga.[30] During these years of Howell's difficulties with his wife's sanity, he more than likely consulted Supt. Green informally.

If the Cobbs liked to get out of town, it was in part because Howell was not particularly welcomed in Milledgeville in 1851 when he was elected governor on a Constitutional Union ticket of Union Democrats and Whigs. In his fourth congressional term, he had served as speaker of the U.S. House, where he was one of the architects of the Compromise of 1850, which would postpone civil war for another decade. He wrote to Mary Ann in 1849 about John C. Calhoun: "God grant that we may be able to floor the old reprobate & thereby preserve the honor of the South, and secure the permanency of the Union."[31] Howell's work on the compromise earned him permanent enmity of states' rights Georgia Democrats. In 1856, they would keep him from becoming senator and in 1861 from being elected president of the Confederate States of America.

Instead, from 1857 to 1860, Howell Cobb joined Democratic president James Buchanan's cabinet in the nation's capital as his secretary of the treasury, and he and Mary Ann set up their Washington home with the best furniture from New York City. The Cobbs would leave Washington with other southerners after Lincoln was elected president. In 1861, Howell became president of the Provisional Confederate Congress in Montgomery, then served as major general in the Confederate army, surviving the war until in 1868 a heart attack felled him on a business trip to New York City with Mary Ann, who would live at least provisionally more happily after his death.[32]

One of the Cobb-Lamar plantations would fare particularly poorly at the hands of General William Tecumseh Sherman, as we will learn in the coming chapter.

PART III

Civil War, Reconstruction, and "Our Disturbed Country"

Indeed I tremble for my country when I reflect that God is just: that his justice cannot sleep for ever; that considering numbers, nature and natural means only, a revolution of the wheel of fortune, an exchange of situation, is among possible events; that it may become probable by supernatural interference! The Almighty has no attribute which can take side with us in such a contest.

—Thomas Jefferson, *Notes on the State of Virginia*[1]

Easily the most dramatic episode in American history was the sudden move to free four million slaves in an effort to stop a great civil war, to end forty years of bitter controversy, and to appease the moral sense of civilization

—W.E.B. Du Bois, *Reconstruction in America*[2]

6

"The Great Interests of Our Disturbed Country": Civil War and the Georgia Asylum

"It is hard to exaggerate the drama of what unfolded in the Confederacy," wrote historian Stephanie McCurry in *Confederate Reckoning*.[3] Lincoln was elected that November of 1860, when the Georgia legislative assembly was in its annual session. With South Carolina's massive, profitable, and brutal slave system at risk, its governor had already called a legislative session that would likely end in an ordinance of secession. How would other southern states respond? That question faced the Georgia legislators assembled in Milledgeville, along with hotly contested differences in opinion as to how to proceed. The controversy was not over abolition, but over whether to secede immediately and probably go to war, or to continue trying other forms of resistance. In 1850, the Georgia triumvarate of Congressmen Alexander Stephens, Howell Cobb, and Robert Toombs had forestalled the "fire-eating" secessionists from war by successfully maneuvering the Compromise of 1850, which guaranteed the Fugitive Slave Act and prohibited Congress from forbidding slavery in new states and territories.

Now in 1860, with Lincoln's election, secession was again in the air, and South Carolina again led the way in December. Of the six slave states of the Lower South, Georgia's move in response was pivotal. Georgia had "more people, more voters, more slaves and more slaveholders than any other Lower South state." But it also had a nonslaveholding majority of over three in five white male Georgia voters. So the 37 percent minority of Georgia slaveholders had to convince the 63 percent nonslaveholding majority to act immediately for secession—which all knew would likely mean war.[4]

Milledgeville sat right on the state's geographic and political fault line. "Thus southern eyes turned on tiny Milledgeville in mid-November, 1860, to see where a divided legislature might lead a divided people."[5] Georgians flocked to the capitol to hear the debates, which all knew would be volatile, and the visitors had their own debates late into the evening. On the secession side, Governor Joseph Brown explosively warned that if the federal government fell into "Republican" hands, events would escalate into a "state of things which must ultimately terminate in a war of extermination between the white and Black races."[6] To stave off a legislative vote to decide secession, Alexander Stephens countered the calls to "seize the sword" with a call to hear "from the crossroads and groceries" before legislative action, which the various factions seized on as a compromise. The Georgia assembly set an election for its delegates for January 2, 1861, and a Constitutional Convention for January 16. This action allowed consultation with the sovereign (white male) Georgia people to determine "the mode, measure and time of . . . resistance," according to the preamble of the Convention Bill they passed.[7] So, for a time, the fierce legislative debates during the day ended, but the public debates at night continued through December.

Surely Supterintendent T.F. Green rode into town to hear these debates. As a prominent local doctor and administrator of a major state institution, Green would have known the secession debates' key players intimately. With other white men from across the state, he would have discussed the portentous decision amid the throngs gathered in the capital. His sons would soon go to war, and a younger daughter would be ardent in her defense of the new southern nation. Secession was highly controversial before it was declared, and Green had to deal with warring politicians in the legislature to secure each year's budget. He seems to have practiced a strategic discretion about secession. But Green believed in the restraining effects of plantation slavery on African Americans, and he owned slaves. The U.S. census from 1840 (before Green became superintendent) showed Thomas F. Green to own four slaves, one male and three female, with ages ranging from ten to twenty-three years old.[8]

Then on January 2, 1861, Georgia's Governor Brown ordered the Georgia militia to take Fort Pulaski, the federal installation in the harbor of Savannah. Brown intended to force the Convention's hand, and momentum did shift toward secession. But in the delegate election the same day, only 51 percent of Georgians voted to elect delegates who supported immediate secession, a fact that Governor Brown suppressed for months, claiming the percentage to be 58.[9] On January 21, 1861, the convention delegates passed its Ordinance of Secession with a vote of 166–130.[10]

A Gamble of World Historical Proportions for a Slaveholders' State

The year 1861 was the year that the oligarchy of about eight thousand slaveholding men took the nation to war.[11] That year, 7 percent of the South's total population owned nearly three million of the 3,953,696 enslaved people.[12] These planters, W.E.B. Du Bois later figured, "had in their hands from 1820 to the Civil War political power equivalent to one or two million freemen in the North."[13] When this southern oligarchy moved to secede, it took a huge risk. As historian Stephanie McCurry explains, it was a "gamble of world historical proportions" when "a class of slaveholders flush with power, set out to build an independent . . . [and] a modern proslavery and anti-democratic state dedicated on the proposition that all men were not created equal."[14] The particular vulnerability of the Confederacy as a slave state was that it excluded from citizenship two-thirds of the people in the territory it claimed—all African Americans and white women.

The intensity of the violence that these oligarchs released was also of world historical proportions. It would "presage the slaughter of World War I's Western Front and the global carnage of the twentieth century," according to historian Drew Gilpin Faust. In comparison with the population, the death rate of the U.S. Civil War was six times that of World War II. Because most of the Civil War was fought inside the Confederacy, three times more Confederate men died than their Union counterparts; "one in five white southern men of military age did not survive the Civil War."[15]

Also, the "total warfare" that Abraham Lincoln, William Tecumseh Sherman, and Ulysses S. Grant practiced by the war's end made southern civilians its game. The ruin of the white southerners' world would in Sherman's words "transmit a psychological message to the whole population, [in order to] to whip the rebels, to humble their pride, to follow them to their inmost refuges and make them feel dread and fear."[16]

As Matthew Carr writes, "More than any military campaign in history, Sherman's March has become a by-word for wartime destruction and cruelty."[17] Historian James McPherson's conclusion of these strategies' total effects is that "the overall mortality rate for the South exceeded that of any country in World War I and that of all but the region between the Rhine and the Volga in World War II."[18]

Today, after more than fifty thousand books have been written on the American Civil War, only recently have historians turned toward dealing with the Civil War's psychological horrors. These recent histories focus less on the great generals who commanded Civil War history through its nineteenth and twentieth centuries' versions, and more on the bleeding and bewildered soldiers who fought them and on "the concept of the Civil War soldier as psychiatric victim."[19] Records show that it was the intensity of fighting that drove soldiers crazy. The U.S. surgeon general Joseph K. Barnes' voluminous *Medical and Surgical History of the War of the Rebellion*, which takes up two feet on a book shelf, provides clinical observations on soldiers because his predecessor William A. Hammond had insisted that Union doctors report the material that Barnes later compiled.[20]

"It was the neurologists, rather than the psychiatrists, who participated actively in military medicine and who profited thereby in experience and knowledge," observes Albert Deutsch. Consequently, the Civil War conflict had "but little impact on the contents of the *American Journal of Insanity*" or on papers presented before the Association of Medical Superintendents of American Institutions for the Insane during the Civil War. One result was that the data and lessons produced from "four years of fratricidal strife . . . were soon forgotten, only to be painfully relearned."[21]

A War Favorable to Mental Health?

As Green and other southern superintendents struggled to negotiate these turbulent events, the *American Journal of Insanity* provided a record of how the Civil War affected northern asylums and their superintendents, with their responses generally shaped by their proximity to combat. By 1860, southern asylums had ended their membership in the Association of Medical Superintendents, and its annual meeting was postponed for a year "on account of the excited state of the public mind caused by the violent efforts to overthrow the established government." When the meeting was held in Providence, Rhode Island, in 1862, eastern Kentucky and Indiana asylums sent regrets, "attendance being required upon the wounded of the army of the Southwest."[22] But many in the profession who were farther from the front shared a view of the upcoming war that romanticized its positive effects. For example, as late as 1863, Dr. John Tyler from the private McLean Asylum in Massachusetts noted that "the 'going to war' . . . [is] not as a hardship, but rather an adventure and almost a pastime [in an effort] calculated to excite in all, a pure and fervent love of country—the whole country—the Union," so that "on the whole, [it has] been favorable to mental health."[23] No one who witnessed or fought in the war's first major battle could hold on to that delusion.

From the declarations of secession onward, the turbulent flood of events swept all before it. By February 4, 1861, Georgia had joined with Alabama, Florida, Louisiana, Mississippi, Texas, and South Carolina to form the Confederate States of America in Montgomery, Alabama, its first capital city. By March 4, Lincoln was inaugurated, and on March 11 the Confederate Congress adopted a constitution that Georgians ratified in Savannah. Vice President Alexander Stephens clarified the new Confederacy's "great truth"—"that the negro is not equal to the white man; that slavery subordinate to the superior race is his natural and normal condition."[24] This conviction would far outlast the Confederacy itself. By April 19, Lincoln had blockaded southern seaports.

Only five days after Lincoln announced the blocade, patients began to show up at the Georgia Asylum with war-related issues. On April 24, 1861, Savannah authorities sent to the asylum a man who had been "seized" by the pro-slavery Rattlesnake Club "as an abolitionist, . . . [and] threatened severely" by the club members. They considered him "perhaps insane" given his convictions, and they managed to have him sent to the Georgia Asylum, which would have required county officials' support in the commitment proceeding.[25] That abolitionist was hardly alone in Georgia, where during the debates leading up to secession strong arguments were made by eminent Georgia politicians against secession. But on the wards this abolitionist probably knew to keep his opinions to himself. Probably Supt. Green enforced such silences given his patients' vulnerabilities to excitement and incitement.

A Field Where Imagination Is Loathe to Follow

Late July 1861 brought the war's first major battle at the Virginia railroad junction of Manassas. In the North, the battle woud be called Bull Run for the creek that ran through the carnage. It signaled to those paying attention how bloody and long the war might be. Spectators from Washington City gathered on the hill above Manassas expecting a Confederate rout. They got a Union one instead as on the fifth death-dealing day, woods and fields shimmering in the July heat, they watched as the federal flank finally caved in to General P.G.T. Beauregard's troops. The Union soldiers turned and headed back toward Washington, not panicking until they met Confederate fire east of Bull Run along roads jammed with gun and ammo wagons and the carriages of fleeing ladies, gentlemen, and congressmen who had come to watch. After that, the Union soldiers fled as a disorganized mass back to the capital, some of them not stopping until they got home to Vermont or Connecticut.[26] The battle at Manassas was fought by three-month recruits, out of each side's belief that the war would result in a quick victory for their side. The delusional phase of the war was over. One Union colonel in the Thirteenth Regular Infantry was disgusted by the chaotic retreat of the volunteer army that "degenerated into an angry mob." His name was William Tecumseh Sherman, and in three years he would help to shape a very different fighting force.[27]

On the day of the Manassas battle, Supt. Green's daughter Anna wrote in her diary, "Our country! God Protect her. Virginia's soil stained with her blood already by one desparate battle that of Manassas plains of Sunday."[28] By the time Manassas was fought, the next-to-youngest of the Green children was a full-blown Confederate nationalist, even if her main preoccupation would be finding a white man to love and marry, a task that the war would make increasingly difficult.

On August 22, 1861, the month after Manassas, a planter from Dooly County was admitted to the Georgia Asylum with "supposed spinal irritation by the Doctor but some of his friends are of the opinion that apprehension of loss of property upon the election of Lincoln" caused his insanity. "He is usually quiet and orderly but has shown disposition to commit acts of violence towards his negroes."[29] The war's effects on southern whites were coming home to the Georgia Asylum, but the slave system's war against African Americans had been going on for centuries.

Weird Copies of Carnage

Manassas left three thousand Union soldiers and two thousand Confederates dead or wounded, their bodies grotesquely littering the battlefield. Soon, Mathew Brady's swarms of photographic assistants would put the new daguerreotype techniques to use in mobile studios and darkrooms to make the carnage clearer to those far from the front lines. "The dead of battlefields come up to us very rarely, even in dreams," a *New York Times* review of Brady's exhibit "The Dead of Antietam" soon reflected of the war's relative abstractness at a geographic distance from the front. "Shadowy fingers point from the page to a field where even imagination is loth to follow." The *Times* writer mused on the "weird copies of carnage": "The same sun that looked down on the faces of the slain, blistering them, blotting them out from the bodies all semblance to humanity and hastening corruption, should have caught their features upon canvas and given them perpetuity forever."[30]

After Manassas, the Civil War swelled far beyond the imaginative capacity of many of its hot-blooded enthusiasts on both sides. The prewar dreams of planters' eternal access to slaves evaporated, for a while at least, as their imaginations turned instead to "dooryards strewn with the dead and dying, and their houses turned into hospitals for the wounded," as the *Times* writer predicted in that same review of Brady's photography.

"Our country's still in the midst of war with all of its terrors," Anna Green noted on June 23, 1862.[31] She knew already what McLean Asylum's Dr. Tyler did not—that the war would not be "an adventure and a pastime," and certainly not "on the whole . . . favorable to mental health."[32]

Her papa knew the same. If Green was by constitution cheerful, as his successor Supt. T.O. Powell would eulogize, he was not so in July of 1863. Green did not have access to Brady's photographs, but his great ledgers laid out on the mahogany desk gave him his own "weird copies of carnage" on which to reflect. Those ledgers show his gradual acknowledgment of the war's traumas on his patients' minds, the most recent pages opened to the latest sad entry. This entry was one of the many white female lunatic-refugees flooding the South as Union armies advanced. Supt. Green noted she came from Williamsburg, site of the first asylum founded in the American colonies, which was now under the possession "of the Yankee General Dix . . . [so that] the patients were all obliged to be removed by their friends."[33]

Earlier that month over the Fourth of July holiday, Union general Ulysses S. Grant had taken Vicksburg after a seige that lasted well over a month, and General George Meade had defeated the Confederate invasion at Gettysburg, with over 43,000 men falling on both sides over three days.[34] Supt. Green's son, Thomas Jr., had fought with the Baldwin Blues at Gettysburg, and Supt. Green, like so many fathers of those soldiers on each side, must have held his breath for days until he got news that Thomas was safe, after that battle at least. After secession, all the state's able-bodied men, including his son, had gone off, mostly to Virginia, where they would spend much of the next years in some of the war's heaviest fighting, if they survived. Trains soon brought coffins back home, bodies wrapped in tar-soaked osnaburg cotton originally woven to make easily identifiable clothes for slaves. Without this wrapping, corpses began to putrify and were buried along the tracks, the smell of death spreading south and west.[35]

In July 1863, Supt. Green noted in one patient's record, the Western Virginia Asylum at Staunton was so overcrowded that "the friends of these unfortunates—unable to keep them are wandering about the country seeking an appropriate shelter for them." One wanderer's husband had brought her to Milledgeville.[36] Previous entries recorded similar war-related tragedies. He recalled from March, four months before, a twenty-one-year-old woman who was admitted after an attack of measles. The family's miseries had cascaded with those of combat:

> About the time of her convalescence, three of her brothers were brought home sick from the army to a hospital in Atlanta and their father went down to aid in nursing them. He contracted the disease and they all died.

Green and his staff at first had been cautious about positing the relationship between individual patients' traumas and the war. By 1863, they were more assertive, as in this patient's entry: "[Her] shock is believed to have contributed materially to orignate the disorder of her mind."[37]

This patient was rapidly followed by another, a thirty-five-year-old woman, eight weeks insane, with five children: "cause unknown unless the absence of her husband who is in the Army and has been for two years." She had "cut her own throat and attempted to kill her children and mother." She was bereft and incontinent, the "call of Nature" the least of her worries. She would live another forty-three years in the Georgia Lunatic Asylum, dying on November 14, 1906, and was buried anonymously in one of its many graveyards.[38]

Supt. Green received some of the Georgian soldiers from the brutal battles. On May 26, 1862, he admitted a twenty-three-year-old man complaining of pain in the head who "has been connected with the Army for seven months." Green turned him out on October 23, 1862, presumably to return the poor devil to the front.[39] A doctor and former patient had entered the service as an assistant surgeon serving at a Tennessee hospital. "Upon his recovery from an attack of fever signs of returning insanity were observed," and he was discharged and committed to the Georgia Asylum on July 30, 1863. Another twenty-two-year-old male who had "always been weak minded" had "about two years back . . . entered the Virginia service and made a very good soldier, up to the last of June 1863 when indications of insanity were perceived." He was admitted on August 1, 1863.[40] Apparently those soldiers with a prior history of commitment were more likely to be discharged into an asylum. No doubt, the mental health crises of countless other soldiers were dealt with at the front, and many did not live to tell the tale.

Living Above a Volcano

As the insanity of war raged outside the asylum, the boundaries between patient and citizen of the Confederacy, between inside and outside of the asylum, became more nebulous. We can observe Anna Green from her asylum perch try to live the life she believed should be hers as a white female with an important papa during the Civil War. From the family quarters on an upper floor she wrote, "I am too excitable. I tremble like an aspen leaf" when she heard a love story. "My whole frame quivers and sharp pain shoots up and down my back and I become so weak I can scarcely lift a hand." Supt. Green may have been reminded of his female patients and of his wife Adeline's soon to be fatal ailments. But Anna had her remedy: "If I could find a strong man yet that loved me with this depth of a passionate nature and perfectly understood me I could rest with quiet confidence."[41]

The Confederate draft policies would make such romantic aspirations much more difficult. As historian Stephanie McCurry observes, "It was not easy for a slave society to wage modern war," given that 40 percent of the Confederacy's male population were enslaved and thus ineligible to enlist or be drafted, and half of the white population were women and so not full citizens. "With a total population roughly one-third that of the Union, that left only 965,000 free white men between the ages of 18 to 45 to draw on for armed service. And that was if every adult white male served, which they could not." Under these demographic pressures, the Confederacy levied the first draft in U.S. history—for white males between ages eighteen and thirty-five, later extended to forty-five, and by the end of the war white men aged seventeen to fifty were being drafted. Nor was the Confederate state ready for the size of Union conscription, which made armies of one hundred thousand possible. Then, after Lincoln's Emancipation Proclamation in 1863, over 180,000 African American men also went into the Union armies, 98,500 of whom had been the Confederacy's slaves. McCurry explains, "At the end of the war the Union had one million men under arms, a number that exceeded the total who had ever served in all of the armies of the Confederacy over the entire course of the war."[42] As a result, "enlistment rates [for the Confederacy] would eventually reach as high as 75 to 85 percent of eligible men"; it was "past the point poor white households could sustain, the welfare rolls grew past what the localities and states could manage, and the howls of protest . . . came up from the farms and workshops of the South."[43] Confederate soldiers' desertion rates escalated, as did the repressive tactics used by the Confederate state to capture and punish them. By the end of the war a need for soldiers forced the Confederate government first to consider emancipation, and in the war's last months to eliminate slavery for African Americans who joined the Confederate army.[44] But this repression of southern white people was not how the Confederate States of America would be remembered by generations of its daughters and sons.

With such a war as her competitor, the odds of getting a husband were not good for Anna Green.[45] But she persevered because the male staff and patients at the hospital provided one of the largest pools of white civilian men in Milledgeville, and they were right under the noses of Anna and her sisters. The first appeared in the person of Dr. Robert Campbell of Augusta, who was boarding privately with the family, so she "spent [time] with him, either reading French, playing chess or talking or riding." Yet Anna feared their time was "spent unprofitably" and was "injurious to a young girl" in unspecified ways. Then came "Doctor Conally," a twenty-three-year-old medical student, whose acquaintance she enjoyed making on a visit to Atlanta in October of 1862. Then there was "Brother Charley," or Dr. Charles Bass, the assistant physician who married Anna's "Sister Mattie," who had also taken advantage of the Georgia Lunatic Asylum's dating pool. And then came "Johnny," who became engaged to Anna's younger sister Fanny, whom Sister Mattie had proclaimed in Anna's hearing "the most beautiful thing in the world," to Anna's chagrin. At one point, Anna went riding with a surgeon from the Confederate army and "fell from the horse into Dr. Bell's arms." This search grew very long.[46] Meanwhile, her journal entries completely disregard the Georgia Lunatic Asylum beneath and around her, and its patients did not appear in her journal until one of them, Sam Cook, became her fiancé.

After Union soldiers blockaded the ports, Supt. Green watched the asylum's funds fall precipitously as pay patients' relatives lost access to cotton markets and could not afford the $70 per year keep. He also had to contend with food prices soaring from war-related shortages and price gouging. Green got through his early widowhood with a near-brutal focus on the crisis under his nose so as to keep his patients as calm, fed, and clothed as he could amid the turmoil. In 1862, Green hired a young Confederate as his assistant physician. Dr. T.O. Powell would take over the helm at Green's death in 1879.

On late nights in his office, Supt. Green stayed steady in his traces as war marched toward him in the person of William T. Sherman. Now half of the Confederacy was in Union hands, and he was caring for refugees from other counties who had fled before the advancing armies.[47] Green must have felt it all coming in his blood and bones, the war to his family's and his patients' door.

A Devastation More or Less Relentless

On a raw and cold November night in 1864, "Uncle Billy," the name Major General Sherman was given by his men, stood before a blazing fire in what he described in his journal as a "good double-hewed log house," warmed as well by his flask of whiskey and comforted by his cigar, as he would write in his journal. He was seven miles outside of Milledgeville, with Union troops bivouacked around the cabin amid the wild plum bushes and the spreading hills at the edge of a plantation, "a row of negro huts close by." His army's campfires lit the whole horizon.[48] He had set out from Atlanta with 62,204 men of the Fourteenth, Fifteenth, Seventeenth, and Twentieth Corps, all "well-bodied, experienced soldiers, well armed, well equipped and provided as far as human foresight could, with all the essentials of life, strength, and vigorous action."[49] Sherman marched this army into central Georgia on parallel tracks, one for Georgia's capital, Milledgeville, one-third of the distance from Atlanta to Savannah and the sea.

Riding out of Atlanta after his army, Sherman had stopped his entourage on a hill "just outside of the old rebel works . . . to look back on the scenes of our past battles." Behind them lay Atlanta "smoldering in ruins, the smoke rising high in the air and hanging like a pall over the ruined city," which had ignited after the arsenal's shot and shell exploded, and so "that night was made hideous by the bursting of shells." After the fires reached the stores near the depot, Sherman later wrote, "the heart of the city was in flames all night."[50] Over seventy years later, Clark Gable's Rhett Butler would lead the wagon carrying Vivien Leigh's Scarlett O'Hara past a massive replica of this same arsenal as it burst into a wall of flame with seven Technicolor cameras rolling. *Gone With the Wind* would join *Birth of a Nation* in bringing the most innovative film technologies to help etch racist interpretations of the Civil War and Reconstruction into the American psyche. In the early 1980s, Jimmy and Rosalynn Carter would build the Carter Center in the same spot from which the general had watched Atlanta burn.

In the distance, Sherman had been able see "gun barrels glistening in the sun, the white-topped wagons stretching away to the South" and men marching "with a cheery look and a swinging pace," with the "Battle Hymn of the Republic" rising from the ranks in the chilled air. Sherman had turned his horse, and they'd rode east. Atlanta had been lost then behind a screen of trees.[51]

Now settled for the night in the hewn cabin outside of Milledgeville, Sherman looked around the room and spotted a small candle box marked "Howell Cobb." When he questioned one of the local African Americans who had come to the camp, he learned that he was at Hurricane Plantation, and he knew that "General Howell Cobb, of Georgia, [was] one of the leading rebels of the South." Sherman ordered immediate confiscation of Cobb's property and instructed his General Davis to "spare nothing."[52] The next morning, November 23, 1864, they rode into Milledgeville, with Hurricane Plantation burning behind them.

"Papa Went Out to Meet Them": The Yankees in Possession of Milledgeville

Supt. Green had his hands full as the federal invasion approached the town, signaled by the smoke and flames from burning plantations along the march's path. He was staying put at the Georgia Asylum with his patients, even as Confederate general Henry Wayne removed the garrison from the capital to Macon, legislators departed for home in a panic, and Governor Brown, for all his earlier secessionist rhetorical bravado, caught the last train out of town loaded down with his furnishings from the governor's mansion plus the collard greens and cabbages he himself, rumor would have it, had pulled up out of the mansion's garden. In November 1864, Green knew for sure what was coming, as did every other person in Milledgeville and those who had gone. Governor Brown fled on a Tuesday with his furniture and collards, and Sherman occupied the barely furnished mansion the following night.[53] In spite of his ignominious retreat, Governor Brown would resurface in postwar Georgia politics, as would his son Joseph M. Brown in the twentieth century as he, among other actions, encouraged the mob that lynched Leo Frank.

Though T.F. Green did not have time or inclination to reflect in personal terms on these events, Anna certainly did. With rumors of nearby villages burned and citizens killed, "bright fire to be seen due west," her father quite sick, and smallpox in the town, "Papa" took Anna with him to view the legislature, and she reported unstintingly: "The scene at the State House was truly ridiculous, the members were badly scared, such a body of representatives made my cheeks glow with shame—what a time it was too for the display of cool, wise, legislation, and undaunted courage and exalted patriotism[;] instead of that they passed a law levying troops in masse excepting the legislature and judiciary. The men paid three thousand dollars for the conveyance to move with speed from this place of danger, when the enemy were approaching. They could [not] stand for the defense of their own capital."[54] In contrast, the Georgia Lunatic Asylum staff would stay in town to stand for their patients' defense.

The Sunday before Sherman's Tuesday arrival, Anna recorded riding with her father on the buggy into town to hear the news, but meeting "wagons loaded with furniture, persons actually breaking up homes and moving, they scarcely knew where. Some to plantations and some to the woods." Four wagons filled with books from the state library were headed to the asylum. Two local women, Mrs. Broughton and Mary White, came out "to remain until the excitement was over," and another Milledgeville resident, Mary Herty, came to hide her valuables. Anna records that her father, her new stepmother, Assistant Superintendent Dr. Powell, and "Brother Charles" Bass were "engaged all night hiding valuables."[55] Dr. Peter Cranford, the chief psychologist who in the 1950s with a research team of patients would write the institution's history, records: "Some [townspeople] thought of the stratagem of committing themselves as patients. Others concealed themselves in the subterranean passages under the Center Building. Local legend has it that the spring supplying the wash house was diverted to permit the burying of large quantities of silver which were later recovered."[56] The annual report would show there were 156 males and 134 female patients as of October 2, 1864, as Sherman approached.[57]

In the capital's conquest there were few shots and no cannons fired to disturb the patients. Anna Green was disgusted at the Confederate incompetence, given that Sherman had outmaneuvered Confederate armies to take Atlanta, and then Milledgeville had fallen without a shot. But the advent of thirty thousand troops on Milledgeville's streets must have made a huge noise that carried in the November air the two miles out to the asylum, as did the explosion when the federals blew up the magazine. And, looking out the windows, those at the asylum would have seen the flames and the smoke from the Union soldiers' burning of Milledgeville's Central Depot and the bridge over the Oconee. At the state penitentiary, its handful of left-behind white convicts probably set it afire and escaped without having to enlist in the Confederate army, as 150 of their penal colleagues had done earlier as their condition for freedom.[58] After the war, the state penitentiary for white convicts never returned, replaced by a convict lease system for African American labor.

Tuesday, when the Union army arrived, Anna reported in her journal: "Papa went out to meet them, and expressed a desire to meet their commanding officer." Supt. Green was taken to Union general Henry Slocum's headquarters downtown at Capital Square. The general "treated him very gentlemanly and volunteered a guard for the institution!" Anna records. Over the next two days, Union soldiers guarded the asylum buildings, which "would have suffered much loss of property but for the efficiency of our guard[s]." Surely, the excitable patients were made more so by the invasion, but apparently the Yankee guards helped.[59]

Raped by Two Soldiers

They did not help Mrs. Kate Nichols, however. As was true of most soldier husbands, Captain James Nichols was not in Milledgeville when Sherman's troops came through. He had gone AWOL from August to October 1861; perhaps like many soldiers he left to check on his family.[60] But he eventually returned to his unit. In November of 1864, Kate was sick and had no other family in the house with her. She was being cared for by an African American male "negro attendant."[61] Kate's African American attendant fled at some point, and two men burst into the bedroom. There, the soldiers apparently took their turns raping her. Eventually, some unspecified person brought her to the asylum, where she stayed until December 1867.[62] Much later, Sherman historian Matthew Carr tersely recorded: "At Milledgeville, Mrs. Kate Latimer Nichols, the twenty-seven-year-old wife of a Confederate captain, was raped by two soldiers while lying sick in bed and later died in a mental institution."[63]

Anna wrote in her diary: "The worst of [the Union soldiers'] acts was committed to poor Mrs. Nichols—violence done, and atrocitiy committed that ought to make her husband an enemy [to the Union] unto death. Poor woman I fear she has been driven crazy."[64] Those slaveholding politicians who pushed the white South to secession had justified the war in part as a defense of southern womanhood. But Milledgeville citizens were too busy burying their silver to remember Kate Nichols and move her to safety. The women of the asylum, we hope, took her in and cared for her.

After four long days, the Union soldiers left toward Savannah, and the townspeople who had stayed emerged, stunned, to survey the damage. That survey turned out to take centuries. Anna Cook's summary after Sherman's departure would prove prophetic of continued white southern resistance: "We were despondent our heads bowed and our hearts crushed—The Yankees in possession of Milledgeville. The yankee flag waved from the Capitol—Our degradation was bitter, but we knew it could not be long, and we never despondent, our trust was still strong. No, we went through the house singing 'We live and die with Davis.'"[65]

The Solgers Her Is Giten Tired of the War

Of course, Anna did not literally live and die with Davis, but very many people did die, North and South. The intensity of death in the Civil War emerged from a new kind of warfare that few of its proponents and combatants (not always the same) could anticipate as the two armies clashed in "the bloodiest battles ever fought on American soil": 23,746 dead at Shiloh, April 6, 1862; Antietam, September 17, 1862, the "single most catastrophic day in American military history," with 22,000 dead; Gettysburg, where over three days 43,000 died; or the Wilderness, "an hallucinatory two-day battle of stunning savagery" that General Grant described as "as desperate fighting as the world has ever witnessed": Union dead 65,000, Confederate 35,000. Carr observes, "The death toll was even more shocking in that it had no obvious impact on the outcome of the war."[66]

The grueling and brutal circumstances broke down soldiers' bodies, then their minds. On the many forced marches, soldiers carried heavy knapsacks with clothes, rations, tent, gun, and ammo in sweltering heat or through rain and mud ten to twenty miles a day or more. Less well equipped, Confederates marched with no boots over gravel roads, often into the night, marching while asleep, to bed with little or no cover, exposed to the elements and waking at times to wet or frozen boots or foot rags. Infectious diseases swept the ranks, killing two soldiers for every battle death, with a total of ten million cases of sickness, each soldier ill an average of four to six times during the war. Often, soldiers were sent directly from such forced marches into battle, terrified to hear the roar of guns and smell the smoke, often breaking into panic or terror, and other times having terror shift to rage, anger, and a weird disembodiment in "intense insane excitement" during the pandemonium of battle. They were ordered to storm heavily armed fortifications by frontal assaults that became scenes of slaughter that left men slipping in brains and blood. On the battlefield, frenzy could drive soldiers to acts of particular cruelty toward their foes. After the battle, soldiers would come back into their bodies, adrenaline surges gone, to drop where they stood and sleep like the dead they fell among, before having to rise and help reassemble their comrades' bodies to bury.[67]

By 1864, as General Grant pursued a policy of "total war" in northern Virginia, casualties escalated as what one soldier called the "Furies of Darkness" came together in combat. "Men were literally driven insane" in the dawn-to-midnight close-range fighting at Bloody Angle at the battle of Spotsylvania. On both sides, soldiers and the doctors and nurses who tended them carried home a set of symptoms that included "intrusive recollections, flashbacks, nightmares, intense anxiety, depression, probably cognitive disorders, and in extreme cases psychotic episodes or permanent psychotic states," historian Eric Dean wrote in *Shook Over Hell*. The 180,000 African American Union soldiers met a different level of brutality from Confederate soldiers and officers.[68]

"The solgers her is giten tired of the war they say they cant stand ite much lounger," one Union soldier diagnosed in a statement that resonated for the fighting men of both Virginia armies.

Surely They Will Not Burn Up Poor Crazy People

As smoke from forests and plantations marked its path, citizens in South Carolina's capital of Columbia experienced the dread that Sherman's way of war inspired. When the Union army finally entered the city, the state's insane asylum provided refuge to patients and citizens alike. The capital's population, ordinarily 8,000 residents, half white and half enslaved Black people, had swelled to 24,000 with refugees.[69] Mrs. Campbell Bryce, whose house caught fire, recalled "We ran out. . . . It was bitter cold, the street filled with blue coats wild with delight at their success. I suddenly thought of the lunatic asylum, and suggested that as a shelter, saying 'Surely they will not burn up the poor crazy people.'"[70] As the massive federal army approached the city, white people poured into the asylum, seeking refuge in the massive fireproof building that was surrounded by a ten-foot wall. Mary Boykin Chestnut, wife of a Confederate officer and herself a noted Civil War diarist, recalled of the atmosphere of panicked bedlam, "Mr. [James Louis] Petigru said all South Carolina was an insane asylum. That will not save us now from fire and sword."[71]

By morning, most of Columbia was smoldering ashes, and even more refugees flocked to the state asylum. Mrs. Bryce described the scene: "The whole front of the enclosure was covered with people, their little effects tied up in sheet, and some few had boxes and small trunks." Another witness described of the "miserable mass of beings" covering the institution's grounds: "Sometimes the permanent inmates of the asylum would elude their attendants and mingle with the new-comers, who in their hasty toilets made the night before, would present such grotesque figures as to look much more in need of the surveillance of the keepers than those for whom they were engaged." Supt. John W. Parker took them in, and some of the refugees remained for weeks, straining the institution almost to the breaking point.[72]

At least one of the Columbia asylum's patients found her way to Georgia. She was a twenty-five-year-old female lunatic and epileptic with "duration of insanity twenty years cause injury received from a fall when about five years old." As Supt. Green's ledger records:

Her disease was much aggravated by the burning of Columbia and the sacking of the City of Sherman's Army. The house the family were living in was burned. She barely escaping death from fire. Her father was in comfortable circumstances until then. . . . Is not known to have had convulsions previous to the burning of Columbia.[73]

Supt. Green, no doubt having heard about Columbia's fate, took her in, as he had Kate Nichols.

Insane Soldiers Found Wandering the Country

In the *American Journal of Insanity*'s section of asylum reports, asylum doctors in the states remaining in the Union reported on the war and commented on its psychic effect. Mostly, the journal's coverage of the Civil War focused on states of mental excitement for whites and the fate of the Union—but never on the fate of African Americans—in ways that were usually determined from 1861 onward by a particular author's proximity to the fighting. In January 1865, one superintendent reported, "The war-excitement does not seem to increase the number of admissions . . . nor has the war given any peculiar character to the delusions of those admitted," perhaps from "the loyal mind deriving an incalculable moral support from a universal sense of the entire justice of the national cause."[74] Here, at least, the war itself had not dissipated the early romantic optimism of its various supporters, in this case that all white northerners supported abolition.

Dr. W.S. Chipley from Eastern Kentucky Asylum in January of 1865 anticipated an increase in mental disorders when the excitement of war subsided. Dr. Chipley had been in the midst of the fighting, and he warned:

> When it is over, and the continued excitement it produces subsides; when thousands of homeless, destitute people, come to look upon the wreck of all that once ministered to their comfort, surrounded by suffering, perhaps starving dependents, bemoaning the loss of sons and brothers, I will be greatly surprised if there is not a large increase of mental disorders.[75]

Chipley's observation here is important because Union veterans would experience acute mental and physical health needs and find them ignored by their neighbors and the federal government. The U.S. surgeon general Joseph K. Barnes provided testimony to the psychic damage the war had already wrought in his memo "Instructions from the Surgeon General

Respecting Insane Soldiers" that was reprinted in the AJI. "Insane soldiers [could be] found wandering about the country, in railroad depots and about the streets of cities, with ordinary and sick furloughs, so insane as to be incompetent to provide for their wants, or find their way home" and those "soldiers on furlough [who have] become violent insane a few days after reaching home."[76]

The veracity of the predictions made by Surgeon General Barnes and Supt. Chipley about the Civil War's immediate and long-term traumas would be rapidly lost in post–Civil War psychiatric practices, even as asylums absorbed individuals whose war-related damage inevitably shaped them. As Deutsch observed, "Organized psychiatry at the time was still confined to a small group of asylum heads, more or less isolated from the main stream of community life. No effort was made within or without the group to mobilize psychiatric talent for the war effort."[77] By the end of the century, the accumulated effect of such professional amnesia would become a vacuum into which enthusiasm for eugenics and theories of degeneracy would compete with the germ theory of disease. Psychiatry's moral therapy—dependent on the patient's relationship with a doctor in a hygienically organized asylum—was no match for modern warfare. Adding insult to injury, moral therapy's emphasis on personal defects, such as accusations of "malingering" or "cowardice," made a soldier's breakdown a stain on his moral character and increased his experience of stigma at home. Historian Eric Dean explains in *Shook Over Hell: Post-Traumatic Stress, Vietnam and the Civil War:* "One of the most enduring lessons of World War II psychiatry was that 'every man has his breaking point.' . . . The army soon discovered that environmental stress put every man at risk."[78]

By spring 1865 in Milledgeville, the stench from carcasses left along the roadside by Sherman's army and the sight of Confederate soldiers picking over meat skins, raw turnips, and parched corn were gone. After General Robert E. Lee's April 9 surrender of his Army of Northern Virginia, paroled soldiers increasingly drifted or staggered into town, where citizens and some soldiers had broken into the Confederate Commissary for two days of looting that kept them afloat but eliminated food for the soldiers, who were instructed to pass on to Macon for provisions.

Then, shockingly, President Lincoln was assassinated on April 14, dying the following morning, and Vice President Andrew Johnson of Tennessee became president. By the end of April, the war was effectively over, and Johnson declared the war officially ended on May 9.

Governor Brown surrendered Georgia's troops in April 1965 and was paroled. But he was arrested again and taken to Washington to spend nine days in Carroll Prison before returning to Georgia. By June, the Military Department of Georgia was established, with U.S. army troops stationed in the state. On June 29, 1865, James Johnson was named provisional governor, and Andrew Johnson's presidential Reconstruction had begun.[79] What W.E.B. Du Bois had called "the most dramatic episode in American history" was over.

On May 1, 1865, Capt. James Nichols was decommissioned at Greensboro, North Carolina, and came home to Milledgeville and his wife, Kate. He took Kate home from the asylum on December 10, 1867.[80]

From 1867, Kate Nichols lived with James and their daughter, Anna, in White County, Georgia, until James' death in 1897. Her status as a widow made Kate vulnerable once again. For the 1900 census, she was back in what by then was the Georgia State Sanitarium, the year she was fifty-eight, and she would die there.[81]

But in August 1867, Kate Nichols was still at the Georgia Asylum when those other refugees, the freedwomen and freedmen, entered the asylum to live in a shoddy building. We know that the African American women and the white women did not share with each other their various experiences of rape, which the African American women knew too well, often at the hands of white women's husbands and sons. For the rest of the nineteenth century, the Georgia State Lunatic, Idiot, and Epileptic Asylum would continue to accumulate these various survivors, perpetrators, former masters, former slaves, paroled soldiers, or those who had engaged in more private rebellions, as ex-Confederates and southern elites mounted a new kind of warfare to regain their Lost Cause.

7

"Separate, Unequal, and Compulsory": Freedpeople Enter the Georgia Asylum

The slave went free, stood for a brief moment in the sun; then moved back again toward slavery. The whole weight of America was thrown to color caste.

—W.E.B. Du Bois, *Reconstruction in America*[1]

An amazing continuity belied the . . . discontinuities and epochal shifts installed by categories like slavery and freedom.

—Saidiya Hartman, *Scenes of Subjection*[2]

Polly sat on her throne and looked around the female ward in the newly constructed Colored Building at the other "freedpeople" just arrived at the Georgia State Lunatic, Idiot, and Epileptic Asylum, although she hardly recognized herself in any of those terms. This was not happening to Polly, who probably would not have known the date (September 5, 1867) or perhaps even where she had been (Fulton County, Atlanta) before this place. In fact, she was not Polly at all. In addition to her "claims to be Victoria Queen of England," her ledger entry noted that she was "liable to paroxysms of excitement and anger, in which she commits acts of violence upon any one who opposes her."[3] How could she not respond vigorously to the pale attendants here who did not respect her status? She, Queen Victoria, could storm, could strike, when it pleased her. This was not happening to Polly. Not knowing Polly's last name, we cannot track her subsequent history through census records as we now can for some of the freedpeople, who, whatever else they were dizzyingly gaining and losing, gained surnames and legal identities after emancipation for what Du Bois would call their "brief moment in the sun."

When African Americans like Polly first entered the Georgia Asylum in August and September of 1867, General John Pope presided over the new Third Military District of Georgia, Florida, and Alabama. Congress had reestablished military rule in the South when it took over control of Reconstruction as a result of white southern recalcitrance and President Andrew Johnson's clear southern sympathies. By Polly's arrival, General Pope had registered 95,214 white voters and 93,475 African American voters in Georgia.[4] They were all eligible to vote in the fall's election for delegates to a new constitutional convention, the first significant election for Black voters in Georgia.

So, the political battle for postwar Georgia was intensifying at the same moment that the first freedpeople were entering the Georgia Lunatic Asylum. In fact, Superintendent T.F. Green allowed them admittance only after the Freedmen's Bureau, backed by military occupation, forced his hand. Polly's rights of citizenship were being struggled out in the Fourteenth and Fifteenth Amendments and would be entangled and diminished in this new setting, where African Americans were housed in newly opened segregated quarters: the Colored Building, with its male and female wings, that sat low behind the Center Building.

Racial segregation emerged as a justifiable practice from the colonial capitals of the British Empire, first in the late 1700s in Calcutta, India, urban historian Carl H. Nightingale explains in *Segregation: A Global History*. "White people almost everywhere had decided it was worth the effort to put into place the types of color lines that are the central focus of this book," Nightingale writes. Its pattern involved a "difficult and complicated process of rearranging whole cities into separate, unequal, and compulsory residential zones for different races." From Calcutta, the capital of British India, then Bombay (Mumbai) and Hong Kong, in the 1890s "segregation mania" spread across the world, shaping monumental colonial capitals but finding its most radical form in the "rapidly industrializing white settler societies" of South Africa and the United States.[5] Under complete state control, the Georgia Asylum could segregate much faster than a city like Atlanta could, given all the "difficult and complicated processes of rearranging" that urban segregation required. Atlanta's difficult rearrangement was probably aided by the fact that Sherman's troops had burned so much of the city. The Colored Building into which Georgia freedpeople Polly and Anna moved portended other forms of segregation that would take the rest of the century to put in place in Georgia's urban centers.

These freedpeople and the other African Americans who joined them in the Colored Building had already experienced massive whiplash, from the joy of emancipation to the realization of how brutal the struggle with white people for power would be in the postwar South. Post-Confederate whites knew that the battle for both African labor and citizenship hinged on the "negro equality question" and that control over its answer would determine their ability to win back their Lost Cause. Psychiatry would be called on to answer whether African Americans' essential nature was unequal to whites. How the profession did so would allow antebellum racism to help shape American psychiatry and U.S. politics into the twentieth and twenty-first centuries.

Maybe those early freedwomen in the Colored Building of Georgia's Asylum Polly and Anna felt those forces amassing.

It Did Not Have to Happen, But It Happens Still

But it did not have to happen that America would slosh into the twentieth and then the twenty-first centuries with slaves' blood still on its boots, or that the maw of a prison system would have consumed 90 percent of today's psychiatric beds. The South and slavery had *lost* the Civil War. After four years of viscious carnage, of battlefields littered with dead and crying boys and men, after burning plantation houses and a smoldering countryside, after African Americans flocked from their plantation gulags across Union lines—finally, on April 9, 1865, in a parlor at Appomattox Courthouse, General Robert E. Lee sat at a delicate oval table, his booted knee ungainly cocked to the side, his sword between his legs, his hat and white gloves next to the papers of surrender. Off to his left, General Ulysses S. Grant and a blue phalanx of officers watched Lee scratch his signature, Grant seated like Lee on another of the parlor's red cloth-bound chairs. For the men there in the parlor, it was an almost prissy scene for the end of such a brutal war. Then Lee's fabled and bloodstained Army of Northern Virginia was no more, and its soldiers began their long treks back south or west to home. My great-grandfather Charles Bosch Segrest was part of this trek, from Virginia to Alabama and the "Big Hungry" caused by war's devastations.

Soon former Confederate president Jefferson Davis was fleeing from another burning capital (this time, Richmond) deep into Georgia with his wife, Varina, and what was left of their children, reputedly on the way to Havana or England, through the charred hallucination from which refugees or marauders could suddenly, dream-like, emerge from the woods or the attic. In Davis' case, he probably intended to make a turn west, hoping to galvanize some severed limb of the Confederate army for another run at victory. The leadership of the Confederate States of America was in flight from its failed, delusional experiment as a modern slave nation, their plantations razed, their families scattered or dead, their Africans emancipated: each and all of the Confederate leadership expecting imprisonment, possibly execution, for treason. Indeed, on May 10, Davis was arrested in Irwinville, Georgia, by a detachment of Union cavalry.

Finally, two hundred and fifty years after the first Africans arrived in Virginia, the South's slaveholding elite was beaten. It was the Year of Jubilee. W.E.B. Du Bois would describe it: "Slowly, continuously, the wild truth, the bitter truth, the magic truth, came surging through":

> The magnificent trumpet tones of Hebrew Scripture, transmuted and oddly changed, became a strange new gospel. All that was Beauty, all that was Love, all that was Truth, stood on the top of these mad mornings and sang with the stars. A great human sob shrieked in the wind, and tossed its tears upon the sea,—free, free, free.[6]

And yet, they were not.

After the war's end, ex-Confederates, by savage violence and political chicanery, would win the peace, and white northerners would let them. And here we are, one hundred and fifty four years after emancipation, still working to find the way beyond slavery's apocalypse.

In Georgia during Reconstruction, asylum psychiatry both established patterns of racial segregation inside the integrated institution and outside its walls made invisible the ways in which a campaign of white terror intervened. It made Black freedom, in Saidiya Hartman's terms, the "transitory" and white violence "the epochal" events during these epochal few years.[7] The number of Black Georgians whom county court processes sent to the Georgia Asylum and the Georgia penal system would grow exponentially. Asylum patients were concentrated in Milledgeville, while the convicts were dispersed across the state in a new convict lease system by which their labor under brutal, slave-like terms would construct the industrial base of the New South. When it was all done, when Reconstruction gave way to triumphant Restoration, the white carnage left the slightest footprint in the Georgia Asylum ledgers, like a mastodon hiding its tracks through a mud flat. Its violence was neither crime nor disease. It was nothing.

Anna McCarly's Strategic Silences

In the Georgia Asylum's new colored building, not-Polly's arrival was surely noticed by Anna McCarly, who had arrived August 22, 1867, among the second group from Freedmen's Bureau hospitals, six days after the first cohort.[8] In the asylum for thirteen days, Anna was already a veteran. Perhaps she recognized Polly, who also came from the Atlanta Freedmen's Hospital with three other women, joined in Milledgeville that day by two freedpeople from the Columbus Freedmen's Bureau Hospital and three from the Macon Bureau Hospital.

Anna was twenty-four, her insanity of about two years' duration, its "cause supposed excitement about the war," which had led in Anna's case to a profound silence. She "has been in the [freedmen's] hospital about five months. Has never known to speak a word since." Perhaps from her quietude, Anna saw in not-Polly a similar kind of strategic retreat. Perhaps Queen Victoria let Anna be, or treated at least this one of her subjects dispassionately.

Both Anna and Polly had departed an Atlanta two years into rebuilding from the ashes of the Union sacking and burning, which occurred after General Sherman had expelled the city's white residents with their enslaved entourages to any and all parts of Georgia not (yet) under Union control. We cannot know how often either woman had fled Atlanta—or what part Anna and Polly might have experienced of the burning of the city, of plantation life, of the slave diaspora driven by precipitous "sale by owners." Then came the added displacements as white owners themselves fled with their human chattel multiple times as federal armies crisscrossed the state, and then as some of the fleeing whites returned home. Nor can we know how many of these freedpeople who had come to Milledgeville had crossed into Union-held territory as soon as the blue-clad soldiers approached the farms or plantations or towns of their servitude.

By 1866, word that, under the administration of the new President Johnson, ex-Confederate former slaveholders had reconstituted Georgia's first legislature and congressional delegation must have reverberated through every Georgia freedperson's body who heard about it. Anna Mc-Carly's insanity, provoked by "supposed excitement about the war," had commenced the month of Lincoln's assassination. Her silence had begun at the end of months in which former Confederates entered Georgia's first and all-white postwar 1866 legislature in their gray uniforms while Black men began to fill the formerly all-white penitentiary.

It was enough to make a person crazy, and mute.

Is there a more cultivated silence than Anna McCarly's entry into the Georgia Asylum, a silence more continually "entangled with the politics of domination" that requires, in African American scholar Said-iya Hartman's terms, our own "struggle within and against the constraints imposed by the nature of the archive"? Hartman instructs us on the "excavations at the margins of monumental history" for the "ruins of the dismembered past" and the need for attending to the cultivated silence, exclusions, relations of violence and domination that engender the official accounts: Polly (no last name given) and Anna McCarly—one's deep silence, the other's delusion-masquerade of Victoria-hood—both display, in Hartman's words, "tactics of resistance, modes of self-fashioning, and figurations of freedom."[9] Anna's and Polly's symptoms are perhaps what Toni Morrison meant when she described to Paul Gilroy what happens to some of her characters as "certain kinds of madness, deliberately going mad . . . in order not to lose your mind," even as slavery made white people "into slave masters, it made them crazy."[10]

"I Want to Make Application for Emancipated Slaves . . ."

It was no small matter for the Freedmen's Bureau to get African Americans committed to the Georgia State Lunatic, Idiot, and Epileptic Asylum. On March 3, 1865, Congress authorized the Bureau of Refugees,

Freedmen, and Abandoned Land, inspired by reports of productivity in liberated areas and alarmed by reports from military commanders and abolitionists about the terrible distress among African Americans in Union territory. That fall of 1865 in Milledgeville, the Freedmen's Bureau set up shop along with the federal garrison in the Masonic Hall at the corner of Wayne and Hancock streets, a well-traveled corner near the Oconee River bridge so recently burned by Sherman's army.

There, Supt. Green pled frequently with the succession of federal officers and bureau agents for a share of the rations. After all, his patients were a kind of unacknowledged refugees from their communities and perhaps from sanity itself. Green had his hands full keeping them fed and housed, with Confederate currency worthless and people reduced to bartering for eggs, corn, vegetables, and what meat there was. It was the Milledgeville Freedmen's Bureau that managed freedpeople's negotiations with former masters and provided various forms of aid, such as food and clothing and health care. The Georgia Asylum was one of its many dependents.

So probably when Supt. Green opened the letter from bureau official J.V. DeVanne dated June 10, 1867, he was not surprised to read: "I want to make application for them [insane freemen] in the state asylum, they being paupers, and request that you will inform me if they will be received under your charge."[11] At the federal level, the Civil Rights Act of 1866 passed over President Johnson's veto had established the legal grounding for state asylums to receive freedpeople, because they had the same right to services as whites. And the same Congress in June 1866 had sent the Fourteenth Amendment guaranteeing due process and equal protection to the states for ratification.

In spite of his semi-dependent relationship with the bureau, Green did not take these first African American patients voluntarily, even though money had already been appropriated for the space to house them. Their decision to fund new "colored" structures did not reflect a newfound generosity of spirit toward the legislators' former slaves. In part, legislators saw the need emanating from the counties for treatment for African Americans.

Also in 1866, a special legislative Committee on the Lunatic Asylum reported that given the end of slavery but not of the "unbridled lust" of slaves, Georgia might anticipate "insanity in the negro much more common under this new dispensation than it was under the old and better code."[12] Freedom was causing new afflictions for African Americans. The fiction of unbridled Black male lust would justify a brutal wave of terrorism and lynching against African American communities. The early stages of Ku Klux Klan organizing in Georgia had already begun, and the claim of Black men's "unbridled lust" would soon justify the Klan's unbridled violence. This is perhaps the process that the legislature seems to wink toward in this passage of the report. Thus the slave apologists' conviction derived from the 1840 census's bad data resurfaced immediately after the war in this intensely contested political climate. Slavery, its apologists still reasoned, had been a beneficial institution for enslaved people, an idea that would resonate long beyond emancipation with the help of Green's successor Dr. T.O. Powell. These old attitudes, expressed freshly, did not bode well for freedpeople.

Nor would the fact that what was left of the torched state penitentiary was filling up with Black men. The fate of the Georgia Penitentiary was being considered at the same time that the legislature was sorting through what to do with its asylum. In September of 1866, Governor Charles Jenkins set up a three-person committee to suggest solutions to its prison system. The legislature's report to Jenkins from November 2, 1866, judged that "from the proportion of Negro Convicts it is very manifest that the new order of things will result in a far greater number of convicts being sent to the penitentiary."[13] In response, the legislature passed laws establishing the county chain gang for prisoners either to work on county roads, to be hired out to private corporations, or to work on the state-owned W&A Railroad. According to Milledgeville historian James Bonner, these laws passed by the first pro-Confederate postwar legislature "would set the pattern of the state's prison system for the next four decades."[14]

But Governor Jenkins, who still favored the penitentiary, refused to act on the law. By 1868, there were 205 convicts sent to the penitentiary, of whom 177 were Black and 28 white. It would be a radical Reconstruction governor, Union general Thomas Ruger, who came to power in January 1868, who instituted the system of convict lease on May 11 by leasing out one hundred prisoners to work on railroad construction near Rome for seven cents per day each. By January 1, 1870, 145 of the men had been leased as railroad labor to the firm Grant, Alexander, and Company, which would oversee most of Georgia's railway construction.[15] By 1870, the entire penitentiary was in Grant-Alexander's corporate control, with its convicts leased to corporations across the state. Convict lease across the South would return to the states a profit of four times the operating expenses of their states' penal systems.[16]

Supt. Green defied the Freedmen's Bureau's request of June 1867 and wrote back to refuse admission to African Americans, as he had been doing for a year. Bureau officials across the South facing such resistance turned to a fear tactic, suggesting that insane freedpeople threatened the white community. Then Supt. Green received a second letter dated June 13: "All the insane are paupers, I insist that the law should apply."[17] So, under considerable pressure from the Freedmen's Bureau, southern asylums opened their doors to freedpeople. As bureau official DeVanne wrote about Georgia to an associate on June 5, 1867: "It is presumed by the middle of August all the insane patients in the Freedmen's Hospital will be taken charge of by the state and the state Lunatic Asylum near Milledgeville."[18] They began to arrive in mid-August, right on schedule. Between August 16, 1867, and December 31, 1867, the Georgia Lunatic Asylum ledgers recorded a total of 74 patients admitted, 30 whites and 44 African Americans (30 women and 14 men). Eighteen of these African Americans came from Freedmen's Bureau hospitals across Georgia.[19]

Historian James Downs explains the likely cause of disproportionate numbers of freedwomen in this first cohort: "Unlike freedmen, who could have been placed into a labor gang and transported to a plantation, freedwomen were displaced from the labor force and migrated from town to town in search of temporary employment and shelter. It is likely that the effects of migration, surviving the aftermath of the war and epidemic outbreaks, and often living without subsistence more than likely caused many freedwomen to appear to Bureau agents as unstable."[20] These women also were ready to "fight if opposed," as we will see in this or similar descriptions in the ledgers, or "except when molested never violent or destructive." In the post-slavery environment of the asylum, these women were doing what they could to protect themselves and to establish limits on how whites could treat them. Whatever else the asylum's pros and cons, there were no whips there. On the other hand, freedwomen's willingness to fight back might also be what got them committed in the first place.

Freedpeople in the Asylum's Wake

For the first African American patients, it was not a particular diagnostic category that brought them to the Georgia Asylum: the ledgers note the same set of questions they had since 1842, and the query about "cause of insanity" could have a range of responses about presenting conditions or underlying causes. Freedmen's Bureau Hospitals had functioned more like almshouses, and most patients who ended up there were too depleted or confused to survive should they be released to the streets. Any page of a bureau hospital ledger recorded the major health issues of the day: variola (or smallpox), diarrhea, dysentery, pneumonia, rheumatism, ulcers, gonorrhea, syphilis, constipation, and catarrh (inflammation of the mucous membrane).

Freedmen's Bureau director O.O. Howard observed of postwar conditions: "The sudden collapse of the rebellion, making emancipation an actual, universal fact, was like an earthquake. It shook and shattered the whole previously existing social system."[21] The breakdown of kinship networks, loss of proximity to sources of food and medicine, and displaced patterns of plantation quarantine established by both masters and enslaved people were devastating. Enslaved African Americans were struck by new illnesses from the major mobilizations or flights of armies and civilians that carried new germs across states and counties, although no one yet understood that germ-driven process. Altogether it amounted to "the largest biological crisis of the nineteenth century."[22]

When the bureau closed these hospitals, the biological crisis was passed on to the Georgia Asylum. Its ledger notes reflect not diagnoses so much as problematic behaviors or conditions: ill treatment by her husband, epileptic, occasional paroxysms of violent excitement, elderly, disposed to do mischief with fire, convulsions. The ledgers consistently note information like a patient's level of excitement, capacity to sleep, incontinence, or seizures—the things that would require responses from the asylum staff. In the chaotic postwar environment, no county or asylum official wrote "slavery" or "war" as the "cause of insanity," even when ledgers for white entries note that "Sherman burned down Columbia" as a cause.

Minnie Ann Pulley arrived from Atlanta Freedmen's Hospital, twenty-seven years old and "usually quiet, never otherwise, except when molested, never violent or destructive." Rifter Wesley, aged fifty-five, entered on August 22, also from Atlanta Freedmen's Hospital, and was "now generally quiet" and "eats and sleeps satisfactorily." Her general health "appears good," but she was dead of consumption in little more than a year. Rachel Luckey, seventy-eight, was brought with Rifter from the Atlanta hospital, her health "rather feeble, but seems to be free from any special disease," but she was dead from consumption in fourteen months. So went the descriptions of African American women for the remainder of the year. Ledgers noted their general health, sleep habits, relative quietness or noisiness, and perceived volatility. Or, as with Rebecca White (August 24, 1867), Jane Campbell (August 24, 1867), and many others: "No history can be furnished by the party bringing her."[23]

Across from the female colored building's single story, the male colored building or ward received the men who had traveled the journey to Milledgeville with the freedwomen. Nathan Grant, twenty, was the first freedman on the register, received from the Columbus hospital on August 22, 1867, and suffering from epileptic seizures. His death was noted on February 3, 1871. Poe White was "about 80 years" when he came, also on August 22, from the Macon Freedmen's Bureau Hospital with "no bad habits at all" and for some months past had been "entirely quiet and orderly."[24]

Lewis Griffin was admitted to the Georgia Asylum on September 14 from the Augusta hospital, the cause "disappointed affection five years since." Lewis had escaped from the Augusta hospital and "took some mans horse, who pursued and shot him about the 15 July, inflicting a severe wound in the thigh, from which he was yet suffering. . . . He is usually quiet, occasionally noisy, never violent or destructive. General health appears good." Henny Williams, the last of the Freedmen's Bureau patients, was admitted on October 8, 1867: "Colored, said to have been left from some of Freedmen's Bureau. We enter here from Baldwin. No History." Henny died on November 18, 1892, after a quarter of a century in the institution.[25]

Of the thirty freedwomen who entered that first year, seven died in the first twelve months, one more at fourteen months. Of the fourteen entering freedmen, four died within the first year. These very high mortality rates (25 percent overall, and 23.3 percent and 28.6 percent for Black women and men, respectively) reflected the deteriorated health in which freedpeople arrived.

Within the same period, of the seventy-seven whites admitted there were ten deaths, for a 12.9 percent white mortality rate. In sum, for four and a half months of African American admissions, the death rate was twice that for twelve months of white admissions.[26] I do not think that these early African American deaths were as much from the new patients' treatment within the Georgia Asylum as from the various conditions in which they arrived. The first white patients also had high levels of mortality because their communities sent the people in the most dire conditions, whom they did not or could not take care of. Nor, coming in such small numbers, would the early African American patients have suffered the overcrowding and resulting diseases that they would experience by the end of the nineteenth century when half of the cases of tuberculosis noted among African Americans were contracted in the institution.

These statistics and stark entries are but one more enumeration of Black suffering, and they deserve at least an epitaph when they enter what contemporary African American theorist Christina Sharpe has called "the wake," in all its currents of meaning. "*Wake: the track left on the water's surface by a ship . . . the air currents behind a body in flight . . . a region of disturbed flow . . .* OR *wake: a watch or vigil held beside the body of someone who has died, sometimes accompanied by ritual observance including eating and drinking . . .* OR *wake: in the line of recoil of (a gun) . . .* OR *wake: the state of wakefulness; consciousness.*"[27] Sharpe elaborates: "To be in the wake is to occupy and to be occupied by the continuing and changing presence of slavery's as yet unresolved unfolding."[28]

The strategy of the Freedmen's Bureau to force southern whites to admit African Americans to welfare institutions worked. After the first thirteen patients from bureau hospitals, in August of 1867 the asylum had also begun to admit African Americans committed by their county processes. Emily Key was received on August 27 from next-door Putnam County: "No history of the case could be furnished." Rose Harris, age seventy, another elderly freedwoman, was received September 5 from Pike County: "Has been insane some years. Is unable to walk at all. In every way feeble." Alsey Redding, thirty, and her little girl, Frances, ten, were received September 30 from Monroe County.[29]

Sweating in their small new rooms on August nights until the heat broke after 2 p.m., those new African American patients, with their one or two roommates, probably slept uneasily or not at all, whether with or without their traveling cohorts from the far-flung bureau hospitals. In the night, from some rooms sounded convulsions, or rapid talking, or forms of fury. From others, rooms probably grouped together, came a silence of exhausted sleep. Or underneath the cover of asylum sounds, some freedpeople cogent and willing to risk engaging with relative strangers late at night or before dawn must have passed on information as they had done for decades and centuries in slave cabins on masters' plantations. Or they did so over meals at group tables, or in the courtyard when they were allowed exercise.

With each new African American admission, they must have hoped for news of family and friends, and they must have listened with increasing concern to stories of the ku-kluxing night riders bringing terror to their emancipation in what many must have recognized as a continuation of the war whose outcome controlled their freedom. In 1867, freedpeople arrived in southern asylums in the midst of a terrible carnage that raged about them, released by President Johnson's early reassurance to white southerners: "This . . . is a country for white men, and by God, as long as I'm President, it shall be a government for white men!"[30] Here we tell that story "of an elusive emancipation and a travestied freedom" by acknowledging the white rage that came between emancipation and freedom. What did U.S. psychiatry have to do with this rupture and this rage, and how is it recorded, or not, in the Georgia Asylum annals?

8

"No History Furnished":
Ku-Kluxing, Lynching, and
Psychiatry's Inter-Psychic Tomb

How does one tell the story of an elusive emancipation and a travestied freedom?

—Saidiya Hartman, *Scenes of Subjection*[1]

Defend the dead.

—M. NourbeSe Philip, *Zong!*[2]

"The person bringing her knows nothing of her and can furnish no
history."

On June 10, 1873, Sally Cunnigan arrived at the Georgia Asylum from
Columbia County, her age about sixty years. She would die February 21, 1875, in the institution.[3] Sally would have been born about 1813,
her birthplace likely in Georgia or, if farther north, she was brought in
one of the coffles of enslaved people from Virginia or the Carolinas. We
do not know how long Sally Cunnigan had lived in Columbia (above
Richmond County, with its seat in Augusta, both eastern Georgia counties on the border of South Carolina). It is a good guess that she had been
in Columbia County at least since 1868.

If so, she would have witnessed an outbreak of violence that must have
shocked even a person who had lived the majority of her life to that point
in slavery. Late nights in the sometimes howling, sometimes whispering
darkness of the Georgia Asylum, she could have passed on the word to
ears intently listening that there had occurred a total of eight lynchings in
Columbia County between September 1868 and December 1869.[4] Her

hearers would have understood the context: the heat of a presidential election in which freedpeople's votes could have made the difference.

African American patients from 1867 onward entered the Georgia Asylum from counties experiencing waves of revolution and of counter-revolutionary violence in response to federal occupation and Black emancipation. Four months after their first arrivals, on December 9, 1867, to the shock of white Milledgeville residents, General John Pope, the Union commander in charge of Georgia at that point, announced the state's second constitutional convention, to be based on the premise of the more radical congressional Reconstruction. It would be held in Atlanta, not Milledgeville as anticipated. In January 1868, General Pope was succeeded by General George Meade, and pro-Confederate Governor Charles Jenkins was replaced by a military governor, General Thomas Ruger, as Andrew Johnson's impeachment and near conviction took place in Congress. The changes were dizzying. From December 1867 to March 1868, the delegates in Atlanta framed a new constitution that established free public schools, gave wives control of their property, formalized voting, and moved the capital to Atlanta from Milledgeville, to the chagrin of Milledgeville citizens. This second constitution was ratified in April 1868, and under the new rules the Republican candidate for governor of Georgia, Rufus Bullock, defeated John Gordon, who was then leader of the Ku Klux Klan in Georgia. In the new General Assembly, twenty-nine of the eighty-four Republicans in the House were Black, and in the state Senate twenty-seven Republicans included three Black senators.[5]

Amid this revolutionary moment, patients came with scant or "no histories" of their symptoms or situations. Most extremely, a five-word entry on September 22, 1870, read: "Lewis. Colored. No history furnished."[6] But new inmates like Sally Cunnigan—if they had their wits about them, as many did—would certainly furnish this news from home about how the South's military defeat and their own emancipation were unfolding in the postwar years to the other African Americans already in the asylum's colored buildings. For us, such notes about "no history" demonstrate a remarkable absence of concern for habeas corpus for white and Black asylum patients, as we have seen repeatedly. More crucially, these stark admissions for the increasing numbers of African Americans in Georgia's asylum certainly do *not* mean that history was *not* happening to them, or that escalating white mob violence back in their home counties did not contribute to their conditions.

That county ordinaries (court officials who took care of more mundane administrative tasks) omitted any references to these traumas of slavery and Reconstruction for freedpeople in the admission process is all the more telling in contrast to the numerous ledger entries that did reference the effects of the Civil War's violence on Georgia's male Confederate veterans and female war widows. There was Mrs. Eliza Busy, a widow with six children, loss of property, and sudden death of her husband, "distress and excitement incident to Sherman's army and Wilson's raid passing through her neighborhood." Eliza "once attempted suicide, by eating sulphate of copper, but taking a large amount was vomited profusely and thereby relieved."[7] Or Miss Mary E. Bynum, forty years old and single, who "is supposed to have become insane decidedly from the loss of all her property, which consisted of negroes." Usually "quiet and orderly," now she "becomes excited and threatens acts of violence. . . . If sometimes noisy and abusive and threatened to burn her brother's house."[8] Also there is James Teat, fifty-six, from Floyd County, "cause supposed troubles of various kinds, the loss of a son in the war, the loss of an office he had long held, and upon which a large family were mainly dependent." James was constipated, excited, noisy, and suicidal. But his anger was not read as basic to his personality: "is not destructive, but handles things roughly as if he would destroy them." Had "threatened acts of violence to others but has not attempted anything of the kind."[9]

Might not an equivalent description for freedpeople have read, *"Cause of insanity supposed troubles of various kinds, enslaved for decades, beaten frequently by master who sold her children away, many relatives separated from family or killed, had a hard time being Mrs. Bynam's property, then her county was wracked with people she knew being lynched by Mr. T's relatives."*

Overall, asylum psychiatry in Georgia maintained a vast silence about the bloodbath all around it, just as before the Civil War U.S. psychiatry had maintained a deadly silence about slavery.

Klan Violence to "Control the Colored Race in Every Respect"

In the years following Confederate surrender, what former Confederate general John Gordon called "a brotherhood of the property holders" was established, extending throughout the state, "for self-protection against the negroes," as Gordon explained before a congressional committee on the "affairs in the late insurrectionary states" on July 27, 1871, even as he disclaimed any personal knowledge of "any Ku Klux organization, as the papers talk about it." His association, he explained, was with the "property-holders, . . . the peaceable, law-abiding citizens of the state . . . [who were] afraid to have a public organization [that might be] construed as antagonistic to the Government of the United States."[10] Many other Georgians who testified before the committee would give very different versions of the story and of the Ku Klux organization.

George P. Burnett, Republican candidate for Congress from Georgia, explained to a congressional committee in July of 1871, two years before Sally Cunnigan entered the Georgia Asylum, that "there have been a good many colored men whipped severely, and also some killed" by "this organization of disguised men that has been going around our county for the last two or three years." Burnett added, "These things occur frequently— so frequently that really I never pay much attention to them. If I hear of a negro being killed, I pay very little attention to it, unless I should happen to know him personally." In response to Chairman Pollard's query, "Is there something of a political character about this organization?" Burnett replied that he considered it "entirely political" because "the parties who are maltreated by these men are generally republicans. I never knew a democrat to be assaulted." He added: "So far as my knowledge goes, the persons who have been whipped, as I before stated, are colored men. There have been no charges of anything wrong against their characters." Pollard asked Burnett the "object of keeping up the Ku Klux organization and operating it as they do?" His reply: "The purpose was to break down the reconstruction acts; that they were dissatisfied with negro suffrage and the reconstruction measures and everybody that was in favor of them."[11]

Regaining the Lost Cause with White Rage

Immediately after surrender, leaders of the defeated Confederacy set about figuring out how to win the peace—in the legislature, by night-riding and sadistic violence, and by ideology. In 1866, on the ideological front, Virginian Edward Pollard devised the narrative sleight of hand by which the Confederate cause would carry its project across the centuries. His book

The Lost Cause conceded that the South "must submit fairly and truthfully to what the war has properly decided," which to him was "the restoration of the Union and the excision of slavery." He then laid out the new terrain of southern white struggle: "[The Civil War] did not decide negro equality; it did not decide negro suffrage; it did not decide States Rights." He set forth what would prove to be the emotional glue to a new white nationalism that we recognize today in the struggles over Confederate monuments: "And these things which the war did not decide, the Southern people will still cling to, still claim, and still assert in them their rights and views." Nor, Pollard wrote, did the Confederacy's defeat decide the right of southern white people to "show dignity in misfortune, and to maintain self-respect in the face of adversity."[12] Edward Pollard's arguments were closely aligned with those revealed in the testimonies of the Joint Select Committee in 1871 about the opinions of the Ku Klux Klan.

It took Edward Pollard only two years to put out a sequel, *The Lost Cause Regained*, published in 1868. He explained how he had "misunderstood" the conflict, which he now saw not as about property or labor but "as a barrier against contention and war of races." Union victory in destroying that barrier "liberate[s] and throw[s] upon the country the ultimate question of the negro" and the specter of race war. In the meantime, "The South still [retains] the Negro as a laborer, and keeping him in a condition where his political influence is as indifferent as when he was a slave."[13] By the 1868 publication of Pollard's *The Lost Cause Regained*, the Ku Klux Klan had already begun its "race war."[14]

In August of 1867, African American patients admitted to the Georgia Asylum came from areas rife with this violent campaign to restore the Confederacy's temporarily Lost Cause. The Freedmen's Bureau was the first to document the scale of violent post-Confederate responses to emancipation. Former Confederate general John Gordon had begun organizing the armed opposition in 1865 and 1866, and the summer before elections rolled around, the Klan was ready to ride. Bureau agents across Georgia compiled a growing list of "ku-kluxing": night-riders' whippings, assaults, and murders; the home invasions into African American dwellings; and the attacks on white Republicans. Many of these violent acts occurred in Georgia's larger cities as freedpeople in large numbers sought to exercise new voting rights after they were registered.

Preserved now online, the reports of white rage poured into the bureau offices around Georgia: "1866 Report of Persons Murdered in District of Griffin, Georgia"; "11 October 1866 Report of Persons Murdered in Marietta, Georgia"; "1866 Report of Persons Murdered in District Macon, . . . in District Columbus, . . . in Districts Rome, Brunswick, Waynesboro, 1865–66." Then came "Report of the number of Freedmen murdered and assaulted with intent to kill in the sub District of Athens year 1867"; and for Harris, Troup, Meriwether, and Columbia counties the mounting murders and assaults.[15] In Camden, the death of Nancy Wright (colored), her "*Supposed Murderer*: DR. WM. WRIGHT (White). *Date of Killing*: 5 May 1866. *Remarks*: The deceased was about 14 years old was shot by DR. WRIGHT when he was drunk. A bill was found against the doctor. He made his escape before being arrested." The next month, Mary Wright (colored) was murdered by N. Parker (white). "*Remarks*: Put in jail with four others for killing a mule. Taken out and hanged to a tree. PARKER was arrested but escaped on his way to jail."[16] The Wright-on-Wright violence probably indicates a former owner killing a freedperson who had been his slave. After emancipation, white southerners took particular pains to assert their right to capricious and excessive anti-Black violence. Their victims, too, were "in the wake."[17] Former Confederate soldiers rode out in the white-sheeted disguise of the Confederate dead to stop dead in its tracks the new powers of citizenship, as happened in Sally Cunnigan's Columbia County.

The Bloodbath in Sally Cunnigan's Columbia County

The relationship I assert here is not an individual, one-on-one connection between a particular lynching and one patient, for instance, lynchings in Columbia County and Sally Cunnigan's documented history.[18] My argument is about communal relationships and effects, because lynchings were acts of terrorism designed to intimidate the larger community and to resonate far beyond the actual tree or road on which the killings occurred. I chose Columbia County because it was the county on E.M. Beck's "Database of Lynchings in Georgia" with the highest number of lynchings, and nearby Jefferson County was second. Those counties had one patient each—Sally and Lucy—who came to the Georgia Asylum fairly soon after the campaigns of violence began in their counties. Even though Sally's ledger entry explained "No history furnished," theirs are blatant examples about the histories that African Americans did bring into the Georgia Asylum that went unacknowledged.

Contemporary activism and scholarship on lynching all assert that such violence had a communal and traumatic effect. After all, that was the intent. Most recently, Bryan Stevenson at the Equal Justice Initiative in Montgomery, Alabama, has established a memorial to lynching victims based on the Initiative's extensive new research into public and private records of lynching. "The Equal Justice Initiative believes that our nation must fully address our history of racial terror and the legacy of racial inequality it created," Stevenson explains. The EJI makes clear these acts were "racial terror whose effects persist today." The EJI report explains that these incidents "inflicted deep trauma and psychological wounds on survivors, witnesses, family members, and the entire African American community."[19]

The EJI report lays out six types of "terror lynching" that are helpful in interpreting the records:

> We found that most terror lynchings can best be understood as having the features of one or more of the following: (1) lynchings that resulted from a wildly distorted fear of interracial sex; (2) lynchings in response to casual social transgressions; (3) lynchings based on allegations of serious violent crime; (4) public spectacle lynchings; (5) lynchings that escalated into large-scale violence targeting the entire African American community; and (6) lynchings of sharecroppers, ministers, and community leaders who resisted mistreatment.[20]

The various incidents across just two Georgia counties in the late 1860s and early 1870s illustrate each of the types of "terror lynching" that the EJI lays out.

By fall of 1868, when the lynchings began in Columbia County, the year was already full of political whiplash. It opened with Republican control of the Georgia legislature, the governorship, and the military. With African Americans registered as Republican voters, in the spring of 1868 Republican gubernatorial candidate Rufus Bullock defeated former Confederate general John Gordon, who was then the leader of Georgia's state

Ku Klux Klan. By that summer of 1868, two-thirds of the states had ratified the Fourteenth Amendment, which incorporated Georgia's ap-
proval on July 21, allowing Georgia to be readmitted to the Union and
to send representatives to Congress. Simultaneously, Georgia Democrats
rallied against congressional Reconstruction, and the power struggle focused on the fall presidential campaign, in which Ulysses S. Grant was
a candidate.

Like other Black people in Georgia in 1868, in the tiny town of Appling on Kiokee Creek in Columbia County, Sally Cunnigan would have
known what was happening and what might come. Columbia was a cotton county, which meant it was a slave county—1850s census records show
that there were twice as many enslaved Blacks as there were whites.[21]
The numbers would have made both whites and Blacks in postbellum
Columbia County more assertive.

On September 6, 1868, in Columbia County, the first spark took fire:
an "unnamed negro [was] lynched." The event is reported in the New York
Herald; the Columbia, South Carolina, *Phoenix*; the Memphis, Tennessee, *Daily Appeal*; the Macon, Georgia, *Weekly Telegraph*; and the Albany,
New York, *Argus*. Clearly word got around the state, and events south-
ward were drawing national attention. From the *Herald*, Augusta, Georgia, September 8, 1868: "It is rumored this evening that a negro man
killed two whites at Thompson [Thomson] in Columbia county, and that
the citizens hung the negro immediately. No particulars as to the origins
of the difficulty have yet been received." By the EJI's categories, this was
a "lynching based on allegations of serious violent crime." The next day's
Augusta, Georgia, *Chronicle and Sentinel* added that "passengers on yesterday afternoon's Georgia railroad train brought information from
Thompson" about the "fearful outrage" (the death of the white men):
"The negro murderer was pursued, captured and hung by his own color. . . .
A good many white men were present." This version elaborated about
which "citizens" had participated.[22] Whether African Americans voluntarily participated in this lynching is unknown, but the "good many white
men present" surely had an impact on how the event unfolded, and organized Black militias in the county made such claims of cooperation with
lynching a Black man unlikely.[23]

Of course, the violence was not restricted to one or two counties. Later
that September, Klan-type riders attacked a meeting of freedpeople in Ca-

milla, a small town in Mitchell County, "killing about a dozen and wounding possibly thirty others"—an incident soon known as the Camilla Massacre.[24] This massacre was the kind of lynching that targeted the entire African American community.

That September there was also a white coup when the white majority in the Georgia legislature expelled all legislators with at least one-eighth "negro blood."

In the November 1868 election, such violent repression paid off in Columbia County and across the state. In the April election, Columbia voters had cast 1,222 votes for the Republican Bullock for governor. But after months of violence, in the November election only *one* vote in Columbia County was cast for Republican presidential candidate Ulysses S. Grant.[25] In Cunnigan's Columbia County, Black and Republican voter suppression was almost absolute. The post-Confederacy knew that white supremacy would not survive one man, one vote. That fall, when Georgia was one of only two ex-Confederate states to vote against Grant in the presidential election, its legislature refused to approve the Fifteenth Amendment, which prohibited denying the vote on account of "race, religion or previous condition of servitude."

Increasingly at the mercy of violent whites, freedpeople in Columbia County organized militia units and drilled openly with their rifles.

On January 8, 1869, the Columbia County lynchers were clearly all white, the victims three African Americans and one white man for the alleged murder of Gabriel Martin and his two sisters (all whites) over the state line near Columbia, South Carolina. It was another case of lynching following the accusation of a freedperson's serious crime. The Macon *Telegraph* informed its readers that three men and their white employer had confessed to the murder of Martin and his sisters and were taken from the jail at Appling in Columbia County and lynched, the victims' alleged motives being robbery. We can imagine such a confession was extracted under considerable duress.

The small town of Appling, the county seat, was Sally Cunnigan's hometown. In the spring of 2019, when traveling to New Orleans and planning to stop at the Equal Justice Initiative Memorial in Montgomery, I drove through Appling to get a sense of its size. It was tiny—the courthouse and jail stood right across from each other and right up a hill from Kiokee Creek. Few other buildings lined the road through Appling—

hardly a town. Sally Cunnigan would have come to the Georgia Asylum via the jail and the courthouse. She would have known the sheriff, the victims, and the lynchers. There is no way these murders escaped her.

Six months later, on June 24, 1869, an Appling lynch mob turned up as a "disguised party [and] took from the jail at Appling, Columbia County, Ga., a negro man and woman, and they were afterwards found dead on the road." The Macon *Telegraph* picked up from the *Constitutionalist* the apparent cause: "The negroes had had a difficulty with a white family." Here the lynching fits another of the EJI types: "lynchings in response to casual social transgressions." Such a motive must have resonated across families and communities of freedpeople as a basic description of their situations as property of whites under slave systems. Any one or more of them could still meet such "difficulties" on any road or in any field in Georgia.[26] And the road on which people died, or the trees from which they hung, assumed legendary status—that was the "lynching tree," families would pass down to their children for generations.

And finally on this list from Sally Cunnigan's home county of Columbia, on December 14, 1869, came the story of Johnson Baker, "A White Man Murdered by Negroes"—supposedly shot and killed by "a party of negroes" on Ray's Creek, a few miles from Augusta: "Tuesday night last, Baker's brother last September had a difficulty with a negro man and killed him, for which offense he was arrested, tried and acquitted. The Negroes in the neighborhood becoming vindictive and menacing, Johnson Baker, who lived in Warren County, was induced to come and reside with his younger brother." Returning from Augusta they were "fired upon [by the freedpeople] and the former killed."[27] The Equal Justice Initiative description that fits here is the "murder of community leaders who had resisted mistreatment"—the neighbors of the white Baker's victim sought their own form of justice for a white man who had killed one of their friends and been acquitted.

Columbia County's eight lynchings were the highest number of any Georgia county on Beck's 1867–1880 list. The history was there, if not the kind Supt. Green would have registered. Columbia County certainly knew other kinds of history. Its Carmel Academy was under the direction of Moses Waddell, former president of the University of Georgia (1819–1829), who was also John C. Calhoun's instructor and brother-in-law. Moses was known as the "Cromwell of the Classroom" and trained southern elite

men in a classical education. All of the eight incidents were widely publicized in local, state, and national newspapers. In Baldwin County, just
three counties over, Georgia Asylum officials would have known this
history.

Lucy Lofley's Jefferson County

On October 24, 1872, Lucy Lofley was admitted from Jefferson County,
the county with the second-highest number of lynchings on Beck's list
and next door to Columbia, joined by roads and backroads and kinship
networks. This set of incidents continues to make the point that history
was happening to Black people in Georgia at a ferocious rate and speed.
Lucy's entry *does* have more information than Sally's—her age fifty-
five years, that she had been an inmate at the asylum in 1867–1868
but had been discharged cured on June 25, 1868, remaining well until
about June 1870, when she relapsed from some "unknown cause" and
was recommitted in 1872. She was generally quiet, "but has occasional
paroxysms of excitement in which she is only noisy." Her health was
generally good. She died on September 25, 1877, in the Georgia Asylum
of "Old Age."[28]

The years before Lucy Lofley's 1872 commitment had been particularly
savage in Jefferson County. The perpetrators of the first incident practiced
the overkill that constituted the egregious sadism so characteristic of
southern lynching, the category that the Equal Justice Institute described as "a wildly distorted fear of interracial sex." December 23, 1867,
"a negro who committed a rape upon a little white girl, on Saturday last . . .
was captured on Monday and burned at the stake by a mixed crowd of
Blacks and whites"; in one account "his ears were first burned off and his
face cut with a knife."[29] Almost three years later, on November 15, 1870,
a quarter mile from Bartow Station near Williamson's swamp, "two
brothers by the name of Creech were taken from their homes . . . by unknown parties and inhumanly murdered and their bodies sunk in the
neighboring creek." According to accounts, both V.A. Creech and his
brother John were "shot and gutted."[30] With no suggestion of Black at-
tackers and no lynchings of Blacks, whites in Jefferson seem to have understood that this violence was white-on-white.

Within two months, on January 14, 1871, another murder and mutilation occurred, this time clearly anti-Black. A "band of disguised men, who are supposed to have been Kuklux," went to the Jefferson County jail. Forcing the jailer to open the doors, they took nine prisoners—five convicted, four charged. All were "whipped severely by the band, and the ears of seven of them were cut off." One of the prisoners, Charles Butler, "who formerly belonged to Dr. Dixon," was "brought back to the jail, shot twelve times and killed." The particular offenses of the nine Black men were not listed.

In yet another incident, on September 16, 1871, Bugs Pierce, African American, was arrested on charges of murdering a white man who earlier with others had come to his home "for the purpose of offering violence to him." (This is an incident based on self-defense.) Pierce had shot and killed Joseph Coleman after he threatened Pierce in his home, and Pierce then fled the state, seeking asylum in New York and Washington, DC. He eventually returned to the county and was arrested on charges of murder. While in custody, "a party of disguised [white] men came suddenly on the scene, bound Pierce onto a cart and carried him away." The spectral cart returned empty the next day. "What fate may have been is only conjectured, but conjecture points very strongly to hanging."[31]

In 1872 and 1873, Sally Cunnigan and Lucy Lofley brought this history with them into the cell-like rooms of the Georgia Asylum when they were sent there from Columbia and Jefferson counties.

By then, emancipation in Georgia was finished.[32] Ironically, when the again-reconstructed Georgia legislature (into which a minority of Black representatives had been restored) passed the Fifteenth Amendment, this act brought Georgia once again and finally back into the Union. That act finally put white Democrats in a position to take advantage of the thorough repression of Black and Republican votes that had by then taken place. In December of 1870, Democrats won control of both houses in new state elections, although they would not take office for almost a year.

In October of 1871, Republican governor Rufus Bullock fled the state under threat of arrest for corruption, and a special election mandated by the new legislature brought Democrat James M. Smith into the governor's office. Democrats Smith, Joe Brown, John Gordon, and Alfred Colquitt would control Georgia for the rest of the century. This was the "Redemption" or "Restoration" by which the Confederates who had lost the war began to win the peace. This project proceeded under the deceptive banner of "The Lost Cause," which by the time it was named was on its way to being re-won. Democrats would rule Georgia for 131 years, until a Republican Party recast on white supremacist lines began to break up and retake the formerly Democratic "Solid South."

In all of their battles, both the ex-Confederates and the radical Republicans had supported the convict lease system, which would soon balloon from 61 white and 324 Black convicts in 1871, to 115 whites and 1,071 Blacks in 1880, to 168 whites and 1,520 Blacks in 1890, to 262 whites and 2,296 Blacks in 1902.[33] Labor historian Alex Lichtenstein summarizes:

> In an era notable for its lack of consensus, the policy of "farming out" convicts to industrialists and railroad entrepreneurs with the goal of stimulating economic development proved amenable to the advocates of Presidential Reconstruction in 1866, the U.S. Military, Radical Republicans, and the "Redeemers" alike.[34]

From immediately after the Civil War until 1930, Georgia's Cotton Belt (containing Columbia and Jefferson counties and Baldwin County itself) proved to be the state's earliest and most continually vicious region, with 202 lynchings occurring between 1880 and 1930, only six of them of whites.[35]

Whites by the 1880s would regain tight control of the Cotton Belt and of the large Black majorities in most of its counties. They forced Black labor into sharecropping and tenancy, controlling crops at every stage of production and the workforce through debt peonage. Paramilitary violence and economic and political repression would continue to be the context of Georgia counties, whose officials and families would send people to Georgia's asylum (or sanitarium or state hospital) for another century at least, with a history that is never available in asylum records.

Psychiatry's Inter-Psychic Tomb

The unprecedented Civil War battlefield violence had disrupted the prevailing formula for causation of insanity: that an underlying predisposition (heredity) was triggered by events in the environment. Supt. Green

explained in the 1868 annual report the belief that when hereditary tendencies exist, "a comparatively trivial cause will develop it." He elaborates,
"Many of the exciting causes would of themselves be inoperable if there
was not an inherited constitutional tendency to insanity."[36] It would not
be until World War II that military doctors would acknowledge the effect of less trivial, in fact massively "exciting causes" such as war, that
challenged and recalibrated nature-nurture equations: "Every [hu]man
has his breaking point," regardless of "heredity.[37] This story of Black patients during Reconstruction shows us that we should make a similar
argument for African Americans subjected to the ongoing brutalities of
slavery, then of lynching and Klan and other terrorist intimidation—all
massively exciting causes that were their own kind of civil warfare.

The repression within Georgia Asylum records of white rage and
anti-Black violence would allow the histories of those people most
violated to be over-written. This palimpsest, this writing over of freedpeople Sally's, and Lucy's, and Polly's, and Anna's histories, left the violence of white rage unnamed as either crime or pathology. Soon both of
these categories would descend not on white elites but on Blacks, immigrants, women, and the poor, who would be cast as immoral, criminal,
and crazy.

But if *they* were *that*, what *was* it then to light the flame again and again
that burned another human body at the stake, or to stand there with your
family to watch and hear and smell that process; what was it to gut and
drop in a creek, to shoot twelve times another human being? What was
that? It was, apparently, a nothing that was everything, such a clanging
silence, such a secret history hidden in everybody's sight, like a white
child picking his daddy's shoes out beneath his Klan robes in a public
march. It was such a profound lack of articulation that, as intended, it
obscured the most important questions. We will explore that process and
its consequences in the following two sections.

But right here, with our finger on the Georgia Asylum ledgers, we can
look into what literary scholar Simon Gikandi calls the "inter-psychic
tomb" into which those events go that we cannot "visibly celebrate as
part of Western identity, because they seem to be at odds with its inform-
ing categories." And yet also we cannot mourn them, "because to do so
would contaminate the modes of our self-understanding as civilized subjects."[38] Psychiatry helped to build this crypt of slavery's empire that

holds our ghosts. Saidiya Hartman speaks of enslaved people as "unthought." Here in the absent archives, we can see that they are also unfelt. Psychologist Jason Silverstein has captured the dynamic in this sentence: "Because they are believed to be less sensitive to pain, Black people are forced to endure more pain,"[39] creating the Negro, post-emancipation, as the "problem," the one to be diagnosed and "treated" in wretchedly segregated institutions, or incarcerated by white people in new forms of state- and corporate-driven slave labor.

The monster of white rage emerges from its crypt—that crowded vacuum—making violence the relentless response that leaves us all (still) haunted by the (continuing) failures of our Reconstructions and grotesque white supremacist attempts at race wars. It leaves us still looking down the barrel, again in Hartman's words, of "the conundrums and compulsions of our contemporary crisis: the hope for social transformation in the face of seemingly insurmountable obstacles" that could in fact become apocalypse because "the failures of Reconstruction still haunt us."[40]

It did not have to happen. It happens still. Psychiatry was there.

"A Witless Woman's Story": Sue Pagan, Jane Stafford, and Belle Mitchell—Solidarity and a Certain Freedom in Atlanta

By the end of 1865, Atlanta's five railroad companies were again running engines and freight cars on restored railroad lines that converged like spokes in a central city, which had its streets laid out at right angles from the tracks. In 1868, the radical Republican government under the command of General George Meade and provisional Governor Thomas Ruger had moved the capital to Atlanta, to the chagrin of Milledgeville residents, both then and now. Atlanta had far better rail lines, a radical press, and an "Atlanta ring" of white businessmen eager to make their fortunes off of the city's economic development.[1] On May 11, 1868, the Republican Ruger had no compunctions about activating the convict lease system to generate workers on the state's railroads and new construction projects to promote the region's industrial development. From 1869 to 1871, 469 miles of railroad tracks were graded by convict labor.[2]

Within a decade of becoming a capital funded by northeastern financiers, Atlanta was in the midst of a huge postwar transition, being rebuilt by Black convict labor as a modern and segregated industrial city, what historian Carl H. Nightingale described as that "difficult and complicated process of rearranging whole cities into separate, unequal, and compulsory residential zones for different races."[3] Rich whites were settling in the city's core, while African Americans increasingly settled in residential clusters like Shermantown above Edgewood Avenue, east of the city center, and in smaller neighborhoods in every ward within the city's three-mile radius. In 1879, Shermantown was described by historian

Tera Hunter as "the most vibrant and largest settlement in Atlanta until the early twentieth century."[4]

In the late summer of 1882 in Shermantown, a drama unfolded with two freed Black women and a white female former Georgia Asylum patient. All three of the women were among the Georgians flocking into Atlanta in the post–Civil War years, during which the meanings of freedom were being shaped and contested. A brief news article on August 2, 1882, in the Atlanta *Constitution* contained the germ of their story. It described the three women's encounter with a white reporter, a councilman, and a policeman, all of whom arrived on their doorstep to intervene in the women's working and living arrangements.[5] The interactions among the six of them give us a look at the smaller possibilities of the Jubilee and newer forms of racial solidarity in the emerging urban geographies after the restoration of white supremacy. It suggests how journalists and state agents were enforcing segregation to disrupt new, contingent forms of freedom in the postwar city. If *Constitution* readers examined the story carefully, it would also give them a cautionary glimpse into the vulnerabilities of one white female asylum patient to her family, the medical establishment, and the state in postbellum Georgia.

A Witless Woman's Story

"Stop! I have a sensation for you," a well-known white Atlanta councilman called out to an Atlanta *Constitution* reporter in early August of 1882. "Out on Houston Street," as the reporter would soon write in the story that began with this piece of local news, "near Storr's School House, there resides a negro family in whose service there is a crazy woman of whom they are making the most abject slave. I have just been talking to a colored man who knows all of the details of the affair and who says the woman is terribly abused. She is crazy and has been for several years on account of the death of her child." A broad grin (that he reported) spread over the reporter's face, anticipating such a sensational story.[6]

Already, the reporter had his next day's story line, its headline to read: "A WITLESS WOMAN'S STORY: A Case Which Deserves Attention—a White Woman the Servant of a Colored Family." He wrote that he and the councilman soon "enlisted the aid of Captain Crim" of the Atlanta police, and off the three marched to 92 Houston Street, "where Jane Stafford and Belle Mitchell, two colored women, resided."

Imagine the surprise of "Sue Pagan," the name the reporter gave to the white woman who emerged from 92 Houston Street "with her arms full of wet clothes, which she had just taken from a wash tub," to see the trio of white gentlemen arrive to accost her in a yard with drying laundry flapping from trees and washing lines that stretched out into the neighborhood. The reporter demanded the name of the "miserable looking object" before him. His description of her as "a woman, clad in nothing but a calico skirt and a body of the same material" makes her seem naked, when she is clearly, if simply, dressed.

"Sue," she replied, as the reporter described, "in that witless way which told of an unbalanced mind."

Captain Crim asked: "Sue, do you want to see your baby?"

"Yes, I do," Sue replied as she dropped the wet laundry.

That question was both cruel and contradictory, given that the councilman's original "colored" male informant had explained that the woman's mind had been disturbed by the death of her child. It implies that Captain Crim was more familiar with Sue's story than he had told the reporter or councilman.

Jane Stafford and Belle Mitchell saw trouble out the window as these three white men accosted their white boarder. They set down what they were doing and pushed open a kitchen door to join the four white people in their yard. What followed the two African American women's entry into the yard that day on Houston Street was described in the ten-paragraph newspaper story as "a conversation," in which the policeman, the reporter, the "two negro women," and the supposedly witless Sue Pagan took part. The reporter conveyed Sue's "pitiable" story in six completely coherent sentences transcribed verbatim from Sue's account to the men.

> She said: "My name is Sue Pagan and I used to live in Macon. About five years ago I was a nurse in the hospital there, and so forgot myself as to become a mother. After the child was born its father, who is now a physician in this city, caused me to be sent to the asylum at Milledgeville, where I was kept for nearly one year. When I came

back I could not find my child, and have not found it yet. I have been living with Jane Stafford two years and she treats me all right. She gives me plenty to eat and wear and I want to stay with her."

Sue here explained that she had been impregnated by a male doctor—to whom she was not married—and shipped off to Milledgeville to be kept quiet and to separate her from the child.

There is no "Sue Pagan" in the entry ledgers for the Georgia Lunatic Asylum in 1877 or 1878, four years prior to this encounter. But there is a "Susan Peyton," listed as a "lunatic from Bibb County," who was admitted to Milledgeville on November 20, 1877, and discharged June 12, 1878—a time frame that roughly fits Sue's narrative.[7] Macon, where Sue was impregnated and committed, is the county seat of Bibb County, and the admission and discharge dates fit the "about five years ago" when the doctor impregnated Sue. This could very well be her.

If so, census records show, she was born about 1841 in Bibb County, daughter of Craven R. Peyton.[8] Susan's mother, Antithy, died between 1850 and 1857, and Craven remarried Ann M. Riddel in 1857.[9] Craven Peyton, like most other white Georgia men, enlisted with the Confederate army. In September of 1862, he was discharged from the 30th regiment because he had passed the age of thirty-five. He then reenlisted as a private in Company D of the 10th Battalion, perhaps after the Confederate state extended the age of conscription to forty-five, to the rage of Confederate wives increasingly left behind without food or support. In 1863, along with many other soldiers in northern Virginia, Craven died of complications of diarrhea, probably in a Richmond hospital, and Sue joined the vulnerable ranks of young women in a chaotic and depressed postwar economic and social environment.[10]

By 1870, like many other postwar southern families, the Peyton family was scattered. According to U.S. census records for Bibb County for that year, Susan Peyton, aged twenty-nine, was living and working as a domestic servant in the Poor House and Hospital in Macon, where perhaps her duties included nursing.[11] Both her parents were dead, and her stepmother lived with her daughter and son-in-law in Bibb County. Sue's brother, John Peyton, her only surviving blood relative, was married with two children. Her residence and place of employment—what the census calls the Poor House and Hospital—was probably the Roff

House, consisting of fifteen buildings on forty-two acres that housed poor and indigent persons of Bibb County.[12] There, apparently, an attending doctor impregnated her in 1877, when she would have been thirty-six. The reporter's cruel question about her baby implies that the interrogators knew her child was not dead, even though the colored informant had told them it was. By Sue's account, the doctor-father was then in Atlanta, where Sue had been searching for her child. She might have talked with him or his family members or friends, or maybe they got wind of her. Perhaps the doctor even alerted the councilman. Sue's hardly witless telling of her own story displaced the white men's "witless" narrative about her not one whit.[13]

The 1880 U.S. census also shows a Belle Mitchell living in Bibb County—its county seat Macon, where Sue was then working in the Rolf House. Belle was twenty-one, and her husband, William, was twenty-nine. In the next household lived Jane Stafford, thirty-five, and her twelve-year-old daughter, Mattie, who was in school. Later census records show that Jane and Belle are mother and daughter, which would make Mattie to be Belle's granddaughter. All these residents could read and write, and Jane and Belle are listed as "dressmakers."[14] Jane was born in 1845, Belle around 1859. In other words, both women had been born into slavery. They had been in Macon in 1878 when Sue emerged from the Georgia Lunatic Asylum to return home to look for her baby. However Belle and Jane had known Sue back in Macon, they had surely known the Roff House, so they knew that Sue was used to working hard at manual labor and that she had no upper-class racial pretensions. Jane and Belle, it seems, had taken Sue in when her brother, John Peyton, had not. By 1882, Sue Peyton apparently had migrated with what the *Constitution* would call "the Stafford crowd" to Atlanta, where the Atlanta City Directory listed William Mitchell, a "colored brick mason," residing at 92 Houston Street, where he was also listed in 1881.[15]

Jane, Belle, and Sue were part of the massive migrations of both Blacks and white people that had swelled Atlanta's population at the time documented by Tera Hunter in *To 'Joy My Freedom*. Whites' numbers grew from 7,600 in 1860 to 11,900 in 1870; African Americans' from 1,900 to 10,000 over the same period to become 46 percent of the city's population.[16] African Americans such as Jane and Belle had fled growing repression, Klan violence, smallpox, and agricultural labor on their former masters' plantations to live in larger concentrations that afforded them strength in numbers. The city provided more opportunities for wage labor, recreation, and cooperative networks. Men took jobs in construction and railroads or in the new hotels and small manufacturing plants springing up across the city. Women were confined to domestic labor in white homes as cooks, maids, and nurses. Laundresses could work at home, an advantage that gave Jane and Belle increased autonomy in relationships with the whites, such as Captain Crim, who might land on their doorstep. By 1880, domestic labor represented 98 percent of Black female labor in the city, and washerwomen outnumbered male common laborers.[17]

In 1881, African American women in Atlanta organized through the Washing Society to hold one of the largest strikes of female domestic workers in the South. Tera Hunter writes:

> Over a two week period in July [of 1881] they summoned 3,000 supporters through the neighborhood networks they had been building since emancipation. The strike articulated economic as well as political grievances: the women demanded higher fees for their services and fought to maintain the distinctive autonomy of their trade.[18]

Sue had been working with Belle and Jane during the strike, and all three likely supported it. The *Constitution* reporter's salacious alarm that Sue was a white woman of whom Blacks were "making the most abject slave" reflected white fears that Reconstruction had upended the racial and gendered order. The story shows the white men's need to convince other white women, who would be reading the newspaper, that such arrangements could only involve "abuse." That a white woman who turned to Black women for shelter and work could only be described in the press as "witless" shows how definitions of insanity could be leveraged at the street level to create and maintain racial segregation. That Sue herself explained how she had been admitted to the Georgia Asylum shows the multiple cultural uses of the institution, particularly for white men who wanted a place to dispose of inconvenient women of both races.

Belle and Jane would stay free. Sue would not.

The mythically named Sue Pagan's story, then, seems to illustrate both the new forms of work and organizing that African American women

were devising in this urban environment and their vulnerabilities to police and politicians. It also shows how the Georgia Lunatic Asylum was
providing a mechanism of control far beyond its confines in this rapidly
changing postwar environment.

That August of 1882 when Sue was confronted by the three white authorities in Atlanta, Jane Stafford and Belle Mitchell both denied to the
white policeman any ill treatment of Sue and expressed a willingness to let
Sue leave when she desired. Sue informed the white authorities that she
wanted to stay on Houston Street with the women and that Jane "treat[s]
me all right." Yet the reporter continued to claim that "the general im-
pression created by Sue's appearance and conversation is that she needs
the protection of her relatives." If we believe Sue, the protection she
needed was from the white doctor from Macon, from whom she had not
been protected at all by her white family, so dispersed by the Civil War.

The reporter recorded the disposition of this afternoon's intervention:
"The result of the conversation was the removal of the white woman from
the custody of the Stafford crowd to the station house, where she will
remain until her case can be resolved." We do not know what happened
to Sue immediately after being taken out of the fold of the "Stafford
crowd." But on May 10, 1884, the Georgia Lunatic Asylum ledger reads:

> Miss Susan Payton
>   Lunatic of and from Bibb Co Ga—Age 40 years. Not married—
> has one child. Duration of insanity about 7 or 8 years. Has been an
> inmate of this institution. Was so much improved, that she was al-
> lowed to go home—Cause unknown. Disposition orderly; talks a
> good deal, especially at night. Not suicidal or disposed to be violent
> at all. Cleanly in her habits. Eats well, sleeps but little.
>   Address John Payton Received 10 May 1884 & UF& Ga RR, Macon
> Ga. Died July 26, 1904.[19]

Her brother had taken Susan back to Milledgeville even though she presented no symptoms of insanity other than insomnia and talking at
night. Sue Peyton spent the next twenty years in the Georgia State Lunatic, Idiot, and Epileptic Asylum. She died there when she was sixty
years old. Her child would have been twenty-seven at the time of her
death. There is no record of what happened to Sue on the inside. Per-

haps her work detail was the laundry, where she could remember the white sheets sailing on the clothes lines in Shermantown and the two Black women who had treated her well.

In the 1900 U.S. census for Atlanta, under the head of household of twenty-one-year-old Stephen Peters at 326 Auburn Avenue (formerly Wheat Street and not far from Houston) are listed his wife Johnnie R. [Mitchell] Peters, her widowed mother, Bell[e] Mitchell, and her grandmother Jane Stafford.[20] Jane, Belle, and their family lived in Atlanta into the new century as free women living in intergenerational families.

But that day in 1882 when the police showed up on their Houston Street doorstep, Belle and Jane must have known they were fortunate not to be caught in the dragnet that took Sue back "home" and eventually landed her back at the Georgia Asylum. Captain Crim of the police, the Atlanta councilman, and the reporter who set out to "rescue" Sue represented one iota of the system of surveillance and arrest of Black people ongoing in Atlanta. In 1880, there were 1,071 Black convicts in Georgia, 115 white.[21] Among these convicts were Black women swept up by Atlanta's Captain Crims. Historian Sarah Haley explains in *No Mercy Here*, "Records from the Atlanta recorder's court reveal that police arrested hundreds of Black women annually in that city after the Civil War. One year after emancipation, women accounted for 17.4 percent of the city arrests. Of the women arrested 776 were Black and 195 were white. By 1888 female prisoners still represented less than a quarter of the total arrests, yet Black women were 5.8 times more likely to be arrested than white women." As Haley documents, eighty-six Black women were arrested between June and July 1886 on charges such as public quarreling and profanity, and judges sentenced thirty-eight of them to the chain gang for failure to pay fines ranging from $1.75 to $25.75.[22] There they would work in brutal conditions of "ferocious state violence," part of a growing Black female prison population in Georgia's convict lease system. Haley explains of her sweeping research into Georgia's penal records in the nineteenth and early twentieth centuries: "State violence alongside gendered forms of labor exploitation made the New South possible, not as a departure from the Old, but as a reworking and extension of previous structures of captivity and abjection through gendered capitalism."[23]

Georgia's postwar invention of a Black penal system arose from the New South's need for a system of labor recruitment after chattel slavery was abolished. That recruitment system required the cover of ideologies of debasement for its justification. Haley explains: "Women's perceived status as deranged subjects proved to be fertile ideological ground upon which constructive normative gender positions flourished."[24] The work of producing "derangement" was the work of psychiatry, and southern psychiatrists would lead the way by the nineteenth century's end. When the Georgia State Prison Farm outside of Milledgeville opened in 1897, once again the Georgia Asylum was balanced by a Georgia prison as a Baldwin County destination. State prisons and the state hospital would continue their carceral duet into the twentieth century and today. The Georgia Asylum (then the Georgia Sanitarium) would provide both sites of containment and ideologies of justification for the earliest manifestation of what we know today as the "prison industrial complex" in a new era of mass incarceration in the United States that today provides 90 percent of psychiatric beds in jails and prisons.

PART IV

New Science, Old Ideas

I'll have to give you my number, 5994
I'll have to give you my number, 5994
Because I'll be there forever,
I have no other place
to go.

—Blind Willie McTell, "Death Cell Blues"

With the morals of the [white] people, their industry is also destroyed.
For in a warm climate, no man will labour for himself who can make
another labor for him. This is so true, that of the proprietors of slaves a
very small proportion indeed are ever seen to labor.

—Thomas Jefferson, *Notes on the State of Virginia*

10

Georgia's Segregated Psychiatric Fiefdom

The object of the [14th] amendment was undoubtedly to enforce the absolute equality of the two races before the law, but, in the nature of things, it could not have been intended to abolish distinctions based upon color, or to enforce social, as distinguished from political, equality, or a commingling of the two races upon terms unsatisfactory to either.

—*Plessy v. Ferguson*, 1898[1]

The most famous photograph of the Georgia Lunatic Asylum shows the Center Building's façade. More like a portrait, it dates from the turn of the twentieth century. The three-story front of the U-shaped building was begun under Superintendent David Cooper in the 1840s and completed by Superintendent T.F. Green in the 1850s with profits from the sale of Indigenous land and Georgia's slave economy. Now it reaches across the entire photographic landscape. Forty windows on each floor mark its white swath with 120 calligraphy-like strokes, behind which lived white patients in the interior of the institutional hieroglyph. Above the façade rides the cupola, giving the massive building the dignity of a capitol building. In the distance, two smokestacks indicate the coal furnace that provides the buildings' heat, although it looks like the chimneys are rising from the Center Building itself, smoke smudging the air around the leftward stack, a nod to the new cotton mills that soon would dot the southern landscape to transform cotton bolls into cloth.

In the right foreground, feathering leaves and branches offset the structure's starkness. In the lower center, they shade a pavilion built for white patients and their families as they walk around the meticulously maintained grounds. The mowed lawns and trimmed shrubs testify to the skill

The Center Building, Central State Hospital, Milledgeville, Georgia, late 1800s
(Courtesy, Georgia Archives, Vanishing Georgia Collection, N GA AR 025)

of Supt. Green's son-in-law, Samuel Cook. A former guard at the notorious Andersonville Confederate Prison, after the war Sam became an asylum patient who courted and married the superintendent's daughter. In the 1870s, Cook's labors as the asylum's chief gardener anchored his sobriety and his marriage to Anna Green. Both Superintendents Cooper and Green would have been pleased about the photograph, as was Green's daughter Anna fast becoming the county historian.

Altogether, the effect of the photograph is formidable: the strength of the newly industrializing postbellum state and its economy arrayed against the forces within of lunacy, intemperance, senility, and disease. But there are also forces that the photograph does not show: the Colored Building in the back, patient numbers for both races growing disproportionate to space available, an expanding farm and textile operation, and crowded "colored" TB wards with germs visible only with microscopes, if and when they had such laboratory tools.

From the collapse of Reconstruction to the final decades of the nineteenth century, the Georgia Asylum expanded into a segregated psychiatric estate, a kind of racial fiefdom. As we have seen, to write about psychiatry in the nineteenth century *is* to write about this asylum structure itself, because for much of the century the chief remedy for the lunatic *was* the real estate—its architecture, engineering, gardening, farming, cooking, and recreations—every bit as much as its superintendents and assistant physicians and matrons and stewards. That was the "moral therapy" of the asylum structured as a space for healing, and as we have traced, this philosophy of asylum architecture and social geography was where psychiatry began.[2] Historians of that moral therapy have traced its decline to overcrowding, which certainly happened in Georgia. But they have not followed moral therapy's continuing uses as a justification of labor regimes more influenced by prisons and plantations than Quakers and *philosophes*.

Annual reports from the 1840s to the 1870s and 1880s ritually claim this noble history. According to Supt. Green, in the late 1840s, the asylum before he arrived was a "species of custodial receptacle for the wretched pauper insane, idiotic and epileptic in the state," its primary goal to relieve home communities from "the revolting spectacles [the insane] daily exhibited" and "the reckless violence of the madman."[3] Records show that the first superintendent, David Cooper, also saw himself as a moral therapist and would have found his successor's description of the conditions during his tenure highly insulting. Green explained in 1873 how his reformed asylum manifested "true-hearted sympathy, and kind offices" through its structures and organization, which included "the most satisfactory classification," "every indoor comfort or convenience that may be desirable" (or that can be allowed), "spacious and beautifully ornamented grounds and gardens," and "a great variety of means of pleasantly occupying or employing them."[4] Superintendent T.O. Powell would similarly laud himself in contrast to Supt. Green.

When state asylums administered moral therapy, they brought the interests of the state to bear directly on the care and treatment of citizens' minds and the definitions of their realities. So, the interests of healing and the interests of state control were both at play, and, if they conflicted, as we will see, the state usually won. Over the next century, Georgia's asylum illustrated what happened to this real estate and its moral therapy when the state enforced a regime of separate, unequal, and compulsory racial segregation in its buildings and landscape, its budgets, its work outputs, and its treatments. Coincident with a rising percentage of colored patients was an expanded agricultural production that would be absorbed into patients' "occupational therapy" in work details structured by race and gender. In other words, over the last decades of the nineteenth century, the asylum-plantation model supplanted moral therapy at the Georgia Asylum. The count of pigs and cows in the farm and garden section of the report is one barometer of this change. It measures the Georgia Asylum's industrial production against Supt. Powell's ideological production, a nexus that locates Georgia at the epicenter of race and psychiatry into the twentieth century. By the century's turn, Supt. Powell would make it clear how slavery and its afterlives would provide the asylum's fracture points and inform its haunting and its hungry ghosts.

Supt. Green Takes the Stand

The defeat of Republican Reconstruction by the southern white "Redemption" initiated a period of institutional stabilization at the asylum, then of repair and expansion of its building and grounds. Annual reports show the asylum becoming increasingly self-contained and self-sustaining, growing into a kind of psychiatric fiefdom that increased its agricultural productivity as it incorporated and segregated freedpeople. In this early period, the African American population grew slowly, its size controlled by the segregated space allotted. These reports also show the asylum's staff and trustees struggling with county governments to control the flow of mostly white patients and battling, often futilely, with the legislature to gain control and obtain adequate funds for patient housing and care.

Before Supt. Green could stabilize the Georgia Asylum, in 1872 he first had to fend off an attack from Atlanta developers attempting to move the institution to the new capital, which was bustling with postwar commerce. The charges they brought against the asylum and Green occurred in the tumultuous months after Republicans were crushed or expelled from Georgia and the new post-Confederate elites were asserting control. The Georgia Asylum's trustees came to the staff's defense, explaining to the legislators the stresses of the job and revealing to us the institution's rhythms:

[The staff's] practice is more unpleasant and hazardous than a general practice. They must visit all their patients every day, and while the revilings of madmen is not regarded, yet to be spit upon, beaten, and kicked and bit, when in the performance of kindly offices, is not pleasant nor to be suffered for nothing. Then the risk of more serious injury, one employee, the head cook, having been killed the present year by a patient, and an attendant killed the year before. They have case-books, record prescriptions and the treatment of every case and make daily reports to the superintendent. They visit the tables at meal hours, to see that the food is properly prepared and given to the patients.[5]

At the legislators' direction, Doctors James F. Bozeman and William H. Cummings would submit separate reports. Bozeman, in historian Peter Cranford's opinion "a person of acknowledged integrity," submitted "a restrained report, in spite of pressure on him [politically] to do otherwise." Finding that in general the trustees and superintendent had served their functions well and that the financial records were in order, Bozeman recommended that subsistence support that was provided in addition to salary be restricted to the superintendent; that the asylum matron be other than the superintendent's wife, Martha; and more generally "if, in the future, the necessity of the country shall demand it, that another institution may be established in the upper section of the State where subsistence and fuel can be more cheaply procured."[6]

Dr. Cummings, in the developers' camp, was far more critical in ways that indicated the institution's shortcomings: an impure water source, lack of access to railroads, insufficient milk from the dairy, and a lack of contributions to scientific research from the staff. Then there was the matter of the 515 gallons of "missing whiskey" from the apothecary, a medicine that he felt the doctors and staff too frequently prescribed for themselves and distributed to visiting legislators. His overall conclusions were damning: "We have commended nothing, and for the simple reason that we saw nothing to commend."[7] This sweeping indictment would later be cited by historian Gerald Grob as the opinion of *both* the doctors examining the Georgia Asylum, rather than that of Dr. Cummings alone.[8] Dr. Cummings worked with his pro-Atlanta faction of legislators to lodge charges against Supt. Green of withholding key documents.

But Supt. Green fought back. His allies arranged a hearing before both houses of Georgia's assembly, and one friend obtained a copy of the charges just before the superintendent mounted the rostrum at the Kimball Opera House (leased by developers to the state to use as a temporary legislative chamber) to speak. Green was a patient man, but he had had enough. Perhaps channeling both Irish parents' political fires and passions, he relived the hospital's history, answered the charges, and turned the attack on Cummings as "the condensation of his exaggeration, misstatement and injustice":

> The concluding paragraph is, we believe, the key: "We can say nothing about the Asylum, but that in the past it has been a failure and now needs a thorough reorganization." Reorganization—exactly! Here we have the milk in the coconut; somebody wants our places.[9]

A majority of the legislators voted to clear Green. Cranford notes that Supt. Green "turned the tide against breaking up the institution," and it would remain in Milledgeville as Georgia's only state hospital for the next century, for better and eventually for much worse. These political battles behind them, the Georgia Asylum's trustees reorganized. They expanded from three members to five and included Dr. Bozeman as board president in 1872.

Dr. Bozeman presided over the increased "administration of lunacy" by modernizing and formalizing the institution's processes, devising and publishing regulations, clarifying rights and duties of officers, and tightening financial controls. Assistant Physician Theophilus O. Powell, who had joined the staff from the Confederate army in 1863, also provided Supt. Green strong support. Through the 1870s and into the 1880s, the asylum reports uplift a full complement of "moral" musical concerts, billiards, picnics, dances, games, and theater performances for patients on the expanding wards. Church services came to mark the rhythms of the weeks and months, and funerals and burials the rhythms of life and death. The reports do not record how the asylum staff performed these services separately for white and colored patients, but we can assume that the colored patients got the attention of local Black ministers, and we hope they got chances for their own recreation. The trustees hired the highly skilled

J.W. Wilcox as chief engineer, and he modernized the facility with "a system of gas, to replace lamps and candles." Wilcox then went to work on a "water works system to replace wells which were becoming a menace to health as the institution was growing rapidly." Then came the new heating plant, the steam laundry, work on the front yards, a bakery, and two small fountains.[10] By 1885, the old buildings had been repaired and modernized and new ones added, including a stand-alone kitchen no longer housed in the basement of the Center Building, where it had been a fire hazard. The Georgia Asylum was growing into its own segregated village.

Classifications Before Segregations

In spite of the heavy racial animus in Georgia in the 1870s, it was not the colored and white distinction that trustees found most compelling in the immediate post-Reconstruction years. It was the founding categories of lunatic, epileptic, and idiot that most concerned Georgia's administrators of lunacy as they confronted the increasingly urgent question of white overcrowding. African Americans were new patients, previously barred from admission, and their admissions were limited by the space that the Colored Building provided. It was white patients whose families were constantly sending them to Milledgeville in numbers that overwhelmed the capacity of the moral therapy, which had depended on a long-surpassed cap of three hundred patients to allow close attention to patients' needs. These white families were the legislators' constituents, and the legislature's reluctance to limit counties' powers to transfer local responsibilities to Milledgeville drove the rising numbers.

When the asylum sought to cull patients because of overcrowding, families often refused to take their relatives back in. Georgians brought to Milledgeville were abandoned there long past the point of curability. They often arrived with one foot in a grave that other patients would soon dig for them on the grounds. As Green explained in 1867, the patients sent by counties and families had become an intolerable burden back home, or they tended to violence, or, given postwar conditions, families could no longer support them. These assessments apply to white families' conditions and practices.

In the 1871–72 report, the trustees declared: "We would most urgently urge upon the attention of the General Assembly the importance of separating the different classes of inmates; it is to us manifest, that every principle of humanity and justice, demands this change." In a moral therapy, he explained, it is the recently afflicted lunatic who can be cured. The best results, he urged, could be achieved in the first three months of an attack, and at least by the first year. "We cannot conceive a state of circumstances less propitious for the convalescent than association with the idiot and raving madman." The trustees lamented the "defects in state statutes" that gave Georgia Asylum officials no discretion on whom to receive. They beseeched the legislature to change laws so that any patient sent as a "pauper" would have actually "received support in whole or in part" from the county, given that counties were allowing many families to avoid paying by mislabeling them. Trustees also requested legislative authority for asylum administrators to discharge harmless and incurable patients back to the "care of friends and relatives." But, they noted, when they did, those folks at home often would not take the relative back in. Some patients, Green noted, had been patients for twenty-eight years, which would have been since 1845, that first cohort along with Samuel Henderson, Nancy Malone, and John Wade.[11]

These long-timers included William Fletcher, admitted May 6, 1846, who escaped twice and returned the second time voluntarily and who lived there until he died in 1898 of "old age." There was disappointed lover Thomas S. Harrison, who at twenty-four years old came to Milledgeville and stayed until his death in 1872. There was Martha Johnson, who at her commitment in December 1844 had endured eight years of "domestic trouble," who died in the asylum in May 1872, her freedom constrained for twenty-eight years by her husband's abuse. Perhaps she and Sarah Comstock formed a bond over the decades, given that Sarah was committed at age twenty for "abuse from her husband" and remained in the asylum until October 1864, when she died of "congestive chill." (To remind us, the husbands were seldom sent to Milledgeville for "abuse.") And there was someone still there whom we know: Alabamian Isaac Rawdon, who on commandment from God slaughtered and burned his disabled son, so his wife sent him far away to Milledgeville with no note of his transgression. Isaac died July 23, 1873, having lived a quarter of a century in the institution.[12]

But Green was right about most patients from the 1840s—the vast majority were dead within a year or two of entering, often from the combination of their own debility on arrival and contagious diseases contracted on the ward.

In 1875, the trustees finally laid down strict rules about overcrowding: "We have reached a point at which something must be done," they declared. Green declined to receive anyone who did not arrive through the formal application process and the waiting list. He insisted that the asylum would take only those people who had "recently become insane," a recommendation he had made for decades.[13] These restrictive moves were protested by county officials and families and censured by the legislature, which asked for a list of possible solutions to overcrowding. The solution was not to add more beds, which would only fill up again; it was to limit the categories of patients they accepted, the trustees insisted.

Their strong recommendation, a long-standing one, was that the "class of idiots" not be sent to the asylum but be kept at home, and that the state should construct an institution that could take care of their particular needs. By 1875, Green pointed to institutions in Europe and the United States that had proved "most praiseworthy benefactions and, in some particulars, truly wonderful":

> In those admirable institutions, individuals whose mental condition, manners and habits had led to their being regarded as among the lowest and most loathesome of God's creatures, may now be seen, neat and cleanly in their persons, quiet and orderly in their habits, learning to read and write; indeed, acquiring knowledge in all primary branches of education, and receiving such instruction in various mechanic arts, as will render them perfectly capable of supporting themselves.[14]

The 1886 annual report showed that the number of cognitively disabled people was 47 for a total population of 1,238, down from a high of 85 patients. From 1867 to 1886 the percentage of "idiots" fell from 17 percent to 3.8 percent, perhaps due to the winnowing process recommended by Supt. Green in the 1870s.

Georgia would not have an institution for what were then called feebleminded people until 1921, but that institution at Gracewood, Georgia, would hardly turn out to follow the "truly wonderful" model that Green extolled. Like what was then the Georgia Sanitarium, its potential (if any) was constrained by legislative penury. Its motive would be sterilization, as we shall see in part V as we follow the impact of eugenics on Georgia's people. In the 1930s, faced with a similar but larger crisis of overcrowding, but this time due to the Great Depression, the trustees would send back home two thousand patients they determined to be "harmless," some of whom had lived in what was then the Milledgeville State Hospital (renamed in 1929) for decades.

Alarming Rates of Insanity in Colored and White

In 1879, Supt. T.F. Green died. Green's family hailed from the Irish Uprising of 1798 against Ireland's colonial domination by the British. In fact, Thomas Fitzgerald Green was named after two martyred Irish revolutionaries. Green's replacement, Theophilus Orgain Powell's family came from southern plantation owners. The differences in how the two backgrounds played out at the Georgia Asylum would prove extreme. By the mid-1880s the trustees' anxieties had turned from (white) overcrowding to race. The 1886 annual report included Supt. Powell's assessment of reasons for the alarming rise in insanity of both white and colored Georgians, and we will examine his process of reasoning out these race questions in later chapters. Meanwhile, as Black patient numbers rose to 30 percent of the total population of the Georgia Asylum, the steward's records show a shift toward levels of increased agricultural production under the rubric of "moral" and "occupational" therapy.

In 1870, the trustees and legislature again considered the possibility of a separate colored asylum in another part of the state, which Green argued was "manifestly desired by the colored citizens generally and would be more satisfactory to them." Green observed that Georgia freedpeople were "almost all wholly unable to provide for one of their relatives such conditions at home or to seek an asylum for them elsewhere," and Green acknowledged that his colored patients were "entitled to claim admissions," in the language of his recent dealings with the Freedmen's Bureau.[15]

The following chart reflects how segregation played out in the expanding institution.

Ratios by Race and Gender at the Georgia Asylum
By White and "Colored," Male and Female[16]

Year	CM	CF	Ttl C	WM	WF	Ttl W	Ttl Pat
1874	44	43	**98**	269	228	**497**	**595**
			Ttl F	**Ttl M**			
			283	**312**			
1886	166	184	**350**	416	472	**888**	**1,238**
			Ttl F	*Ttl M*			
			656	*582*			
1897	332	321	**653**	705	810	**1,515**	**2,168**
	15.3%	14.9%		32.5%	37.9%		
			Ttl F	*Ttl M*			
			1,131	*1,037*			

Overall, annual reports show that after the end of the war the number of African American patients grew slowly for the first fifteen years, then hit a tipping point by the mid-1880s.

In 1871, the asylum had 1,250 acres and 375 patients, with an annual budget of $91,268, with 130 people in county jails "begging for admission."[17] Given the lack of attention during and immediately after the war, all of the buildings were dilapidated and "crowded beyond their utmost contemplated capacity." The Center Building held 323 white patients, and the two-story Colored Building, with separate male and female wings, held 52 colored patients in a space that was "insecure and not adopted for the purposes for which it was then and now used." The legislative appropriations from the previous year ($50,000 for additions to accommodate 150 more white patients, and $18,000 for fifty additional beds for African Americans, both of which would soon bring overall capacity to over 500) were rejected by contractors as too low: "No contractor proposed to do the work which was absolutely necessary to making these additions for the sum appropriated by the General Assembly," leaving it difficult to "convey a correct conception of the comparative advantages" of the buildings requested and the obviously more inferior ones "which we have caused to be built."[18] Adding additions rather than new structures was a fiscal consideration that allowed the builders to take advantage of plumbing and heating systems already in place, but at the cost of the quality of the structures and lives of the patients.

In 1874, the annual budget was $105,000, and there were 595 patients. Dr. Bozeman was in place as president of the board of trustees. For the first time, the report provided a breakdown of white and colored patients by gender. White patients totaled 497 and made up 83 percent of the total patient population, with 98 colored patients making up 17 percent. Overall, males totaled 312 patients at 52.4 percent and females 272 at 47.2 percent, a ratio that would shift to majority female as the century wore down.[19] By 1874, the grounds expanded to 2,987 acres.[20] This doubling of the asylum's size gave the institution access to additional wood for heat and timber, to better sources of water, and to agricultural land that would increasingly produce vegetables, meat, and eggs for use inside the institution and later for sale as cash crops. Almost three thousand acres of state land did not auger well for future patient workloads. By 1886, seven years into Powell's tenure, the Black population jumped to 28.3 percent and held near 30 percent for the rest of the century, even as total numbers grew. By 1897, the total population was 2,168 patients, of whom 1,515 were white (70 percent) and 653 were Black (30 percent). By the century's end, Black patients' numbers had increased by 660 percent, given that the institution until 1867 was all white; and white patients increased by 317 percent. But whites still outnumbered Black patients by 862 patients. In general over the last thirty years of the nineteenth century the rate of women and of Black patients rose, with the number of white men falling. The numbers of Black men and women would remain closely aligned, with those numbers affected by the growing numbers of African Americans arrested into Georgia's convict lease system.

"Raised at the Asylum": Pigs, Pork, and Piecework

The consolidation of the African American population at the Georgia Asylum to about 30 percent by 1886 coincided with an expanded agricultural production that would be increasingly absorbed into "occupational therapy" structured by race and gender. This happened as asylum modernization proceeded apace, with engineer Wilcox hard at work installing a new plumbing system with better drainage, new water closets, hot water tanks, and vertical covered radiators rather than the old system of bare stovepipes. The 1879 report shared the institutional desire "soon to accommodate all the colored insane of the State" with additional housing. It was the year that Supt. T.F. Green collapsed on the ward, dying soon thereafter, and the shift to Supt. Powell's leadership was under way. The newly installed Supt. T.O. Powell again extolled the "moral treatment" as "all those means that tend to lead the mind into a normal healthy channel, thereby directing the thoughts from the morbid, self-contemplations, insane delusions, etc." These moral therapies included "a variety of occupations, amusements, and entertainments." (Powell was particularly glowing about "useful employments.") As he explained, "Man's powers, mental and physical, were given for use." Such places of moral employment included "the kitchen, laundry, engine house, . . . flower garden, yards and vegetable garden, and . . . in the female department in sewing," with particular job assignments "according to [patients'] tastes and habits."[21]

Nor did the report specify who determined patients' "tastes and habits" for their work assignments. The early 1900s annual reports would explain the division of labor: white men were gardeners, 120 Black men lived and worked a "colony farm" that was "destined to be of valuable assistance to us in the reduction of the expenses of the institution," opened in 1903; white women were seamstresses and colored women worked the laundry.[22] It is safe to assume that in 1879 these perceived "tastes and habits" were in play and that segregated patients did not get to choose their work details.

The results of these jobs are tallied in "Farm and Outside Labor," a new Abstract G appended to the 1879 annual report.[23] The abstracts showed big production increases in the new Powell regime across the Georgia Asylum's 2,800 acres. In 1874, the annual report had listed "two hundred head of hogs" that the asylum is "having . . . killed for patients." That same year, the garden's produce was valued at a savings of $1,300.[24] By 1879, there are no hogs enumerated. But the steward reported "issued from [his] office . . . [and] raised at the Asylum" 3,082 pounds of beef and 7,446 pounds of pork.[25] That year the garden had produced, for example, 5,300 heads of cabbage and 5,600 ears of corn, and the women had produced 1,007 dresses, 1,021 shirts, and 666 pairs of pants.[26] The transition from hog to pork signaled a move toward industrial-level production on the asylum grounds, not good for hogs or for patients. By 1886, production had leaped: beef from 3,082 to 4,486 pounds; pork from 7,446 to 10,417 pounds; and corn from 560 ears to 28,000 ears. The matron had the women busy: dresses increased from 2,007 to 2,188 pieces; shirts from 120 to 2,738; pants from 666 to 2,212. In 1886, cows produced 7,893 gallons of sweet milk, and the chickens were hard pressed too, with 4,533 eggs for the year.[27] By 1886, 350 Black patients were holding at 28.3 percent of the population, and Supt. Powell was enthusiastic about housing "all of the state's colored insane" at Milledgeville, even as his institution reported a doubling of production for key commodities over the previous six years. The 1886 report does not specify who is producing all of this. There do not seem to be big increases in labor costs to process the increased food, and the per diem cost increased only slightly from 32.9 cents to 33.75 cents—both of which indicate that free labor was likely picking up the slack.[28]

Annual reports during the years between 1879 and 1885 are not available currently, but it seems likely that patient labor happened in the "Farm and Outside Labor" as well as the "Gardening" categories in Powell's report, where we can also note that Supt. Green's son-in-law Sam Cook had risen to head the Farm and Garden Department.[29] Perhaps if the reports provided more specificity about what all patients were doing, it would undercut the Georgia Asylum's claims to be "Georgia's #1 Charity," and perhaps white families would have balked at family members' being worked in forced conditions under such proximity to African Americans. By 1950, the Milledgeville State Hospital had an abattoir, a slaughterhouse that increased the hospital's production exponentially and grotesquely.

More Blacks "Convicted" to Corporate Lease Than "Committed" to Asylum

The statistics on race and gender in the postwar years show how segregation was proceeding at the Georgia Asylum. To recall, segregation was a "difficult and complicated process of rearranging whole cities into separate, unequal, and compulsory residential zones, for different races," in

Carl H. Nightingale's global history of segregation. In most cities across Georgia, this process would not be completed until 1910.

But in Georgia's asylum and prisons, the state had complete control of inmates and patients and could "rearrange" for different races. As we saw, asylum trustees put a ceiling on the proportion of Black patients, first at 17 percent, then approaching 30 percent. But the convict lease system absorbed increasing numbers of Black men with no need for the limits that segregated housing imposed on Georgia Asylum populations. Corporate labor camps provided the space for the new racialized prison system to be the solution to the Black labor problem after emancipation. By the end of the twentieth century, given the collapse of psychiatric treatment into the system of mass incarceration, it is important to understand the degree to which the state always created a proximity between prisons and asylums, which shared administrations and state land.

The effects of segregation on Black patients also registered in per patient costs. Over the years as the percentage of Black patients rose, the

Summary of Asylum and Convict Data with Asylum Land and Budget Data, 1868–1897[30]

Year	Asylum Total Patients	Asylum White # (%)	Asylum Black # (%)	Acres	Budget Request ($)[31]	Convict Total Inmates[32]	Convict White # (%)	Convict Black # (%)
1868	389	389	51[33]		77,911	245 (1865)*	245	0
1871	375	323	52[34]	1,250	91,268	385	61 (16%)	324 (84%)
1874	595	497 (84%)	98 (16%)	2,987	116,800	614	90 (15%)	524 (85%)
1879	754	644 (85%)	110 (15%)		116,250	1,108 (1877)*	114 (10%)	994 (90%)
1886	1,238	888 (72%)	350 (28%)		178, 208	1,527	149 (10%)	1,378 (90%)
1893	1,666	1,146 (69%)	520 (31%)		204,442	1688 (1890)*	168 (10%)	1,520 (90%)
1897	2,168	1,515 (70%)	653 (30%)		254,448	2,357 (1896)*	193 (8%)	2,164 (92%)

per diem expenses fell. (It had started in the 30-cent range in the 1840s.) Reports attributed this decline to administrators' frugality and to economies of scale as the patient load increased. But they were also due to the disparities in spending for Black patients in the segregated psychiatric fiefdom, although asylum records were not kept in such a way to document this assertion. In addition to being consistently cheaper in provisioning African Americans, the low per capita figure probably reflected increased production on the asylum land, achieved by increased patient labor.

At the end of the Civil War, the asylum and the penitentiary had about equal numbers of white inmates, the asylum 275 and the penitentiary 245 people. By 1871, there were in total 375 patients, 52 of whom were Black (at 13.8 percent), and 385 convicts, with 324 Black prisoners, who constituted 84 percent of the convict population. By 1879, the prison population outpaced the asylum by 1,108 convicts, 90 percent of whom were Black, to 754 asylum patients, 15 percent Black. By 1896 in Georgia, there were 2,357 convicts, 2,164 of them Black (92 percent), and by 1997, 2,168 patients, 653 of them Black—still holding at 30 percent. By the end of the nineteenth century, the number of African American convicts was about equal to the total number of asylum patients, and African Americans were 85 to 90 percent of Georgia's convicts. By national comparison, "In 1886 there were 64,349 prisoners in the United States, 9,699 under the lease system." In Georgia, only 100 to 150 of the 1,527 convicts worked in agricultural labor, as the rest were building Georgia's transportation system, mines, and cities.[35] If the asylum did not match the brutal labor system of convict lease, by the turn of the century its annual reports of "Occupational Therapy" do show an increasingly industrialized approach to patient labor influenced both by prisons and by the plantation model. In 1897, when Georgia established a prison farm for convict labor outside of Milledgeville, the state's prisoners and its asylum patients came once again into proximity on state land in Baldwin County.

While the Georgia Asylum allowed its African American patient population to climb to 30 percent—most likely for the additional labor those patients provided the institution—this increase was accompanied by what we might consider a "psychiatric panic" at the alarming rise in rates of insanity in Georgia and across the country. The Georgia Asylum trustees called on Supt. Powell to account for why so many Georgians, colored and white, seemed to be going mad. His reasoning would reinforce the emerging logic of segregation that the U.S. Supreme Court would articulate in *Plessy v. Ferguson* in 1898—that the Fourteenth Amendment "could not have been intended to enforce a social, as distinguished from a political, equality; or a co-mingling of the two races upon terms unsatisfactory to either."[36]

11

Dr. Koch and Supt. Powell:
Bacillus or Emancipation—"The Problem"?

In Berlin's Imperial Health Office in 1882, medical officer Dr. Robert Koch leaned over his microscope. He adjusted the lens over a concave glass plate, on which he had tried a new dye for a solution with tissues that contained a tubercule growth. Of the immense number of bacteria on Earth and in the body, the *tubercle bacillus* was among the deadliest because the white blood cells that were chief guardians of the human immune system could not destroy it. The methylene-blue slide might have struck him as oceanic, beautiful, were he not so focused on the few tiny rods now swimming into view. Koch was in search of the elusive bacteria for tuberculosis, the disease that caused one out of seven deaths in Europe. He reached for a pipette with which to add a brown counterstain, then the caustic potash with the ammonia he guessed would make the microscopic creatures visible. Then, the rod-shaped bacteria filled his eyepiece. Koch was euphoric—he had finally identified the *tubercle bacillus*.[1]

His laboratory in the Imperial Health Office provided him with the best equipment, although years before in the makeshift lab in the back of his house in a mining community of northwestern Germany he himself had developed many of its components. Key to the new bacterial science was his slide-plate technique, which sealed infected tissue in a drop of liquid on a concave slide. He had also developed the material in which to grow pure cultures for examination of bacterial growth over a series of days, and he had developed the dyes to bring the tiny swimmers into view. To increase the visibility of these tiny organisms, Koch had refined the microscope itself in terms of its resolution and illumination. Koch was brilliant and relentless in his determination to bring this invisible world into human view and discover its implications for health.[2]

Back in Wöllstein, he had also discovered the *bacillus* that caused anthrax, and in so doing became "the first to link a specific bacterium with a specific disease."[3] He began to distinguish the spores that carried bacteria from the bacteria themselves. In this way, Koch discovered that contaminated spores in the soil could cause anthrax for years after the bacteria within them died. From such an insight came the preventive measure to burn diseased animals or bury them in cold soil. Koch would go on to apply his instruments and his meticulous experimental method to studying wound infection and cholera. Contemporary medical practitioners and scholars agree: Robert Koch's work led him to the summit of scientific achievement.[4]

In Germany, Robert Koch's careful experiments and innovations were making breakthroughs that would transform human life on the planet, while across the Atlantic Supt. Theophilus Orgain Powell was engaged in a very different epidemiology in the Georgia State Lunatic, Idiot, and Epileptic Asylum. The post-emancipation southern struggle to wrest back white control was coinciding with the advent of this new scientific revolution developed by figures such as Robert Koch that was transforming medicine. In 1885–86, the asylum's trustees had asked Powell to explain the precipitous rise in insanity across Georgia in the two decades after the end of the Civil War, which in the 1890s he would link to a rise in tuberculosis, the deadliest of the nineteenth-century killers.

Koch had explained TB's devastating impact: "If the number of victims which a disease claims is the measure of its significance, then all diseases, particularly the most dreaded infectious diseases, such as bubonic plague, Asiatic cholera, etc., must rank far behind tuberculosis." Koch estimated that the disease killed one-third or more of the most productive middle-aged population and one-seventh of all humans.[5]

For most of Powell's years as superintendent, U.S. doctors were absorbing the new science. Supt. Powell instead would infuse debunked and defeated antebellum arguments about Black mental and emotional capacities into national psychiatric conversations and major professional organizations. As he did so, he neglected the most recent medical developments that could not yet cure TB but could help to prevent it. Nor would Powell be deterred by objections by Dr. Thomas S. Hopkins from within his board of trustees about methods of TB transmission. When Powell's institution eventually hired a pathologist in the late 1890s, the effects of his study would also be turned to racist uses.

With such obtuseness, he rose to the top of his profession, and in 1897 T.O. Powell delivered the Presidential Address to the American Medico-Psychological Association on the topic of psychiatry in the southern states. Powell's work would help to consolidate the racism that in Georgia was justifying convict lease, and it would contribute to Lost Cause arguments about Negroes' inferiority that were used to justify new forms of inequality such as segregation and voter disenfranchisement. Because U.S. superintendents habitually deferred to southern doctors on questions of African American treatment, these arguments easily made their way into the psychiatric mainstream.

Powell did not do this by himself, of course. But again, the Georgia Asylum events give us insights into how this American medical counter-revolution happened.

The Germ Theory, Scientific Medicine, and the Lost Cause Regained

In the nineteenth century, medicine had advanced on many fronts: dissection brought its more exact description of human anatomy, the microscope brought tiny disease agents into view, applications of physics and chemistry began to explain unique processes of organs and blood circulation, the new stethoscope amplified acute clinical observations, and sterilization and anesthesia ended many of surgery's tortures. For much of the nineteenth century, the best U.S. doctors (such as the first *American Journal of Insanity* editor, Amariah Brigham) had traveled to Europe to learn the new scientific medicine. At the time of Supt. Powell's tenure, germ theory was bringing medicine into "coexistence with a world of living microbes unseen by the naked eye," according to historian Nancy Tomes. The germ theory, Tomes summarizes, is "the belief that microbes cause disease and can be avoided by certain protective behaviors . . . [against] a wide variety of organisms, referred to colloquially as 'germs,' [that] are capable of causing disease; they include bacteria, viruses, rickettsiae, parasites, and fungi."[6] Contemporary medical historian Roy Porter observed of the impact of this nineteenth-century revolution today, "No one could deny that the medical breakthroughs of the past 50 years . . . have saved more lives than those of any era since the dawn of medicine."[7]

These insights would reshape the treatment of asylum patients, given that it was from paradigms of science that asylum doctors prescribed medical treatments for patients, many of whom lived in the asylum for decades. Medical paradigms generally overlay each other, with contradictions between the newer and older sets of ideas. As we recall, the Georgia Lunatic Asylum's first superintendent, David Cooper, could describe his patients as both "legionized" (a biblical reference to the "legions" of wild spirits that Jesus cast out from humans into pigs) and "sanguine" (one of the bodily humors from the Hellenic period, around which medicine in Europe was shaped for two thousand years): one a religious reference, the other medical. The new scientific medicine was a far cry from this older medical belief in bodily humors with its "heroic measures" that included purging and bleeding, heavy metals, and the use of opium, all of which severely curtailed the healing powers of Enlightenment institutions, such as those powers were. The new medicine was also a merciful departure from the lack of treatment available to the thousands of soldiers who had died of infection in Civil War hospitals because of lack of sterilization for wounds and amputated limbs.

Scientific medicine opened up an ecosystem of microbic environmental forces that caused disease. In so doing, it showed new ways of preventing sickness by eliminating germs. These changes implicated asylums, where burgeoning numbers of patients crowded into insufficient space. The germs in these institutions had, of course, always been there, as we can see from the records of the earliest patients.

Poignantly, our friend the loquacious wanderer Nancy Malone died in 1848 of "dysentery and inflammation of intestines succeeding measles."[8] Of the first one hundred patients, her death was one of eighteen others resulting from digestive infections, some explicitly leading to "marasmus" or wasting from the inability of the intestines to absorb nutrients. Marasmus is listed by itself in five other of the first hundred deaths. Six patients died from "consumption" or TB, four from "general paralysis" from syphilis, and one from typhoid. Altogether, in the first one hundred deaths, thirty-five were from communicable diseases, and the twenty-four from dysentery and marasmus were directly related to unsanitary conditions within the asylum itself. In contrast, four patients died from seizures, one from "maniacal exhaustion," and one severely disabled twenty-three-year-old from exposure on the journey to Milledgeville.

In sum, only six patients' deaths arose from the conditions of lunacy, epilepsy, and idiocy for which the asylum was founded. The majority were from dysentery. Such endemic dysentery, we now know, comes from fecal contamination of food and water and is carried by the *Shigella* bacterium or by an amoeba.[9] Surely these intestinal diseases were caused in part by the heroic regimes of purging asylum patients with laxatives and nauseants. Superintendents Cooper and Green could not know this information about germs in the 1840s. But Supt. Powell assumed responsibility for the Georgia Asylum at a time when the best practitioners knew this new information, and he was not among them.

If asylum entries in the 1870s could read "no history" as lynching raged in patients' home counties, the new science with its powerful technologies, such as those Koch innovated, were uncovering a different kind of history of disease in the tiny ecosystems of the body. However structured an institution might be, however many walks and dances and newspapers it might offer its (white) patients as moral therapy, if the institution neglected basic sanitation or continued to house patients in grossly overcrowded wards, they sickened and died. In 1886, when Powell was rehashing proslavery arguments about rises in insanity, he neglected the latest information on how organic causes of psychiatric symptoms might be flourishing in his own institution. This institutional environment was asylum administrators' primary responsibility, but Powell's intellectual commitment to racist ideology pointed him in exactly the wrong direction. His allegiance to Old South ideologies not only left all patients unprotected, it also leveled blame on them for their suffering, adding insult to injury.

Law professor and race theorist Dorothy Roberts' *Fatal Invention* describes the overarching dynamics of this end-of-the-century juncture. "Defining the political system of race in biological terms," she argues, "has been a constant feature of U.S. society for centuries, but the precise mechanisms for re-creating race have changed to reflect current sociopolitical realities." These realities emerged not so much "in response to scientific advances in human biology," but rather to "sociopolitical imperatives."[10] The history of Georgia's asylum illuminates the precise mechanisms by which new scientific advances were subverted by the South's post-Reconstruction imperative of reasserting white control and winning back its Lost Cause. The "negro equality" question that Edward

Pollard, T.O. Powell, and the ex-Confederates refused was at heart also the "negro humanity" question, and psychiatry, with southern influencers such as Supt. Powell, would continue to serve as one arbiter of Black humanity. In doing so, southern psychiatry played its role in conveying slavery's anti-Black racism to re-create the U.S. system of race in biological terms into the twenty-first century, as we will see in chapter 12. The Lost Cause would be won over and over again.

Why So Many Insane People in Postwar Georgia?

By 1886, when Robert Koch was in India investigating a cholera outbreak, T.O. Powell was ten years into his tenure as superintendent of the Georgia State Lunatic, Idiot, and Epileptic Asylum. His annual report from 1885–86, in which he enthused about "occupational therapy" as a cure, also contained his report "On the Increase of Insanity and Its Supposed Causes" that demonstrates a rising anxiety over race among the trustees and superintendent. Supt. Powell had already had one physical breakdown from the work overload caused by his expanding patient base and would experience a second in 1887. "On the Increase of Insanity and Its Supposed Causes" was his first stand-alone analysis of the forces impacting him and his institution. By Powell's count, in 1860 the ratio of insane-to-well white Georgia citizens was 1:1,323. By 1870 it was 1:1,007. By 1880 it was 1:635. The number of African Americans declared insane was burgeoning along with that of whites. According to the 1880 census, Georgia had 725,133 colored citizens—more than any other state in the Union. In 1860, the ratio of sane-to-insane Negroes in Georgia was 1:10,584. By 1870, it had risen to 1:4,225. By 1880, 1:1,764.[11] Notably, in 1880 white rates of insanity were still two times those of Black rates.

Why were so many people in Georgia seemingly going insane in the postwar years? Or were they? These would have been potent questions for the professional and political class, given the state's increasing responsibility for "lunacy administration" and its interests in shaping the understandings of how human minds perceive reality and suffer history. Such an upsurge in insanity was bound to catch the state's attention.

Two dilemmas immediately faced Powell. First, given that both Negro and white rates of insanity were rising, were white and Negro minds biologically the same? If so, what might that mean about the much-vaunted innate white intellectual superiority? Second, how did his almost religious belief in the importance of heredity in causing insanity stand up against medical reports that seemed to show only a handful of insane slaves in the years before the war, then exponential rates of increase afterward? If such reports were accurate, they at least pointed to environmental factors moving at a much faster rate than heredity could. Such data tended to undercut arguments about hereditary differences between the races and thus of inherent white superiority. Could he have it both ways? If he did, would anyone notice?

How Powell set out to resolve these contradictions provides important insight into those "precise mechanisms for re-creating race" that law professor Dorothy Roberts identifies in *Fatal Invention*. So, at the risk of pedantry, let us look over Powell's shoulder as he sat at his solid desk with its carved floral embellishments in his Center Building office as he went about figuring out how to solve these quandaries.

First, Powell reasoned that "negro brains" were not afflicted like whites' were with the tensions of modernity. Perhaps he went back through his ledgers as he enumerated white afflictions: "losses sustained in commercial speculation, or in any other ways." Nor were Negroes bothered "over brain work, or increased tension of the brain by any of the business callings of modern life," like creating the wealth that led to "brain overwork," or the demands of "wealth or luxury"—situations that were certainly not dangers to Georgia's African Americans.[12] His argument here echoed Amariah Brigham's assertion that rising rates of insanity in the United States among whites indicated superior white minds' exposure to the stresses of modernity and industrialization. As to the condition of the "negro brain," Powell wrote:

> Their remarkable mental and physical health and their immunity
> from certain diseases while in slavery, was entirely due to the health-
> ful restraints that surrounded them from childhood through life. . . .
> In slavery all the laws of health were generally enforced.[13]

As we now know, differences in vulnerability to disease did arise when a particular group (e.g., British colonists, African slaves, indigenous people) had either developed immunity to a disease or experienced a dis-

ease to which they had no prior immunity. For example, early white settlers in Georgia were decimated by malaria because they had no prior
exposure. And some African Americans had a survival advantage against
malaria due to a particular sickle cell hemoglobin, as a 2011 study
showed.[14] But in this passage, Powell assumed that any health advantages
that African Americans might have experienced from factors such as
relative immunity were "entirely due" to slavery's "healthful restraints."
Whatever limited immunity a Black person might have had, the Civil
War and Reconstruction created a new biological crisis for African Americans resulting from massive dislocations, new forms of confinement, and
diseases that spread rapidly by troop deployments. None of these debilitating factors were due to emancipation, but rather to war's effects and to
violently repressive efforts by southern whites. But here Powell attributed
all of freedpeople's woes to emancipation itself. Analyses such as Powell's turned freedom into a disease factor, and any illness for freedpeople
was a function of character, not of environment or history.

Powell's 1886 report made the remarkable but not unusual assertion
that, absent slavery's restraints, "[Negroes] are frequently led into excesses
which produce insanity, the legitimate result of constant mental and mus-
cular excitement, insufficient sleep and rest for the recuperation of the
brain and nervous system," as well as alcoholic intemperance.[15] In other
words, Powell believed that, post-emancipation, the essential character
of "the negro" had reemerged—a popular argument of southern slave
apologists about freed African Americans in the North, with its origins
in antebellum debates over abolition. In asserting slavery's beneficial effects, Powell drew on old and refuted arguments from the 1840 census
that free Blacks in the North suffered more insanity than enslaved Blacks
in the South, a "fact" that proved slavery's positive influence on slaves.
As noted statistician Dr. Edward Jarvis had lamented in his 1844 critique
of the census data: "We confess, we are disappointed, we are mortified;
nor are we alone in this feeling. . . . So far from being an aid to the
progress of medical science . . . it has thrown a stumbling block in its way,
which will require years to remove."[16] His statement proved prophetic.
Such a reassertion of slavery's hygienic effects was necessary in order to
demonstrate the negative effects of emancipation on African Americans,
a key element in contradicting Negro equality to regain the Confederacy's
Lost Cause.

Having fallaciously distinguished the "white mind" from the "negro mind," Powell then sorted through a set of mostly white circumstances to conclude that insanity among whites was not really on the rise in Georgia. First, he listed the post-emancipation lack of "servants [who] could be controlled and used as nurses for such cases," an insight into how formerly slaveholding white families were suffering the stresses of having to care for their own people absent slave labor. Particularly impactful, in 1877 the legislature had made the hospital free to all citizens (no more "paying patients"), so people were being sent by relatives "upon the slightest mental disturbance"—perhaps another indication that for white patients the Georgia Lunatic Asylum was taking the place of the work of emancipated Black caretakers. Additionally, Powell argued that improved asylum care raised public confidence, and the growing reputation of the Georgia Asylum led white families to return relatives from asylums in other states.[17]

Finally, and to Powell's mind importantly, he cited a "continued extension of the boundary lines of insanity," so that "a large number are now received in the hospitals for treatment who years ago would not have been regarded as insane, but simply peculiar or odd."[18] That the merely "peculiar" people were becoming understood as "insane" shows the ways in which the asylum was enforcing new standards of normality on Georgia's citizens. Still, the vast majority of overcrowding came from the weak and sick rather than the peculiar. These factors added up to an institution that was increasingly a catchall for Georgia's unwanted people. Powell's reasoning ignored not only the multiple traumas of slavery and its aftermath for African Americans, but also the considerable trauma of Civil War violence to whites, which for Powell the "continued extension of the boundary lines of sanity" did not encompass, even though he had witnessed the effects of the war from the asylum itself.

Historian Edward Shorter, seeking to explain the worldwide swelling of cases of severe mental illness with which the Georgia superintendent grappled, argues that there was an actual increase in brain diseases. First, an epidemic of venereal disease swept Europe and North American in the nineteenth century, "following the great military campaigns," so that neuro-syphilis, involving psychosis and paralysis in its last stages, "carved its path through the public asylums of the nineteenth century." Second, a rise in alcohol consumption and alcohol-related psychosis, attributed to a rise in the standard of living and the availability of cheap sugar beets for alcohol, created insanity from what came to be called "alcoholism." Third and most significantly came what Shorter argues was a rise in psychosis from schizophrenia marked by hallucinations, frank psychosis, and delusions. It was a "clearly genetically influenced disease of brain development, beginning perhaps in traumas of childbirth," although he does not speculate on what might cause an increase in such traumas (perhaps doctors' delivery of babies by forceps, lack of oxygen to the baby's brain during birth, or maternal starvation—all factors in rises in infant mortality as we will see) or how they would influence a person's genetics.[19] Trauma-induced symptoms from the Civil War or other of the "great military campaigns" also do not factor for Shorter, a telling omission typical of nineteenth-century and contemporary accounts of the Civil War's effects. By our mapping the history of white supremacy onto the history of U.S. psychiatry, such connections emerge.

Hereditary Taint? The Fates of A and B

In 1886, as he tried to think through how this rise in insanity was playing out in Georgia, Powell's faith in narrowly interpreted biological causes of mental disorders elevated the role of heredity over environment as a cause of insanity among his patients. In fact, heredity was one of the few explanations in his toolbox. He found at least half of his patients brought "hereditary taint" and quoted a "distinguished [but unnamed] alienist": "nine-tenths of all the insanity is the result of hereditary taint."[20] Powell explained the relationship between factors of "exciting causes" in a person's immediate environment, such as ill health, failure in business, domestic troubles, and so forth, and "predisposing causes" that existed prior to environments and underwrote the effects of its "excitements." A hereditary "predisposition to insanity," Powell reasoned, accounts for why if "A and B engage in business; they fail. A becomes insane. B bears his misfortune with the courage of a man. . . . Bad environments foster and develop the defects, while good environments might modify, improve or eradicate them."[21]

So, Supt. Powell's parable exhibits a process of what Darwin called natural selection: Why *would* humans A and B both fail in business in the competitive economy of post-Reconstruction Georgia (for example)—but only A would "become insane" from "hereditary taint," while B would not, "bearing his misfortunes with the courage of a man"? Human B must have been "naturally selected" to survive if he could offset his deficits and not go insane. Yet heredity was not entirely fate in Powell's drama, because "bad environments foster and develop the defects, while good environments might modify, improve or eradicate them."[22] Human A might be more defect-prone than the courageous and manly human B, but perhaps (male) human A had the hope of good environments to offset his hereditary deficits. (For Powell, slavery had offered Black people such an environment.) But if Supt. Powell had been tending to Koch, he might have then asked himself what factors in the environment of his asylum would offset or complicate what he assumed were hereditary deficits of his patients? One simple answer would have been "sanitation," for which he, the trustees, and the State of Georgia were responsible.

But Powell's thought processes were running on another track and in the opposite direction. His 1886 paper was shaped by the belief that hereditary traits were also "degenerative," a process that multiplied heredity's negative effects over shorter time spans. He wrote, "In each succeeding generation, these morbid tendencies increase out of proportion to the increase of the population."[23] It was easy for him to reason inductively, from stereotypes about slaves or women or the poor, to explain the different fates of Georgians that landed some people in his asylum. Under the wrong circumstances, the best ancestral processes of natural selection could not defeat these exciting environmental causes. As white southerners had learned on the Civil War's killing fields and as Europeans learned in the trenches of World War I, wars could override evolutionary advantages.

That Powell made this turn to heredity at the very moment that overcrowding was increasing the environmental dangers to his patients was particularly tragic for those Georgians trapped in the asylum. Powell was not unique in this thinking. Psychiatrists shared this belief that mental illness was directly heritable. Historian Shorter explains:

> Psychiatrists of the nineteenth century pioneered the modern understanding of the genetics and biology of neuroscience. But then they went one step further. They asserted that not only do the major

mental illnesses have a heavy biological and genetic component, but that these illnesses get worse as they are passed from generation to generation, causing progressive degeneration within family trees and within the population as a whole.[24]

The theories of degeneration would help to make Powell's asylum into an increasingly confined space for people from social "Group A's," such as African Americans, women, cognitively disabled people, homosexuals, and people variously disabled by poor health. Powell's arguments did not account for the germs within and around these people and invisible to the naked eye, or allow how their effects were magnified by the acute poverty, sexism, and racism in Georgia; in other words, for the emerging insights about "public health." Within a hereditary framework, his patients' sicknesses became deficits of "family fitness" or of "manly courage," not repeated exposure to pathogens in overcrowded and nutritionally deprived conditions. Such logic, or the lack thereof, marked the late-century shift in psychiatry away from "moral therapy" toward a version of morality that blamed marginalized people for their own vulnerabilities because of their and their families' moral failings. The eugenics movement would amplify this blame and devise solutions for "populations" that it found degenerate. It happened to my Daddy and Aunt May.

Within these contradictions, African Americans were denied the benefits of any doubts. They were protected by slavery, harmed by emancipation, exposed to grotesque levels of violence, afflicted by hereditary degeneration, denied basic rights and safe employment, worked on the asylum farm, vulnerable there to overcrowding that exposed them to germs, starved by inadequate diets, and vilified as carriers of rapidly spreading contagious diseases into the houses of white families. But Supt. Powell was not interested in contradictions, which can be exploited best if they are not named.

The Epidemic in Tuberculosis and Dr. Hopkins' Other Theory

In 1895–96, Powell wrote to physicians across the state about links among tuberculosis, insanity, and African Americans. By 1894 and 1895, Powell was extending his analysis of the rise of insanity in Georgia to the epidemic of tuberculosis, with his signature negative focus on African American patients. Within the American South, TB was particularly devastating to African Americans, and in the 1890s it was on the rise. By 1906, Atlanta University's Conference for the Study of the Negro Problems would report, "[The] greatest enemy of the Black race is consumption," with a TB rate three times that of whites, standing above the other four leading causes of death in its complex symptoms and the havoc it rendered.[25]

As he reached out to other doctors, the superintendent particularly valued Dr. T.S. Hopkins' opinion because the older man had "a larger experience in the care and treatment of consumptives, perhaps larger than any other man in the state," as Powell explained. He was also an asylum trustee. Powell looked to Hopkins to affirm his own belief in the absence of cases of consumption among African Americans during slavery, which he claimed demonstrated slavery's beneficial effects.[26]

Back in his Thomasville office, Hopkins pulled down the old plantation journals, which went back to 1783. He looked through records that he must have brought with him into their new home in the southwest corner of Georgia from McIntosh and then Wayne County along the coast to Thomas County when he and his family fled Sherman's March. Hopkins could find no references to consumption among slaves in the ledgers—"When the negro is referenced, he is placed among the immunes."

Hopkins then posed the question that Powell seemed to be asking: "Why, then, is it that the negro, who was until a recent period exempt in a great measure from consumption, is now the chief sufferer from that disease in the same climate where he was born?" He offered to Powell: "Finding nothing of interest in these old records on the subject, I propose to give you my own experience after an active professional life of fifty years." (An independent opinion was *not* what Powell had requested.)

In our cities which have become popular resorts for the consumptives the negro is the chief sufferer . . . with all the consumptive resorts of which I have any knowledge. Consumption among the negroes [in these cities] commenced among the chambermaids, laundry women, bellboys, and waiters at our hotels and boarding houses where consumptives spend the winter. They contact the disease from the visiting consumptives, and have disseminated it through their kin and kith among our negro population. I do not believe that consumption is a palpable contagion but that it is a communicable disease I have no doubt. I believe that it is to some extent a preventable disease.[27]

In other words, the answer of Dr. Hopkins to Powell's query about African American vulnerability to disease was *not* emancipation. Historian Tera Hunter enumerates the reasons why such claims about antebellum immunity do not hold up—factors such as alternative diagnoses like "Negro Poisoning," unreliable childhood memories of white doctors or treatment by other whites, and the racial biases and lack of experience of white plantation doctors.[28] In the nineteenth century, few white southern physicians would take that stand. Dr. Hopkins was paying attention to what was under his nose: white-to-Black transmission.

On the surface, Hopkins was not a likely candidate to make such a break with the superintendent's antebellum thinking. Powell's father had been a Virginia planter, and Hopkins' was a large landholder on the Georgia coast with ties back to the earliest settlers. Both had served in the Civil War. Powell served for only six months before being recruited by Supt. Green. Two decades older, Hopkins was in the U.S. military for many years before he joined the Confederate army; he fought in Georgia's Okefenokee Swamp during the Second Seminole War and enlisted during the Mexican War.[29]

During the last years of the Civil War, Hopkins served as assistant surgeon with the Engineers Department at the Confederate military prison at Andersonville, Georgia.

Andersonville Prison's Morass

Perhaps Dr. Hopkins was immune to Supt. Powell's suggestions of Negroes' inherent degeneracy because his military service at Camp Sumter, what most people knew as "Andersonville Prison," taught him the debilitating effects of increasingly wretched conditions for any human. Camp Sumter opened in February of 1864. That summer, General John H. Winder assigned Hopkins to inspect the site to determine "the causes of disease and mortality among the federal prisoners" and to make suggestions to prevent them in what had become the size of the fifth-largest city in Georgia. Hopkins went into the prison stockade on July 28 for his in-spection and soon submitted a letter to the prison's chief surgeon, Dr. Isiah White. Hopkins would have seen the double stockades of logs that rose from the countryside in a rectangle enclosing thirteen acres, with the ironically named "Sweetwater Creek" cutting through the middle. Up had gone the guard towers, which peered over the stockade walls at frequent intervals to enforce the "dead line" around the circumference in which any prisoner who wandered would be shot. The prison designed for 10,000 captives would swell at its height to 33,000 men, naked or in ragged clothes, without enough space to lie down. He saw the ground and the stream that had filled with their excrement and refuse. Smoke from what firewood they could gather hung above the prison and covered the prisoners in soot. When the wood was gone, what foodstuffs that were left had to be eaten raw from lack of firewood.

Because July 28 was his only day spent in the prison, perhaps he did not know how white Confederate deserters and Black soldiers and their officers received particularly lethal attention from the prison staff. Under such conditions, some prisoners stole from and preyed on others. Other prisoners tried to enforce a more humane order and to establish some bare standards of sanitation and nutrition. But their efforts were futile.[30]

After he completed the inspection and turned in his report, he worked until September 8 as a surgeon assigned to the engineering de-partment. Whether from the stockade walls or the engineering depart-ment, Dr. Hopkins saw the effects as prisoners became the walking dead. He probably saw that the same wagons that brought in their meager corn rations carried out corpses, a total of 13,000 dead prisoners. Trapped in what seemed like the end of the world in southwest Georgia, Hopkins would have seen white men break under its pressure, losing sanity. For one day, at least, Dr. Thomas S. Hopkins was there officially to witness the effects of this Confederate death camp.

Dr. Hopkins testified for the prosecution on September 22, 1865, in Washington, DC, in the Union military tribunal against the Camp Sumter commander, Captain Henry Wirz. Hopkins presented a copy of his "Inspection Report of the Andersonville Prison, July 1864" that he had written to Confederate brigadier general John H. Winder on Au-gust 1, 1864. It noted "CAUSE OF DISEASE AND MORTALITY" (overcrowding, absence of vegetables, want of barracks, badly cooked

foods, filthy conditions, "morbific emanations from the branch . . . a morass of human excrement and mud") and "PREVENTIVE MEA-
SURES" (removing 15,000 prisoners, either grow vegetables on site or
have the army's agents buy them, furnish wood and dig wells, erect shelter, put prisoners into bathing squads, buy them clothes or ask the
Union to, cover the "morass").[31] Dr. Hopkins explained to the tribunal
that his report apparently never made it up the chain of command to General Winder, who had submitted a second report made by another officer
that was "rather different," in Hopkins' words, and less critical than his
own. Consequently, none of the reforms Dr. Hopkins recommended were
made. In the engineering department, Dr. Hopkins was assigned to the
"1,000 to 1,200 negro men," where he reported that none of his workers
died. Hopkins testified, "I was never at any time on duty as a surgeon in
the hospital or prison at Andersonville."[32]

Capt. Wirz was found guilty and executed on November 10, 1865.

Then, after the war, Dr. Hopkins went home. Whatever else he carried away, he had seen the importance of clean water, sanitation, nutrition, and clean air. These were the forms of "moral therapy" being
promoted by the emerging emphasis on public health. Geography, terrain,
and space did make a difference in making people sick or well. Andersonville made that grotesquely clear.

"Consumptive Resorts of Which I Have Knowledge"

When Hopkins wrote to Supt. Powell of "consumptive resorts of which I
have knowledge," he exhibited remarkable modesty, given that almost
single-handedly he had brought consumptive visitors to Thomas County's hotels and boardinghouses, where they could spend the winter.
Under his tutelage the county became a health destination. Dr. T.S.
Hopkins did not further research the insights about white-to-Black
transmission that he shared with Powell. Nor has he been a subject of historians' research. So I pursued this idea for him across Georgia and into
Thomasville.

After a stint at Savannah's Georgia Historical Society and a weekend
on Jekyll Island, both of which were haunts of Hopkins' youth, I drove
across south Georgia past the Okefenokee Swamp with its gators and

moccasins and into the western part of the state on a highway marked with the derelict trailers and rusted cars in front yards that can signify southern hardship. The landscape changed in southwestern Georgia, where huge fields of cotton that bloomed white on both sides of the highway signaled an antebellum kind of wealth. Then I drove into the still "quaint" town of Thomasville, where in front of one antique store the owners had constructed a bent figure made out of overalls and a flannel shirt packed with cotton, clearly stooped to pick cotton's blossoms and not intended to represent a white person. I could have sworn I heard Paul Robeson singing "Ole Man River" from a cloud somewhere. The Thomasville Genealogical, History, and Fine Arts Library had ample material on multiple generations of the socially prominent Hopkins family.

After the Civil War's end, settling into his new Thomasville home, Dr. Hopkins took the lead in setting up local and regional professional organizations. These associations established a fee schedule for local doctors; convinced the city to respond to an outbreak of the dreaded Asiatic cholera; and oversaw the removing of rubbish, cleaning of privies, and providing of people with lime to spread over "night soil" to cut down on flies feasting on uncovered feces and spreading hookworm larvae. He also served on the county's board of health.[33] Hopkins increasingly emphasized the impact of climate on health, inspired by Hippocrates, whose writing had influenced European doctors for over two thousand years. The Hellenic philosopher's *Airs, Waters, and Places* argued that environmental influences such as sunshine, soil, water supply, and human habits shaped health. This emphasis on environmental factors fit well with the prevailing explanation of many diseases rising from noxious gases they called miasma—not from the disease-causing bacteria that were decomposing into the soil or the water supply.[34]

In those climate regards, Dr. Hopkins found his new county most excellent. The county had escaped many of the epidemics of coastal areas, a benefit that Hopkins attributed to the scent of pine trees, but more likely was the result of its absence of mosquito-breeding waters. Hopkins extolled the region's "climactic advantage" before the Georgia Medical Association and as president of the South Georgia Medical Society, which he helped to organize.[35] Hopkins' promotion of the area as a health resort for consumptives was as much a prescription for the county's economic health as it was for the patient-clients he hoped to attract.

It was an era in which fortunes could be made. By the time Dr. Hopkins settled in, Thomas County already had a growing business as a pleasure resort for wealthy northerners looking for the ideal place to avoid cold northern winters with their medical complications. In Thomasville, entrepreneurs built fifty massive Victorian "grand winter cottages" and put out the word to their friends about the possibilities of fishing, hunting, socializing, and taking the cure with their social class way down South in Thomas County. A decade after the Civil War ended, Yankee dollars were flowing south and Gilded Age capitalists bought out former plantations for their pleasure and health—hunting, fishing, yachting, gentleman farming, carriage riding, and staying or getting well. Dr. Hopkins' son Harry became both a local judge and a real estate agent to facilitate the shift of cotton land to hunting land, profiting considerably. In the 1890s, the Rockefellers, Vanderbilts, and other of the era's Robber Barons turned the Jekyll Island Yacht Club into the most exclusive resort in the world.[36] In the same years in Atlanta, the pharmacist Asa Candler bought the rights for a tonic and headache remedy called Coca-Cola. With its early potent combination of sugar, caffeine, and cocaine, his company would become the world's most recognized brand.

Hopkins' vision was to medicalize Thomas County's emerging tourism infrastructure with a campaign for consumptive travelers. In the last quarter of the century, through Dr. Hopkins' considerable energy, Thomas County became known as the "Winter Resort of the South," along with other competing Georgia health resorts, such as Warm Springs, Indian Springs, and the scenic Tallulah Falls in northern Georgia. In 1882, Atlanta *Constitution* editor and New South promoter Henry Grady commented, "Dr. T.S. Hopkins has been a pioneer in setting forth Thomasville's claims, and to him, as much as any man, is due her present preeminence as a health resort."[37]

In a pamphlet, *Thomasville: Winter Home for Invalids*, Dr. Hopkins publicized his case for Thomas County's climate. He extolled its temperature—in the summer, 86 degrees at the highest, with nights "delightful" for sleep—and its location, 200 miles from the Atlantic Ocean, 60 miles from the Gulf of Mexico, and 330 feet above sea level, away from the dangers of the coastline, where excessive humidity, sudden shifts in temperature, and the moist and salty atmosphere could be dire. The consumptive in Thomasville was also safe from the equally dangerous mountains, whose altitudes required possibly fatal exertions of the lungs. Hopkins particularly lauded his county's distance from rivers or lakes (and, he did not yet know, the malaria-carrying mosquitoes that standing waters breed) and its pine forests, which infused into the dry and balmy air the soothing smell of sweet resin.[38]

In a letter to a white Pennsylvania pastor written to entice his flock to visit Thomas County, Dr. Hopkins pulled out all the stops of prose and persuasion, hoisted the American flag, and claimed the Union as native soil. It was a New South paean of which his supporter Atlanta *Constitution* editor Henry Grady was no doubt proud:

> During the winter and spring months nearly all of the States in the Union are represented here, and Canada and Cuba aid in recruiting the "invalid brigade." When this army of invalids turn towards their far-off homes, and see their lovely vales and beautiful grass covered hilltops overspread with winter's icy mantle, they have reason to and do rejoice that there is one section of country, on their own soil and under the protection of their own flag, where winter quarters can be found with almost continuous sunshine, and here they will meet with a cordial welcome.[39]

No Lost Cause here. The "invalid armies" of northerners that Dr. Hopkins summoned to Thomasville were well provisioned. There were plenty of rooms, as the town's summer residency of 5,500 swelled to 12,000 with the winter influx, many of them carrying disease.[40]

So the issue that Dr. T.S. Hopkins raised with Supt. T.O. Powell for Powell's 1896 essay "The Increase of Insanity and Tuberculosis in the Southern Negro Since 1860" was a short paragraph, but not a small matter. He argued that it was not heredity or emancipation that sickened post–Civil War African Americans, but their exposure to highly contagious tuberculosis in the wealthy white clients in the hotels where they worked. There for two decades, Hopkins implied, they had spread the deadly disease through kinship networks—as we know, already made vulnerable by violence, poverty, and repression. It was seven years into Thomasville's medical-tourism expansion that Robert Koch first discovered the *tubercle bacillus*, although the information was not fully assimilated into the U.S. medical establishment for two decades, at the end of the century. But by 1895 Hopkins' attempted intervention with Powell most likely came from his subsequent awareness of the unintended effects of his health tourism that brought so many germs into his county.

This point of view on white-to-Black transmission was later uplifted with the "Germs Have No Color Line" campaign of African Americans in Atlanta. As historian Tera Hunter observed, "Privileged people who could afford to hire servants reaped the benefits of well-being by having someone else perform their 'dirty' work. Particularly during severe epidemics that necessitated extreme caution, hired help became more imperative."[41]

In spite of Hopkins' information and Koch's discovery, Powell persevered in explaining rapidly rising post-emancipation rates of disease with the increasingly popular theory of degeneration. He believed that "inherited [but yet unmanifested] tendencies" during slavery caused this "insane and consumptive [tendency toward TB] . . . to widen and deepen . . . from generation to generation, unless the laws of health are properly appreciated, carefully and cautiously considered and conformed to." By implication, white people did not have such an inherent tendency. Given this degenerate acceleration, Powell could anticipate when "the number of colored insane in the Southern States will soon be as large, if not larger, than the whites in proportion to the population."[42] What Powell does not consider in his linkage of TB to insanity is the fact that TB can infect the brain, so that symptoms of insanity characterize TB's late stages. Its symptoms are not a separate disease. As we will see, such symptoms increasingly show up in his institution in the 1900s.

President Powell and the Southern Specialty of Race

Georgia Asylum Supt. Theophilus Orgain Powell stood at the podium in the Hall of the Medical and Surgical Faculty of the Johns Hopkins Medical School in Baltimore before the 53rd Annual Meeting of the American Medico-Psychological Association. It was May 11, 1897, and he was there to give the Presidential Address. Looking out at the distinguished crowd, Powell must have felt immense satisfaction at his ascent to the top of his profession after thirty-four arduous years in Milledgeville. Powell's topic that day was "A Sketch of Psychiatry in the Southern States," which had been suggested by the meeting's national planning committee in order to give "due credit" to the southern pioneers in the field of asylum care.

That afternoon, Powell had sketched out five periods of southern psychiatric history, from demonic possession to the present. Only then did Powell turn to a brief but defining section on "The Colored Insane," from which this book takes its title:

> In one particular alone does lunacy administration at the South differ from the same problem elsewhere in our country. What the race problem is to our section, so is the question of the colored insane to our speciality. Provision for this has always been a separate and peculiar problem.[43]

Powell's ticket into the New South rebirth was his self-proclaimed expertise on the Negro, who was fast becoming considered the nation's problem. Powell was building a reputation in Georgia as the administrator of the state's "leading philanthropy." However, Powell was not the most notable of the superintendents in the room. He did not have the credentials of the previous year's president, Edward Cowles, who had studied at Johns Hopkins, been a clinical instructor at Harvard Medical School, served as superintendent of McLean Hospital from 1879 to 1903, and there had "almost single-handedly guided the professional transformation of the community of American Alienists or asylum physicians, from a marginal sect to a respected biomedical specialty in U.S. general medicine," as the *American Journal of Psychiatry* proclaimed at his death in 1919.[44] Nor did Powell have a long association with the Medico-Psychological Association (which had succeeded the Association of Medical Superintendents of American Institutes of the Insane), of which he was now president.[45]

In 1894, the Georgia Asylum's annual report had again noted the danger of chronic overcrowding; this time Powell explained that such overcrowding had "destroyed the original aim and object of the male and female convalescent building" by disturbing "those two factors that yield the most results"—"proper classification and surroundings."[46] No germs in sight, but classifications. Only three years later, in 1897, Supt. Powell proudly reported that what had been renamed the Georgia State Sanitarium had outfitted a pathology department "complete in every particular" for "suffering humanity and the benefit of science."[47] In fact, by 1897 the recently renamed Georgia State Sanitarium's new pathologist, Dr. T.E. Oertel, had almost single-handedly brought science to the facility by setting up the pathology lab, with Dr. John Mobley as his assistant.

That year, tuberculosis in the colored female ward was the institution's greatest health problem because of its "alarming prevalence" in those wards, where women faced "rapid and fatal decline." There were twenty-four deaths among African American women in 1897.[48] The cause of death was now confirmed by "post-mortem evidence," or autopsies. The lab conducted eighty-six autopsies that year.[49]

Robert Koch's innovations were finally showing up in Milledgeville, microscopic procedures that in 1897 Oertel explained had "been in use . . . for a number of years [but] . . . it does not seem to have become well known." By 1897, the pathology lab had new microscopes and collections of diseased tissues on glass slides "for future study." There were two operating tables "under modern aseptic precautions." When a case of TB was suspected, doctors "examined that patient's sputum for the tubercle bacillus" with slide techniques practiced at Johns Hopkins Hospital.[50] In the colored female wards, patients who tested positive for TB were put into quarantine, and "all possible precautions [were taken] towards disinfection of sputum and the rooms occupied by this class."[51] In his pathology report that year, Dr. Oertel was gratified to note that these practices had brought down the mortality rate for pulmonary tuberculosis in the colored female wards from 78.57 percent of deaths the year before to 30.76 percent (a downward trend that reversed into the early twentieth century).[52] Dr. Powell concluded in the 1897 annual report, "Our claims to being an advance in psychiatry is justifiable and from it we confidently expect scientific progress."[53] These advances most likely formed the basis of his daytime report to the Association of Southern Hospitals for the Insane and his claims as president of the national association.

The Association of Southern Hospitals for the Insane & the Lost Cause

In 1896, as the *American Journal of Insanity* noted the next year, Powell was also a founding member of the Association of Southern Hospitals for the Insane, which had met that year in Asheville for the second time, with thirteen doctors attending from six southern states. This Southern Association meeting provides both context for Supt. Powell's growing role in the national association and insight into how the new advances in science and pathology were shaped by old ideas of the Lost Cause, a difference quite literally of day and night.

The science came in the daytime. Baltimore's Superintendent Charles Hill of Hope Mountain Retreat gave the 1896 session's Presidential Address, "What the Clinical Laboratory May Contribute to Psychiatry," and the conference included two presentations on chemical analysis and laboratory work in asylums. One of these was a paper by our Dr. T.E. Oertel, who had set up the lab at the sanitarium. In such sessions, the new Southern Association brought appropriate attention to the applications of the scientific medicine that had come from European clinics, labs, and universities. But an evening session attended by major southern players had a very different purpose and message. It demonstrated the degree to which these scientific medical techniques were already being deeply corrupted by racism.

That nighttime session at the Association of Southern Hospitals for the Insane provided space for giving attention to that southern "speciality" that Powell would soon claim nationally from the Johns Hopkins podium. With science out of the way, the title of the session was "Has Emancipation Been Prejudicial to the Negro?" The session began "by a carefully prepared paper by Dr. J.F. Miller" of the Eastern North Carolina Asylum (for Black patients), which concluded with a post-Confederate flourish: "While enslaved the negro had improved in healthfulness, prolificness, and sobriety. Now he was degenerating in all these respects. . . . I express here the opinion that the mental inferiority of the negro as thus shown in the midst of the environments which have surrounded him since the war is a leading factor in the development of his insanity."[54] This was a succinct summary of the special knowledge from the region's "peculiar institution" that white southern psychiatrists such as Powell were bringing into the national discussion at the century's turn. Powell's skill in its elaboration was demonstrated in the same *American Journal of Insanity* issue, which abstracted what the editor described as his "thoughtful paper" on the "Increase of Insanity and Tuberculosis in the Southern Negro Since 1860." The editor's summary quoted Powell's description of the development "on the part of the race of 'a highly insane, consumptive, syphilitic and alcoholic condition, which predisposes them to diseases which formerly they were free from.'" With their denigration of African American intelligence and morality, the southern psychiatrists "asserted in their rights and views" a refusal of Negro equality with whites, a refusal that Pollard's 1867 Lost Cause argument had granted them the privilege of.[55]

It is remarkable that southern superintendents such as Powell and Miller posed their question in terms of *emancipation*'s impact on the African American's mental well-being—not of slavery's impact, nor the impact of lynching and other forms of Klan terror, or convict lease, or sharecropping. This obfuscation was possible because these same superintendents had systematically kept those traumas out of their African American patients' records when they came in from counties roiling with Klan terror, their ledger entries reading "no history noted." With such erasures, Black suffering in the postwar years was made to seem to come from the emancipation that was heartbreakingly being withdrawn by these same southern white elites and their northern counterparts. Powell and Miller disregarded scientists like Robert Koch and the information so lauded that very afternoon in Asheville at the Southern Association meeting. Science at Milledgeville would be read through this antebellum frame of emancipation's prejudicial effect, a reading itself that had prejudicial effects.

Powell's underlying prejudices would make eugenics a more compelling argument to him in the last years of his life, the first decade of the twentieth century. As long as "emancipation" was the cause of every Negro's insanity or disease, no patient or vulnerable citizen would be spared the lethal effects of such willed ignorance. Supt. T.O. Powell was not a firebrand racist; he had no reputation as a ku-kluxing nightrider that I have found. He was a gentleman and a Christian and, by white accounts, a kind man. For precisely this reason, he was an able carrier of this strain of white supremacist ideology. Wanting someone to speak about southern psychiatry's accomplishments, the national planning committee of the American Medico-Psychological Association had to know that Theophilus Orgain Powell was the man for that job.

By 1898, the United States had entered its imperial era with its provocation of the Spanish-American War. The southern psychiatric "speciality" of anti-Black psychiatric racism was one of the new American Imperialism's most needed currencies. Long abandoned was Dr. Amariah Brigham's quaint idea that American white people were the most insane because they were the most intellectually advanced, in comparison to their primitive slaves or conquered native foes, who lacked the emotional capacity to feel the pain of slavery and genocide or to have feelings of affection for family and friends being separated or slaughtered. By the early twentieth century, funded by the most wealthy families in the United States, the Eugenics Record Office at Cold Spring Harbor on Long Island would launch the U.S. eugenics movement as it directed the medical gaze onto those denigrated populations increasingly marked as sick, insane, and perverse—for study, for control, and, in 1930s Nazi Germany, for elimination.

12

Turn-of-the-Century Dreams:
The Fire This Time, the Asylum
Farm, and Supt. Powell's
"Operation of a Certain Class"

I got the dark night blues,
I'm feeling awful bad.
> —Blind Willie McTell, "Dark Night Blues"[1]

But at least in the asylum the old man had learned caution and when
he got out he put everything he had in the service of his cause. He proceeded about the Lord's business like an experienced crook.
> —Flannery O'Connor, *The Violent Bear It Away*[2]

Three years before Superintendent T.O. Powell gave his Presidential Address in Baltimore, Georgia Asylum steward J.L. Lamar was prepping
his section of the asylum's 1892–93 annual report, documenting how the
goods acquired through his department were distributed across the institution. Lamar's efforts give us a more quotidian way to measure how segregation was proceeding at the Georgia Asylum. It operated via his
precise allocations across wards at the same time that tuberculosis was
sweeping through colored women's wards made vulnerable by overcrowding. As the 1890s moved forward, segregation also informed the
trustees' allocations of building space, and before the rollover to 1900 its
aspects would burst into fiery view in the Atlanta *Constitution*'s yellow
journalism accounts of a gun-wielding patient and the asylum's "fire this
time." As the nineteenth century prepared to dump so much of its refuse
into the twentieth, it carried its bizarre unrealities in such minute details

as those Lamar stewarded and could do so because the official accounts lied, and those lies lay like a pall over its institutional narrative.

A Georgia Asylum Sampler of Who Got What

In Milledgeville in September 1893, the steward accounted for how he distributed the state's bounties and deficits across asylum wards organized by race and gender. Segregated wards made such distributions almost natural and highly efficient, as they were intended to do. From Steward Lamar's master list, we can create our own subsets for the 603 white females, 543 white males, 284 colored females, and 246 colored males (the African American men reduced in asylum numbers by their presence in convict lease). In total, 1,146 whites were 68.4 percent of the asylum population, and 530 colored patients were 31.6 percent. Here is a Georgia Asylum sampler of who got what, although these entries do not reflect nearly all of what the steward recorded.[3] It has its own sad poetry:

What white wards got:

Palmetto fans white men 50, white women 51

Envelopes white men 2,603, white women 3,269

Writing pens white men 345, white women 110

(colored women 12)

Soap cakes white men 2,783, white women 6,486

(colored women 2)

Masquerade suits white men 28, white women 20

Spectacles white men 32, white women 40

(colored men 1, colored women 0)

Sheets, Paper white men 6,353, white women 3,818

Toothbrushes white men 5, white women 2

What white men's wards got:

Table linen 9 yards

Shaving brushes 30

Razors 6

Razor straps 15

Bugle 1

Playing card decks 142
<u>What white women's wards got:</u>
Backgammon Boxes 8
Capes 26
Cologne bottles 2
Carpets 12
Gowns 1,138
Rugs 206
<u>What women's wards got:</u>
Bonnets white women 322, colored women 51
Chemises white women 799, colored women 507
Dresses, rough white women 831, colored women 610
Dresses, calico white women 959, colored women 35
<u>What men's wards got:</u>
Coats white men 1,147, colored men 358
<u>What colored's women's wards got:</u>
Irons 9
<u>What colored patients' wards got:</u>
Jim Crow cards 13 for men, 8 for women[4]
<u>What all got:</u>
Books white men 26, white women 20,
colored men 13, colored women 11
Brooms white men 449, white women 577,
colored men 153, colored women 189
Water buckets white men 59, white women 63,
colored men 32, colored women 68
Scissors white men 15, white women 9,
colored men 7, colored women 7
Hose, pairs white men 25, white women 2,411,
colored men 0, colored women 168
Lead pencils white men 300, white women 161,
colored men 120, colored women 24
Slippers white men 153, white women 228,
colored men 20, colored women 23
Wash pans white men 471, white women 741,
colored men 550, colored women 864

The African American Building, Central State Hospital, Milledgeville, Georgia, 1894 *(Courtesy, Georgia Archives, Vanishing Georgia Collection, N GA AR 030)*

From such a listing we can surmise how asylum administrators allocated privileges and labors across the wards and buildings and how the state separated out white people from African Americans even when they were all in dire conditions. Such allocations enforced the racial inequalities that Lost Cause post-Confederates insisted on. These calibrated disparities worked on patients to internalize white supremacist interpretations of worth. They also constructed the bizarre combination of benefits and insults that shaped the existence of white women, who were the largest demographic group in the asylum. In 1898, the Supreme Court would uphold in *Plessy v Ferguson* the social inequalities necessary to prohibit a "commingling as to the two races upon terms unsatisfactory to either."

As examples, we can see that white men and women were allowed to read and write; they were given pens, pencils, books, and ink and had access to spectacles—at times the men got twice as much as the women, although white women were sixty more in number than white men. When colored women got feminine items like bonnets (also protection

Superintendent Powell in his office, seated next to his steward, Georgia Lunatic Asylum, 1890 *(Courtesy, Georgia Archives, Vanishing Georgia Collection, bal179-85*

in the sun), white women got six times more, although they were only twice as numerous as colored women. All women got "rough dresses," more or less proportionate to their ward numbers. But for more decorative calico dresses, white women got almost one thousand and colored women got a negligible thirty-five. In total, white women got six dresses each, colored women two. Overwhelmingly, white women got hose, with 2,411 pairs to colored women's 168, also a negligible number for 284 colored women.

White people got the items of sanitation and comfort: slippers, soap cakes, gowns, shaving materials (although how 543 white men shared six razors is hard to imagine, or five toothbrushes). Think for the African American patients—bare feet on cold floors, grossly inadequate provisions for bathing, and the grit and danger and insomnia of that, for the men no shaving day in and out. White women got the slippers and also carpets and rugs, reminders through the soles of their feet each day that they were at least one comfortable step above the colored people. Perhaps the men got coats because they did the "outside work" while the women were mopping, sweeping, and sewing. But did any of the women go outside in cold weather? Colored men and women got "Jim Crow cards," which were hair combs repurposed from weaving looms (not a Black deck of playing cards as I imagined).

On the moral therapy front, white people got the entertainments, minimum as they were: for men the 142 decks of playing cards, for women the eight backgammon boards, for men a bugle, probably for some old Confederate veteran to play reveille or taps, for white people the "masquerade suits" for the periodic masquerade balls—for example, at New Year's celebrations—one effect of which we will see shortly. Clearly items such as 28 masquerade suits for 543 white men or 35 calico dresses for 284 colored women or one pair of spectacles for 246 colored men cannot be used by all in that ward. Such structured shortages raise the issue of how these rare items were distributed within the wards, how they were subsequently shared among ward mates, and what jealousies or generosities they created. How they actually played out, we cannot know. Of such minutiae was the asylum's Jim and Jane Crow constructed.

No New Building for Colored Patients

As segregation at the Georgia Asylum proceeded with the steward's quotidian distributions, it also operated at the structural level as far as which people got which buildings in an institution predicated on overcrowding. "Every available space in the white men's and colored men's and female departments is now occupied," Supt. Powell wrote in the 1893 annual report, a familiar refrain, with an added warning of "much evil and danger" if conditions were not remedied.[5] This "available space" was no longer the first Colored Building behind the Center Building but a much larger and more isolated structure. In July 1892, the trustees met with the Joint Committee of the Legislature to figure how best to meet the expansion needs created by a patient population that still continued to grow. The legislative committee again rejected the idea of starting a "second institution in a distant part of the State" that trustees had recommended. The trustees figured that a new institution would cost $500,000

The Day Room, Central State Hospital, Milledgeville, Georgia, 1894 *(Courtesy, Georgia Archives, Vanishing Georgia Collection, N GA AR 035)*

to build, with administrative costs of up to $10,000 annually. But additional construction at the Milledgeville institution would be in the $100,000 range. The special committee and trustees suggested the cheaper option of allocating $100,000 to construct a new Negro building, adding $20,000 to renovate the old Negro building so that white male patients could inhabit it. The engineer drew up plans and revised the budget up to $130,000.[6] The trustees had done the right thing in prioritizing a new Negro building.

But the legislature balked at giving new construction to Negroes. The next year, the legislature cut the allocation by 23 percent to $100,000, which made for "an entire change of plans" on the dismayed trustees' part. As a result, the Negroes lost the new building, which instead would be given to five hundred whites. Instead, there would be two annexes added to the already large colored building, adding 370 patients and a dining room for

770.[7] The trustees regrouped and lauded "the cost of the buildings now being erected . . . [as] vastly less according to capacity than any similar building ever erected on the Asylum grounds." In other words, the cost reflected a new low even in Georgia for already cheap facilities. Their funds would provide white patients with "sun rooms, dining rooms, kitchen, steam heating apparatus, including boilers, kitchen furniture, gas pipes, bathrooms and water closets." For the Negro building there were new additions of steam heating, sunrooms, and dining rooms. To save funds, the grading for both buildings "will be done largely by patients and the regular employees of the institution."[8]

By 1897 the new buildings were completed. The total colored population that year was 893 patients, all housed in one huge place. "PICTURE SHOWING FRONT AND ONE SIDE OF BUILDING OCCUPIED BY NEGROES" from the 1900 report shows a formidable structure, taken from a distance of open ground, isolated up the hill against the skyline.[9] There are twenty-six rooms per side on each of the three floors. Unlike the Center Building portrait with its gardens, trees, cupola, portico, and pavilion, the building occupied by Negroes is stark and prisonlike. A smaller building sits in front of one side.[10]

But that's the picture of the Negro building rebuilt *after* the fire. The horror of that day and night of fire was the outcome of a quarter century of segregation of African Americans at Georgia's asylum. Fortunately, no one died in its terrible flames.

Asylum on Fire

On November 9, 1897, a fire broke out under the roof of the old part of the Negro building on the female side. There are two accounts of this asylum fire, the event most dreaded by superintendents. The official one is told in the annual report from 1898; the yellow journalist version came out immediately from an Atlanta *Constitution* reporter. By Powell's official 1898 account, the fire began at 12:15 p.m., and the asylum fire brigade responded promptly to an alarm and with "commendable zeal" got the patients to safety. Nurses and other staff carried some out with "no casualty or escape." The Milledgeville Fire Brigade, then the Macon brigade, arrived "as promptly as possible" (how promptly was that?) and worked to put out the fire late into the night, pumping a million gallons of water in the process. "The fire gutted the greater part of the building occupied by the females, and burned off the roof of the building occupied by the males." But the firewall built with the new construction protected the two additions—no firewalls having been included in the old building.[11]

The next morning, the Atlanta *Constitution* blared:

ASYLUM ON FIRE;
COMPLETE LOSS
Negro Lunatic Asylum of Georgia
Completely Destroyed By Fire.
WILD SCENE AMONG INMATES
Driven Out and Corralled Like So
Many Cattle
After Three Hours Hard Fighting
Partial Success Comes—Inmates of
White Asylum Doubled Up[12]

By Remsen Crawford
Milledgeville, GA, November 9, 1897 (Special)
At high noon today a furious volume of flames burst through the roof of the eastern wing of the negro building at the Georgia lunatic asylum, and with stubborn resistance has baffled the combined powers of the fire departments of Milledgeville and Macon until it has completely laid waste the colossal structure in which the state had housed nearly a thousand colored lunatics.
Hustling Out the Lunatics
Without a moment's delay after the fire was discovered, the guards were summoned in the scene, the huge gates flung wide open, the cell doors bursted loose and the hundreds of negro lunatics driven out of the door of the building into the yards to the rear where, like cattle, they were guarded until other buildings could be vacated for their custody.

"It was a wild scene of consternation which beggars description," reporter Remsen Crawford wrote. "The mad throng was driven into the corners of the yard the males on one side, and the females on the other, and were guarded by the platoons of attendants until the two white detaches could be vacated, when they were corralled there, and in the old assembly hall of the asylum known as 'the old thirteenth.'" Here, Crawford took full advantage of racist stereotypes and white readers' fears. He also recorded with such gross stereotypes what must have been the genuine terror of the African American patients captured in the fire:

> Madmen leaped high in the air, pell mell over each other, screaming, shouting, singing and praying, many of them being murderous fiends sent to the asylum instead of the gallows by the craft of shrewd lawyers, and many dangerous, depraved wretches no better than brutes. Shouting and singing, crying and laughing in fiendish/idiotic glee, while the flames leaped high . . .

This *Constitution* reporter used the descriptors "dangerous," "depraved," "wretches," "brutes," "criminal," "murderous," and "fiendish" all in one paragraph to describe the African American patients. These passages give us a glimpse into the projections of the white imagination about African American people and what had brought them to such buildings and made their lives in such conflagrations so nightmarish.

Of course, the raw experiences would have been wildly scary and traumatic. Those nine hundred African Americans saw, felt, and heard the "furious volume of flames" that sprouted so rapidly within their intensely overcrowded and isolated building—located, as the newspaper reported, "in a remote southern corner of the grounds." To this awful scene Crawford added the gathered townspeople, out to view the spectacle. "Nearly everybody has left the city tonight to witness the fire," he wrote—but not, apparently, to help. His description projects the fears of the white onlookers: "citizens here fear[ed] the lunatics might break out from the control of guards after they were liberated from the building and [might then] enter the town." African American citizens would have also assembled, with a different set of fears for the patients and of the white crowds.

In an account of an asylum fire in Ohio in 1872, the townspeople showed no such fear of the mostly white patients. As soon as possible, the Ohio staff organized efforts to gather them together and care for them: "The people of Newburg did nobly, throwing open their houses for the reception of the sick. . . . They extended every facility in their power for tending the terrible exigencies of the occasion."[13] Decades after the Ohio fire, Powell reported that there was no damage to the "White Buildings" in Georgia. But displaced African American patients were in "greatly overcrowded conditions in the annexes," which were "simply packed" with 650 patients in spaces built for 270. They were also confined in "many of the jails throughout the State."[14] No one mentioned the obvious stress this put on already sick patients, or the overcrowding that increased the tuberculosis contagion.

In either Georgia account—the official record or the yellow journalism— where might we find these humans among the burned-out psychiatric ruins? Amid his fantasies, Remsen Crawford did report one small figure who provides another perspective from which to view the events. "While they arrived on the scene the crowds of lunatics had been carried out of the way and safely housed, one patient, Rebecca Arnold, falling dead on the way," he writes. The writer had so fixated on the fiends and the flames that the white *Constitution* reader has little attention or sympathy for this small figure of Rebecca Arnold collapsing into the moment of her death. But, here given a name, Rebecca Arnold stands in for the nine hundred souls, although Powell claimed there were no casualties in the fire. Asylum ledgers record that Rebecca Arnold was received on June 23, 1881, believed to be forty years old at the time. Back in Fulton County, Zack T. Reid, a local policeman, had petitioned for her commitment. The duration and cause of her insanity were not known, and she was "quiet and orderly." A year after Rebecca Arnold, Reid also committed Fannie Luckie.[15] Rebecca Arnold was buried in the Negro cemetery at the Georgia Sanitarium on November 9, 1897, the day of the fire. She was fifty-seven years old at her death.

The Fire This Time

Amid Crawford's prose there was another familiar voice that emerged from the patients—that of the anonymous "pyromaniac."

Lunatics Enjoyed the Blaze

Dr. Powell is greatly disturbed. He is fearful of further work of destruction by the inmates. All over the grounds tonight from the windows could be heard such screams as

"Let the fire alone!"

"Let it burn the whole place down, and we will go home from this hell!"

It could easily be detected that the officials were alarmed at these shouts. Whether the fire was the work of an inmate or not is the question.

One of the negro women patients claimed responsibility for setting the blaze. Powell thought the fire started from a tinner working on the roof who accidently allowed a coal or spark to fall into the attic, although the tinner denied he had been at work the day of the fire.

Yet here the voices came from "all over the grounds." If Remsen Crawford is accurate, it was not only the colored patients who would rather burn to death than stay in the sanitarium.

Amidst its conflagration, their voices rang.

The "New" Old Negro Building Rises from the Ashes

By October 1898, Powell and the trustees were putting the best face on the fire and its aftermath for the institution if not the patients. Powell reassured the governor and the public that the $40,000 provided by insurance had allowed them to build back a structure far better than the old one and even have $3,000 left over. The new old Negro building now had eleven fire walls from basement to roof and doors between; floors laid with pine; remodeled steam heating in the female room; larger flues and better radiators; and steel ceilings over 30,612 square feet of building. The contractors, the public was reassured, had rebuilt as much in sections as possible, given that the patients had been crowded into the annexes.

Also, "there will be added a small structure of brick in the rear for surgical purposes"—28×36 feet with an instrument room, a sterilizing room, two bedrooms, and one operating table. Additionally, the female wing contained a 10×21–foot room for surgery with "an operating table, fixtures for sterilization of instruments used in genito-urinary investigations," and instruments for viewing the eye's interior and the larynx. Dr. W.H. Doughty Jr., of Augusta, had already completed four hysterectomies and one ovariotomy on Georgia Asylum Black women. All were done in sterile conditions, thanks to the advent of germ theory in Georgia.

But, sterile instruments or not, there would be other types of sterilizations via "genito-urinary investigations" in such operating rooms in the coming decades. Nor is the lauded Dr. Doughty Jr. from Augusta reassuring. Doughty was a faculty member at the Medical College of Georgia in Augusta, having joined his father, Dr. Doughty Sr., in 1881 on the faculty as "assistant demonstrator of anatomy and clinical assistant." Dr. Doughty Jr. held the chair of pathology, with special attention given "to post-mortem examinations, . . . with the opportunity of studying morbid Anatomy to the best advantage."[16] The elder Dr. Doughty died in 1905, and his son took over as dean of the Medical College in 1910, serving until 1923.[17]

Both men, then, would have been at the Medical College during the now infamous period of robbing African American graves for bodies that white medical students then used for dissection. These thieves were the infamous "Night Doctors" or "Resurrection Men" who operated across the South in antebellum and then the postwar years, exhuming African American graves for southern medical schools.[18] In 1989, almost ten thousand human bones, three-quarters of them African American, were unearthed in the basement of what had been the Medical College of Georgia. The 1989 discovery became the subject of *Bones in the Basement: Postmortem Racism in Nineteenth Century Medical Training*. In the nineteenth century, freelance robbers brought the unearthed corpses to school labs, where they were preserved in whiskey, then dissected, or put into the school's anatomical collection, or buried in the basement.[19]

These events help us to understand the highly praised Georgia Asylum pathologist Dr. T.E. Oertel's parting observations as he left his position in 1900 for a job at the Medical College of Georgia:

Preserved patient brains found in old closets at the Central State Hospital and displayed in the Central State Hospital Museum, Milledgeville, Georgia *(Photograph taken by the author)*

Perhaps the most important work so far carried on in the laboratory [at the Georgia Sanitarium] is the forming of a collection of negro brains for the purpose of future study and elaboration of statistical data which cannot fail to interest the scientific world at large, and it is hoped add somewhat to the sum of human knowledge.

He also lauded "the seventy-five (75) specimens thus far preserved." Dr. Oertel bowed out with his observation: "Nowhere in the world does such an opportunity for collecting brains from insane negroes present, and if the pathologist were to devote his entire time and energy to the prosecution of the work begun, he could not spend them in a more interesting or valuable research."[20]

On my visit to the Central State Hospital museum around 2010, staff had recently turned up in one of the hundreds of closets a number of brains cut to their cross section and preserved in square glass containers—perhaps from this "interesting and valuable" collection? It is not clear where they are currently stored. It was not only the *Constitution* reporters' yellow journalism that tipped the Georgia Sanitarium's story toward the Gothic and the haunted. Nor were the Resurrection Men and the "bones in the basement" the only racist horror.

LUNATIC PULLS PISTOL, Patient Osborne and T.O. Powell

The fire did not provide the only excitement for *Constitution* readers that year.

Less than two months after the fire, on January 3, 1898, a tired Supt. Powell was walking past the female convalescent building, where a New Year's masquerade ball was in full swing in the amusement hall, its revelry spilling out from the open door into the winter night. From Steward Lamar's 1893 records, we know that there were at least twenty white women and twenty-eight white men with "masquerade suits" for such occasions. This type of "lunatic ball" was a familiar spectacle in late-nineteenth-century asylums—newspapers covered them with headlines like "DANCE OF THE LUNATICS."

But Supt. Powell was not partaking of the masquerade that evening. He was on the way home to the Center Building when he heard the shots.

The noise pulled his attention to the person with the pistol rushing toward him. Had T.O. Powell been a cursing man, as he recognized the approaching figure he would have let it rip. It was the notorious white "patient Ben Osborne." As we would say today, Powell had an active shooter on his grounds.

According to the copious news accounts in the Atlanta paper the next day, as Osborne raced toward the superintendent Powell turned "and put himself squarely in the fleeing man's path," in one of his better moments.[21] Osborne raced within a few feet of Powell, lifted the pistol, and fired at him—but missed! Osborne ran past Powell but turned to fire again, the second shot also whizzing past the doctor's head. Powell's heart must have been racing, but he was alive and unhurt. "The escaped lunatic made his way out of the asylum and has not been seen since." The next day the *Constitution* blared:

LUNATIC PULLS PISTOL
AND FIRES ON DR. POWELL
Osborne, the Notorious Atlanta Murderer, Escapes
From State Lunatic Asylum
SUPERINTENDENT'S CLOSE CALL FOR LIFE
Desperado Dashes from the Dancing Hall
While Reveling with Asylum Lunatics,
And Is Now at Large . . .
Thrilling Story
Of the criminal Career of Osborne.

The Atlanta *Constitution* had followed the story of Osborne since 1896, when he had killed Theodore Schrader, the foreman of an Atlanta lithography company who had recently fired him. Vowing revenge, Osborne had shot Schrader down in the street, and the prosecution argued that the homicide was retaliation for the firing. But Osborne claimed that Schrader had stolen his soul and given it to a dog. Osborne's defense team pointed out that their client had a history of mental problems—in spite of the fact that his labor problems seemed more pressing. The *Constitution* coverage played on the ambiguities of the "insanity defense" as its own kind of masquerade.[22] Hired by the defense, Dr. Hugh Hagan visited the prisoner and concluded that Osborn was "undoubtedly insane" in the form of "periodical insanity," so they would get him "sent to the asylum, but just when is not known."[23] Three days later, the *Constitution* reported, "He is now a raving maniac."[24]

Building up the paper-selling drama, citizens learned that despite his returned appetite, he "STILL DEMANDS RETURN OF HIS SOUL." The *Constitution* explained that the prisoner "Was Not Hypnotized as a Dog," according to "the hypnotic performer" Professor Lee, because "the whole time Professor Lee remained in Atlanta no subject was put under a spell."[25] Supt. Powell, who prided himself on his decorum, had no doubt watched with dismay as the story progressed to his doorstep. But the inmate-become-patient had not given Powell any trouble—until the night of the dance of the lunatics.

However, no doubt consoled by his wife after his near miss, Powell was not prepared for the newspaper two days following the escape:

LUNATIC OSBORNE
WRITES A LETTER
Mailed the Constitution a Long
Epistle from Milledgeville,
TELLS A REMARKABLE TALE
A Crazy Man's Frightful Story of Alleged
Cruelties at Asylum
WROTE LETTER BEFORE HIS ESCAPE
He Evidently Contemplated His Daring Act When He Penned
the Strange Missive in his Lunatic Cell—Why He Fired at
Dr. Powell

The newspaper published his letter in full, the very day after his escape and attempted murder of Powell. Was the escape the act of a lunatic, or was it the calculated ploy of a killer who had saved himself from hanging by a wily game? Whichever, the *Constitution* gave Osborne's missive full play. Osborne larded his claims against Powell with unlikely disclaimers that not wishing "to bring myself into prominence," he was "sacrificing himself to unpleasant notoriety" in order to reveal to Georgians "the real modus operando" of the Georgia lunatic asylum at Milledgeville:

Under the guise of law I have been entombed in this prison for the insane for many months. Dr. Powell pronounced me cured three months after I came here, yet I was allowed to remain a burden on the state, and now through gross insults and mistreatment I am on the verge of insanity again. I am deprived of any fresh air, exercise and sunshine, the three most essential properties for health, and I am utterly deprived of any enjoyment whatever; thus I am deprived of those privileges of life, liberty and the pursuit of happiness which the constitution guarantees to every citizen.[26]

Osborne knew how to play it all ways—suffering from "temporary insanity" when he killed his former boss, he escaped prison or execution. Now allegedly sane enough to be released, the asylum made him mad again by its deprivations, so he shot at Powell. And it was all Supt. Powell's fault for his escape.

He continued that the terrible asylum diet was "cooked by a bevy of worthless Africans." Extraordinarily insane patients were "choked to death by the doctors," murders covered up when legislative committees visited, he alleged. "He Offers Proof" of other patients who had played "the insanity dodge" more successfully than he had, then declared the "Whole State An Asylum" and signed off with his plan to "shuffle off this cognomen and physiognomy," lamenting his failures to realize his potential: "But for my adversity I would have been a combination of Wren Pitt, Dean Swift and John C Calhoun without the profligacies. But all is gone, the world is against me." Although the asylum did not yet have the diagnosis, Osborne seems a bit of a narcissist.

We last hear of Ben Osborne in a *Constitution* story from January 14, 1898, that read "OSBORNE MAY BE NEAR AUGUSTA: Escaped Lunatic Heavily Armed, Passes Through Harlem," a town in Georgia, where "armed to the teeth [he] terrorized the people of Harlem tonight and had women and children hiding in their houses behind locked doors. He passed on through the town and disappeared and many believe it was Osborne, the Atlanta murderer."[27]

Such yellow journalism as that exhibited in the shooter and fire stories facilitated the growth of the American empire on the century's cusp. Less than six weeks after the Osborne incident at Milledgeville, the *USS Maine* hit a mine in Havana harbor, and the competing "yellow" coverage in Hearst's and Pulitzer's newspapers would help push the country into the Spanish-American War. "The rise of yellow journalism helped to create a climate conducive to the outbreak of international conflict and the expansion of U.S. influence overseas," the U.S. State Department's Office of the Historian would explain.[28] On the local level, state lunatic asylums offered ample opportunities for sensationalized coverage of such "notorious, lunatic, desperado murderers" as Osborne. Such were the events back home within a year after Supt. Powell's Presidential Address: a literal firestorm.

Done responsibly, journalism improved the lives of patients and accurately informed the public. For example, in 1887, Nellie Bly's ten-day undercover assignment in the asylum on New York City's Welfare (now Roosevelt) Island put mental institutions into the public eye. Her early example of muckraking journalism was published later as *Ten Days in a Mad-House*. Bly revealed neglect and physical abuse at the institution, and her book resulted in important reforms, including a separate Department of Public Charities, a much larger appropriation for patient care, stronger supervision of health care workers, and regulations against overcrowding and fire.[29] But in Georgia, the lunatic-desperado-madman-genius-undercover agent Osborne drew on this genre of exposé to get himself into the asylum rather than the prison and then to attack Powell in the press. The only results were public entertainment, Osborne's escape, and Powell's increased chagrin. Had Osborne, as Milledgeville Muse Flannery O'Connor would later write about another wily male patient, "proceeded about the Lord's business like an experienced crook"?

Burning buildings and celebratory dances in response to arson were not new to Georgia. Some of the patients in the colored building had been alive when General Sherman's army blazed across the Georgia landscape, a pyromaniac's heaven and a slave's sign of redemption. Burning plantation houses would also light up the pages of William Faulkner's novels far into the twentieth century and inform the title of one of James Baldwin's prophetic books, in which he would write to Black people like Rebecca Arnold: *"Please try to remember that what they believe, as well as what they do and cause you to endure, does not testify to your inferiority but to their inhumanity."* He called that book *The Fire Next Time*.[30]

13

Plantation—Asylum—Prison

The habitual criminal is the product of pathological and atavistic anomalies; he stands midway between the lunatic and the savage.
—W. Douglas Marrison, quoted in T.O Powell[1]

In 2010, when Central State Hospital closed its doors under federal court order, what had been at various times the largest state mental hospital in the United States—and at times in the world—was replaced at every level by a prison. Today, the Baldwin County Jail, the Fulton County Jail, and Chicago's Cook County jail are the largest in their respective U.S. governing units (the county, the state, and the nation). These prisons and jails are the concrete, brick, and mortar equivalents of the twenty-five thousand bodies stretching into the Baldwin County woods as far as the eye can see—or the bodies that have had their bones brought up in the roots of trees, so the stories go, in a monster storm. These living and dead bodies in the ground or behind bars are not coincidences, but old patterns of harm unbroken across the centuries—and such patterns, or "afterlives," are what eventually constitutes the haunting of psychiatry in this book's title. Here at the century's turn, the Georgia Asylum-cum-Sanitarium is slipping its Enlightenment moorings and (re)turning to the Gothic, the grotesque, the repressed. As the brilliant southern literary critic Patsy Yeager described a century later: "Trauma has been absorbed into the landscape . . . of repudiated, throwaway bodies that mire the earth: a landscape built over and upon the melancholic detritus."[2]

So, in the late nineteenth century, the insanity plea I suspect that patient Osborne copped was not the only issue that linked the asylum-sanitarium to Georgia's expanding penal system. By the turn of the twentieth century, the plantation was their primary intermediary. The rising numbers of African Americans in the convict lease system and in the asylum in the 1870s and 1880s offered their own synchronicity, their less than coincidence that starts to feel uncanny. Baldwin County's dethroned status as state capital made it handy for the state when it wanted to use or acquire state-owned land for other types of confinement, which Georgia did in 1897 with the State Prison Farm. By the late 1880s, the asylum's population makeup, with its 30 percent African American patients, coincided with an increase in the Georgia Asylum's agricultural production—measured precisely in pounds, bushels, quarters, and dozens. These things together pointed to a social geography becoming less "morally therapeutic" and more like a plantation whose various tasks offered its involuntarily committed patients "occupational therapy," since little other therapy was available.

Like distributions of goods, patients' work was also structured by raced and gendered political economies. In 1893, the steward J.L. Lamar reported the results of the year's labors across a "variety of departments . . . [that] have given employment to quite a large number of patients of both sexes." The matron's report that year reflected "a large amount and variety of work done by female patients, such as making, repairing, etc" with the "garden and dairy, grading and excavation" all giving "outdoor employment to many of the male patients." Neither the steward's nor the matron's reports specify how many patients worked for how long per day or week or year, as Superintendent David Cooper had done (with far fewer patients).[3]

But a closer look at the annual reports provides some suggestions about who was doing what work. These production figures reflect a considerably larger operation than "garden" implies. For example, the "outdoor work" of the "garden" staff and patient workers produced 27,014 gallons of sweet milk for a credit of $5,402.80, with a favorable balance of $2,470 above the milk provided to patients and staff. The garden produced a credit worth $5,059.46, its largest crops 1,810 bushels of sweet potatoes for $905 in credit and 26,982 cabbages for $809.46 in credit, in addition to turnips, collards, radishes, onions, cucumbers, beets, potatoes, tomatoes, butter beans, pears, field peas, green corn, cantaloupes, watermelons, and hay. (None of the fresh produce turned up on the allocations to patients that same year.) The garden had a favorable overall balance of $2,570.67. Overall on the livestock front, there were 29,728 pounds of pork slaughtered and prepared, at a credit of $2,378.28, with a balance of $2,247.06. The total profits that these "outdoor" operations produced was $7,288.18, after having provided food, meat, and milk to patients and staff. One Inflation Calculator turns this $7,288 into $207,424 in 2019 dollars—to give us a sense of how much work and its worth were actually involved.[4]

Occupations listed for white patients prior to commitment included seventy-seven farmers, one daughter of a farmer, and one son of a farmer. Colored patients' occupations included twelve farmers, twelve farm hands, and fifty laborers. At most, the total patient "farmer" population was 101 patients, with a son, and daughter, and fifty laborers thrown into a possible labor pool.[5] From all of these statistics we can also assume that the free labor of patients was helping the institution's much vaunted balance sheets and lowering its per capita per diem figure, which in 1893 was 31 $^{95}/_{100}$ cents, a historically low figure but for one other year, as the report boasted. The equivalent per annum figure was $116.[6]

The production units are clearer on the female side. The matron was in charge of the female wards and work outputs, measured in a total of 29,258 pieces, including 1,305 chemises, 1,531 homespun dresses, 1,977 pairs of drawers, 2,004 pillow covers, 3,159 sheets, 3,410 shirts, and 1,164 towels. If all of the work was done by no more than 887 women in a year, they produced an average of 33 pieces each.[7] Given the ill health or disposition of many of the women, those healthy enough to work produced considerably more pieces per year.

In 1898, the trustees reorganized their committees to reflect a growing plantation-industrial model that included "Executive Committee"; "Auditing Committee"; "Committee on Farm and Outside Business"; "Committee on Buildings, Machinery, and Repairs"; "Committee on Sanitation"; "Committee on Dairy"; and "Committee on Rules and Regulations, Laws, etc." Tellingly, there is no mention of patients' welfare or treatments in this new institutional structure. The 1899 annual report finally made the division of patient labor clear: "Many of the white females are employed in the sewing rooms, and the men in the gardens and various other departments of the Institution. The colored females are generally employed in the laundries, and the colored males in grading and in the fields, dairies, etc."[8] (By 1900, the colored males would be moved to the asylum's "colony farm.")

By 1900, the trustees had reorganized the now sanitarium's businesses even further. The Executive Committee became the Prudential Committee; the Auditing Committee became the Finance and Auditing Committee; the Committee on Farm and Outside Business stayed the same, as did the Committee on Buildings, Machinery, and Repairs. The Committee on Sanitation added the Welfare of Patients; the Committee on Dairies added Hog Raising; the Committee on Rules and Regulations, Laws, etc., stayed the same; and a committee on Medical and Dispensary Service was added.[9]

By the century's turn, then, three committees oversaw the farming operations, with hogs in a parallel position to patients. Only half of one committee references "welfare of patients," but at least medical services were also an executive consideration. Also telling, the pictures in the 1900 report featured buildings, a herd of cows, and a pen of pigs—the only human an African American man standing beside the strung-up carcass of a slaughtered hog.[10] In all, the psychiatric-estate form of patient care carried a lot of overhead when its main focus was its farm and the opportunities for "work therapy" its operations provided Georgia patients. For Georgia lunacy administrators, the plantation model was still too close at hand. And it would get closer still.

Georgia State Prison Farm Comes to Baldwin County

In 1897, Georgia's prison system and its asylum once again came into proximity to each other when the State of Georgia built the Georgia State Prison Farm on four thousand acres in Baldwin County. The asylum was south of town, and the prison farm was located on the west side of Milledgeville on the road to Macon. It was the first centralized prison in Georgia since the Reconstruction government closed the all-white Georgia Penitentiary in 1868. Subsequently, African American inmates lived in convict labor camps across the state in dire conditions, subjected to the cruelest treatments in a new regime of hybrid agricultural and industrial labor. In 1897, the Georgia legislature reorganized its prison system, reducing the sentence limit on convict lease from twenty to five years. The state opened the Georgia State Prison Farm to house all convict females and young, old, and disabled males—although any and almost all of the people in these categories could be "disabled," given the way they were worked. In 1907, Georgia would add to Baldwin County's carceral acreage a reformatory for youth on the prison farm grounds for the adolescents caught up in convict lease. By 1908, under pressure from reformers, the convict lease system was abolished and replaced by an equally brutal system of county chain gangs.

Talitha L. LeFlouria and Sarah Haley's recent scholarly books on women in Georgia's prison systems during convict lease and the chain gang have been foundational in understanding the understudied role of women in Georgia's penal system.[11] Neither scholar makes the comparison between the experiences in the prison farm and those in the asylum-sanitarium, even though both institutes were in Baldwin County. But their work provides a basis for us to do so.

The system of convict lease decentralized Georgia's penal system in labor camps across a range of industries and counties. These camps mixed races, genders, and ages, with African American males disproportionate in the population. The few white people were generally given special privileges (the white men, for instance, got guns). There could be as many camps as corporations would pay for. As we saw in the tables in chapter 10, the population of convicts grew in Georgia from 385 in 1871 to 614 in 1874 to 1,108 in 1879 to 1,527 in 1886.[12] In 1886, the Georgia Asylum had 1,238 patients, 350 of whom were Black. Of the 1,527 total convicts in Georgia in the same year, 1,378, or 90 percent, of them were Black.

The Georgia Lunatic Asylum–State Sanitarium centralized the collection and treatment of people that the counties judged to be lunatics, epileptics, and idiots, as well as senile people, alcoholics, misfits, and local citizens suffering from debilitating sicknesses. Repeatedly, when implored to open other institutions in order to give more specific care to cognitively disabled people, or to separate out convicted criminals or inmates who took the "insanity plea," or to segregate African American patients in "their own" institution, or to move patients closer to home, the legislature refused for budgetary reasons. It was cheaper just to expand the Milledgeville fiefdom.

At the prison farm, labor was anything but therapeutic, and prisoners were anything but the old idea of penitents. There, African American women and boys provided its primary workforce, although all disabled people were expected to work too, and the state refused to grant clemency short of the deathbed. At the asylum, according to its records, African American women worked in the laundry while white women were seam-stresses. The distribution of labor stayed within raced and gendered roles. At the prison farm, African American women worked across domestic service, agricultural labor, and skilled, more industrial work. Their strength and multiple abilities were sufficient for their keepers to put aside tradi-tional gendered work roles. The women's new labor hybrid, Haley argues, "made the New South possible, not as a departure from the Old, but as a reworking and extension of previous structures of captivity and abjec-tion."[13] Across convict lease camps and at the Georgia State Prison Farm, Black women experienced, in Haley's terms, "staggering violence."[14]

Asylum reports listed the numerous occupations for patients as evidence of the latest in moral therapy. But as farming operations expanded into state acreage, the "plantation" was there to replace the "asylum" as a model of confined labor. Such a shift marked the end of the Enlightenment-inspired idea of the therapeutic use of space that U.S. asylums had long outgrown. If the Georgia Asylum did not operate primarily as a labor sys-tem like the state farm did, the ideological production of administra-tors like Superintendent T.O. Powell in his essays and speeches bolstered the psychiatric rationales necessary to justify the idea of the degenerate criminals whose function was to provide a cheap and controlled labor force after emancipation.

Operation of a Certain Class

While patients and prisoners supplied agricultural, industrial, and domes-tic labor, Supt. Powell continued his ideological tasks into the early twentieth century.

In 1901, his last essay, "Marriage, Heredity and Its Relations to Insan-ity and Allied Morbid Conditions," pushed his antebellum-based critique explicitly toward the new theory of eugenics, a term coined in 1883 by Charles Darwin's cousin Francis Galton. Eugenics means "well born," a concept Galton drew from the breeding of livestock. Galton wanted to hurry evolution along by encouraging the "best families" to intermarry and the rest not to reproduce. Charles Darwin had coined "natural selection" as a parallel to the "artificial selection" of breeding stock. Both prisons and asylums had plenty of animal stock at hand, and perhaps the proximity of hogs and cows to patients and convicts allowed too easy a linkage to the "natural selection" of what came to be called Social Darwinism. By this thinking, evolution meant that whoever survived (however armed with killing weapons and ideas) was the fittest. By the turn of the twentieth century, the rediscovery of Gregor Mendel's work with pea pods showed their regular patterns of "dominant" and "recessive" factors over generations. This research hardened hereditary arguments, with the analogy between people and pea pods.

Powell's 1901 essay came much closer to Galton than Mendel in its emphasis on marriage. Powell concluded: "Many of the most alarming diseases and conditions to which the human race is subject can be traced directly to improper marriages," continuing:

> In my opinion there is no subject of such vital importance to the human race mentally, morally and physically and perhaps none so much neglected, as marriage, heredity and its relation to insanity and other morbid tendencies, inherited and acquired, that are readily transmitted, and it should be remembered that they are not manifested in a stereotyped form, but in an endless variety of morbid forms.[15]

Powell's last essay was filled with the dread of "the natural tendency of defectives [that was] degeneration" of humans "dominated by their morbid, depraved and selfish natures" that led them to "violation of God's inexorable laws."[16]

If the "positive" requirement to certify "the mental and physical condition of the parties . . . before they could obtain marriage licenses" should fail, Powell wrote, "then an operation with a certain class—say, the most depraved and some of the epileptics; would this not be a source of true benevolence? The people, however, will have to be educated up to the necessity of such a course."[17] The coyly indirect reference here is to sterilization. In 1899 in Indiana, Dr. Henry Clay Sharp had become "the first person in the world to impose a vasectomy on a person in custody."[18] Apparently news of "an operation with a certain class" in order to sterilize them was traveling fast among white U.S. medical men.

In advocating marriage control, Powell advocated what was being termed "positive eugenics." But his promotion of the operation on the depraved was "negative eugenics," which took corrective measures against those people regarded as degenerate. He wrote this essay three years *after* Georgia Sanitarium officials rebuilt its burned down Negro building to encourage Dr. W.H. Doughty Jr. in his "genito-urinary investigations." It was written three years *before* the now infamous Charles Davenport would corral Carnegie money and researchers from Harvard, the University of Chicago, and Columbia into the Carnegie Institution's Station for Experimental Evolution, which opened in Long Island's Cold Spring Harbor in 1904.[19] In 1910, Davenport and Mrs. E.H. Harriman, widow of the Union Pacific Railroad fortune, would add the infamous Eugenics Records Office to the Cold Spring Harbor compound. All of these eugenic developments come into play in part V. But their roots are here in work such as Powell's in Georgia. There are six years between Dr. Doughty's surgeries and Carnegie's initial support of eugenics. On eugenics, our superintendent, with his "operations on a certain class," was ahead of his time.

Trustee Nisbet's Journey of Comparisons

At the turn of the twentieth century, Georgia Sanitarium trustee president R.B. Nisbet made an official trip to three asylums to get perspective on how Georgia was faring, an expedition from which we can draw our own comparisons.[20] He chose institutions in Washington, DC, North Carolina, and Virginia. The National Hospital (or St. Elizabeth's) held 2,020 patients from the District of Columbia, the U.S. army and navy, and "the Soldiers' Homes of the Northern States." Nisbet reported: "The hospital was well equipped with every appliance for the care and cure of its inmates—able physicians, abundant attendants and trained nurses, there being one attendant to every eight patients." And yet, "the only thing that commended itself to me was the Department of Pathology." It had two doctors, a photographer, and a morgue in which the doctors had dissected two thousand cadavers "not claimed by [their] friends." Congress paid the National Hospital $220 per capita annually, or 60.3 cents per day—about double Georgia's miserly per capita expenditure over most of its history. Perhaps it was the Union veterans or the ample funding and federal control that discomforted Nisbet.[21] It is not hard to conclude that Nisbet was more impressed by patients' remains than their condition while alive, which he himself concludes were well resourced. Cadavers were popular for Georgia doctors.

Next, Nisbet traveled to Morganton in the foothills of the Blue Ridge Mountains. There, in 1883, the Western North Carolina Institution had opened to accommodate the overflow from the Dix-inspired Insane Asylum of North Carolina, which had opened in 1856 outside Raleigh, the state capital. At the same time, the Eastern North Carolina Insane Asylum was also opened in Goldsboro to accommodate the colored insane, the first of whom the Raleigh asylum had admitted at General Sherman's insistence after he occupied their grounds.[22] Nisbet was quite taken with the Western North Carolina Institution, nestled in the Blue Ridge foothills with perfectly terraced access and its grounds grassy and shaded by trees. "Like Jerusalem of old," he declared. Nisbet found it remarkably spacious, having "almost double the floor rooms of ours," with large, well-ventilated and heated rooms lighted by electricity. Patients ate in "congregate dining halls" separated only by sex, and they were equitably fed and waited on.[23]

Nisbet then turned east to Petersburg to tour the Virginia Hospital for the Colored Insane, and the comparison did not bode well for Georgia. "Both in North Carolina and Virginia better provision is made for the colored insane than here," he concluded frankly. But his recommendation was not to improve the provision in Milledgeville; it was to give the space allotted to African American patients (those 900 rooms in the formerly burned-out-but-now-improved-with-insurance-money-and-surgery structure) to white patients: "[Colored patients] should be in a separate locality, and have plenty of outdoor occupation. In a few years we shall need every foot of room now occupied by our colored population for whites."[24]

For once, a Georgia trustee explained how much the state saved per capita by segregating African Americans in inferior quarters:

It is true that [building a colored asylum] would make a decided change in the rate per capita, but this would not be a loss to the State as it would be saved by the less per capita in the negro institution, which average in North Carolina and Virginia only about $88.00 per annum.[25]

The colored buildings were cheaper, their patients' clothes were cheaper, their paper was nonexistent, and they were worked harder. That $88 per annum at Petersburg came to 22 cents a day, two-thirds of Georgia's already rock-bottom per diem. The "equal" in separate but equal, as everyone knew, never applied, and these data came two years after the *Plessy v. Ferguson* decision upheld segregation as long as it was "separate but [supposedly] equal."[26]

Nisbet also cited North Carolina's "special wards for the criminal insane," inspiring the Georgia Sanitarium trustees' president: "The State has in our immediate vicinity its Convict Farm in most successful operation, and here, where there is already guards, physicians, and strict government, these people can be easily provided for."[27] But progressive reformers were already exposing the actual brutalities of this "strict governance" at the Georgia State Prison Farm. Helen Pitts Douglass, Frederick Douglass' widow, lamented of Georgia's convict lease: its "cruelty and vice and filthiness unutterable; insufficient and filthy food; beds and people alive with vermin; inhuman punishment . . . Bastard children—25 in one camp." Mary Church Terrell of the National Association of Colored Women found Georgia's convict camps the most "shocking and cruel" in the South. Such activism by progressive reformers, led by African American women, would lead to the abolition of convict lease in Georgia in 1908.[28]

Finally, Nisbet brought back observations from the National Psychological Association of America. There, "the most important fact" seemed to be "the rapid increase of insanity, especially among the negroes of the South, and the foreign born of New England States." Nisbet was also impressed by the report from a Canadian doctor of 260 operations on the "female Genito-Uterine organs" thought to cause insanity in females, given that Nisbet had "always recognized the intimate relations between these organs and the mental condition of women." But to his great surprise, "the consensus of opinion of the Association was antagonistic to this treatment." He noted that the Delaware superintendent gave patients more access to fresh air and the out of doors and "escapes were rare, even less than when strict confinement was maintained."[29] He also noted how cheap Georgia was compared to "the vast amount that is annually expended by the various States."

Nisbet, for the record:

> I was glad to see that there was a decided opinion against the old way of erecting great prison-like structures such as we have here. In our desire to accommodate our increasing numbers we have been compelled to sacrifice everything to that end—not how comfortable we could make them, but how many we could house. The plan now is to colonize the patients in distinct buildings, airy and open, with large halls and balconies. . . . The saddest sight to me on approaching an asylum is [that of] the melancholy faces pressed against the bars like so many convicts. We must do all we can to differentiate in every way possible an asylum from a prison.[30]

Among these revelations and confessions, Nisbet made an odd comment in noting "the almost universal opinion" among the professionals at the conference: "It is not relief to a patient to be taken from his room to be caged in a hot enclosure, without shade with the reflection from brick walls and earth. See ours."[31]

What might that mean, "See ours"? See what?

I might not have lingered on page 36 of the annual report had it not been for the convergence of two memories. The first was an advertisement posted on the Friends of Central State Hospital Facebook page by one of the institution's boosters, my friend Edwin Atkins. I remembered a replica of an ad from 1915 by the Manly Portable Convict Car: "The Car That Has Made Possible the Economical, Safe and Human Housing of Convicts at Night on Public Road Work." I did not recognize a connection of this old advertisement to the sanitarium until I saw what looked like a replica on a visit to "Cherry Hospital," the abandoned remains of what began as the Eastern North Carolina Insane Asylum founded in 1883. (Cherry Hospital, by which it is known now, came much later when the institution was renamed for a former governor.) My friend musician Tift Merritt (a Grammy-nominated singer and songwriter) was artist in residence for the year at the Dorothea Dix Conservancy, and she brought a group of artists and scholars over to see the hospital's remains. The museum in which I had expected to view artifacts similar to those I originally found at Milledgeville had been cleared out after a recent hurricane and flood (a frequent occurrence for the low-lying Black institution located in the bend of a river). All that was left in the museum was "The Cage," which we hurried over to see after our tour guide casually mentioned it. It was a six-by-nine-foot wooden replica that looked very similar to the Manly Portable Car in its latticework of metal bars, and our guides explained that it was used for "constraining" difficult patients. Its label told as much:

> The Cage: This 6′ × 9′ wooden replica is modeled after the iron crates that were once utilized to contain highly disturbed and aggressive patients. If necessary, a patient was locked up in the straw-filled cage until they were calm. Dr. M.M. Vitos, Superintendent, removed the cages in 1956.

Our tour guides explained that patients would be left in the straw-lined cage in the summer sun for lengths of time. Dalton, Georgia, specialized in "Jail Building and General Prison Work," and their Convict Cars "had demonstrated success in over 200 of the best arranged and most economically managed camps in the Southern States."[32] On closer examination, one could see that its ad pledged that these cars "represent for you the latest and best results in 'PORTABILITY, ABSOLUTE SECURITY, PERFECT SANITATION, INCREASED EFFICIENCY, COMFORT TO PRISONERS, AND COMPARATIVELY LOW COSTS.'"

"See ours," Nisbet had nodded to those who knew. With prison and asylum in such close proximity, such devices as Manly Convict Cars, "portable" as they were, apparently proved their uses in both institutions. Georgia Asylum's patients, like so many convicts and slaves before them, were caged in the Georgia sun. The moral therapy was a long time gone.

But the prison system was in place for the century. By 1948, journalist Albert Deutsch in his exposé on state mental hospitals wrote that the Milledgeville State Hospital functioned "like a prison" for all of its patients. Chief psychologist Peter Cranford wrote at his arrival in 1950, "Like a prison, [the hospital] functions largely through the work of the inmates. Help patients do everything from hard manual labor to secretarial work."[33] *Ebony* magazine in 1949 said that for white people it was like a prison, but for Black people it was more similar to a Nazi concentration camp, or "the lower levels of Dante's Inferno."[34] Apparently, Georgia Asylum trustee Nisbet's resolve against the old way of "erecting great prison-like structures" did not last his journey. We will see how this legacy of incarceration manifested by 1950 at what was then the Milledgeville State Hospital abattoir in this book's epilogue.

PART V

Jim Crowed Psychiatric Modernity

It was thus that race science was staged between performances of burlesque and horror . . . . Race presents all the appearance of stability. History, however, compromises this fixity. Race is mercurial—deadly and slick.

—Cedric Robinson, *Forgeries of Memory & Meaning*[1]

14

"It Must Be the Boss at the Other End": Psychiatry's Black Atlantic

> The time has come for the primal history of modernity to be reconstructed from the slave's point of view.
>
> —Paul Gilroy, *The Black Atlantic*[2]

When I first opened the files in the reading room of the Georgia Archives in which patients finally articulated their own assessments of sanitarium conditions, voices poured out of the musty boxes and into the room. I could almost hear them dusting themselves off and saying to me, "My God, what took you so long?" It was one of the most powerful moments I experienced on this Milledgeville journey.[3] These case files join psychiatry to what critical race scholar Paul Gilroy called the Black Atlantic. Gilroy's groundbreaking 1993 study asserted that understanding the history and culture of the African diaspora—so shaped by racial slavery and imperial conquest—required us all to rethink modernity's times and spaces, in other words as Gilroy suggests to rethink modernity from the slave's point of view. We are fortunate that in Georgia this modernity coincided with a verbatim typed archive that preserved the actual words and intonations of Georgians on the threshold of the state sanitarium. What they reveal in a series of liminal moments is a defiant counterculture with "its own critical, intellectual and moral genealogy in a partially hidden public sphere of its own."[4]

I Never Seen Such a Place as This

Stork Hardly's experience at the Georgia Sanitarium offers an example of psychiatry's Black Atlantic. Hardly, an African American man, was

admitted on June 10, 1910, with symptoms of epilepsy that had been getting worse for seven or eight years. In response to the doctor's questions, Hardly explained that he had been working as a pilot and cook on
a boat. He had never been to school and "never tried to remember" anything like the names of governors or presidents. But he did know how
much he could make in a day (between $1.50 and $2.50). When the doctor asked if he'd had syphilis, he said no but then described being sent by
the boss of the boat to the hospital where "they had all that on their legs."
"You had bad blood?" the doctor asked about this sign of syphilis. He replied, "Yes, sir." The doctor noted: "This history rather confirms the examiner's belief that this patient had had syphilis, and that these
epileptiform attacks are probably syphilitic in origin, rather than true epilepsy." Hardly was diagnosed with epilepsy at the staff meeting a month
after he was admitted.[5]

But we do not have to stop there, because the Georgia Sanitarium case
history that contains Hardly's medical file also contains a verbatim transcript of his entry interview. In these interviews, sanitarium patients answer a range of questions from the doctor to enable the staff to diagnose
them. In their exchanges, the patients also have their say. For example,
the doctor's summary of his findings omitted Hardly's story about how
he arrived at the sanitarium:

> I was on the street one evening, and it was about nine o'clock and I
> sat down by a man and a little dog was there and he began barking
> at me, so I got right up and goes down there and then the white folks
> all run behind me, and then I run in a yard to get out of the way but
> they come and took me and locked me up.[6]

He was kept in jail for three weeks before he was brought to the sanitarium. When the doctor asked him, "Are you worried about anything?"
he replied:

> I never seen such a place as this. I want to get back to the doctor so
> bad I don't know what to do. I thought this place was like the Savan-
> nah hospital but it is not. I went to the other end of this house and a
> man told me to go and sit down on a bench, and I got up to go and

another fellow run into me and threw me down, like that. I don't think I can stand it. I never seen such a place as this in my life.[7]

When the doctor quizzed him about his emotional state, Hardly continued to talk about how he felt about the sanitarium itself:

Are you afraid of anything?
    Yes sir, I am afraid of these people here.
Is there nothing in particular worrying you now?
    No, sir, that is the only thing.
Are you sad or happy?
    I feel all right.
Do you feel happy?

At this point, Hardly let his impatience show and asked his own question of the doctor:

Happy? What is that?
Have you never felt happy?
    I been happy round home. (Laughs). If I could get well and somebody would tell me what time I was going home I would feel happy. I don't want to stay in here.[8]
Why was it that brought you in here?
    He must be the boss at the other end.[9]

Irony is a powerful force, either dormant or articulate. The terrors of slavery, then of Jim Crow, birthed vast contradictions in which terrible ironies resided. So resounding silences, masks, and indirections were integral to the "partially hidden sphere" of the Black Atlantic's counterculture. A Black person who let a white person know she was in on the deception could put a life in danger, or a community. The sanitarium itself was only the latest version of Hardly's problems, and the white doctor was an equivalent of a long sequence of "bosses at the other end." For Hardly, the issue of his happiness would not be resolved within the institution, by whatever diagnosis the doctor might assign him to justify his stay. It would come from his release from captivity, so that he could go home.

The doctor did partially get this point. On July 9, he noted in a "Mental Summary":

> His general behavior has been that of a normal man. The replies to questions asked him show him to be in excellent touch with his surroundings. They are concise, coherent, and show no tendency to distractibility, volubility or fright. He tells freely of his past life, of working around Darien and on the wharves. . . . He is only afraid of the patients here. Has nothing in particular to make him happy. But seems to be more or less amused when the question is asked.[10]

Stork Hardly's ironic laughter indicated his open acknowledgment that an agent of the white state's claim to care about a poor, ill Black man's happiness was patently absurd, and Hardly let the doctor know it. Long ago, one of the asylum's first patients, Samuel Henderson, learned the hard way the dangers of irony in a slave culture after his white brothers chained him to the floor for nine years for being, among other things, "facetious in his prayers."

Also, for future reference for the story of pellagra, Hardly was asked (as many patients were) what he had for dinner. "Had hominy and light bread, corn bread, and a little beef soup."[11] This was a sparse meal, particularly when set against the bushels, and gallons, and pounds of food that male patients were growing in the farm and garden operations.

The Georgia State Archives, now held in the Atlanta suburb of Morrow, contain boxes of largely unexamined case histories from 1909 to 1924. (Fortunately, the Georgia Archives are now under the University System of Georgia, moved there after in 2012 the Georgia secretary of state's office tried to close the Georgia Archives down completely, ostensibly for "budgetary reasons.") These files include intake medical exams and psychiatric interviews, then notes on patients' progress—or more often the lack of it. There are also occasionally lab reports such as urinalyses and Wasserman tests for syphilis, and occasional autopsies provide final punctuation to the life record. The first files from 1909 are handwritten, but soon they become typed verbatim documents. However fragmentary these files often are, the verbatim interview transcripts provided my first opportunity to "hear" the actual voices of the people who became patients at the Georgia institution. The advent of the typewriter that allowed this emergence also seemed to mark a particular institutional moment of bureaucratization, in this case the use of the new machine to fulfill a compulsion to codify the new Jim Crow regime in an age of mechanical reproduction.[12] But what emerges is something different than bureaucratic mania.

A Molehill Out of a Mountain

In 1909, Sigmund Freud had only just made U.S. landfall at Clark University "with novel and bewildering feelings . . . in the New World, lecturing before an audience of expectant enquirers," as Freud himself explained.[13] His ideas would not land in Milledgeville for a good many years, and the sanitarium's patients never got the psychoanalytic couch, which was far too comfortable a resting place and far too labor intensive a doctor's process for the burgeoning patient loads. The treatment available at the Georgia Sanitarium was the era's psychiatric norm.

In 1910, the year that Stork Hardly was admitted, sweeping changes were under way in the quality of administration and patient care at the Georgia Sanitarium. There were 3,347 patients, with twelve physicians, or a 1:275 doctor-to-patient ratio.[14] In 1907, Dr. L.M. Jones had taken over as superintendent at the death of the venerated Dr. T.O. Powell, and Supt. Jones presided from the old Center Building, which was renamed the Powell Building at Supt. Powell's death. In historian and chief psychologist Peter Cranford's opinion, the new superintendent was making "a molehill out of [Dr. Powell's institutional] mountain." The white patient amusements that Powell had begun in the 1870s were dropped, there were three suicides, attendants were fired over mistreatment of patients, there was greater use of seclusion rooms, supposedly therapeutic devices were used for disciplinary purposes, and "more patients returned home dead than returned alive":

> It was clear there was a change of attitude toward the patient. The pressures that were placed upon the patient to work were no longer motivated primarily by the effect which an occupation would have on his emotional progress. There was more and more talk of brutality.[15]

Supt. Jones was more interested in the institution's farm than in its patients. The farm produced massive amounts of food, much of it for sale, along with the cotton that the Black men grew, all of which functioned as the sanitarium's cash crops.

By 1909, allegations by a white male former patient of abuse at the institution played out on the pages of state newspapers. Two legislative investigations confirmed some of the charges, apparently including rape of female patients, although the papers withheld names of the perpetrators.[16] The trustees fired back to the legislature and the governor that they were underfunded and needed financial support to fix the institution. They included facts from (yet another) subcommittee's tour of similar asylums across the country. "From a close and careful analysis of the per capital (per diem) of seventy-nine insane hospitals in this country, the cost of the Georgia State Sanitarium is the lowest with but two exceptions—i.e. Louisiana State Hospital, 34 cents, and the Central State Hospital (negro), Petersburg, VA." Of eighty-six sanitariums they surveyed, "only two spend less per capita per diem than the Georgia Sanitarium," while only three contain more patients. In 1909, the per diem at the Georgia Sanitarium was 37.28 cents. The trustees recommended raising this amount to 50 cents, and they uplifted long-standing recommendations, particularly around correcting the mixture of the insane with epileptics, alcoholics, and "the feeble-minded" (many of them children, others old people suffering from hardening of the arteries), along with the criminally insane and acutely ill patients, often with highly infectious diseases, in all the wards.[17] Once again, the legislature did not heed their call.

Such crowded conditions in underfunded state institutions were a recipe for accumulating disasters.

New Diagnostic Categories and Therapeutic Pessimism

The sanitarium transcripts emerged at the same time as a new system of classifying mental illness did. It represented a huge shift within psychiatry, with new diagnostic categories codified by Emil Kraepelin making their way from Heidelberg, Germany, through successive editions of his *Clinical Psychiatry: A Textbook for Students and Physicians*. "It is Kraepelin, not Freud, who is the central figure in the history of psychiatry," historian Edward Shorter argues.[18] The doctor's questions to Hardly were being asked of all Milledgeville patients because they reflected Kraepelin's diagnostic categories.

"Prognosis, not cause, is the single most important word in understanding Kraepelin," Shorter writes.[19] Kraepelin compiled, sorted, and analyzed thousands of cases on a set of notecards, looking for patterns of how the symptoms progressed. He sorted the cards into a set of diseases and turned them into successive editions of his text. In the sixth edition of *Clinical Psychiatry*, published in 1899, Kraepelin divided all psychiatric illnesses into thirteen groups, with the two most important categories determined by whether or not they had an affective, or mood, component. The first of the two he termed "manic-depressive psychosis" and the second "dementia praecox," which in 1908 would be relabeled "schizophrenia" by psychiatrist Eugene Bleuler.

Kraepelin worked at a time when "therapeutic pessimism" characterized psychiatry in Germany and elsewhere. Overcrowding had destroyed institutions' potential for the "moral cure" of a structured environment and close physicians' care, and such pessimism rose from the profession's lack of other solutions, prescriptions, or cures. Kraepelin's classification filled this diagnostic gap in late-nineteenth-century medicine. In the absence of knowledge about origins or possibilities of treatment, Kraepelin directed his efforts away from subjective clinical experience, instead simply delineating onset, course, and outcome of psychiatric diseases. Since Kraepelin sought simply to classify and observe disease, his system did not lead to meaningful therapeutic results. This vacuum led to "the predominance of prevention and neutralization," contemporary scholar Michael Shepherd writes.[20] In this pessimistic framework and always with a strong allegiance to the German Fatherland, Kraepelin viewed forms of mental illness as social disorders from which the German body politic should be protected. Criminal behavior, for example, arose from "a congenitally inferior predisposition."[21] This emphasis on the prevention and neutralization of psychiatric diseases helped to set the stage for sterilization and euthanasia. Supt. Powell in Georgia, as we have seen, was also working on the same ideological stage set.

Kraepelin's diagnostic system would prove a pivotal moment in psychiatry's modernity, and versions of it have persisted into the twenty-first century. In 1921, the American Medico-Psychological Association (AMPA) became the American Psychiatric Association (APA) that we know today. After 1921, the *American Journal of Insanity* became known as the *American Journal of Psychiatry*. In 1918, the AMPA published a *Statistical Manual for the Use of Hospitals for Mental Diseases* with the Bureau of Statistics of the National Committee for Mental Health. In 1952, the *Statistical Manual*'s categories would provide one model for the American Psychiatric Association's *Diagnostic and Statistical Manual of Mental Disorders*. The first two DSMs were highly infected by Freudian psychoanalysis, which prevailed in U.S. psychiatry from the 1930s to the early 1970s. DSM-III marked a return to the biomedical model on which subsequent editions have elaborated, including DSM-5.

Germany Come to Georgia: Too Much Coke, or Manic Depression?

Stork didn't know who Emil Kraepelin was as he set out to explain his opinion of Georgia's sanitarium. Kraepelin's influence had been over a decade in getting to Milledgeville. In the 1890s across the United States, "a whole squadron of young researchers . . . regularly traveled back and forth from the Heidelberg clinic" where Kraepelin worked. That squadron included Adolf Meyer and August Hock, who made the journey when he was working as a pathologist at the McLean Hospital in Massachusetts. By the mid-1890s, Hock had persuaded McLean to adopt Kraepelin's system. In 1896, Meyer brought the system to the state hospital in Worcester, Massachusetts, where he worked as a pathologist. In 1910, Johns Hopkins University offered Adolf Meyer a professorship in psychiatry, from which he shaped a German-style psychiatric clinic based on Kraepelin's clinic in Munich.[22] Such changes at Johns Hopkins across the medical field inaugurated a new era in American medical education that brought together the university and the clinic.

So in 1910, responding to what they understood as American psychiatry's best practices, Georgia doctors reshaped their understanding of patient behaviors according to Kraepelin's categories. The differences were profound. For example, the 1888 annual report by Supt. Powell had noted "Cause or Supposed Cause of Insanity" (with "whites" and "coloreds" listed separately). This list willy-nilly mixed the effects of diseases (syphilis, epilepsy, attacks of fevers) and other conditions (such as "idiocy," "menstrual derangement," old age) with responses to life events (disappointed affections, failure in business, death of a child, fall from a house, financial trouble, eating peach kernels) and habits thought to be mentally unhygienic (masturbation, excessive use of alcohol, overstudy, religious excitement, taking opium).[23] The 1909 report looked almost the same. But with a nod to Atlanta's most famous beverage, it did include one incident of "excessive use of Coca Cola." By only one year later, in 1910, the table of "Causes or Supposed Causes of Insanity" was dropped, leaving only the table "Forms of Psychosis," with descriptions of each diagnostic category.[24]

That year, these understandings of psychiatric categories informed the Milledgeville interview protocol experienced by Stork Hardly. Questions regarding affect or mood that might signal manic-depressive psychosis became: "Are you happy or sad?" To detect dementia praecox, with its delusions, hallucinations, and disordered thoughts, the questions included: "Ever hear noises or voices?"; "Ever see strange things you cannot account for?"; and, in some cases, "Do you ever talk to God?" and "Does God ever talk to you?"[25] As we will see in the interviews, the doctor starts off with "Are you sad or happy?" and goes on to clarify his answer with "Why?" and queries on, for example, whether a patient cries. One suspects that no one else of authority in these Georgia patients' lives had ever paid quite so much attention to whether or not they were happy. It is not so clear that the doctors cared either, except to diagnose them (when they did).

The case histories, the new psychiatric categories they contained, and Stork Hardly: all crossed the sanitarium's threshold at a fraught historic moment of colonial and anticolonial movements. Milledgeville, Georgia, was at their psychiatric crossroads.

An Epicenter of Race and Psychiatry

W.E.B. Du Bois wrote from Atlanta in his classic *The Souls of Black Folk*: "Not only is Georgia thus the geographical focus of our Negro population, but in many other respects, both now and yesterday, the Negro problems have seemed to be centered in this State." In 1900, he carried this message to Paris when *The Georgia Negro: A Social Study* was the first plate of the *Exposition des Nègres d'Amérique* that became part of the U.S. government's offerings to the French Exposition Universelle. The entire exhibit was developed by African American educators, journalists, and activists to illustrate their progress since emancipation. A set of graphs, charts, and maps by W.E.B. Du Bois and his team of Black sociologists in Atlanta helped to frame the Black exposition from their study of *The Georgia Negro*. As Du Bois elaborated, "No other State in the Union can count a million Negroes among its citizens,—a population as large as the slave population of the whole Union in 1800; no other State fought so long and strenuously to gather this host of Africans."[26]

Census data and Du Bois' graphics help us to understand how the Georgia Sanitarium was central to an understanding of how Kraepelin's theories applied to race. The U.S. Census Bureau did a separate count of insane and feeble-minded people housed in U.S. institutions in 1904 and 1910 that gave more accurate data than the regular census.[27] In 1910, these showed that Georgia had the largest Negro population of any state in the nation, with Mississippi second. Both states had over one million African Americans, although Mississippi's percentage of the total population was higher: 56.17 percent to Georgia's 45.11 percent. In 1910, Georgia's African American population was 12 percent of the national total, and the state had 142,174 more African Americans than it had in 1900. Nationally, in 1910 Georgia had the greatest number of institutionalized African American patients (979), who constituted 31.3 percent of the total Georgia Sanitarium patient population.[28] Comparisons with states outside of the former Confederacy from the same census data show that the overwhelming concentration of institutionalized people of color was in the South.[29]

So, in the United States, "colored insane" generally meant "Negro," and "Negroes"—both in the general population and in the committed insane—were overwhelmingly southern. The southern state with the largest number of both "Negroes" and "Negro institutionalized insane" was Georgia—precisely the point that Du Bois was making about the overall census data. Given the predominance of Black people in the South, psychiatrists outside the region deferred to white southern asylum doctors as experts on African Americans' mental health. All of this is to say that Milledgeville was the epicenter of transatlantic psychiatric practices as they applied to "Negroes."

This arrival of new psychiatric categories at an institution that held the largest number of Black patients in the nation happened at the very moment in Georgia when Jim Crow's concrete was set and hardened. By 1910, after brutal campaigns of paramilitary violence across the South, whites had regained their Lost Cause by stripping African Americans of voting rights, the right to a jury of their peers, and the right to hold elective office. They had held the line on an acceptance of "Negro equality" by infusing antebellum white ideas about freedpeople into such discourses as psychiatry. By the first decade of the twentieth century, resurgent white political power in cities like Atlanta and towns like Milledgeville had curtailed Black freedom of travel and access through laws segregating housing, neighborhoods, and public services. Southern whites accomplished these things by legislative fiat, by enforcing a degrading racial etiquette, and by continuing the flagrant police and paramilitary violence we examined in the Reconstruction years. Between 1882 and 1930, only Mississippi surpassed Georgia's toll of 458 lynching victims. By 1910, Jim Crow practices were a "common and pervasive feature of life in all Georgia cities."[30] Cedric Robinson, director of the Center of Black Studies Research at University of California–Santa Barbara, underlined the significance of this moment when "the contours of the social practices which came to characterize twentieth century American society were fixed."[31]

Forty years later, white Georgia writer and activist Lillian Smith made one calculation of the human costs of Jim Crow:

Some step off the sidewalk while others pass by in arrogance. Bending, shoving, genuflecting, ignoring, stepping off, demanding, giving in, avoiding. . . . So we learned the dance that cripples the human spirit, step by step by step, we who were white and we who were colored, day by day, hour by hour, year by year until the movements were reflexes and made for the rest of our lives without thinking.[32]

This "dance that cripples" would not be captured in Kraepelin's diagnostics. Nor would Georgia Sanitarium doctors inquire as to segregation's lethal effects, because they themselves were part of its system.

Across the globe, colonized peoples were on the march, and European imperialism was reaching a boiling point. In the United States, a new era of struggle emerged. In 1893, Ida B. Wells-Barnett would launch an international campaign against lynching. In 1896 the National Association of Colored Women (NACW) formed, bringing together "race women's" clubs and organizations into a national body. The NACW would work on women's suffrage and on fighting emerging Jim Crow practices. Between 1905 and 1909, in the Niagara Movement W.E.B. Du Bois and William Monroe Trotter brought together African American leaders in order to denounce segregation and to strategize on regaining political rights. By 1911, Niagara Movement leaders founded the National Association for the Advancement of Colored People (NAACP). In 1900 the Pan African Congress was established and under Du Bois' leadership convened in 1909 and four times thereafter to bring together activists and intellectuals in the African diaspora to work against racism and imperialism and increasingly in the 1950s and 1960s for national independence. The year 1911 in South Africa also brought the beginning of the African National Congress, and in that decade Mahatma Gandhi led a campaign of Indian South Africans against growing racist restrictions for "coloreds." Gandhi would carry this anticolonial organizing back to India, where a broad nationalist movement would expel the British in 1948.

Eugenics and the White Atlantic

The eugenics movement of a White Atlantic was also on the move. In 1883, Francis Galton, Darwin's cousin, had coined the term "eugenics" to describe his work to eliminate humans with "poor heredity." In 1901, steel magnate Andrew Carnegie sold out Carnegie Steel Company to bank magnate J.P. Morgan and became a philanthropist, giving away $350 million. In 1902, he founded the Carnegie Institution with $10 million, adding additional wealth to what Congress soon chartered as the Carnegie Institution of Washington: a premier scientific organization, with twenty-four of the country's most respected scientists, politicians, and financiers on its board of trustees. Harvard biologist Charles Davenport was already working to establish eugenics as a science through the ongoing study of livestock at the American Breeders' Association, which had added a eugenics committee in order to elevate "superior blood" and to eliminate "inferior blood" in livestock. In 1902, Davenport wrote to the Carnegie trustees to ask them to sponsor a Biological Experiment Station at Cold Spring Harbor for "the analytic and experimental study . . . of race breeding." Davenport enticed the Carnegie trustees with the prospects of "build[ing] a wall high enough around this country so as to keep out these cheaper races" and a suggestion, failing Negro self-improvement, to "export the black race at once."[33] The Carnegie trustees agreed to fund his proposal, so on January 19, 1904, the Carnegie Institute opened the Station for Experimental Evolution of the Carnegie Institution at Cold Spring Harbor. Thus, the Carnegie prestige and fortune fell in behind American eugenics.[34]

Next, Davenport approached railroad magnate E.H. Harriman's widow, Mary, to fund a second institution, the Eugenics Records Office (ERO), also at Cold Spring Harbor. It opened in 1910, sponsored by Harriman money and the American Breeders' Association. The Eugenics Records Office's new director, Charles Davenport himself, would send out ERO investigators (in Edwin Black's words) to "quietly register the genetic backgrounds of all Americans, separating the defective strains from the desired lineages." His chilling list included "our 42 institutions for the feebleminded, our 115 schools and homes for the deaf and blind, our 350 hospitals for the insane, our 1,200 refuge homes, our 1,300 prisons, our 1,500 hospitals and our 2,500 almshouses."[35] This work would show up almost immediately in Georgia and across the South, as we will later examine.

In 1912, the first International Congress for Eugenics was held in London, drawing attendance from eight European countries and the United States, and whose participants included Alexander Graham Bell, Cold Spring Harbor's Davenport, Harvard president Charles W. Eliot, and Stanford president David Starr Jordan.[36] Madison Grant, chairman of the New York Zoological Society, captured their anxieties in the title of his 1916 book, *The Passing of the Great Race or The Racial Basis of European History*. It was a paean to the role of race, which "implies heredity and heredity implies all the moral, social and intellectual characteristics and traits which are the springs of politics and government."[37]

Leo Frank and the Rebirth of the White Nation

Hyped by yellow journalists and white hysterias, the new diagnostics were traveling fast throughout the culture. Only five years after Kraepelin's diagnostic categories showed up in Georgia, they sounded in the steamy August courtroom for one of the most infamous trials of the new century—that of Leo Frank. In 1913, the Jewish American Leo Frank was convicted of the murder of white thirteen-year-old Mary Phagan, who worked at the pencil factory in Atlanta, where Frank was director. The other possible suspect in the murder was Jim Conley, an African American janitor at the factory. A popular ballad laid out the choices: "Now, while in that building, / Though virtuous and modest too, / She was brutally murdered / By the Negro or the Jew."[38] The case was sensational and became headline fodder for yellow journalism of the type that Remsen Crawford had penned about the Georgia Sanitarium fire. It sent the Leo Frank trial story throughout the country.

His trial in the summer of 1913 in a crowded August courtroom and out its windows into the listening streets offered pornographic testimony to the centrality of race and gender to Georgia's body politic. The Phagan family had recently come down to Atlanta from the hills, searching, like many other poor white people, for industrial work. Mary Phagan had operated a machine that put metal tips on pencils and had recently been laid off because of a shortage of metal. On the Saturday of her murder, Confederate Memorial Day, she had gone by the factory to pick up her last payment of $1.20 from Frank. The killer accosted and killed her, then dumped her body in the factory basement that was covered in soot and grime. As lawyer William Schley Howard explained to Governor John M. Slaton: "The body was black, could not be distinguished." One policeman "in order to determine whether she was white or black . . . took a piece of paper and wiped the grime from her face."[39] Had it not come off to reveal white skin, Leo Frank would probably have lived.

Nor was only the body of Leo Frank on trial—his mind was, as well. Frank's lawyer explained: "I shall undertake to prove by the evidence before us that not only was Frank not a pervert, but he was the very opposite of perversion—he was a perfectly normal man; normal in body, *normal in mind* and normal in character—the opposite of Conley," upon whose testimony the prosecution's case rested.[40] The new diagnostic categories introduced in 1910 at the Georgia Sanitarium included "Constitutional psychopathic state" and "Constitutional inferiority": "weakness of judgment, indifference to consequences, lack of sound moral instincts, criminal tendencies or sexual perversions."[41] In 1911, in this Constitutional Disorders and Inferiorities category, all "manifested an instability of character, were incapable of steady application, evinced a preference for the companionship of their social inferiors, and had been for years sources of anxiety and mortification to their relatives. All of them showed criminal tendencies, one sexual perversion."[42] Doctor's testimony as to the presence or absence of sperm in Phagan's vagina approached pornographic, and proceedings often took a scatological turn. Rumors and reports of Leo Frank's sexual practices and treatment of young women circulated wildly around Atlanta, inflaming the public and linking Frank with perversion.[43]

Frank's defense team failed to persuade the jury that Conley killed Mary Phagan; in September 1913, the jury convicted Frank and sentenced him to hang. Frank was imprisoned in the Georgia State Prison Farm outside of Milledgeville. But in 1915, then Georgia governor John Slaton commuted Frank's death sentence, calling the trial unfair and further inflaming Mary Phagan's "defenders." On the night of August 16, 1915, a lynch mob calling itself the "Knights of Mary Phagan" kidnapped Frank after his wife, Lucille, had left his bedside, where he was recovering from a stab wound inflicted by one of the inmates.

As revelations much later would show, a high-level lynch gang of twenty-five white men, mostly from Marietta (the Phagans' hometown), had assembled after Slaton commuted Frank's death sentence. Henry Clay, the oldest son of a former U.S. senator, was a former mayor of Marietta and current solicitor general of the Blue Ridge Circuit in which the lynchers would have been tried. John Tucker Dorsey was newly elected to the legislature and put onto the House Penitentiary Committee, which gave him leverage on Warden J.E. Smith and the State Prison Farm's three prison commissioners. Lawyer Fred Morris's connections reached into the state militia. Bolain Glovery Brumley's cousin Richard Bolain Russell would soon be on the Georgia Supreme Court (and his son, Richard B. Russell Jr., would go on to serve as a Georgia senator and governor). Judge Morris had been speaker of the Georgia legislature and was a judge on the Blue Ridge Circuit. Former governor Joseph Brown—whose father served as governor and fled with the legislature and his turnips as Sherman approached—provided the link to Tom Watson, whose shameless white populism spewed from his paper *The Jeffersonian* to inflame his white Georgia base against Frank.[44]

Most of these men's family connections reached back into the short-lived Confederacy as they planned a "rear-guard action in the Civil War," as historian Steve Oney termed it. Dorsey's role on the Prison Commission provided the lynch gang entrée to Frank's place of captivity. Dorsey had blackmailed the warden with the negative results of a recent inspection of the State Prison Farm. They were no surprise to Georgia legislators but made Warden Smith and the three (nonlegislative) prison commissioners overseeing him vulnerable to a bribe, which came in the form of a $30,000 appropriation that would build a new colored wing. And so the Marietta gang could waltz in and out of the Georgia State Prison Farm with Leo Frank, which they did on the evening of August 16, lynching Frank the next morning at Frey's Cotton Gin. As word went out across the state, upwards of three thousand increasingly frenetic white people gathered before ringleader Morris, and his men got the body back to an Atlanta funeral home. The legislators, judge, and prosecutor in the lynch gang, along with the white people in Marietta, were able to protect completely the identities of Frank's killers, who were never prosecuted. The lynching of Leo Frank inspired the founding of the Anti-Defamation League to protect Jews against anti-Semitism, and it became a rallying point for the reemergence of the Ku Klux Klan as a national movement. The new "Negro wing" of the Georgia State Prison Farm, funded by the legislative bribe-threat that gave the Marietta lynchers access to Leo Frank, would in 1924 become the site of "Old Sparky," Georgia's first electric chair located conveniently to execute 162 people before it was moved to Reidsville in 1938. One hundred and thirty of these men executed were Black.[45]

Newspapers across the United States responded to the barbarism of the act and the transparency of the cover-up, such as this from the *San Francisco Bulletin*: "Georgia is mad with her own virtue, cruel, unreasoning, blood-thirsty, barbarous. She is not civilized. She is not Christian. She is not sane."[46] There is no evidence of what the actual arbiters of Georgia sanity at the Georgia Sanitarium thought about Leo Frank's abduction and demise. "No history furnished" there.

Re-Whiting of History: Birth of a Nation

The same year of Frank's lynching, D.W. Griffith's film *The Birth of a Nation* opened in U.S. theaters, and it would again catapult Georgia racism to the national stage. The year 1915 was the fiftieth anniversary of the

Civil War and the second year of World War I. In the context of the times, Griffith brought technical mastery to what Black scholar Cedric Robinson calls a "re-whiting of history" in the first U.S. blockbuster movie. It mesmerized white audiences with its close-ups, fadeouts, battle sequences, tinted scenes, and three-hour orchestral score. The film birthed, in Robinson's terms, "a new, virile American whiteness." It would be "unencumbered by the historical memory of slavery, or being enslaved." After Griffith's film, he said: "No moral claim would dare challenge the sovereignty of race right."[47] Shortly after the film's release, President Woodrow Wilson (who spent part of his youth in Georgia during Reconstruction) sponsored a showing in the East Room of the White House for himself, his family, and members of his cabinet. Using his southern connections, Thomas Dixon—the North Carolinian whose novel *The Clansman* inspired Griffith's film—arranged a showing for members of the Supreme Court, the House of Representatives, and the Senate.[48] Dixon wrote to Wilson's press secretary, Joseph P. Tumulty, "Every man who comes out of the theater is a Southern partisan for life!" To President Wilson himself, Dixon wrote, "This play is transforming the entire population of the North and the West into sympathetic Southern voters. There will never be an issue of your segregation policy!"[49] Robinson summarized the impact of Dixon, Griffith, and Wilson: "[They] impersonated history, transferring the crimes of the slave order onto their fantastic myth of Reconstruction."[50] The new film industry had injected the Confederacy's "Lost" Cause into the veins of twentieth-century American culture.

As Griffith no doubt intended, life would follow art. On Thanksgiving Day, 1915, Georgia native William J. Simmons led fifteen comrades, including several responsible for Frank's lynching, to the top of Stone Mountain, east of Atlanta, to light a flaming cross, visible in every direction for miles. There they proclaimed the national rebirth of the Ku Klux Klan. In Simmons' words: "The Invisible Empire was called from its slumber of half a century to take up a new task and fulfill a new mission for humanity's good."[51] The reborn Klan would attract five million members at its peak in the 1920s with its white supremacist, anti-Catholic, anti-Semitic, and anti-immigrant beliefs added into the original anti-Black racism. As *Birth of a Nation*'s subtitle had explained: "The former enemies of North and South are united again in common defense of the Aryan birthright."[52]

Eugenics would enact the same reunion. America's Jim Crow and the Nazi party in Germany would soon unite in an Aryan embrace, and psychiatric patients would be on the front lines of their race wars. By the opening of *The Birth of a Nation*, the long arm of eugenics had already reached from Cold Spring Harbor on Long Island into the little segregated town of Milledgeville, Georgia.

The Gospel of Eugenics

The Georgia Sanitarium was a prime target for proponents of eugenics, because at the time its 3,200 patients made it the largest such facility in the world, according to historian Edward Larson.[53] There and elsewhere, eugenic framing of patients left them more vulnerable to contagions in the institution itself even as it stigmatized mental illness as the result of "morbid, depraved and selfish natures," as Powell had written in 1901 and to which others easily added "criminal" to the mix. Eugenics arrived at the Georgia Sanitarium at almost the same moment as Kraepelin's new diagnostic categories got there from Germany. These diagnoses would provide the questions by which Stork Hardly and all the other patients would be examined. This particular confluence of new diagnostics and eugenics shaped the Black Atlantic's experience of psychiatry, and psychiatry's treatment of the Black Atlantic's Georgia people. That Georgia, as the "epicenter of race and psychiatry," as I have argued, was experiencing such a degree of racist turbulence is one more example of the "bedlam" that flowed between the sanitarium and the broader culture.

In 1912 (the year before Phagan's murder), the Georgia Sanitarium staff were given a presentation called "Sterilization: The Only Logical Means of Restricting the Progress of Insanity and Degeneracy." The next year, as Frank's case went to trial in Atlanta, a Georgia Sanitarium staff doctor examined the institution's admissions and concluded "heredity is the greatest pre-disposing etiological factor in insanity," even though the epidemics of tuberculosis and pellagra were actually responsible for sending many people to the sanitarium and sickened many people already there.[54] Influenced by the work of the Eugenics Records Office at Cold Spring Harbor, Georgia Sanitarium officials began a decades-long effort lobbying for a compulsive sterilization law for Georgia. A prominent southern critic of eugenics was Supt. E.C. Williams of South Carolina State Hospital, who pointed out, in Larson's words, the "lack of supporting scientific evidence for the theory, especially as applied to specific types of mental illness." Williams held out for real treatment, rejecting the "popular idea of hospitals for the insane as a place for the segregation of the mentally afflicted rather than a place for scientific treatment in the hope of restoring to normal the alienated."[55]

Because there was less public support for sterilization, many eugenics organizers, such as the Mississippi State Medical Association's Thomas Haines, strategized that the state could use the new colonies later to "manage the sterilization successfully."[56] Supportive state officials for all feeble minded advocated an "added tax" and that institutions be staffed by existing mental health professionals, often in proximity to existing state hospitals. A standard pattern of eugenics activism emerged across the Deep South, as usual later than in the rest of the country for advances considered "progressive." But Georgia, with the nation's largest state mental hospital, took the lead. Georgia Medical Association president W.B. Hardman proclaimed at the 1914 annual meeting:

> What is the medical gospel of the 20th century? It is the gospel that is calling for eugenic laws, so that the creature of the future may be a better specimen of manhood and womanhood; that there may be fewer inebriates and cripples, that our alms houses, hospitals and penitentiaries, chain gangs and asylums may have fewer inmates, and that our streets may be free of beggars and perverts.[57]

The "creature of the future" would find its own grotesque form in Nazi Germany's Aryan ideal.

Encouraged by the mental health and medical professionals, in 1918 the Georgia legislature commissioned the National Committee for Mental Hygiene (already working across the country on eugenics) to gather information that would help promote eugenics legislation. The result was the most comprehensive such survey in the Deep South. The national committee sent eugenicist V.V. Anderson to Georgia with a research team, which took a representative sample of inmates in Georgia's public institutions, for each of whom they compiled a personal case history with psychiatric exam and the new IQ test. Not surprisingly, given Georgia's eye to cheap or slave labor, its recommendation was a farm colony devoted to "mental defectives," where a large proportion of them could "be usefully and profitably employed." The NCMH sent the report to the legislative commission, which sent it to the governor, who submitted it to the legislature.[58] With the support of the Georgia Federation of Women's Clubs, the legislature created the Georgia Training School for Mental Defectives, which opened near Augusta in 1921 and came to be known as Gracewood State School and Hospital.

Yet there *were* therapeutic solutions for both TB and pellagra, they just required that a legislature being galvanized to support eugenics would open its coffers to protect, house, feed, and cure the Georgians confined in its care. Case histories explored in the upcoming chapters show how those diseases played out and what might actually be done to prevent or cure patients suffering from them.

15

Abraham Lincoln Jones, Dr. Goldberger, and the Asylum's Epidemic Violence

These performances constituted acts of defiance conducted under the cover of nonsense, indirection, and seeming acquiescence.

—Saidiya Hartman, *Scenes of Subjection*[1]

An African American man from Glynn County who looked to be in his fifties or sixties quietly entered the examination room of the Georgia State Sanitarium on April 28, 1910, and took his seat in front of Dr. Saye, greeting him cheerfully. But they soon disagreed over the patient's name. The patient had been admitted as "Jim Jones," but he claimed, "My regular name is Abraham Lincoln Jones," by which he was "known all over the world and both South and North." He insisted: "They committed me wrong. I knows my own name."[2]

For patients entering the Georgia State Sanitarium—or any of the other eighty or so state mental hospitals in the United States at that time—their sense of reality was immediately in question. Abraham insisted on his own name, but he also knew that "I lost my mind in January. . . . I noticed it myself. . . . by being forgetful. I couldn't think of what I was doing at times. I know I lost my mind all right. They took and put me in prison and said they were going to send me down here." The jail provided temporary holding that could last for months for people committed to the sanitarium. There is no sign that Jones was sent to a county chain gang, where convicted prisoners were dispatched to work on local construction projects after the system of convict lease to corporations was abolished in 1908. When queried, Abraham Jones knew the doctors and the difference between the attendants and the patients—"Oh, yes, to be sure I do." Such power relationships did not escape him. He knew that he was in "the place they call Milledgeville where they send [people] to be treated . . .

[where] a lot of them have lost their minds and a lot of them are getting their minds back gradually."[3]

Abraham's case file contains his medical examination from 1910 and later his autopsy from February 22, 1915. His records reveal that he carried in his body an epidemic violence prevalent in the general culture and heightened within the sanitarium walls, where crowded, unsanitary conditions and a semi-starvation diet generated illness. Case files such as Abraham Lincoln Jones' show that the men, women, and children in the Georgia Sanitarium were afflicted with alarming rates of tuberculosis, syphilis, parasites, and pellagra. This range of diseases resulted in such symptoms as memory loss, delusions, and hallucinations that could result in involuntary commitment by counties' lunacy commissions. We now know that these diseases had various origins—airborne (TB), dirt-borne (parasites), transmitted sexually through body fluids (syphilis), afflicted via insect bites (malaria), or through nutritional deprivation (pellagra). These vectors of disease point away from the idea that heredity was responsible for the "moral depravity" of the patients, as Superintendent T.O. Powell's brooding eugenics theories had held. Instead, they reveal a public health crisis in Georgia and its overcrowded institution created as much by Georgia legislators as by anyone.

This crisis was large, long, and complex, but its contours become clear upon examination of the three best practices of the time to respond to disease: germ theory, a growing awareness of nutrition, and the frameworks of public health and epidemiology. The juxtaposition here is between the evidence-based practices that would save millions of lives in the twentieth century and therapeutic nihilism and bogus eugenic beliefs that helped no one and harmed many. The story of one epidemic, pellagra, shows how acute this gap was, and it shows us how, despite the political odds stacked against them, the best medical practitioners used scientific medicine to help patients at the sanitarium. In Georgia, these practitioners came from outside the sanitarium and outside Georgia's Jim Crow culture. Dr. Joseph Goldberger from the U.S. Public Health Service was in charge of its pellagra investigation, and his insights on disease were humane and nuanced, his work at the Georgia Sanitarium and across the South still cited as one of the touchstones of the best work on epidemics in the field of epidemiology.

But let us first look at Abraham Jones' account of himself.

Abraham Jones' Errors of Madness

According to the intake form filled out by the Glynn County Ordinary before Jones was sent to Milledgeville, "Jim Jones" was a fifty-five- or sixty-year-old single Black man, which would have put his birth between 1850 and 1855. He had worked on Georgia's docks and railroads, and on his intake form his religious beliefs were described as "none." He was being admitted for his first attack of "forgetfulness," and he had no convulsions or mental weakness as a child. The only serious disease was given as "pox." Under "Remarks," the ordinary in Jones' home county had noted, "This man has been in the county jail 4 months under treatment, has no relations here and am unable to locate any."[4] He was interviewed at the sanitarium on May 12, 1910. The doctor conveyed Jones' sense of himself as "of a restless disposition all his life" but "quite cheerful with it all." Jones said that he had not been sick, but was in "the bloom of health."[5]

Later in the interview, when asked specifically about particular sicknesses, he answered yes to having had syphilis, smallpox, typhoid, and malaria. He went to school "a right smart but I never took much interest in it" because his mind was "mostly on work and money." He made friends easily. He was never married, but "I used to have a good time with the women." The doctor summarized his patient's early history: "He went to school as a child and got along quite well, except for Mathematics, which caused him some trouble. As a child and adult he associated freely with his fellows and has never been in many fights. He was easily approached and has many friends among both races."[6] Jones knew how he got to the hospital, where he lived, who had brought him there, and that he took a bath and changed clothes when he arrived. For breakfast he had syrup, bread, and coffee—a typical diet at the institution, where "I aint had a good meal yet." All in all, he strikes the reader as having his wits about him except for the question of "memory attack."[7]

The doctor then began the series of questions in the interview protocol about patient affect or emotional state:

Are you sad or happy?
 I feel happy.
Why are you happy?

Why my good old Marster, you know. He makes me feel happy.
What is your good old Marster? Who is he?
I think everybody ought to find out who he is.
Who are you speaking of?
The Almighty God.
Have you any reason to complain about anything or anybody?
Why, no sir.
Did you ever get sad?
Yes sir at times.
Why?
Any God fearing man gets sad sometimes.
. . .
Did you ever cry much?
No sir.
Ever laugh a great deal?
Yes sir.
What do you think of yourself as a man?
I think a great deal of myself.[8]

The next section of the examination was designed to reveal problems
with the patient's sense of reality, indicated by ideational issues such as
delusions, hallucinations, and disordered thoughts, which could point to
dementia praecox or schizophrenia.

Have you got any wealth?
Yes sir, I have got a great deal of wealth.
Where is it?
Savannah and Brunswick.
How much are you worth?
I couldn't tell exactly how much I am worth. I know I own a house
and I have money in the Banks.
How much have you in the Bank?
I have money in three different Banks in Savannah and Bruns-
wick. I have a fine house in Brunswick and I am building another one
to be four stories high. . . . . .
Own any horses?
Yes sir, I own stock.

How many horses have you got?

   I don't know exactly, I own part of a Livery Stable in Brunswick.

Aren't you lying, Abe?

   No sir.

Do you mean that?

   Yes sir. I mean that from my heart. You can write to Brunswick and find out.[9]

The doctor seemed to think that these claims to wealth were delusional thinking. The doctor encouraged the patient to elaborate:

You own anything else?

   Yes sir . . . I own property, plenty of property . . .

Do you own anything else?

   Money and property that's all there is to own.

Knowing more about ownership than his patient, the doctor prompted him with other possessions, and Jones extended his claims:

Have you got any Steamboats?

   Yes sir. I own Steamboats.

Own any automobiles.

   No sir, I was building an Automobile house and had ordered some automobiles but the Building got burnt down before I could get the automobiles in. . . .

You really don't think you have all these things?

   I know I have.[10]

Abraham also had conversations "through the air," particularly with a man named Louis Carter in another building.

There is not such a person as that down here?

   Yes sir. There is.

He is just an ordinary person?

   Yes sir, just like I am.

He is not an imaginary person?

   He is a natural man just like I am.

Abraham Jones also claimed to talk to people "all over the world . . . specially to Europe." These voices talk to him "plainly."[11]

> What did they talk about?
> About how I was getting on. I said I was becoming a little dissatisfied. I had lost my mind but I was getting it back and I thought it was right for me to get out from there and they said Yes.
> Do these voices ever frighten you?
> No sir. No special voice ever frightens me.
> Do they ever tell you to do things?
> Yes sir.
> What?
> Tell me to do things that is all for the good.
> What kind of things do they tell you to do? . . .
> They tell me "Friend be of good cheer."
> Do they ever tell you to kill anybody?
> No sir. . . . They tell me to pray and be of good cheer.[12]

Abraham Lincoln Jones' special voices seemed to provide a kind of "talk therapy," ideally part of his doctor's job and not unlike prayer might do. These were not voices that tormented him or instructed him to violate his own conscience, or to hurt himself or someone else. In fact, they seem quite cheerful and wise in their instructions, including advising him to get out of the hospital if possible.

The interview protocol was designed to reveal paranoid distortions of thought involving enemies. When asked if he has any "special enemies," he responded, "no more than any one would have."

> Does everybody treat you well?
> Yes sir, so far as I know.
> Have you any enemies?
> I suppose everybody has enemies.[13]

Abraham's place in the world seems benign.

How would the doctor have used this conversation to diagnose his patient? For Emil Kraepelin, whose diagnostic categories were reshaping Milledgeville protocols, disturbances of perception were either hallucinations or delusions. Hallucinations involved events of perceived sight or sound with "no recognizable external stimuli," whereas delusions were "falsifications of real precepts" such as "delusions of grandeur." Kraepelin gave myriad examples of delusions, and Abraham went into the "expansive" categories that included the idea that a person had "untold wealth and vast estates, including whole continents or the world itself."[14] To the doctor, Abraham's voices were auditory hallucinations, distinct enough for him to maintain a conversation in another building and another continent. The doctor argued that no such patient as Louis was in another building at the sanitarium. In terms of his claims to wealth, Abraham did not claim to have his boats or automobiles actually in the room with him, so he was not hallucinating them. His conviction of his great wealth was, by the doctor's thinking, a delusional distortion. Abraham also believed he was 120 years old, which would have put his birth around 1790. His age on his admission form was given as fifty-five or sixty, which would have put his birth at 1855 or 1850. So his claims to great age are also delusional distortions of thought.

But the doctor, hardly dispassionate himself, found his Black patient's claims to wealth somewhere between irritating and preposterous, and that discussion takes up a significant portion of the interview. Nor did he concede to Mr. Jones his own version of his name.

Jim, if you have got so much money why don't you wear better clothes?
  I do. I wear good clothes. I have plenty of fine clothes at home, enough to last me a life time. Sometimes I just take a notion and I buy another fine suit.
You don't mean that, do you?
  Yes sir, I do.[15]

The doctor seems offended that Abraham would assert any wealth, nor does he allow that Jones might have a different take on fashion. Perhaps he was also offended that "Abraham" claimed the name of a U.S. president. Abraham Lincoln Jones did seem happy to assert or imagine as many possessions as he could within his limited knowledge of forms of wealth. Jones seemed to be enjoying this particular part of the encounter, and his capacity to call up and describe wealth probably gave him a kind of power in the doctor-patient exchange and an accompanying pleasure in jousting with the doctor. In Jones' vernacular, with its high value on word games, he is "signifying." "To signify, according to the jazz musician Mezz Mezzrow, is to 'hint, to put on an act, boast, make a gesture.' The novelist Zora Neale Hurston defines signifying as 'a contest in hyperbole carried on for no other reason.'"[16] The doctor's search for his patient's grasp on reality is met by Jones as a challenge for boastful hyperbole.

His "delusions" call to mind Polly ("no last name given"), whom we visited at the Georgia Asylum in 1867. Polly believed she was Victoria, Queen of England. Describing the European context in the time of King George III, Foucault asserted that "'believing oneself to be a king' is the true secret of madness."[17] But in the American context, royalty was replaced by class, gender, and race power structures that could inform delusions. In American terms, then, believing oneself to be rich when one is not, or white when one is Black or brown, is the relevant "error of madness," increasing the doctor's perception of the patient's distorted perception, and thus the doctor's irritation, exponentially. The patient-doctor interviews were struggles over the nature of reality and how knowledge of it is acquired, with dire consequences for poor patients, Black and white, who had little to no hope of winning this metaphysical encounter. They could not decide that they did *not* belong in the sanitarium or that they had a condition that could actually be treated. I have found it fruitful to analyze their exchanges through "speech acts" or "language games" that "may be play, or it may be combat," as Jean-François Lyotard puts it. "But it necessarily involves taking up positions relative to one another, as well as some form of exchange, and some rules of engagement."[18] Such a framework gives the patients a bit more of an even playing field, if only retroactively, in which to joust. Patients did not know the diagnosis, but they knew the game. As Hartman observes in the epigraph to this chapter, their responses can be viewed as "acts of defiance under cover of nonsense."

Abraham's file contains two physician's notes from Dr. Saye. On September 16, 1912, Saye noted the patient was "disoriented for time and place. Judgment impaired. No delusions or hallucinations developed. Does not assist in ward work. Quiet." Abraham Lincoln Jones had lost track of where and when he was—impairments probably made worse from the monotony of institutional life. He was not working in the fields or inside the institution, nor did they force him to.

The second note about A.L. Jones by Dr. Saye was made on December 10, 1914, and read: "Pellagrous symptoms have cleared up, although his nose is still roughened. Has convulsions." This note indicates that Jones had been one of the many patients in the hospital suffering from pellagra, the symptoms of which included butterfly-shaped lesions on the skin. There was also a laboratory report from August 26, 1913, that contained results of a Wasserman lab test, indicating a "positive" finding for syphilis. His file also contains the record of his autopsy on February 22, 1915, after "4 years, 9 months, 15 days" in the hospital. He had a bed sore over either buttock, indicating lack of attention from staff. The first diagnosis of the coroner who performed the autopsy is given as "paresis," generically a loss of movement but specifically a complication of syphilis.[19]

In sum, the autopsy shows Abraham as having chronic meningoencephalitis, pulmonary tuberculosis, and chronic nephritis at his death, in addition to the typhoid, smallpox, and malaria he reported that he had suffered earlier and the syphilis and pellagra indicated in the doctors' notes. Abraham Lincoln Jones was a walking epidemic. The contrast is stark between the dialogue that Abraham had with his doctor, in which he seemed to give as well as he took, and the medical reports and autopsy, which present his vulnerability to a range of diseases that affected his mental capacities.

His various afflictions paint a history of transmission, understanding, and treatment of diseases that flourished in the South over Abraham Jones' lifetime that sharply conflicted with the ever more popular theory of eugenics. Jones' diseases could have been prevented or treated by a better diet, a less-crowded institution, and better medical care, when eugenic sterilization (not the sterilization of medical instruments, to be clear) was emerging as the solution. But feeding patients better and providing new buildings to relieve overcrowding required more funding than Georgia legislatures would allow.

So let's look at his some of his afflictions.

First, Abraham had tuberculosis, the disease about which Supt. Powell had written extensively, concluding that it was the result of heredity and degeneration. We now know that tuberculosis is a highly infectious and often deadly disease caused by micro-bacteria spread through the air that infect a sufferer's sputum. It usually attacks the lungs but can affect other parts of the body, such as the nervous system. Its presence in the nervous system affects a patient's memory and perceptions of reality, which are read as psychiatric symptoms. Most infections are latent and asymptomatic but can progress to the active disease that, if untreated, kills half of its victims. In the asylum's 1895 annual report, as we saw, Powell explained that more African Americans died of consumption within the institution than all other deaths in Baldwin County. By 1910, hundreds of tubercular patients were treated in seven segregated pavilions. "About half had contracted the disease outside the hospital; the rest had contracted it by infection from other patients," historian Peter Cranford reports.[20] Crowded conditions increased transmission because sufferers coughing in crowded rooms spread the bacillus. Being Black and/or female made a patient more vulnerable to contracting serious diseases in the institution. We do not know whether Abraham Lincoln Jones came into the sanitarium with tuberculosis, but it is possible he contracted it there.

Abraham Lincoln Jones also had syphilis. "General paresis," also known at the time as "general paralysis of the insane of paralytic dementia," is caused by a syphilis infection of the brain and central nervous system. In the nineteenth century, "general paresis" was considered a psychiatric disorder, because patients usually presented with dramatic and sudden psychotic symptoms. In 1905, Fritz Schaudinn and Erich Hoffman, a zoologist and a dermatologist, respectively, discovered that syphilis comes from bacterial spirochetes in the brain, or *Trephonema pallidum*. The next year, the Wasserman test was devised to diagnose the disease, and the antimicrobial arsenic drug Salvarsan was tested in 1907 and marketed by 1910.[21] But syphilis was not effectively treated until penicillin was mass-produced in 1940. The U.S. Public Health Service's now infamous "syphilis experiments" in Macon County, Alabama (where I grew up), withheld treatment from infected African American men even after penicillin offered them a cure that would also have saved their families and intimate partners from contagion. (This infamous study was conducted within a decade of when Goldberger finished his exemplary work for the U.S. Public Health Service (USPHS) on pellagra. Penicillin would cure both tuberculosis and syphilis and in fact was probably the most effective antipsychotic medication developed in the twentieth century.)

Meningoencephalitis, another of the findings of Jones' autopsy, is inflammation of the brain covering, the meninges, that causes fevers, headaches, and seizures. Seizures can be a complication of syphilis, and it is possible that in this case the convulsion that Jones' doctor noted in 1914 was from the meningoencephalitis that resulted from syphilis. The Georgia Sanitarium's 1910 annual report shows that there were a relatively small number of cases of "demented paralytics." Peter Cranford attributes that to "the fact that admissions to this institution are chiefly from the villages and from the rural districts" where syphilis "is less common than in the densely populated localities [where] opportunities for dissipation are few."[22] That male and female patients were segregated had the effect of minimizing transmission within the sanitarium.

Abraham Lincoln Jones also had pellagra, a mysterious and deadly disease that in 1907 swept the southern states, striking asylums with lethal force. Pellagra's mysterious origins, its swift emergence, and its wretched course wrought a new terror among southerners that soon had a name: "pellagraphobia." In the first decade of the century, the disease spread rapidly through southern states. The epidemic would last into the 1940s, with 100,000 deaths and three million cases. It reached across the races and particularly afflicted the working poor.[23] Outbreaks of pellagra occurred in southern mental institutions, orphanages, cotton mill villages, and some urban and rural areas. Annually, outbreaks began in the spring and continued through the summer months. Pellagra brought weight loss, then eruptions of blisters and rashes, intestinal problems, and a "melancholia" that sent its sufferers to the nearest well or spring with rocks in their pockets, or out to barns with rope, in an epidemic of southern suicide.

In the early twentieth century, recently absorbed information on germs made people who were afraid of affliction wonder: was pellagra contagious? If the cause was not germs, what was it? For over two centuries, pellagra had existed in Europe, where the suspected cause was eating spoiled maize. Atlanta physician Dr. H.F. Harris first reported the disease in the United States in 1902. His white patient had maintained a corn-based diet and for fifteen years had suffered a recurring debilitating sickness in the warm-weather months.

Supt. James Woods Babcock of the South Carolina State Hospital for the Insane pioneered the study of southern pellagra. In 1908, he traveled to Italy with the notoriously racist Senator "Pitchfork Ben" Tillman in order to visit pellagra hospitals. Both men returned convinced that the disease in Italy was the same as the one in the South Carolina hospital, where the superintendent examined his records from as early as 1834 to find possible cases. In 1909, Supt. Babcock organized the First National Conference of Pellagra in Columbia, the capital of South Carolina and site of the asylum to which residents had fled when Sherman's troops burned down the city. In 1912, two northern philanthropists funded the Thomas-McFadden Commission, which weighed in early and often on the belief that pellagra was an infectious disease—a thesis that would soon prove in Milledgeville to be wrong.[24]

Of all the diseases carried by Abraham Lincoln Jones, pellagra was the one that put Milledgeville in history books as an example of epidemiology at its best. This happened through the work of Dr. Joseph Goldberger, who was placed over the U.S. Public Health Service's pellagra efforts in the South.

Dr. Goldberger Comes to Milledgeville

When he arrived in the fall of 1914, Joseph Goldberger looked out over the Georgia Sanitarium dining hall, absorbing its pandemonium of pots clanging, conversations among staff or between patients and imaginary people in other buildings or on other continents, or sudden quiet spaces from shy corners and nooks. Amidst the cacophony of sound, he was tracking the food. What people first saw in his intelligent face were his eagle's eyes, made more prominent by his wire glasses. Goldberger's penetrating gaze looked at what was right in front of him but that others had not seen.[25]

Goldberger's observational skill came from his outsider status as a young Jewish émigré from Austria who grew up in New York City, where he went to medical school. Soon after graduation, he joined the U.S. Public Health Service. His work took him to New Orleans, where he met and married Mary Farrar, recognizing in her an intelligent partner who shared his idealism. Mary was the grandniece of Confederate president Jefferson Davis, but she was of a different generation and mind-set. By 1914, Goldberger had an impressive résumé. Since being hired at the Public Health Service in 1902, he had fought yellow fever, typhoid, dengue fever, and typhus. Traveling in and out of Louisiana, Puerto Rico, Mississippi, and Mexico, over the decade he had also contracted yellow fever, dengue fever, and typhus—badges of honor in his profession. The Georgia Sanitarium would become one of the most important sites of Goldberger's work, along with two orphanages and a white men's prison in Mississippi and asylums and mill villages in South Carolina. He would bring the accumulated skill of his work across the Americas. Desperate, the Georgia Sanitarium staff welcomed his presence and gave him their full cooperation. And well they should.

The Georgia Sanitarium's 1908 annual report noted that "a new disease, with mental and physical symptoms, appeared in the [Georgia] sanitarium . . . pellagra." Twenty-three patients had already died of it that year. There were forty cases in all, all African American women.[26] The sanitarium's 1910 annual report cited sixty-seven cases of "Infective-Exhaustive Psychosis," noting: "This group is larger than has formerly been the case . . . due to the fact that pellagra has increased in frequency and is so often accompanied by a delirious type of reaction."[27] By 1911, Georgia Sanitarium trustees pled with the Public Health Service for attention. In early 1914, the federal agency sent Doctors William Lorenz and D.G. Willets to Milledgeville to investigate "pellagra psychosis." By then, the Milledgeville institution was "the largest asylum in the South," with frequent cases of institutional origin, making the Georgia Sanitarium, in Goldberger's words, "an endemic focus of the disease."[28]

In December 1914, three months after Goldberger's arrival, Abraham Lincoln Jones' doctor would note his "pellagrous" symptoms. Jones had been in the sanitarium since 1910, so he likely contracted pellagra during his stay. Goldberger would be in and out of Milledgeville in 1915, the year that the lynch mob kidnapped the also Jewish Leo Frank out of the state prison in Baldwin County, although I have found no reference to this coincidence in my readings. Surely Goldberger and his wife, Mary, discussed the Frank case privately.

Goldberger was on the track of a cause and a cure. He first made a quick tour of the South, including the newly established Pellagra Hospital in South Carolina, the U.S. Marine Hospital in Savannah, and asylums, orphanages, and mill villages across the region. Then he laid out the direction that the Public Health Service (PHS) pellagra research would take to prove that pellagra was not communicable and that it was related to an as-yet-undiscovered aspect of southern diet. He created an innovative research plan that would confirm or deny this hypothesis. Dr. Goldberger would give pellagra his scrupulous empirical and experimental attention for over a decade, proving the links between the disease symptoms and what became recognized as vitamin deficiency. Unlike Supt. T.O. Powell, who never absorbed decades-old information about the bacillus that caused tuberculosis, Dr. Goldberger worked on the edge of new medical understandings, aware of the latest medical breakthroughs that might provide answers to his questions.

So in 1914, Goldberger looked around the Georgia Sanitarium dining hall with care, made detailed notes, and soon started to write his first pellagra article, focusing on the question: "If pellagra be a communicable disease, why should there be this exemption [of sickness] of the nurses and attendants?" He thought the answer was connected to food distribution. Goldberger had a keen eye for class distinctions: "The writer from personal observation has found that although the nurses and attendants may apparently receive the same food, there is nevertheless a difference in that the nurses have the privilege—which they exercise—of selecting the best and the greatest variety for themselves." He knew pellagra to be a rural disease associated with poverty. He understood the relationship between the countryside and the pellagra epidemic—that "the very poor of cities have a more varied diet, than the poor in rural sections." He noted what must have been obvious but unstated: "Vegetables and cereals form a much greater proportion in [institutional diets] than they do in the dietaries of well-to-do people; that is, people who are not, as a class, subject to pellagra."[29]

No physician at Georgia's Sanitarium before Joseph Goldberger had such a perspective on economic class or such relentless advocacy for an institution's poor patients over its professionals. Goldberger made the research implications of his observations clear:

> It might be well to prevent the disease by reducing the cereals, vegetables, and canned foods [that patients eat] and increasing the fresh animal foods, such as fresh meats, eggs, and milk; in other words, by providing those subject to pellagra with a diet such as that enjoyed by well-to-do people, who as a group are practically free from the disease.[30]

He set about planning his 1914 field studies to "put this suggestion to a practical test." It does us well to remember here the records of the institution's farm production, measured in bushels, tons, gallons, pounds of meat, vegetables, and dairy products. How much of that food did patients get, anyway? If their accounts of their breakfasts in the intake interview give any evidence, they got very little.

This test of the "diet of the well-to-do" would be its own small revolution. Goldberger did not argue, as Powell had done, from assumptions that white people and Black people had different physiologies, or that African Americans did not really suffer, or that their problem was emancipation from slavery. He did not privilege the white men with the extra food. He was convinced that pellagrins suffered from a particular kind of starvation, and he set about to identify it. Generally, his public focus was on class more than race. But his method in Milledgeville was racially egalitarian.

If Supt. Powell had stayed twenty years behind the medical curve, Goldberger was at its forward edge. Research into beriberi and scurvy was demonstrating that diseases could be caused by nutritional deficiencies, a factor "X" for which, in 1913, biochemist Casimir Funk in London coined the word "vitamine" [sic]. Vitamin A, the first such substance, had recently been identified. Goldberger and his public health associates thought that these "vitamine" deficiencies and pellagra might be linked. Like earlier resistance to Dr. Robert Koch's findings on TB, the new ideas about vitamins and pellagra would meet with a period of opposition.

*Let Them Eat the Diet of the Well-to-Do! The Women
in Wards 23 and 24*

The Georgia Sanitarium trustees, superintendent, clinical director, and staff were desperate. In 1914 they would have 365 pellagra cases with 190 deaths—as the annual report explained, "slightly more than one death from pellagra every other day for the whole year."[31] The institution gave Dr. Goldberger and his colleagues access to all of their records and placed wards 23 and 24 at their disposal—a colored women's and a white women's ward. Each housed forty adult pellagrins who had fallen sick the previous year and were "of a much deteriorated, untidy class," in Goldberger's words. Under Goldberger's supervision, both wards of women were fed the diet of the "well-to-do." The nurses were instructed to give "more than ordinary care" in supervising the feeding. A similar regimen was established in two orphanages in Mississippi that suffered high rates of pellagra. No other changes in routine were made with these groups across the institutions being studied, which is to say there was no "control group" beyond all those who ate the established sanitarium diet—no other depravation than the normal.[32]

We do not know the names of the women in wards 23 and 24, nor have I found reports from these participants on what the experience was like. It must have been a significant one when their diet changed so dramatically. They went from their daily diet of "meal, molasses and fat back meat" with coffee—a meal reported across case files when patients were asked what they had for breakfast—to Dr. Goldberger's new menu, which included, for example, on Mondays:

> Breakfast: Grits, sweet milk, sugar, broiled steak, hot rolls, biscuits, coffee.
> Dinner: Roast beef, gravy, peas, potatoes, rice, biscuits, buttermilk.
> Supper: Stewed apples, light bread, coffee, buttermilk, sugar.[33]

Given how sick they were, they might not have noticed at first the details of this "treatment." But they must have noticed that they were getting the sudden close attention of the sanitarium attendants. At some point, the women must have begun to swallow more consciously and to notice when their taste buds kicked in. They would have also felt their health improve and their strength return. I hope they savored their sweet milk, hot rolls, roast beef, stewed apples, and buttermilk. We do have records that the children in the Mississippi orphanages expressed their gratitude to Dr. Goldberger, crowding around him when he appeared on campus and imploring him to keep the food coming. At Milledgeville the experiment was extended for two more years and included an additional ward of colored women, who on two wards were two-thirds of the patients Goldberger fed.

In October 1915, with great satisfaction, Goldberger reported the results from the two initial wards: "Of the 36 colored patients, 8 have histories of at least 2 annual attacks; of the 36 white patients, 10 have histories of at least 2 attacks. None of this group of 72 patients has presented recognizable evidence of a recurrence of pellagra."[34] The doctor was elated. For him, the results were clear: "The conclusion is drawn that pellagra may be prevented by an appropriate diet without any alteration in the environment, hygienic or sanitary."[35] Goldberger wrote his wife, Mary (back at home with his children as her husband traveled the South), his conviction that "we surely can stop pellagra by a correction in diet." He anticipated "a mile-stone in the history of preventive medicine," gratified that "the knowledge we have gained is sure to save thousands of lives annually, thousands of your own Southern people not to mention the misery of many years of suffering and ill health of thousands of others."[36] The Public Health Service distributed pamphlets recommending that southerners should own a milk cow and chicken for home consumption, grow diverse food crops in their gardens, and have access to butcher shops. Goldberger also included at the end of his recommendations in 1915: "Improve economic conditions; increase wages, reduce unemployment."[37]

Emil Kraepelin in 1920s Germany complained that "the masses" were driven by the "primitive urges of hunger, pleasure, hate and fear, oblivious to the consequences for their own and others' public well being."[38] For Goldberger in Georgia, hunger arose from the lack of sufficient food to sustain health and life—and he was on a diligent search for the "X" factors or "vitamines" that could alleviate particular starvations. Goldberger and his political economist research partner, Edgar Sydenstricker, saw hunger as a function of poverty, not a source of "primitive" urges. Dr. Goldberger's solution was always to alleviate hunger, not to eliminate the hungry.

For over a decade after leaving Milledgeville in 1918, Goldberger, Sydenstricker, and their team worked in selected South Carolina mill villages to understand the connection between the incidence of pellagra and economic conditions. They worked with data from the Federal Bureau of Labor Statistics, the British Board of Trade, and their own house-to-house surveys. They compared the results of their surveys with information on mill village families' food purchases at the mill store to find the prevalence of pellagra in a range of circumstances. They determined that in the first decade of the twentieth century, the increase in urban population was greater in the southern states than in any other section. Wage earners increased during that decade by 50.8 percent, or by 380,000 people. In 1907 and 1908, when pellagra broke out across the South, white southerners had left their farms for mill villages in time for an economic downturn that occurred when fluctuating cotton prices led to wage cuts and factory closings. Low or no wages reduced the amount a mill family could pay for food and thus the quality of the food they could purchase. Local sanitation laws kept these white mill workers from owning livestock or gardens to compensate when retail food prices rose and wages fell. Mill families subsisted on cheaper food and sacrificed animal proteins.[39]

Public Health Service research showed that the people who could maintain their diets escaped pellagra's scourge. It found that pellagra also did not happen to workers living near fresh meat and vegetable markets or with access to farm carts that brought this food into their communities. Also, the worst places had the most cotton—the cash crop that ate up room for small gardens and livestock At the root of the pellagra epidemic was the South's old devil, the monoculture of cotton that literally grew up to the steps of many mill villagers' little houses.[40] The Public Health Service urged southerners to have a milk cow, to eat animal proteins when they could, to consume beans, and to avoid the diet of molasses, cornmeal, and fatback that was so prevalent in the region. Southern states widely distributed these suggestions.

Goldberger and Sydenstricker's research was not perfect by any means. Sydenstricker's background as a labor economist made the racial and gender inequalities in pellagra sufferers invisible, and his emphasis on men as heads of household left him ignorant of how food was actually distributed within families, or to what happened to kinship groups headed by unmarried individuals or of single people outside of heterosexual units. "As a consequence, pellagra's partiality for women remained unexamined," historian Harry M. Marks concludes, and the data ignored the damage pellagra did to African Americans, who did not get mill jobs and worked in other capacities, including as domestics for mill families.[41]

Goldberger's Georgia Sanitarium studies were more egalitarian than their mill village work: Goldberger insisted on feeding women, both white and Black, and used only women's wards in his Milledgeville work. But the U.S. Census Bureau's first reports of pellagra deaths in 1914 showed that non-white deaths accounted for 50.3 percent of the total and women of all colors for 69 percent. Perversely, the people most responsible for feeding families starved the most.[42]

The Georgia Sanitarium during the Jim Crow years would be many things, often absorbing all of the region's and the nation's worst inequities. But none of that was fated—the relative clarity, intelligence, and humanity of a single person could shift the environment for patients—for better and for worse. For example, in 1922 on the other side of the Atlantic, Emil Kraepelin, in "Psychiatric Observations on Contemporary Issues," lamented the "psychopathological" types whom he saw as those "individuals with distinctly hysterical traits" who "in one way or another fall outside the bounds of normality." These individuals were "dreamers and poets, swindlers and Jews." He elaborated ideas of anti-Semitism that were similar to the ones that had killed Leo Frank on the other side of the Atlantic: "The active participation of the Jewish race in political upheavals has something to do with this [morbidity]." It was the rising anti-Semitism that killed Leo Frank, and people in the Georgia Sanitarium knew how lucky they were to have Goldberger's poetic medical dreaming.[43]

16

Dora and the Kindergarten Teacher: (Dis)Abilities and Eugenics

It is the land where he is buried, the place she
spent her whole life, the room
where they made it impossible
for her to have children.
> —Molly McCully Brown, "The Central Virginia
> Training Center (Formerly Known as the
> Virginia State Colony for Epileptics and Feebleminded)"[1]

Dora Williams came to the Georgia Sanitarium from Dodge County on June 25, 1910. We do not have her interview with the doctor. The file describes her this way:

"MENTAL STATUS": Attitude and Manner: The patient had to be brought to the ward, and since admission has manifested no intelligence whatever. She is mute and has been unable to articulate any words at all. She is not able to dress herseld [*sic*], and has to be fed by the nurses. Her mental reaction is absolutely nil. On account of her lack of mental function the mental examination was not attempted, she having no insight, judgment, retention, attention or information of any nature.[2]

To the doctors, Dora Williams was a blank slate, the tabula rasa of a mind on which nothing had been written. Her diagnosis: "Idiot," or "Idit," as the ordinary had written. This chapter explores issues of cognitive ability embedded in such terms as "idiot." Dora Williams helps us to understand how such labels played out in people's lives and how the eugenics movement developed these labels to justify the segregation, congregation, and sterilization of people based on their perceived and then measured lack of intelligence. These are the spiritual descendants of Nancy Malone, the wandering griot whom we met in the earliest chapters. Yet we also see in the 1910s another kind of response to cognitive differences in the work of an unnamed kindergarten teacher reacting to the needs of the children around her. She probably never met Joseph Goldberger on his Milledgeville rounds, but their spirits were similar.

Reflections on Terminology, a Recap

From the institution's founding through Dora Williams' admission and after, "idiot" was the term for what we more recently call cognitive, intellectual, or developmental disability. In 1975, under pressure from a new disability movement, "developmental disability" became standard. Now cognitive, intellectual, and developmental disability are used interchangeably. Today, people who were once labeled "idiot" or "feebleminded" might include someone with Down syndrome, autism, ADHD, traumatic brain injury, or any number of learning disabilities or differences. Some contemporary writers use the term "neurotribes."[3] Disability historian James Trent explained that the "long history of condescension, suspicion, and exclusion . . . . is unavoidably manifest in the words we now find offensive," which led him and others to use the words that we now find offensive, as appropriate to the historical context.[4]

No #MeToo for Dora

The paperwork that Dora brought to the institution provides important information, not only about her, but also about what happened to feeble-minded people in their home communities at the time. Her form read:

Make Answers to Questions as Definite and Complete as Possible
Have Blank Filled Out By Family Physician Whenever it Can be Done.

Ordinary G.F. Coleman in Eastman, Georgia, had filled out thusly:

DATE June 25, 1910. From *Dodge County*, Ga.

Native of *Georgia* . . . . Age *18*, ~~Married~~, Single or ~~Widowed~~?
If female, state number of children born and date of last birth *one born dead last November 1909*
Occupation *Nothing*
Give as near as possible date of first symptoms of this attack *From birth*
What symptoms of insanity were manifested? *Idit.*
State in full the probable cause of this attack *Weeke minded From Birth* . . . . Give number of previous attacks and duration of each *Patient is Dumb But can hear* . . .
Has patient's marital relations been congenial? *Yes.*

According to the rest of the form, Dora Williams had never had convulsions, did not have constitutional diseases when a child, was not blind, deaf, or paralyzed. No relatives had suffered from insanity, epilepsy, idiocy, deaf mute-ism, alcoholism, consumption, syphilis, suicide or homicide, addiction, or mischief with fire. But the court ordinary had marked the form *yes* for "Congenital deformity" and for "moral depravity" of relatives. Since arriving at the sanitarium, the patient had been both violent and destructive and was not sleeping satisfactorily, but had not been confined.

Neither the Dodge County Court's ordinary G.F. Coleman, nor the sheriff who took her from Dodge County to Milledgeville, nor the Georgia Sanitarium's Dr. Gerrard, who made notes on her case, nor Dr. Green, who read the terse diagnosis of "idiot" at the sanitarium staff meeting: none of these officers of the State of Georgia noted the disturbing fact that an eighteen-year-old mute woman who was described as having what they termed "no intelligence whatever" had been impregnated, and six months before her arrival had borne a dead child. None of these men would note the rape of Dora Williams, probably by some white male member of her family or her community. Apparently, such intercourse was so habitual that it would not be noted.

Such gaps and amnesia as those that surround the rape of Dora Williams show one of the effects of the eugenics movement on disabled people.

As far as the state and the sanitarium were concerned, if these women were impregnated they should be sterilized, and that solved that. No predatory male behavior would have to change. None of the official white men in contact with Dora found any contradiction between her rape and their supremacist ideals of Western civilization, of Georgia's "fittest" white men, and of the "Great Race" of Nordics, whose passing eugenicist Madison Grant would lament in his 1916 book *The Passing of the Great Race*.[5]

Dora was described as a "portico patient," indicating that the patients who required Dora's level of care were kept on the "portico," or porch. Dr. Gerrard noted in August of 1912 how she "sits on the floor most of the time. Runs about in portico. Makes peculiar noise at times but has never been heard to speak. . . . Sits in a fixed attitude before examiner, fingers in mouth, silly smile. . . . Has to be lead about." Gerrard's last note—"No change since last notes"—was from September 4, 1914.[6]

But we should not leave Dora there on the portico without working to better comprehend her circumstances. A 1921 Georgia Department of Public Welfare report explained the state's perspective on the idiots in its care. "What shall it profit Georgia if we stop the loss from the boll weevil and fail to stamp out the germs of dependency and delinquency that eat the heart out of the human family itself."[7] The heart *was* being eaten out of the human family, not by "germs of dependency," but by the state's equation of acutely vulnerable people with the boll weevils who were leaching "profits" from the state of Georgia. Everything in Georgia still came back to cotton and to profits. Yet the syntax derives from Mark 8:36: "For what profits a man if he gains the whole world but loses his own soul?"

A Delicate Little White Woman and Her Lively Active and Interesting Pupils

Two years after Dora's admission, in the spring of 1912, another white woman entered the sanitarium. We don't know who it was for sure, but from a review of that spring's entry ledgers the likeliest candidate would have been Miss Mamie Bonner. The ledger describes her as a fifty-three-year-old single female lunatic from Houston County and a native of Ohio. Census and other records suggest that she moved with her brothers from

Xenia, Ohio, to Georgia in 1894.[8] In 1916, the Atlanta *Constitution* reported the story in the gendered terms of white female fragility:

> There was sent to the sanitarium a delicate little woman, suffering from a temporary mental disorder due to ill health. She had formerly been a kindergarten teacher. As she slowly regained her strength and began to wish for some form of employment, she asked to have a few of the feeble-minded children each day in order to see if she could not help them in some way.[9]

This kind and stalwart volunteer was so successful in her initial efforts to improve the children that the sanitarium officials decided "to establish a little school for both boys and girls as an experimental measure," reported the sanitarium's clinical director to the Atlanta *Constitution* in the same article. So they all set up a classroom at the end of a large hall for a select group of feeble-minded children, who were given kindergarten work. Given the segregated nature of the sanitarium, most likely all of these children were white.

They did so well that their teacher gave them more "ambitious" tasks, first "games as well as simple useful work," then classes in reading, writing, and arithmetic. "They became more active, better behaved, and when left to themselves they would plan games on their own accord." With such success the little school moved to a "little cottage at the rear of the institution, fitted with tables and chairs, its walls filling with its pupils' decorative handiwork." Seeing its growing success, other patients looking for meaningful activity began to volunteer, their help rendering a "valuable service . . . with much benefit to themselves," the reporter explained.

At some point another white female patient, a "young girl [also] trained to be a kindergarten teacher," was hired to join Mamie. From the school's opening in 1912 to June of 1916, their classroom served thirty-five girls and thirty boys who had "the benefit of patient, personal teaching" in Mamie's schoolhouse—with its little table and little chairs, and the perhaps crimson, lime, yellow, vermillion, orange, black colors from her students' artwork around its walls. Over four years, Mamie and her helpers transformed children who presented to the world as "stolid, stupid, and untidy" into "active, lively, interested and interesting boys and girls." This transformation took vision, structure, patience, attention, and love. The *Constitution* summarized their accomplishments:

> These two women now have charge of the school and their pupils are active, lively, interested and interesting boys and girls who are capable of leading useful if circumscribed lives, presenting a marked contrast to the stolid, stupid, untidy group to whom their first efforts were given. . . . Some of them have been engaged to return to their homes. The whole credit for the work is due to the patience and persistence of these two self-sacrificing women who have given themselves to it.

We do not know if Dora Williams made it from the portico into Mamie's school. I hope that she did.

Mamie Bonner's best practices in such limited circumstances at the Georgia Sanitarium grew out of an earlier period of institutionalization for feeble-minded people in the mid-nineteenth century, with its strategy of educating the mostly young people for productive roles in their communities. Disability historians Stephen Noll and James Trent write of this era's intents: "To educate idiots was to lead them out of the absence of intelligence. Once idiots showed they could learn, they became worthy of understanding, and they became worthy of care."[10] This was the theory behind the founding of "idiot schools," which followed the trend of asylums that over time became increasingly custodial facilities. By the nineteenth century's end, the focus had shifted from "the child as burden" for its parents and the state to "the adult as menace" to society. Under growing public fears of degeneracy, popular perceptions of the parents of these children shifted from sympathy to blame for offspring who now seemed violations of natural law. The state's late-nineteenth-century concerns were succinctly stated: "An idiot child in the family of a laboring man is a burden weighing heavily upon him, and may indirectly be the means of rendering the whole family dependent on the state for support."[11]

Mamie Bonner, then, was in part a throwback to a time before the shame of "degeneracy." But she was also a forerunner of the disability rights advocates of the twentieth century who would bring such children as Mamie taught back into schools and communities. These were the institutional abolitionists—they included Central State Hospital (CSH) survivors and their families and friends, the social workers and journalists, the Atlanta Legal Aid lawyers, and Georgia Advocacy Office staff. A range of Georgia disability activists would build on the 1990 Americans with Disabilities Act to win the *Olmstead v. L.C.* decision in 1999, arguing successfully before the Supreme Court that the segregation of disabled people is a violation of their civil rights.[12]

By 2010 they would close down the central focus of our study, what was by then called Central State Hospital at Milledgeville.

Ta-ra-ra-boom-de-ay: Enter the IQ Test

But such effective advocacy was decades away. In the early twentieth century, the machinations of the eugenics movement led the public to institutionalize feeble-minded people as a step toward sterilization. As we saw, the Carnegie Foundation helped to fund two institutions on Long Island at Cold Spring Harbor—the Station for Experimental Evolution in 1904 and the Eugenics Records Office in 1910. From Cold Spring Harbor, these institutions would promote eugenics across the United States and the world, and we saw the immediate effects of this in Georgia in previous chapters. In the short run, American eugenicists knew that increased institutionalization required better justifications, more uniform definitions, and a scientific-sounding rationale. They filled this need with the IQ test, promoted by none other than the eugenicists at Cold Spring Harbor. In 1906 in France, psychologist Albert Binet first developed diagnostic tools to measure different levels of ability among feeble-minded children. Out of these materials he and French psychologist Théodor Simon created the first "intelligence test." Binet and Simon intended that their set of thirty questions would measure feeble-minded children's functioning in order to raise their abilities and thus improve their subsequent scores.[13] Education for improvement, not heredity as fate, was their premise, as it had been Mamie Bonner's.

American eugenicist Henry Goddard, head of the research lab at New Jersey's Vineland Training School for Feebleminded Girls and Boys, flipped Binet and Simon's script with his premise that "no amount of education or good environment can change a feebleminded individual back into a normal one."[14] Goddard was closely associated with the Eugenics

Records Office and made the children under his questionable care available for its research. Starting in 1909, Goddard used Binet's test questions to set up three levels of mental retardation based on levels of functionality, each with an equivalent "mental age." He coined the term "moron" for the highest functioning individuals, with imbecile and idiot in the lower tiers. With these changes, American eugenicists turned a designation of functionality that could have led to education into a warning of public danger. "Indeed," Noll notes, "it was in the moron classification that the belief in feeble-mindedness as deviance reached its full fruition."[15]

Eugenics-friendly researchers in the United States quickly built upon Goddard's work. In 1916, Stanford University's Lewis Terman used the test on a much greater number and range of students and added the concept of "intelligence quotient," or IQ. This became known as the Stanford-Binet IQ Test. In this way, the IQ test was born to sort and stack mental defectives into three tiers:

Mild (IQ 55–70)	Moron Educable
Moderate to Severe (IQ 25–55)	Imbecile Trainable
Profound (<25)	Idiot Profound [untrainable][16]

With remarkable speed, the well-funded Cold Spring Harbor networks diffused the idea of IQ, the assumption that it could be measured, and the veracity of the Stanford-Binet test. Through the Cold Spring Harbor efforts, eugenics "rocked through academia, becoming an institution virtually overnight," as Black explains. By 1914, forty-four of the most reputable universities offered eugenics in their courses of instruction, and high schools soon followed suit.[17] By then, eugenics ideas were so widespread as to seem common knowledge. It was an academic coup.

With World War I raging across the globe, President Robert Yerkes of the American Psychological Association seized the day and worked with Goddard and Terman at Goddard's Vineland Laboratory to design army intelligence tests, which the surgeon general rapidly approved. In 1917, the United States army administered two versions of the IQ test to all males entering the military services: an Alpha Test for men literate in English, a Beta Test with pictures for those who were not. The results of the military testing of draftees was alarming: 47.3 percent were graded as feeble-minded, with 50 percent of male southerners scoring as imbeciles. Of ten southern states, Georgia ranked fourth from the bottom.[18] These figures alarmed the military, policy makers, and politicians. In the South, the IQ scores were an impetus for the opening of a flurry of new institutions for the feeble-minded in the 1920s. This was exactly the eugenicists' intent—to institutionalize more people as a condition of sterilization, which could more easily occur once the feeble-minded were congregated and segregated, a process that eugenicist Goddard admiringly called "colonization."[19]

Eugenics advocates were passionate about their cause and proud of their ideas. They were the Cold Spring Harbor Boys, the Eugenics Gang. They even had a song that they sang each morning before starting work:

> We are Eu-gen-ists so gay,
> And we have no time for play
> Serious we have to be
> Working for posterity
> Ta-ra-ra-boom-de-ay.
> We're so happy, we're so gay,
> We've been working all the day,
> That's the way Eu-gen-ists play.[20]

A Boy Born to Millions Is Altogether a Parasite?

The IQ tests and sterilization procedures proved highly controversial. It was not a stretch for politicians or the public to imagine themselves scoring low on tests and so putting their testes or their fallopian tubes at risk for the scalpel, or their children for institutions. On the high culture front, Walter Lippmann in *The New Republic* attacked the IQ test as a "gross perversion by muddleheaded and prejudiced men." In 1924, noted psychologist Abraham Myerson joined the fray, warning of the use "by certain people—not to advance science or in the scientific spirit, but for race discrimination and in the spirit of propaganda."[21] Nor were Myerson's "certain people" hard to detect: the self-appointed genetic-financial elites.

But the rage for sterilization built on a popular fear of the danger posed by the most functional of the three categories, the moron class of women and girls, who were targeted first for sterilization. "The feeble-minded girl is vastly more dangerous to the community than the feeble-minded boy," explained Hastings Hart, the director of the Russell Sage Foundation's Child Helping Division at a 1913 New Stork State Conference on Charities and Corrections. This danger rose from "her inability to protect herself" and her lack of "regard for the consequences which restrain normal women," Hart opined.[22] Such was Dora Williams' fate.

Feeble-mindedness certainly made self-protection difficult for women like Dora, but so did poverty, misogyny, and racism. Rape epitomized "the consequences that restrain normal women."[23] But white men had few consequences, and many had no restraints. Dora was not in the "moron class," whose relative functionality might offset blame for the men having intercourse with her, since Dora did not speak and "manifested no intelligence whatever." For the rapists of Dora Williams, there was no possible excuse. Across the board, feeble-minded females were convenient scapegoats for an unchecked, predatory white male sexuality that in the South had long constituted white masculinity. Sterilization was the "answer" to the wrong problem.

The Eugenics Gang and their advocacy for sterilization prompted a large and loud countermovement. Echoing the backlash against eugenics, in October 1915 Hearst's San Francisco *Daily News* issued an editorial broadside against the Rockefellers and Carnegies who funded eugenics efforts:

> We see that our moneyed plutocrats can own the governments of whole states, override constitutions, maintain private armies to shoot down men, women and children, and railroad innocent men to life imprisonment for murder, or lesser crimes. . . . And IF WE SUBMIT TO SUCH THINGS, we ought not to be surprised if they undertake to sterilize all those who are obnoxious to them.

The editorial board then aimed its fire at the children born into wealth, whom it called "another sort of 'defective,' who is quite as dangerous." The editorial's authors gleefully described the heirs to Gilded Age wealth:

A boy is born to millions [of dollars]. He either doesn't work, isn't useful, doesn't contribute to human happiness, is altogether a parasite, or else he works to add to his millions, with the brutal, insane greed for more and more that caused the accumulation of the inherited millions. Why isn't such THE MOST DANGEROUS "DEFECTIVE" OF ALL? Why isn't the prevention of more such progeny THE FIRST DUTY OF EUGENICS? Such "defectives" directly attack the rights, liberties and lives of millions.[24]

Such turnings of the tables can be satisfying, and it illuminates the processes that underlie stereotypes of what Freud was coming to call "projection": the tendency of a person or a group to find in the powerless the precise set of their own unacknowledged feelings. But such turned tables also reinforce the same stereotypes. In the short term, such sentiments protected institutionalized people from the surgeon's knife for a while. But that did not mean these patients got the right care in their new institutional homes.

Gracewood, or Graceless?

In 1921, the Georgia Training School for Mental Defectives in Gracewood, Georgia, was opened as a result of the eugenicists' efforts in the 1910s with IQ tests. Like other southern states, Georgia chose a rural location for its institution in order to remove its charges from the temptations of city life—which was code for removing them from the urban genetic pool before they could reproduce—and to provide them the "opportunity" to do farm work. Gracewood was as poorly funded as the Georgia Sanitarium at Milledgeville. Historian Noll explains:

> Caught in a bureaucratic no-man's land (the institution was placed under five different governmental agencies from 1921 to 1940), forced to compete for limited funds with a mental hospital established before the Civil War, and saddled with appropriations that, according to a State Board of Health Report, were "far less" than those of states that made "any effort to care for their mental defectives," Gracewood remained small and underfunded throughout its first twenty years of existence.[25]

In 1928, with ninety patients, Gracewood was the South's smallest public institution. The Georgia Department of Public Welfare noted that Gracewood was "heavily handicapped in its efforts to instruct the trainable types" because it did not separate children into small groups that allowed intensive training at appropriate levels.[26] By 1939, Gracewood Supt. Edward Schwall reported that one-third of the population was "untrainable" and therefore only custodial. That same year, a fire in the moron boys' dormitory at the school killed six of its twenty-four inhabitants.[27]

But Mamie Bonner and her volunteers had proved that with humanity and care and sufficient funds, such schools might have produced "interested and interesting boys and girls"—rather than incinerate them.

Buck v. Bell *and Cutting off Fallopian Tubes*

As feeble-minded people were collected in institutions such as Georgia's Gracewood, the Eugenics Gang launched the last of its strategic trifecta, its court strategy to get the U.S. Supreme Court to affirm its model sterilization law. Its machinations take us from Georgia to Virginia, from Dora Williams to Carrie Buck and her family. Harry Laughlin of the Eugenics Records Office was the legal strategy's mastermind, and his success would fall onto an eighteen-year-old white female in Virginia. The success of *Buck v. Bell* would profoundly shape Carrie's life and would open the floodgates of eugenic sterilization in the United States, a tide that would land at the Milledgeville State Hospital in 1937 and last into the 1970s.

In 1922, Laughlin completed *Eugenic Sterilization in the United States*, a 502-page compilation of each state's eugenics laws that included a new model sterilization statute, complete with a guide for advocates and legislators for how to implement it. Eugenics allies in the Municipal Court of Chicago issued the tome. Laughlin sent a copy to Supt. Albert Priddy of the Virginia Colony for Epileptics and Feeble-Minded. In the fall of 1923, Priddy and Virginia Colony attorney Aubrey Strode wrote up legislation using Laughlin's model, and it was passed by both legislative chambers to take effect in Virginia on June 17, 1923.[28]

Carrie Buck at that time was the seventeen-year-old daughter of recently widowed Emma Buck. Charlottesville authorities had earlier removed a three-year-old Carrie from her mother and had given her to a local police officer, J.T. Dobbs, and his wife, Alice. Emma Buck was then committed to the Virginia Colony as feeble-minded, which her records show she was not. The Dobbses soon used the young Carrie to provide them with extra help around the house. They allowed her to go to school until the sixth grade, where her school records show her performance as "very good-deportment and lessons."[29] Then the Dobbses withdrew Carrie and put her out to hire in the neighborhood for household chores. By age seventeen, Carrie was pregnant—she said toward the end of her life it was by a Dobbs nephew, who "forced himself on her." Officer Dobbs immediately filed commitment papers, claiming that Carrie was both feeble-minded and epileptic—which she was neither. Like Dora, Carrie Buck was raped, and Dobbs wanted her out of town.[30]

On June 23, 1924, Justice of the Peace C.D. Shackleford presided over a hearing in which the Dobbses testified about their charge's "hallucinations and . . . outbreaks of temper." Shackleford declared Carrie feebleminded and ordered her taken to the Virginia Colony, where her mother, Emma, had resided for four years. Carrie could not be admitted as long as she was pregnant, and on March 28 she gave birth to her daughter, Vivian, whom she was forced to give up, and Vivian was taken in by the Dobbses to the very home in which Carrie had been raped.[31]

By the time Carrie arrived at the Virginia Colony, Priddy and his ERO colleagues considered her a prime test case with which to establish the legality of Laughlin's sterilization law, given her mother Emma's prior commitment. Priddy had a man named Robert Shelton appointed her legal guardian, and Colony attorney Aubrey Strode had Shelton appeal Carrie's case in order to test its constitutionality. Shelton hired Irving Whitehead as Carrie's lawyer—a "staunch eugenicist, founding father of the [Virginia] Colony, and an advocate of sterilization."[32] In other words, Carrie's defense against the eugenicist onslaught was designed by them to fail. Carrie Buck—raped, vulnerable, and alone—was caught in nets woven by money from some of the richest, most powerful men on the planet Earth, the gift of the Robber Barons to the twentieth century.

Supt. Priddy also arranged to have Vivian declared a "mental defective" because, as Priddy wrote to Supt. Joseph DeJarnette of the state hospital at Staunton (also a eugenics activist), it was "the case of Carrie Buck's child on which the constitutionality of the sterilization law depend[ed]." Priddy encouraged Supt. DeJarnette to read up more on the eugenics literature. Priddy had DeJarnette travel "over to Charlottesville . . . to get a mental test of Carrie Buck's baby. . . . We are leaving nothing undone in evidence to this case." Laughlin provided his own deposition to the consideration of the tiny Vivian's status that the Bucks "belong to the shiftless, ignorant and moving class of anti-social whites of the South."[33] As we have seen, these same whites were starving in mill villages, orphanages, and asylums alongside African Americans, but were encouraged not to identify with them. Carrie was of the same class, race, and age as that other white daughter of the South used for elite white men's ends Mary Phagan, for whose death Leo Frank was lynched by some of the most powerful white men, the most "fittest families," in Georgia.

On April 13, 1925, the Amherst County Court upheld Carrie Buck's sterilization, and her so-called lawyer Whitehead appealed to the Virginia Court of Appeals. His was a five-page brief for Carrie's side, against which the Colony's lawyer Stroud turned in forty pages. When this court also upheld the sterilization, Carrie's lawyer Whitehead, dutiful to his eugenics bosses, appealed to the U.S. Supreme Court, which took the case. Were it to be upheld, in Black's words, "the floodgates of eugenic cleansing would be opened across the United States."[34]

Standing at this floodgate was one of the country's most noted jurists, Oliver Wendell Holmes, a Boston Brahmin and a thrice seriously wounded Union soldier who wrote to his sister about how he "loathed the thick-fingered clowns we call the people."[35] Holmes had been shaped by Herbert Spencer's texts with the redolent phrase "the survival of the fittest," the interpretation of which helped to feed Social Darwinism, which justified economic and social success by making them agents of evolutionary advantage.[36] As a member of one of Boston's "fittest families," Holmes rose rapidly through the Massachusetts judiciary and set his sights on the U.S. Supreme Court, to which, with a boost from distant relative and Massachusetts senator Henry Cabot Lodge, Theodore Roosevelt appointed him in 1901.

Two years later, the still new Justice Holmes wrote the majority decision in *Giles v. Harris*, a major voting rights suit brought by the plaintiff Giles on behalf of more than five thousand Negro citizens of the County of Montgomery, Alabama, "similarly situated as himself."[37] Giles challenged the fact that in the election of 1902 he and others were "refused arbitrarily on the grounds of his color together with large numbers of other duly qualified negroes," to be able to register while all white men were registered. "The same thing was done all over the state." This exclusion from voting lists would subject them to the new set of taxes, tests, and requirements and was applied prejudicially to create a permanent disadvantage for Black voters. "The white men generally are registered for good under the easy test, and the black men are likely to be kept out in the future as in the past," *Giles* explained, as Holmes summarized, "the wholesale fraud . . . by the state—that is, by the white population which framed the Constitution."[38] Giles asked that Alabama strike the relevant sections of the new Constitution of Alabama because they were "contrary to the Fourteenth and Fifteenth Amendments of the Constitution of the United States." To Giles' pleas Holmes remarkably replied: "If the conspiracy [of the State of Alabama] and the intent exist, a name on a piece of paper will not defeat them. . . . [u]nless we are prepared to supervise the voting in that state by officers of the court."[39]

In 1903, the "conspiracy" against them was still too great. Justices David Josiah Brewer and John Marshall Harlan dissented: "The plaintiff is entitled to relief in respect of his right to be registered as a voter [and] . . . . It is competent for the courts to give relief in cases such as this." Such relief would have to wait another sixty years and would indeed require federal intervention over such permissions, as Union veteran and Boston Brahmin justice Holmes protected the Jim Crow voting rights conspiracies in states across the South.[40]

Almost a quarter of a century later, Carrie Buck's Fourteenth Amendment rights to due process and equal protection did not have a chance against Justice Oliver Wendell Holmes. *Buck v. Bell* was decided in May 1927, with Justice Holmes writing the majority opinion in favor of Carrie's sterilization, regardless of the Fourteenth Amendment. Thus, the nation's most renowned jurist would give the highest court's imprimatur on sterilizing a poor, raped young white woman whose mother and child had also been taken from her.

By the 1910s, eugenics' siren song had drawn in major white women leaders of the movements for suffrage and birth control. Angela Davis explains: "The fatal influence of the eugenics movement would soon destroy the progressive potential of the birth control campaign."[41] By 1919, Margaret Sanger and others abandoned their focus on poor and working-class women's efforts to control their reproductive lives in favor of the growing "race suicide" panics, which were succinctly articulated in the title of eugenicist and Harvard-educated Lothrop Stoddard's *The Rising Tide of Color Against White World-Supremacy*, its introduction by Madison Grant of the New York Zoological Society and the Museum of Natural History.[42] Stoddard was awarded a seat on the American Birth Control League's board of directors, and an article by Sanger in the ABCL's journals touted "more children for the fit, less for the unfit."[43]

Holmes' opinion in *Buck v. Bell* accepted the assertions that Carrie Buck was feeble-minded and had been committed to the state colony "in due form"; that her mother and daughter were likewise feeble-minded, with mention of illegitimacy but not of rape; that the surgical "salpingectomy" would come with no "menace to life"; and that her own welfare and the welfare of the state were at risk if she were not sterilized. Holmes famously climaxed at the conclusion of the narrative determining the fate of the Buck females' reproductive rights:

> It is better for all the world if, instead of waiting to execute degenerate offspring for crime or to let them starve for their imbecility, society can prevent those who are manifestly unfit from continuing their kind. The principle that sustains compulsory vaccination is broad enough to cover cutting the Fallopian tubes. *Jacobson v. Massachusetts*, <u>197 U.S. 11</u>. Three generations of imbeciles are enough.[44]

It was a chilling prescription that states would rapidly follow to "bring all within its lines . . . and so fast as its means allow." Between 1907 and 1925, there were 6,244 sterilizations of men and women, three-fourths in California. By 1940, the total was 35,878 people, 30,000 since *Buck v. Bell*.[45]

Carrie Buck and her family represented the poor and working white people considered by white elites as "less fit" just as those white workers in mill villages starving from mill wages had been. With *Buck v. Bell*, the white poor too were swept up into the eugenics net. But those opened floodgates would sweep up many more women of color than white women, as Angela Davis and other feminists have made clear. In North Carolina, for example, of 7,797 sterilizations between the 1930s and the 1970s, 5,000 of them were of African American women. A Princeton study from

1970 showed that nationally 20 percent of all Black married women had been sterilized. By 1976, research indicated that 24 percent of native women of childbearing age in the United States had been sterilized; by the 1970s, over 35 percent of all Puerto Rican women of childbearing age had been surgically sterilized. In 1972, data showed that 100,000 to 200,000 sterilizations had been funded by the U.S. Department of Health, Education, and Welfare (HEW) that year, leading Davis to ask, "Is it possible that the record of the Nazis, throughout the years of their reign, may have been almost equaled by U.S. government-funded steril-izations in the space of a single year?"[46]

Carrie Buck was formally discharged from the Virginia institution on January 1, 1929. Finally free, after three years of courtship she married a sixty-three-year-old widower, William Eagle, in 1932. Seven weeks later, the eight-year-old Vivian died from the measles in the Dobbses' home, although for months no one informed Carrie of her daughter's death. Carrie never succeeded in getting her mother Emma out of the colony. After William's death, Carrie moved to Fort Royal, supporting herself with housework and picking apples. In 1965, she married again, to an orchard worker, and they eventually moved back to Charlottesville, where in 1980 the director of what was by then the Lynchburg Training Center reunited Carrie and her sister Doris, who had also been sterilized as part of the *Buck* case. Together, they put flowers on Emma's grave and visited the building where surgeons had sterilized them. Carrie remained devoted to her husband Charlie, and they lived together in a District Home, a home for indigent elderly people, where she died in January 1983.

For the thousands of individuals sterilized over the decades, the loss of generations set these families up for indigence of the kind that Carrie and William experienced: a loss of the kinship networks that enable survival and resilience in the face of poverty's socially induced hardships. This was the impact over the century of what Supt. Powell termed these "operations of a certain class" in all those institutions' "rooms that make it impossible for her to have children," as Molly McCully Brown's poem in the epigraph laments.

Historian Adam Cohen summarizes from his study of the *Buck* case: "The final theme running through Carrie's life was precisely what the Supreme Court had refused to see: a quiet intelligence. Carrie's lively mind is preserved for posterity in the many letters she sent to the colony. Neatly written and well composed, they reveal a thinking, caring woman with a love for life."[47]

Patients arrived at the Georgia Asylum-cum-Sanitarium with a broad range of cognitive abilities and mental faculties. They were committed to the institution because, for whatever reason, they had failed to function in their home communities, and in the age of eugenics, such failures were deemed deeply threatening to society—they were perceived to eat "out the heart of the human family," they took profits out of the Georgia economy, and they made families dependent on a state whose legislators refused to tend to their care. This was the justification for an age of confinement that would eventually produce a new generation of abolitionists.

17

"Exalted on the Ward": Mary Roberts and the Asylum's Epistemic Violence

For nothing can be sole or whole
That has not been rent.
　　　—"Crazy Jane Talks with the Bishop, William Butler Yeats"

On July 17, 1911, Mary Roberts entered the Georgia Sanitarium from a county in south-central Georgia, where she and her husband, Jim Roberts, were living in the country. Thirty-four at the time of her commitment, she was born in 1877, as Reconstruction was transitioning to Jim Crow in the South. The sanitarium's Dr. Peter Cranston first noted that she was a small, light-skinned woman whose racial description was "colored." She measured 5 feet 3 ¼ inches and weighed 121 pounds. Cranston's case notes described his other observations: "Forehead rather high. Face symmetrical. Hair black. Eyes hazel. Nose straight. Teeth regular." Her expression was "bright." He knew from her medical report that Mary Roberts had no drug habits, and her "usual physical health [was] good." Her memory was "uniformly good."[1] In comparison with some other entering patients, Mary Roberts was highly functional.

Dr. Cranston began what was for him by now a familiar conversation.

Why were you sent to this place?
　　I wanted to be examined to see if I was crazy.
What had you been doing to make them think you were crazy?
　　I was at home praying.
Were you very much excited at that time?
　　Yes sir. I would pray, shout and sing and then sometimes I would cry.
What do you think of yourself as compared with other people?

I don't think I am any better.
Do you think you are a Missionary?
   Yes sir.
Do you think you are especially appointed by God?
   Yes sir.
How long have you felt that way?
   A long time.
Do you think that God has especially appointed you to preach for him?
   Yes sir.
In what way did he reveal that thought to you?
   I can't exactly tell.
Have you any property?
   No sir.
Do you think you are rich?
   No sir, I know I aint rich.
Do you think you can do anything better than anybody else?
   No sir.[2]

Mary Roberts' praying, singing, shouting, and crying had disturbed the authorities back home, and her ability to remain "exalted on the ward" perturbed her doctors. Cranston's file on Mary shows how the doctors confused Mary's spiritual practices, with which she responded to her life's losses, with symptoms of disease. The transcript shows how the doctors struggled to apply Emil Kraepelin's new diagnostic categories to Mary Roberts in the Georgia context. They never did decide on which of the two major diagnoses set out by Kraepelin fit her most accurately: dementia praecox or manic depression, which the Milledgeville doctors called "manic depressure" in the case file.

Real Things, or Living Things?

Dr. Cranston conducted the usual questions.

Are you worried about anything?
   I am worried all the time.
Why are you worried?

> I can't help it. I am easily worried but I don't stay worried over one
> thing long.
> Is there anything in particular that is worrying you?
> Not now. If I was at home though I would feel better.

The doctor summarized: "Being detained here depresses her but otherwise she is not depressed. She is not suspicious."[3] No paranoia, and any
depression was situational.

The doctor's sentences were primarily interrogatory, and Mary Roberts
and other patients had little institutional power in these exchanges. She
could not command, advise, promise, swear, congratulate, thank, or excuse.
The doctor next asked questions related to her "general mental attitude."

> Has anything strange happened to you?
> No sir, not much.
> Ever hear voices talking to you?
> I have always heard them.
> How old were you when you first heard them?
> When I was about 6 years old.
> Whose voice was it?
> I couldn't tell.
> What did the voice say?
> It sounded like my dead brothers and sisters' voices.
> What did those voices say to you?
> They didn't sound very plain; just a kind of mumbling voice.[4]

Perhaps these voices were "mumbling," but perhaps Mary Roberts at
this point was exercising a bit of the rhetorical power allowed her. She
could not refuse outright, but she could indirectly assert her voices' mumbling unintelligibility within the framework of the doctor's questions.
The doctor asserted these to be auditory hallucinations, which would be
convenient when it came time to diagnose her.

The doctor asked next:

> Do you see strange things?
> I don't now but I have seen them.

What kind of strange things have you seen?

Anything that people see. Dogs and people with their heads off and people laughing and hollering and making a strange noise. You can see that any time.

Dr. Cranston pressed his point, giving the patient a chance to recant:

When you see those things, do you think they are real things?

No sir.

You just imagine you see them, don't you?

But then Mary Roberts seems to have decided to stick to her guns and not allow Dr. Cranston to bully her. In so doing, she moved the discussion up a notch into the metaphysical, taking Dr. Cranston to school. She explained to Cranston:

They are real things, but they are not living things.

Mary is challenging Cranston on what philosophers call "epistemology," or how we know things, and "metaphysics," the question of what is real. But Mary was not in control of the terms of debate or her circumstances. But if this were a debate, by my way of thinking Mrs. Roberts would have won it here. The doctor pressed again, seeking to clarify the difference between imagining and physiologically hearing:

Do you really hear those voices, or do you just imagine that you hear them?

I think they are actual voices.

Have you heard any lately?

Yes sir.

. . . . Do those voices tell you what to do?

Yes sir. . . .

Do you have to obey them?

No sir.

Do those voices control your life?

No sir.

Roberts asserted that she does not lose her autonomy to her voices, and they were not malevolent. She took Dr. Cranston to school again:

Whose voices do you think they are?
   I think they are my dead people's voices. My dead sisters and brothers.
Do you think it is possible to hear the voice of a dead person?
   Yes sir.
How can you hear them if they are dead.
   I can see them too. That's not strange about hearing a dead person's voice. A lot of people die and then come back and talk.
. . . . Have you ever done anything that you just had a feeling that you can to do and couldn't help it?
   No sir. I can't do any harm.
Why can't you do any harm?
   Because I can't.[5]

At Home Praying

Mary Roberts was described as a "housekeeper," presumably for a white family. Her husband and his father were farmers. According to her husband, James, she had no drug habits, was "bright as a child, obedient and cheerful. Nothing unusual in puberty." He said that she "learned readily and advanced to the 6th Grade." The doctor reported, "Her marital relations have been congenial." On the test for "Retention," she remembered four out of five phrases exactly after six minutes and got all but two of the eight "counting and calculation" questions. She answered correctly the governor of Georgia, the capital of Georgia, the largest cities in the state, the principal crops raised in the South, who Abraham Lincoln was, that Emancipation Day was in June and "it's the Day that the Negroes were freed." She knew George Washington was a president, although she did not know the current president of the United States. She knew how she got to Milledgeville and how long she had been in the hospital. She had "no defect in conversation" and no convulsions. Her heart and lungs were sound.[6] The 1900 census showed that the Robertses had a two-year-old and a three-year-old and that the family included James' seventy-year-old mother.[7]

It is not clear who sought Mary Roberts' commitment. Later in the interview, she explained to the doctor that "they said I hit my daughter, but I hit her because they was trying me to carry me to jail." In this answer, "they" here seem to be whites with authority to jail her, but nothing about the altercation was clear—whether "they" had a relationship to the daughter or to the rest of Mary's family, or what preceded the event. Nor is it clear whether her husband, James, was there when she was taken to jail. But he did give the county ordinary or clerk considerable information about her history during the county commitment process. The statement that the couple's relationship was congenial seems supported by the way that Roberts' husband respectfully served as her memory and that she did not complain about him. The extent of information about Mrs. Roberts in her case file allows us much fuller possibility of insight into her life.

Mary Roberts' file illustrates the dangers of being a poor female in rural Georgia; or, as the doctor summarized, "A few stigmata of degeneracy are noted." We learn from the record of her medical exam that she had a "general feeling of lassitude" and "headache in frontal region." Her teeth were decayed. "Her mother's sister was crazy," one part of her history noted. Since she was fifteen, she had occasional attacks of excitement in which "she wanted to speak but would be unable to do so." One of her two children "ha[d] fits." There were times when she "[could not] control her movements." Tuberculosis killed her maternal grandfather and her father. Her mother was healthy, and she had four healthy siblings, although four others were dead, one probably from tuberculosis. She had birthed eleven children in twelve years, "two children living and nine dead," and had "several miscarriages, at which time she was confined to bed three or four days."[8] Her youngest child was born February 1911, five months before her commitment.[9]

When the doctor asked why she had been committed, she replied: "I wanted to be examined to see if I was crazy." When the doctor asked what she had been doing "to make them think you were crazy," she answered: "I was at home praying."

Roberts was a cooperative patient when she was not singing, praying, crying, and shouting. She went "unassisted about the Ward; perform[ed] her own toilet; sociable with the other patients. She came into the Examining Room quietly, accepted a seat and cooperated with the Examiner."

But she was also convinced of her own mental soundness. When asked, "Do you think there is anything the matter with your mind now?" she replied, "No sir." When asked, "Do you think that there has ever been anything wrong with your mind?" She replied, "I don't believe so."[10]

Mary Roberts' file contained the typed transcript of the staff meeting in which the doctors were to diagnose her. (Not all the files contain the record of such sessions, but they are illuminating when included.) After Dr. Cranston conducted his interview, the medical staff at Milledgeville discussed Mary Roberts at a meeting, as they did all their new arrivals. It must not have taken long—its full transcript was half a typed page. Their confusion provides insights into the limits of Kraepelin's biological approach to psychiatric illness.

The meeting was held on July 29, 1911, and her interviewing physician, Dr. Cranston, presented her history. There were eight doctors in the room, with no first names given. Dr. Kelley started off with the declarative sentence toward which the case history moves: "I make a diagnosis of Manic Depressure [sic]." None of the doctors noted the typo, at least to correct it in the transcript, and the slippage between "depression" and "depressure" stands. Kelley based this diagnosis on the "fact of her being depressed, crying, shouting, hallucinations, and her attitude." Dr. Yarbrough agreed with Kelley "on account of her volubility, psychomotor activity," but he noted the doctors "can't lose sight of Dementia Praecox in this case." Doctors Echols and Cline vacillated between the two major Kraepelian psychoses: "I had thought mainly of Manic Depressive Insanity. It may turn out to be a case of Dementia Praecox," said Dr. Echols. Dr. Tanner and Dr. Weeks stepped up to declarative utterances of either a "diagnosis" or a "provisional diagnosis" of "Manic Depressure." This diagnostic conversation was typical of those in the case histories. Often doctors did not agree, and the transcript seldom was longer than half a page. The consultation ended with Dr. Green's "I had thought of Dementia Praecox but I rather favor Manic Depressure." Five-sevenths of the statements recorded on the transcript did not rise to the level of declaration/diagnosis, and there was no attempt to resolve the uncertainty or ambivalence of the doctors. Nor was there any recommendation for treatment, which might have included "prescribing" medicines or "instructing" nurses.[11]

The 1907 edition of Kraepelin's *Clinical Psychiatry*, co-authored with A.R. Diefendorf, defined manic-depressive insanity as a "recurrence of groups of mental symptoms throughout the life of the individual, not leading to mental deterioration." According to their text, the explanation in 70 to 80 percent of the cases was heredity, and women were more vulnerable to the diagnosis, making up two-thirds of all patients. The first episode could occur during menstruation, subsequent episodes occurring during successive periods of childbearing. Mary Roberts could have met these criteria.[12] *Clinical Psychiatry* went on to explain that depressive symptoms included psychic retardation, a dearth of ideas, depressed emotional attitudes, and stupor. Manic symptoms included psychomotor excitement, flight of ideas, distractibility, and unstable emotional states that included elation, happiness, exuberance, boisterous laughter without sufficient cause, incoherent speech, mischievous tricks, lack of control of thoughts, persecutory delusions, and self-accusations or exaggerated self-esteem. Kraepelin's manic patients "prattle and shout at the top of the voice . . . drink . . . smoke . . . boast . . . frequent saloons . . . read trashy novels [and] . . . fall in love."[13] Mrs. Roberts hardly fits the specifics of these descriptions.

Manic-depressive patients could predominate as more manic or depressive, and Mrs. Roberts' dancing and praying put her in the former category, but her crying in the latter. But her speech was coherent, she was focused in the interview, and her thoughts were under control; she preached but did not "prattle." She was humble but not self-denigrating, and she did not seem boisterous or happy, and there were no saloons or trashy novels available. Overall, the doctors' summaries of her behaviors focused on religious practices assumed to be symptoms: "Praying, shouting, singing and crying were indications of insanity on her part which led to her being sent here." The other basis for her diagnosis was "hallucinations of hearing . . . and of sight."[14]

The Georgia doctors' rudimentary efforts showed how a diagnostic system developed in Germany would fare in circumstances in rural Georgia—two places that were radically different in terms of culture, but that often seemed eerily similar in terms of power dynamics. Whatever the cultural differences between Milledgeville and Munich, they were united in their understandings of race and complicit in the history of European imperialism. In the twentieth century, those transatlantic ideas of racial supremacy once again crested cataclysmically. Ten years after Roberts entered the sanitarium, Adolf Hitler rose in conditions of bitter defeat not so different in intensity and effect from those that white southerners felt after the Confederacy's surrender left the South in smoldering ruins. In Germany, the Nazi Party would have its own agenda of "Lost Cause Regained," which Hitler would spell out in 1925 in *Mein Kampf.*

The failure of the doctors' diagnosis to lead to treatment was poignantly apparent in the twelve subsequent doctors' notes in the file:

> From May 15, 1913: "Dances, sings, etc. She appears quite exalted today."
>
> January 1914: "Has had two attacks of excitement. During these attacks was destructive. Would not wear her clothes. Had to be secluded. Recognizes when she is in these attacks and requests that she be secluded. Rather exalted at this time. Assist [sic] with ward work and laundry."
>
> August 7, 1914: "Is subject to attacks of excitement in which she dances, preaches, prays, psychomotor activity marked and she becomes somewhat stubborn and hard to control, but at present she is quiet."
>
> March 19, 1915 (the last note): "Patient is lazy and indifferent. Lies avout [sic] on the ward and sleeps through the day; talks to herself; untidy and uncleanly. Denied hallucinations. Gave month correctly and day of week but didn't know the year or the day of the month. Has no insight."

And with that, her record ends.[15] There is no autopsy in her file.

As her environment and physical condition deteriorated, Mary Roberts requested seclusion and resisted efforts at institutional control. Mary Roberts had lived in Georgia one version of the history that would play out in Germany in the 1920s and 1930s. On Thanksgiving Day of 1915, as Klansmen lit their fires atop Stone Mountain, a hundred miles to the southeast, Mary Roberts had finished the last phase of her own battle, from which she did not retreat. And a white woman patient, Mary Gay, entered the sanitarium suffering from the advances of old age. Almost a quarter of a century later, her *Life in Dixie During the War* would provide a prototype for Scarlett O'Hara in *Gone With the Wind.*[16]

If Mary Roberts was having a debate with Dr. Cranston and the other doctors at Milledgeville, let us bring in outside judges to even it up a bit. Flannery O'Connor would find such disparagement of the spiritual and supernatural to be an anathema. The Clines, the maternal side of O'Connor's family, were from Milledgeville; their white-columned family home was next door to the governor's mansion. In 1952, when O'Connor was diagnosed with lupus at the age of twenty-five, her disabling illness brought her back to Milledgeville, where she lived at Andalusia, the family farm on the other outskirts of town from the Milledgeville State Hospital, with her mother, Regina. O'Connor, a devout Catholic, wrote short stories and novels that quickly entered the American literary canon. Her stories were galvanized by an ambivalent attraction to her collection of backwoods Protestant prophets afflicted with the "wise blood" of fervent evangelical faith (mixed with not a little degeneracy). In her sympathetic rendering of their interpretations of God's special spiritual influences, she created a cast of characters whose "religious excitement" seemed to propel them right out of the Georgia Sanitarium and into the pages of her fiction. She chose the lunatic preachers over the social scientists and the hospital doctors every time. O'Connor would have understood Mary Roberts' supernatural encounters better than Dr. Cranston could have. In fact, she might have gored him with a bull or, should he take a wrong turn, allowed a psychopath to shoot him in the woods.[17]

In the 1950s, Alice Walker was growing up in her childhood home in Putnam County, about thirty miles from the state hospital as the crow flies. In 1983, Walker wrote in "In Search of Our Mothers' Gardens" about the women that Jean Toomer found when he traveled the South in the 1920s: "[Their] spirituality was so intense, so deep, so *unconscious*, that they were themselves unaware of the richness they held." Walker described them:

These crazy Saints stared out at the world, wildly, like lunatics—or quietly, like suicides; and the "God" that was in their gaze was as mute as a great stone. . . . They dreamed dreams that no one knew— not even themselves . . . and saw visions no one could understand. . . . Our mothers and grandmothers, some of them: moving to music not yet written. And they waited.[18]

Mary Roberts was from this generation of Walker's people. But, given Roberts' resistance to recanting in the face of the doctors' questions, she *did* seem aware of the spiritual riches she held. Alice Walker also wrote *The Color Purple*, whose main character, Celie, writes letters to God as she works her way out of abusive relationships with the help of her lesbian lover, the jazz and blues singer Shug. I can imagine Alice's Celie answering the doctor's question: "Do you talk to God?" with "Does writing to God count?"

Spirits of the Dead and Agents in the Story

To understand Roberts' life, we need to understand African cultures in the Americas as much as we do Kraepelian psychiatry from Germany. The sanitarium doctors struggled to put Mary Roberts' symptoms into either manic depression (psychomotor activity) or dementia praecox (her conversations with the dead). Historian Edward Shorter explains Kraepelin's crucial either-or distinction between these two "neat camps": "Patients with manic-depressive illness had a circular disorder that naturally would improve; patients with dementia praecox would deteriorate."[19] Within this system, the diagnostic choice was an either-or.

But within Mary Roberts' own spiritual tradition, the activities of dancing, singing, and praying—signs of manic depression—were hardly antithetical to talking with ancestors—seen as a symptom of dementia praecox. None of these behaviors were considered abnormal among her own people.

In the African cultures in the Americas, ancestors were ever present. In *Medical Apartheid*, Harriet Washington describes slave medicine on plantations, practices that included "enlisting the help of departed spirits, especially the intercession of ancestors."[20] On antebellum southern plantations, these ancestors had had the same experience that their children and great-grandchildren did of post–Civil War plantations. In another realm, these ancestors might offer a different kind of power, advice, and help. Their presence also provided company and conversation, in the same way that Mary could talk with her departed brothers and sisters. The spirits of the dead are active agents in the story.

The "psychomotor activity" that disturbed Mary's doctors and nurses had elements of the "ring shout"—a form of worship in churches along the Georgia and South Carolina coasts, which is where kidnapped Africans were last smuggled into the Americas, so that those communities (called Gullah in South Carolina and Geechee in Georgia) maintained the most cultural continuity with their various African origins. Historian Erskine Clarke writes in *Dwelling Place: A Plantation Epic* of the ring shouts on the plantations in Liberty County north of Savannah:

> More incantation than song, the shouts were mystical and powerful, drawing the singers into a kind of ecstasy as emotions from deep currents surged like a turbulent sea. A number of dancers would form a circle and move counterclockwise to a rhythmic step: feet flat on the floor, heels tapping, hips swaying, shoulders stiff, arms close to the body, hands forward with palms up as a supplication, and all the while an undulating flow of song: *"Day, day Oh—see days' a-coming/ Ha'k'e'angels . . ."*[21]

A survivor of slavery interviewed in the WPA Federal Writers' Project of the 1930s recounted a story from Ibo Landing along the Georgia coast in which newly arrived enslaved Africans revolted, then committed suicide by drowning. In Kongo cosmology, this act of freedom was transformed into flying. In the dialect of the WPA accounts: *"All ub a sudden dey git tuhgedduh an staht tuh moob roun in a ring. Roun de go fastuhnfastuh. Den one by one dey riz up an take wing an fly lak a bud."*[22] Althea Sumpter, an ethnographer native to the Gullah Geechee culture on the coast, observes: "The word shout is thought to be derived from saut, a West African word of Arabic origin that describes an Islamic religious movement performed to exhaustion."[23] Performing to exhaustion would have looked like mania to the psychiatrists at Milledgeville, and conversing with one's departed dead was read as hallucination.

Nor did Mrs. Roberts get the benefits of Kraepelin's proposed treatments. According to Kraepelin, treatment for such perceived manic-depressive patients should include "large doses of bromides . . . quiet and rest in a regulated hospital . . . warm baths . . . exercise in the open . . . gentle friendliness in suitable moments . . . abundance of nutritious and easily digested food at regular intervals . . . hot baths at night . . . gentle massages . . . and rational conversation and encouragement,"[24] none of which, except perhaps the bromides or sedatives, was available to Mary

Roberts at the Georgia Sanitarium at 37.28 cents per patient per day in emerging Jim Crow Georgia, where "therapeutic nihilism" reigned.

Mrs. Roberts' psychiatrists needed to consult an anthropologist. They might have benefited from the perspective of Zora Neale Hurston, who would not get to Columbia University until 1925, where she would work with anthropologist Franz Boas as well as his students Ruth Benedict and Margaret Mead. At the time of Roberts' commitment, Hurston was working as a maid to the lead singer in a Gilbert and Sullivan traveling show.[25]

Instead, the sanitarium's doctors had highly racialized thinking about the primitive nature of African Americans to guide them. Dr. E.M. Green, one of the doctors at Mary Roberts' diagnosis meeting who had waffled between dementia praecox and manic depressure, explained as much in his article "Manic-Depressive Psychosis in the Negro," published in the *American Journal of Insanity* in 1916. It drew on a study of Georgia Sanitarium patients that would have included Mary Roberts. Like Supt. T.O. Powell, Green considered the South an optimum location for research because there "the average negro lives under conditions which are natural to him." He noted "negro characteristics" of being "overactive, vivacious, stirring, or as intense and easily excited, high strung and enthusiastic and sometimes of violent temper. On the other hand they may be inclined to blue spells, to fight battles over again, prone to worry over trifles and borrow trouble." Green concluded: "It would appear that this race possesses the very traits which should lead one to expect that manic-depressive psychosis would hold a prominent position among the mental disorders affecting it and that, furthermore, it would more frequently be manifested in the manic form which, as a matter of fact, it is."[26] Why bother to diagnose individuals when you have diagnosed an entire culture? Such research went far beyond mere expediency in underfunded circumstances. It exposed again how the tenets of the profession were informed by virulent strains of racism in the general culture.

To add insult to injury, such preconceived biological explanations often displaced actual medical diagnoses. In the discussion following the presentation of Dr. Green's paper at a professional conference, one of the physicians in audience, Dr. M.L. Graves, challenged him: "Until we can eliminate the factors of syphilis, alcoholism . . . and other nutritional disturbances associated with tuberculosis and with pellagra, it will not be safe to classify the emotional reactions of the negro as representing a definite clinical entity called manic-depressive insanity."[27] Graves, like the Public Health Service's Dr. Joseph Goldberger, believed in looking broadly at a patient's conditions and countering his colleagues' overtly racist pronouncements; for example, in Goldberger's case, the meals fed to the "well-to-do." Both Dr. Graves and Dr. Goldberger were in line with trends over the previous decade to view issues of mental health and mental illness more broadly in terms of "behavioral health," as sessions at the Carter Center's Program on Mental Health explored in 2016 as "The Widening Circle of Health and Wellness: The Central Role of Behavioral Health."[28]

Mrs. Roberts came to the increasingly dysfunctional and overcrowded state hospital, not any of the private spas and sanitariums that had sprouted in Georgia and elsewhere, nor did she recline on the archetypal Freudian couch. The "moral treatment" that envisioned a curative environment was being turned on its head: "asylum" had become its own oxymoron. The distorted biological thinking about degeneration that was the legacy of T.O. Powell was given a laser focus through Kraepelian diagnostics. Kraepelin's legacy as a mentor helped to shape three German psychiatrists who would contribute to the Nazi program of genocide three decades after Mary Roberts entered the Georgia Sanitarium.[29]

The Language She Cries In

What else might the Georgia Sanitarium doctors have taken into account in Mary Roberts' case? Her spiritual expression, beginning so shortly after the onset of childbirth and child death, surely included her grief for these losses. Her medical exam shows that she was pregnant at least thirteen times in as many years, with only two children surviving. We do not know the names of her nine dead babies, but she did.[30] Her epidemic was not tuberculosis or pellagra but the devastating scourge of infant mortality among African American women in the South into the twentieth century, an additional effect of the poverty and multiple forms of starvation that Goldberger documented.[31]

In addition to tuberculosis and heart disease, infant and maternal diseases were the third major killer of southern Blacks from 1900 to 1930.

"Most tragic because they were mostly preventable, deaths of mothers and babies were a measure not only of the despair that marked the lives of most families but also of the ineffectiveness of Southern public health work in the early decades of the century," explains historian Edward Beardsley. Sociologist E. Franklin Frazier explained the effect of white southern race and class biases on public health for everyone: "It has been well nigh impossible in the South to get communities to adopt health programs when it was thought that the Negro would share the benefits."[32] Infant and maternal mortality in the South would not improve substantially until the 1935 Social Security Act, a part of the New Deal that brought federal resources and attention into local areas. Georgia benefited immensely, and by 1940, 55 of the state's 169 counties had local public health units, serving 61 percent of the population.[33] But that progress would not hold.

Mary Roberts would recognize conditions that journalist and professor Linda Villarosa recently summarized in "Why America's Black Mothers and Babies Are In a Life or Death Crisis" in the *New York Times*.[34] In 1850, the U.S. government first began to keep records of infant mortality in the first year of life, in a seemingly faraway era when "babies died so often that parents avoided naming a baby in the first year."[35] Those 1850 records showed a Black-white divide of 340/1000 (deaths per thousand) for African American babies and 217/1000 for white babies.[36] From 1915 (when Mary still danced on the Georgia Sanitarium ward) to the 1990s, infant mortality rates *fell* 90 percent, a reduction "unparalleled by other forms of death," because of vast improvements in nutrition, advances in clinical medicine, and improvements in access to health care, to educational levels, and to standards of living.[37] When applied to the causes of infant mortality, these factors save mothers from having to experience such grief in the first place. But in the twenty-first century, the tide of infant mortality turned again, driven largely by the deaths of Black babies. By 1960, the United States ranked eleventh among developed countries in the rate of infant mortality.[38] The United States now ranks *thirty-third out of thirty-six* in infant mortality rates among the wealthiest nations.[39] Black infants are now more than twice as likely to die as white infants in the first year—11.3/1000 for African Americans and 4.9/1000 for whites. "This racial disparity," writes Villarosa, "is actually wider than in 1850, 15 years before the end of slavery when most black women were considered chattel." If that is not an "afterlife of slavery," what is? In fact, "a black woman [today] with an advanced degree is more likely to lose her baby than a white woman with less than an eighth grade education."[40] It follows these wretched circumstances that if Black babies are dying, Black mothers are too—by hypertensive disorders of high blood pressure and cardiovascular disease that lead to preeclampsia and the seizures of eclampsia itself.

And these numbers for mothers and daughters cannot be attributed to "heredity" or "poverty." Villarosa elaborates the research:

> But recently there has been growing acceptance of what has largely been, for the medical establishment, a shocking idea: For black women in America, an inescapable atmosphere of societal and systemic racism can create a kind of toxic psychological stress, resulting in conditions—including hypertension and pre-eclampsia—that lead directly to higher rates of infant and maternal death. And that societal racism is further expressed in pervasive, longstanding racial bias in health care—including the dismissal of legitimate concerns and symptoms—that can help explain poor birth outcomes even in the case of black women with the most advantages.[41]

Dr. Arline Geronimus, professor at the University of Michigan School of Public Health, was the first researcher to link stress and Black infant mortality. She developed a theory of environments—what she called "weathering." Geronimus explains in contemporary terms what we have signaled by the term *trauma*: "the kind of toxic stress [that] triggered the premature deterioration of the bodies of African American women as a consequence of repeated exposure to a climate of discrimination and insults. The weathering of the mother's body," she theorized, "could lead to poor pregnancy outcomes, including the death of her infant."[42]

Mrs. Roberts' psychomotor activity was, to cite the title of a documentary about Gullah culture, "the language she cries in."[43] Mary Roberts continued to dance, pray, sing, and cry her way through the asylum in the steady, trance-like movements of the shout dance to achieve for herself "states of exaltation" on the wards that offered her nothing for comfort, cure, or care; and she refused to the end to say that the voices she communed with were not real. The doctors concluded of her: "has no insight."

But how could they know? They never asked her why she was crying, or what she prayed for. Fortunately, in spite of brutal, extractive systems, humans always leave other tracks. Her case record tells us that Mary Roberts died without "insight." Of course, we cannot know for sure, but perhaps at the end as time receded Mrs. Roberts had *only* insight, and perhaps the ability to rise up and take wing:

> *Day, day Oh—see days' a-coming / Ha'k'e'angels.*
> *Den one by one dey riz up an take wing lak a bud.*[44]

Kraepelin's categories were one of many such "precise mechanisms," in law professor and race theorist Dorothy Roberts' terms, by which U.S. psychiatry found new ways to identify, justify, and prove race as a biological category, this time as a harbinger of modernity in the global age of Jim Crow. Like other colonizing processes, U.S. psychiatry extracted history itself from humans who lived it, such as Mary Roberts and Abraham Lincoln Jones, like Nancy Malone and Samuel Henderson and Polly and Sue Pagan. It then individualized and misconstrued the markers of American suffering and ignored the broader historical drivers that were themselves "pathological," if anything was, or perhaps more aptly, deeply unjust. In this context, Mary Roberts to the end performed the Black Atlantic politics of transfiguration.

Psychiatry's Afterlives of Slavery, Our Ecologies of Sanity

Eastward and westward storms are brewing—
great ugly whirlwinds of hatred and blood and cruelty.
I will not believe them inevitable.
I will not believe that all that was must be—
that all the shameful drama of the past
must be done again today
before the sunlight sweeps the silver seas.
        —W.E.B. Du Bois, "The Souls of White Folk" (1920)[1]

We have come far enough in the Georgia hospital's history to answer the questions that drove me to commit myself to this study. How does a culture that justified slavery, and Jim Crow, and Muscogee and Cherokee removal decide who is and is not sane? It does so flagrantly, mindless of its own contradictions. Power does not have to justify itself; its violence is its justification even as it erases its tracks in official records and buries its bodies in the woods. I set out to explain how the "afterlives of slavery" haunt American psychiatry in two primary regards. First, Georgia's history shows that the collapse of psychiatric treatment into prisons and jails was not "incomprehensible," as the National Sheriffs' Association lamented in 2014. It was as old as slavery and the plantation system itself. Second, I wanted the reader to understand that a diagnostic system based on a "bio-medical model" denuded of history is bankrupt because what fills history's void is pro-slavery apologists, eugenics, and racism always complicit in misogyny.

I have studied this history during the administrations of three U.S. presidents—George W. Bush, Barack Obama, and now Donald Trump, with most of the writing done in the buildup to the Trump presidency and through it. A third lesson I want the book to leave is how powerful, corrosive, and complex in their engorgement with other systems of denigration the various strategies, tropes, and forms of racism are. Its templates have been nourished over the centuries so that they are still there to build on, or regress to.

Such circumstances as traced in this book over decades create cycles of stress and cycles of grief that are the "socio-cultural variation," the lack of which humanistic psychologists and psychiatrists name as the chief and disqualifying limit of DSM-5. This is the *context, the history* that this book works with others to restore, as it does to link these contemporary conditions to the ongoing legacies of settler colonialism and of eugenics that haunt us today and hover dangerously around the new vacuum—the nineteenth and twentieth centuries' hungry ghosts. They are all too available for any fool with a Twitter account to enact.

Likewise, I want to affirm that throughout this narrative the "afterlives" of psychiatry's slavery have consistently been balanced by countervailing forces, what I am calling here "our ecologies of sanity."

"It turns out that how a people in a culture think about mental illnesses—how they categorize and prioritize the symptoms, attempt to heal them, and set expectations for their course and outcome—influences the disease themselves," journalist Ethan Watters observes in *Crazy Like Us: The Globalization of the American Psyche*. Watters examined how, as DSM diagnoses began to appear across the globe in local cultures, people's symptoms migrated into the newly announced categories. As a result, he posited, "in teaching the world to think like us, we have been, for better and worse, homogenizing the way the world goes mad."[2] While Watters overplays his arguments and does not account for recent scientific research on maladies he traces, his alternative to this "homogenizing" is helpful in the longer view of this book. "Symptoms of mental illness are the lightning in the zeitgeist, the product of culture and belief in specific times and specific places."[3] Across the globe, this range of healing practices in response to local geographies and histories of suffering constitute, Watters suggests, a remarkable diversity, not unlike the diversity of our ecosystem.

Mary Roberts' dancing, singing, and praying were a part of her cultural (Gullah-Geechee) ecosystem that she refused to abandon. Someone raised in a different culture would have different practices. They would not have substituted for adequate medical treatment—but they were vital because she had none (as many people today do not have). But, Watters warns, both our eco-diversity and our diversity of symptoms are "rapidly disappearing," displaced by "a few mental illnesses identified and popularized in the United States—depression, post-traumatic stress disorder, and anorexia among them—[that] now appear to be spreading across cultural boundaries and around the world with the speed of contagious diseases." Their effect is to "bulldoze . . . indigenous forms of mental illness and healing" that are themselves as valuable as the natural resources of the Amazon rain forests are to our survival.[4]

This idea of ecology, I began to sense, provides a more nuanced view of the context of symptoms and treatment—one less caught up in the binaries of heredity/environment—to describe the *sources* of patients' traumas. State asylum psychiatry obfuscated them in part because the state did not want the actual costs of settler colonialism in pain and suffering to become evident. Diagnoses denuded of histories could be redirected to attack the sufferers and justify their circumstances; and, freed of the baggage of history, they could travel much faster across borders to achieve their effects. That was colonialism's intent and its effect on both psychiatry and the telling of psychiatry's history: its haunting.

Although some of my friends may disagree with me, I hold that early psychiatry's "moral therapy" belief in a structure's restorative powers has not been disproved. It rather was displaced by the practices of heroic medicine, by gross overcrowding that created its own epidemics, by therapeutic nihilism, and by eugenic descriptions of suffering intended to end the reproductive capacities of already marginalized people, and in places and times, to eliminate those people directly. They were corrupted by the hatred of women, poor people, Black and native people, immigrant people, and the emerging "homosexual" among all of whose practices were those of basic psychic housekeeping—for instance, staying exalted on the ward. At the same time, marginalized people *should* have access to the best medicine and science, a goal for which it is crucial to fight. These best medical practices and scientific knowledge *should* travel across borders. But that political struggle for equity in medicine and health in the United States and globally is not won, and may not be for a while. Most people do not have access to the best practices and practitioners, so sadly lacking today in the State of Georgia for many of its people.

Given the shameful subsequent history of the asylum, going back to it—to forced segregation and concentration of people considered abnormal in state or private hospitals over long periods, as some suggest—is not an option. Nor is a deliberate recourse to the worst historical mistakes.

Also, an emphasis on "ecologies" makes it clear how racism dooms careful observation of environments, because it imposes cruelly obtuse and impractical theories (about savages, Africans, Indians, women, queer and trans people, poor people, immigrants) between the eye and the brain. Consequently, any solution the brain arrives with is simply its own terrible shadow. The state has the power through institutions such as Georgia's asylum–sanitarium–state hospital to shape such questions and direct the public gaze into these lethal fictions of race (and race-gender-sex etc.). That kind of fictive science is the real Lost Cause, and it can kill anyone.

"Ecologies" also puts on our communal "psychiatric" radar screens the climate change that will have increasingly profound effects on our minds and bodies and communities. As this history of Milledgeville clarifies the original questions, it also raises others: how in the name of "mental health" do we preserve our ecosystems as best we can and organize our communities to respond to their devastations? Again in Du Bois' prophetic terms, we cannot believe "that all the shameful drama of the past must be done again today."[5]

Onward to the Present

But having come this far, we cannot leave it here without at least a hop, a skip, and a jump into today. After all, much more happened in that twentieth century that can seem now quaint and distant.

In the 1930s, the "Little New Deal" came to Georgia with Franklin Delano Roosevelt, whose treatments for polio at Warm Springs had already taught him about the rural poverty that presaged the 1929 economic collapse. In Georgia, FDR's New Deal programs were met immediately with opposition by often-times governor Eugene Talmadge, who fought

The Whittle Building, Men's Day Room, Central State Hospital, Milledgeville, Georgia, 1940s *(Courtesy, Georgia Archives, Vanishing Georgia Collection, N GA AR 026)*

throughout the 1930s and 1940s with New Deal governors over the role of the state. Should there be extended welfare functions for vulnerable people, or a low-tax, laissez-faire state? In these struggles within the one-party Democratic South, Talmadge also brought a dictatorial governing style and a stony racism to rouse white voters in Georgia's still agrarian counties. In the 1936 presidential election, FDR openly courted Black voters (formerly loyal to the Republican Party of Lincoln), and thousands of northern Blacks responded by switching allegiance. In reaction, a splinter group took shape that included Christian Nationalist and far-right clergyman Rev. Gerald L.K. Smith, *The Clansman* novelist Thomas L. Dixon, Eugene Talmadge, and wealthy right-wing industrialists. It opposed the New Deal's "socialistic programs," "big government," and welfare in favor of "states' rights." As Talmadge reportedly explained to a federal agent, "The way to handle a relief program was like Mussolini was handling it in Italy, namely, to line these people up and take the troops

and make them work."[6] In the 1930s, Hitler defended Germany by pointing to segregation and immigration laws of other nations. "Russia is our
Africa and the Russians are our Negroes," he explained.[7] Many southern
congressmen were glad to oblige the comparisons.

As events played out in Germany, New Deal and anti–New Deal factions in Georgia swapped power throughout the 1930s and 1940s, with
the Milledgeville State Hospital (as the state's largest charity) often in the
crosshairs. The 1933 annual report at the beginning of Governor Eugene
Talmadge's administration cited 29 percent cuts in revenue, resulting in
similar drastic reductions in salaries and personnel. Superintendent R.C.
Swint warned of patients sleeping three people to two mattresses on hospital floors. Overcrowding, he explained, "sometimes result[s] in physical
conflicts and serious injuries."[8] He warned, "The old asylum idea must
be banished from the face of the earth," and said that clinics should be
placed in every congressional district.[9] This decentralization had little
support because of the patronage and votes that the increasingly large
hospital provided to county Democratic political bosses in the one-party
South. The idea of local clinics would resurface in the 1960s, when President John F. Kennedy called for federal money to provide for "community
care" that would make the exit of patients from state hospitals seem a
constructive solution had the funds actually been supplied. The *Constitution* reported in May of 1939, "The verbal war over what to do with Fulton
County's 350 exiled mental patients developed color and intensity yesterday as the healthiest county commission mobilized its healthiest minds
for a conference next week to discuss a final solution."[10] When patients
were dropped off presumably by Milledgeville staff or a sheriff on the
courthouse steps, the Fulton commissioners called a special meeting.
"Don't let 'em in!" exclaimed one Fulton County commissioner of the patients at the door. [11] Fulton County administrators refused them, given the
continuing strain of Great Depression unemployment on the city's relief
rolls.[12] By July 1938, the relevant authorities had arranged a swap of violently insane patients from county jails for harmless inmates at Milledgeville State Hospital who could be brought back to their home counties,
and the hospital built a temporary structure for three hundred persons to
relieve congestion.[13]

One response to the swelling patient loads was eugenic sterilization.

Georgia's Eugenics Commission

Late to the eugenics game, in 1937 Georgia established its Eugenics Commission under New Deal governor E.D. Rivers, former governor Eugene Talmadge having refused to sign the authorizing legislation because he realized its possible dangers to and reactions from his populist base. Eugenics had long been sold to Georgians as a progressive response to regressive populations. Georgia's Eugenics Commission would involuntarily sterilize over three thousand patients by the 1970s. Eugenic strategists had positioned sterilization as a cost-saving measure, particularly appealing in cash-strapped Georgia. Stephen Michael Smith summarized his 2010 study *Eugenics Sterilization in 20th Century Georgia*: "Recently revealed documents from the Georgia Department of Archives and History show that social deference, the scientific expertise, bolstered by legal coercion, poverty, or lack of education, was a major reason for the eugenics movement in Georgia."[14]

By 1939, New Deal money had built a new TB hospital and enough beds to decently house the people counties continued to send to the hospital.

In 1938 the *Constitution*'s Lamar Q. Ball had his tongue far up in his cheek when he wrote of how "the healthiest county commission mobilized its healthiest minds for a conference next week to discuss a final solution." Although the resonance is most likely coincidental, the following year Nazi Germany began its own "final solution" with the Aktion T-4 program. Aktion T-4 was Hitler's first effort at systematic eugenic extermination, and it was aimed at disabled people, whose capacities did not match Aryan standards. From the fall of 1939 to the summer of 1941, Hitler's doctors gathered up the people on their eugenics lists and in their institutions—Germans with mental illness, retardation, epilepsy, chronic illness, blindness, deafness, and other disabilities. They were considered *lebens unwertes leben*, "life unworthy of life." There are no accurate numbers for disabled people put to death in these first Nazi extermination camps or more informally across German-held territories. Doctors administered lethal treatments to those considered unworthy of life of all ages or they were shot by the SS or swept up indiscriminately in a "wild euthanasia."[15] But for the official Aktion T-4 killings the total was 70,243. In 1939, there were 300,000 mental patients in Germany.

In 1946, there were 40,000. Journalist and scholar Gregory Gallagher writes: "It has been estimated that no more than fifteen percent of the mental patients of Germany survived the killing programs of the Third Reich . . . It cannot be doubted that the euthanasia program swept out entire wards, cleaned out entire hospitals. It decimated the entire German population of the severely disabled and the chronically insane."[16]

Kraepelin had died in 1926, but his influence reached into these events. In 2015, the doctors Rael D. Strous, Annette A. Opler, and Louis A. Opler would assess the meaning of Kraepelin's contribution to Nazi extermination in a letter to the *American Journal of Psychiatry*:

[Emil Kraepelin] mentored three prominent Nazi psychiatrists: Robert Gaupp (1870–1953), Paul Nitsche (1876–1948), and Ernst Rüden (1874–1952). Gaupp echoed the thoughts of Kraepelin when he wrote that he felt wrong caring for "his patients when people of 'full value' were starving to death in the world outside." Nitsche was the director of the Sonnenstein hospital where tens of thousands of mentally ill were killed under the guise of mercy killing (euthanasia), and he later headed the entire T4 euthanasia program [the first Nazi extermination program, directed in 1939 against disabled people amassed from Rüden's lists]. Rüden, president of the Society of German Neurologists and Psychiatrists, was author of the 1933 "Law for the Prevention of Hereditary Diseased Offspring" and was referred to as the "Reichsführer for Sterilization." Rüden, who acknowledged the "eminent Kraepelin as his teacher and collaborator," wrote that "thanks to Hitler has our 30-year-long dream of translating racial hygiene into action become a reality."[17]

In these ways Nazi Germany enacted the most extreme version of "negative" eugenics: mass extermination.

On the United States front, then came the Japanese attack on Pearl Harbor in December of 1941, and rapidly World War II drew off doctors, nurses, and other staff. The profound labor shortage took what was then Milledgeville State Hospital into another period of profound crisis. In 1942, Superintendent L.P. Longino reported: "Many of the wards are carrying twice the number of patients for which they were originally designed to accommodate." Longino continued: "The Medical Staff has reached a point where it is practically impossible to render even the minimum care to the individual patient," Longino reported of a 1:900–1,000 doctor-patient ratio. The list of causes of death included "strangulation by hanging," the beginning in a rise in cases of suicide during the decade. By 1943, "the resignation of our best employees has been almost a daily occurrence." By July 1944, Supt. Longino understated, "We have been forced to employ those whom we would not have employed in normal times."[18]

In this depleted environment, electroshock came to the Milledgeville State Hospital. The 1942 report showed 219 patients were given 2,332 shock treatments. By 1946, with a patient load of 10,789 and thirteen doctors, 1,508 patients received 13,435 shock treatments. By 1947, total shock treatments climbed to 18,034, with a patient load of 11,031. In 1948, 2,170 patients received 18,867 shock treatments.[19] Electroshock quieted patients, ending the feeling of bedlam from contagious excitement—a change that a harried and overworked staff appreciated. Given the dearth of doctors, the decision on who got shocked was left to nurses and attendants. "The words 'punish' and 'shock' were often synonymous," historian and chief psychologist of this era Peter Cranford writes.[20]

At the end of World War II, the opening of the Nazi concentration camps revealed the extent of the fascist violence to those people who had managed not to see the Third Reich's efforts to exterminate the Jewish people while it was happening. The Nazi extermination of disabled people in the 1939 Aktion T-4 Program was its own part of that horror that was followed by mass extermination of Jews and other racial and political minorities.

In the United States during the war, three thousand conscientious objectors (COs) documented horrors inside U.S. state hospitals. Journalists like Albert Deutsch in *Shame of the States* and magazines like *Ebony* drew on their documentation to illuminate national conditions. The COs also modeled humane and intelligent treatment supported by the networks of "peace churches" and notables like First Lady Eleanor Roosevelt, Pearl Buck, Reinhold Niebuhr, and Helen Hayes. In the postwar years they educated the public on mental illness, worked against its stigma, and advocated best practices.[21]

On the very worst practices front, in the early 1950s, the "lobotomist" Dr. Walter Freeman came through Milledgeville on his national tour intended to teach the state hospital's doctors how to give lobotomies through the eye socket—a practice that lasted through the 1950s until longitudinal studies proved its harmful effects.[22] My friend Richard Brookins, who worked as a young man at the Milledgeville State Hospital, remembers assisting in two surgeries in which Dr. Freeman performed lobotomies in the Georgia facility.

The height of Georgia eugenics would take place in the 1950s under Supt. T.G. Peacock, who also served as chair of the Georgia Eugenics Commission. In another Milledgeville exercise in the surreal, Supt. Peacock (a known alcoholic) would write letters back and forth to himself asking for permission as representative of the Milledgeville State Hospital, and giving permission in his role as head of the Georgia Eugenics Commission, to sterilize Milledgeville and Gracewood State Hospital patients.[23] Apparently, he never turned himself down. Dr. Peacock was the official "king" of eugenics in Georgia, and after he was forced out there were never again the numbers of sterilizations that there had been under Peacock. The policy was officially stopped in the 1970s.[24]

The Abattoir

In 1950, the Milledgeville State Hospital's annual report showed the hospital's extensive use of patient *and* convict labor. "Without the aid of the patients' help, there would be a great need for about three times as many employees as we have; but without this form of therapy the patients would be denied of their greatest aid in the construction of mental health," the Occupational Therapy Department report explained. "Patients work on the farms, in the gardens, chicken projects, garages, bakery, beauty shops, and in short in every department in the hospital." Such work was intrinsically therapeutic, the Occupational Therapy administrators elaborated: "The idle mind is the devil's workshop."[25] In this regard, this institution was not so different than it had been in 1900. But it was considerably larger.

In the Farm and Dairy Division section, a fuller picture emerges of exactly what this 1950-era work entailed. Its ambitious plans involved prison labor, mainly for construction projects. Seventy convicts working under supervision over the previous year had built a large brick dining hall and a kitchen at the Colony Farm, a grist mill, seven three-bedroom brick homes for doctors, two brick police stations, dairy barns, bleachers for six hundred people at the baseball field, a five-room house for the chief of police, and concrete fire escapes for the Powell Building. "I want to take this occasion to thank the prisoners for their fine work," the Farm and Dairy supervisors wrote of the prisoners under their direction, who "saved the State of Georgia thousands of dollars."[26]

The savings from patient *and* convict labor was more in the hundreds of thousands of dollars of savings. For 1950, the total income for Milledgeville State Hospital was $7,263,966.19. Expenditures for Medical and Hospital Care were $1,484,416. In other words, the Milledgeville State Hospital spent approximately five times more on its farming operations than on its patients. By comparison, income from the Departmental Sales of the Farm and Dairy Division was approximately $1,312,000. Of this total, $632,342 was from the abattoir; $199,381.43 was from the dairy; $273,484 was from the farm; $8,288 was from the poultry farm; and $198,318.15 was from the cannery.[27] Profits from these enterprises totaled $390,124: Abattoir $106,226; Dairy $107,176; Poultry $2,177; Farm $124,728, Cannery $49,817.[28] And the income from its Farm and Dairy Division almost offset the costs of its medical services. That patients were saving the hospital three times their current employees meant that they were mostly paying for their treatments in labor, in the name of their "therapy."

So, what might this work have looked like, therapeutically?

The report assured its legislative readers that patients worked in all aspects of the hospital. They would have staffed the production in the buildings for which convicts built the structures. In fact, patients did two-thirds of the institution's work, if we apply the formula that the hospital would have needed three times the number of employees without patient labor. So, what were they doing? The Broiler Project brought 24,000 broiler chickens a year into the convict-built broiler houses, to allow the consumption of two thousand chickens per week, which allowed one serving of chicken weekly for each patient. These chickens had to be fed and slaughtered, and we can assume that patients did that work. In the laying house, twenty thousand hens labored to yield twelve thousand eggs per day, yielding one egg per day per patient. That's feeding chickens and retrieving eggs daily, not to mention the hens' assembly line.

The abattoir brought the Milledgeville State Hospital the distinction of being the only state agency with a slaughterhouse.[29] Six pages of the

1950 report detail its work slaughtering 3,346 hogs with a "live weight" of 649,610 pounds. Patients there were presumably instrumental in producing 6,282 pounds of liver, 1,345 pounds of hearts, 18,625 pounds of fat, 35,140 pounds of hog heads, and 1,755 pounds of trimmings. Workers at the abattoir also slaughtered 2,619 cows, for 2,025,403 pounds of "live weight" and $320,539.82 of "live cost." Once slaughtered these pigs and cows became livers, hearts, tongue, oxtail, cheek, brains, and hides, not to mention steaks, ground beef, sausage, bacon, and ribs.[30] In 1900, as we saw, pork had been at approximately 29,728 pounds. By 1950, pork production was 649,610 pounds—almost twenty-two times as much.

That the Milledgeville State Hospital was the site of the only state abattoir in Georgia and that the production numbers listed in the annual report were so high indicate that this slaughterhouse was a large-scale operation; it would have used the pigs and cows being raised in the hospital's three thousand or so acres. There is no indication in the 1950 report that these workers were anything other than Milledgeville State Hospital patients. Slaughtering these large animals—killing them, skinning and gutting them, chopping them up, taking out their hearts, livers, removing their heads, disemboweling them for sausage, de-hairing them, refrigerating them, and disposing of their carcasses—was dangerous, bloody, and exhausting work.

But how much so? A report from the *Monthly Labor Review* in 1943, "Injuries and Accident Causes in the Slaughtering and Meat-Packing Industry," gives us details of what happened to animals and humans during the slaughter, and these help to fill in the *Ebony* writer's remark that conditions at the Milledgeville State Hospital for Black people were similar to the lower levels of Dante's Inferno. Workers killed the animals on the upper levels of the slaughterhouse structure so that still live animals, then their whole carcasses, then the severed parts descended rapidly by chutes to the next level, where workers standing in water and blood and holding lethally sharp knives waited in what must have been terror for a still live and kicking animal or some version of its afterlife emergence as "meat." At every level of the operation the dangers compounded. One sample suffices of what happened after the "shackler" had shackled the hog's hind legs so that a chain could suspend it off the floor and move it along the assembly line:

The animal is then killed by an employee, called the "sticker," who cuts through its jugular vein. As the sticker must stand in the blood which drains from the animals, he must wear boots and be very careful of his footing on the slippery surface of the blood pit. . . . Another hazard . . . is the possibility of being kicked by the forefoot of the suspended animal. . . . Against the hand in which he holds his knife [that] sometimes will drive the knife into his other hand or arm or even his body.[31]

The Bureau of Labor Statistics reported that in 1943 Georgia's average rate of injuries in meat processing was "nearly 40 percent higher than the average for any other State."[32] Work in slaughterhouses was profoundly dangerous, putting workers at risk of "psychological disorder and pathological sadism."[33] Overall crime rates, including violent and sexual crimes in surrounding communities, also rose.[34] Putting workers in such risk in Georgia's state abattoir in 1950 was wrong whether done by hired workers, prisoners, or hospital patients. For patients, surely it would have been especially harmful. They were, in effect, worse off than prisoners.

In the three-thousand-acre MSH campus, only 132 acres accommodated hospital buildings. The rest formed this huge gulag of a psychiatric farm. The 1950 annual report recommended that the hospital acquire an additional ten thousand acres for pasture land and food. "It is our opinion that the Hospital with sufficient acreage could using patient labor produce practically all the livestock needed for slaughter, with a considerable savings."

By comparison, the three thousand acres of the Milledgeville State Hospital grounds in the early 1950s was already larger than the county's largest antebellum slave plantations with the exception of Stith Myrick's 3,200-acre holdings in antebellum Baldwin County.[35] An *extra* ten thousand acres would be *three* times Myrick's antebellum plantation. That's a lot of unpaid labor for a psychiatric hospital whose budget for medical services was only 20.4 percent of the hospital's total expenditures.[36]

One poignant item in the budget uplifts the legacy of the plantation: "rewards for escaped patients $578.25."[37]

The abattoir of Milledgeville was one measure of its infernally lower levels of inhumanity, where workers' blood mingled with that of cows and pigs on the low levels of the abattoir's floors.

This was, in fact, the devil's work. Nothing about it would have been "therapeutic."

Whatever the conditions, there were always in these hospitals decent staff people working to help their patients. At the Milledgeville State Hospital, our often-quoted historian-employee Peter Cranford was one of these people. He was hired as chief psychologist in 1951 and lasted two years. He offered humane care and collected six highly functional patients to help him assemble archives and write the history often cited in *Administrations of Lunacy*. History always being risky in Georgia's hospital, Cranford was fired by Supt. Peacock and went on to live a long and productive life, finally publishing *Milledgeville! But for the Grace of God: The Inside Story of the World's Largest Insane Asylum* in the 1970s, then letting the Georgia Consumer Council republish it in the 1990s to support its work establishing the memorial cemetery. African American staff also worked as best they could to ameliorate the severe conditions of Black patients.

Thorazine, a Miracle Drug?

By the 1950s, half a million people in the United States lived in state mental hospitals, on which was spent $500 million annually to support patients, many of whom the public knew did not belong there because of all the postwar exposés and the experiences of thousands of families. The journalist Albert Deutsch summarized for these hospitals: "Minimum standards set by the APA in *all* major aspects of care and treatment" have never been met.[38] The system had been in failure for half a century. But when its transformation came, a process that came to be called "deinstitutionalization," it would not be for the best.[39]

The roots of deinstitutionalization started when the French drug company Rhone-Poulenc synthesized Chlorpromazine in 1950 from a class of compounds that had previously served as dyes, then insecticides, then were used during surgery to numb the nervous system, allowing a doctor to operate without anesthesia. Within a year, the drug was used to calm manic patients at St. Ann's Hospital in Paris. Its effects were marked by "apparent indifference," "affective neutrality," and a "vegetative syndrome," or extreme passivity. The "neuraleptic" drug also had side effects similar to Parkinson's disease, as doctors in both the United States and Europe recognized. As Robert Whitaker in *Mad in America* summarized, "During this initial period, psychiatrists did not perceive Chlorpromazine as having any specific antipsychotic properties."[40] That it hindered brain function was seen as a positive on the crowded wards that housed too many patients with too few staff, the solution for which had included electroshock and lobotomies.

In 1954, Smith-French-Kline (SFK) began to market Chlorpromazine in the United States as Thorazine. Its development cost $350,000. In 1953, SFK had a revenue of $53 million; by 1970, its revenue was $347 million, $116 million of which was from Thorazine.[41] Within a decade, this drug that blocked brain functioning to produce a kind of "hibernation therapy" would be announced in *Time* magazine and across the United States as a wonder drug that would free mental patients from suffering and free state legislators from allocating the $500 million annually to keep them institutionalized.

The first effect of this infusion of drug company cash was on psychiatric journals, whose money from dues and journal subscriptions went from $5 million to $16 million in the 1950s, with $8 million coming from advertisements. As Whitaker describes, "As this change occurred, the AMA dropped its critical stance toward the industry. It stopped publishing its book on useful drugs, abandoned its seal of approval program, and eliminated its requirement that pharmaceutical companies provide proof of their advertising claims."[42]

Inspired by possibilities of "new knowledge and new drugs," President Kennedy announced the basis of a "wholly new emphasis and approach to care for the mentally ill."[43] His Community Mental Health Act, also known as the Mental Retardation and Community Mental Health Centers Construction Act of 1963, was the last major legislation passed before his assassination. It provided $329 million to build 1,500 centers for treatment, prevention, research, and education for both mental illness and what was then called "mental retardation." These centers were to provide in-patient and out-patient care, partial hospitalization, emergency care, and educational services to the community.[44] Basic to this act was use of federal funds in the first five to eight years, with declining federal funds to be replaced by third-party payments and state support. But such "government spending" was the anathema of the anti–New Deal forces in Georgia and beyond: the funds would not come through to implement the program.

By 1959, these old and new developments played out publicly at Milledgeville State Hospital, which was once again brought into public scrutiny through a series of news articles in the Atlanta *Constitution*. The *Constitution* uncovered a host of scandalous practices. For example, under the supervision of a MSH doctor being paid by pharmaceutical companies to conduct research, doctors were giving unapproved experimental drugs to patients without the knowledge or permission of the patients' relatives or patients themselves, some of whom were unable to communicate with their doctors.[45] Additionally, a quarter of the doctors employed at the hospital were found to have a history of drug and alcohol addiction; some had been hired after they were discharged as patients. Doctors had been witnessed working while intoxicated, while others had been held for treatment while still employed there.[46] The *Constitution*'s editorials focused on the impossible situation the staff faced while the newspaper called for reforms. The editorial staff also noted that the same recommendations made by a recent committee had been repeatedly made by the Medical Association of Georgia, beginning in 1916.[47] The Medical Association of Georgia reluctantly gave its endorsement of a state report on conditions at the hospital, and eight doctors resigned.[48] Jack Nelson and the Atlanta *Constitution* received a Pulitzer Prize in Journalism for their coverage.

Things were changing. In 1958 Ernest Vandiver won the gubernatorial election in a landslide against Marvin Griffin, a segregationist whose administration had been particularly corrupt. Vandiver described segregation as "the most over-riding internal problem ever to confront the people of Georgia in our lifetime." In 1961, Vandiver would oversee the integration of the University of Georgia after 175 segregated years. Also under his administration, nine Black students integrated formerly all-white Atlanta schools.[49] Given the crisis at the Milledgeville State Hospital, Governor Vandiver moved it from the Department of Welfare into the Department of Health; as his biography explains, his improvements included hiring additional personnel, raising hospital pay levels, upgrading medical care for patients, improving admission processes, and beginning a chaplaincy training program.[50]

In 1972 in *Wyatt v. Stickney*, a case arising from Alabama's mental health system, Judge Frank M. Johnson of the Third U.S. Circuit Court ruled that "people who are involuntarily committed to state institutions because of mental illness or developmental disabilities have a constitutional right to treatment that will afford them a realistic opportunity to return to society."[51] The ruling led to sweeping reforms in the nation's mental health systems and the creation of minimum standards of care and rehabilitation for people with mental illness and developmental disabilities. It also contributed to the exit of patients from state hospitals whose systems would not meet those standards.

Mental health professionals were also challenging diagnostic categories from within. In 1973, a campaign by gay and lesbian psychologists and their allies produced an important shift in the DSM when the American Psychiatric Association removed "homosexuality" from its list of psychiatric disorders in the second edition of the APA's *Diagnostic and Statistical Manual*, or DSM II, making homosexuality not a "paraphilia" but a "variant of normal sexuality." DSM II left gender nonconformity as a diagnosis—one that would become necessary for gender reassignment surgery but also as medicalizing of nonbinary gender expressions and identities as epistemic struggles over gender and sexuality moved into a new era.[52] It was one of the early important victories of the nascent gay rights movement, freeing up gay men and lesbians from the stigma of disease. DSM-III, published in 1980, marked the turn from Freudian psychoanalysis to more medical-biological descriptions of mental illness. This approach was often described as "neo-Kraepelian."

At the same moment, an uprising was also being fomented by psychiatric patients themselves. Perhaps their exit from the institutions gave them this voice. In 1972, the first *Madness Network News* went out to eight hundred readers, its design "to bring together and disseminate information about the psychiatric system and alternatives to it." The newsletter would be chock full of educating and advocacy tools. Its goal was "to put an end to the degrading and alienating practices of the psychiatric system and to create instead a process that validates human beings and their right to express themselves."[53] Former patients in the psychiatric empire had finally begun to speak back, and their numbers and voices would grow stronger over the coming decades as some of them emerged as influential professionals in the mental health field.

One of the foremost of these was Pat Deegan. Deegan was eighteen years old in her third hospitalization. Her doctor finally explained to her that she had "a disease called chronic schizophrenia," then elaborated: "If you take medications for the rest of your life and avoid stress, then maybe you can cope." Her reaction was profound:

> In essence, the psychiatrist was telling me that my life, by virtue of being labeled with schizophrenia, was already a closed book. . . . [He merely] recognized me as the schizophrenic who had been handed down through the generations by Kraepelin and Bleuler. He did not see me. He saw an illness.

Here was the old nemesis of therapeutic nihilism dressed up for a new century. Her doctor's dismissal of her life's possibilities stirred the eighteen-year-old Deegan to an outrage that sparked a new hope: "I decided that I wanted to get a powerful degree and have enough credentials to run a healing place myself," she resolved. It was the "survivor's mission" that turned her life around and that she would clarify for others as being key to their actual recovery.[54]

Deegan elaborated that the goal of such recovery "is not to become normal" or to "get mainstreamed," but to "embrace our human vocation of becoming more deeply, more fully human." She summarized its practices: "Choice, options, information, role models, being heard, developing and exercising a voice, opportunities for bettering one's life—these are the features of a human interactive environment that supports the transition from not caring to caring." Deegan and others were making a case for "revolutionary" and peer-run alternatives to the medical model.

These alternative models began as outliers, but over the decades became increasingly important because JFK's plans for "community care" were not materializing for lack of being funded. The work of another Georgian, Rosalynn Carter, would identify the gaps opening up in communities and track the shift from "deinstitutionalization" that assumed community care to "trans-institutionalization" that resulted from its lack. In the gap between deinstitutionalizing and trans-institutionalization, the severely mentally ill would fall through very large cracks.

Mrs. Carter Goes to Washington

In 1972, on the campaign trail when Jimmy Carter ran for governor, he and Rosalynn received many poignant queries from ordinary Georgians asking them for help with mentally ill relatives, and Carter promised that Rosalynn would help make Georgia's mental health system "the best in the country." Rosalynn Carter's reputation as an advocate for people with mental illness and developmental disability emerged with her husband's political ambitions; today she is recognized as a national leader in advocating on issues of behavioral health.

Jimmy and Rosalynn Carter brought a sensitivity to issues of mental illness to the governor's mansion based on family experience similar to many other families across the state. Jimmy's cousin Linton Slappey probably would be diagnosed with bipolar disorder today but could have lived a normal and productive life with today's "modern medicine." However, "he was a problem for his parents," and his antics made Plains folks nervous when he walked the streets as a "knowledgeable and unrestrained public commentator on the most sensitive happenings in the community." Carter wrote:

> Linton made brutally frank comments, often at the top of his voice. . . . If a man had been fired from the railroad, couldn't pay his grocery bill, or was secretly visiting a widow or another man's wife, Linton was likely to know and to promulgate the news, and not in diplomatic language. The shock[ed] or embarrassed townspeople would finally convince Uncle Jack to let Linton go back to the state mental institution, until he calmed down and was permitted to return home. Some of us looked forward to those times when Plains was enlivened with his presence.[55]

After they were married, Jimmy and Rosalynn visited Linton at the Central State Hospital and observed personally what Jimmy Carter called the "medieval" conditions there. Carter entered his governorship with a nuclear engineer's determination to make government more efficient, his own desire to make it more humane, and a growing ambition to run for president.[56] But it was Rosalynn who took on the crusade for mental health.

As Georgia's first lady, she made mental health her signature project. She took leadership in researching the issue and finding solutions. Carter formed the Governor's Commission to Improve Services to the Mentally and Emotionally Handicapped, composed of "mental health professionals, laymen, parents, and concerned citizens." Rosalynn attended the meetings of the commission while visiting mental hospitals around the state and volunteering at the Georgia Regional Hospital. After months of research, the commission produced a comprehensive report; its thrust, as Mrs. Carter explained,

> was to shift the emphasis away from the large institutions to the smaller, more intimate community mental health centers. This would allow some of those who were afflicted to live at home, surrounded by loved ones, yet have somewhere to go during the day to learn and be cared for. We wanted a center within reach of every person who needed help, and we almost accomplished that.[57]

In three years, the number of community mental health centers in Georgia increased from 23 to 134, with the number of resident patients decreasing by 30 percent by the end of Carter's term. In addition, twenty-three group homes served mentally retarded patients who had nowhere else to go.[58]

When the dark horse candidate Carter won the presidential election in 1976, Mrs. Carter took on her "one and only campaign promise: to study the mental health needs of our nation."[59] Demystifying the problem, Rosalynn asserted in her 1984 autobiography the conditions that still exist today:

> Each of us at one time or another will be affected by marital problems, delinquent children, drug- or alcohol-related stress, the inability to deal with death or a serious accident or illness, or simply by low self-esteem. Many will also experience the tragedy of a severe mental illness, in ourselves or in our families. Perhaps we will be able to cope. Perhaps not.

Jimmy Carter formed a President's Commission on Mental Health, its intent to shape needed legislation on issues of mental illness and mental health. The commission held public hearings across the country and organized more than 450 volunteers on thirty task panels who "developed comprehensive statements in specific areas of concern such as research, prevention, and the needs of special populations." What became apparent in this process was the degree to which "deinstitutionalization" had taken place without sufficient community care and relied on drugs with significant and insufficiently acknowledged side effects. Mrs. Carter summarized the commission's findings:

> What we learned was sobering. Federal and state programs were fragmented and fraught with bureaucratic problems. . . . And over and over again at every stop we heard of the plight of the chronically mentally ill who were returned to their communities . . . only to live marginal existences. Often these people remained jobless, homeless, feared by society, and even hungry because no adequate community services were available to them.[60]

Communities had been prevented from receiving federal funding for mental health as a result of amendments to the Community Mental Health Centers Act of 1963. In addition, health insurance programs didn't cover mental illness. Meanwhile, people with mental illnesses often feared the stigma and consequences of seeking treatment. These findings were shaped into legislation, and in 1980 Congress passed the Mental Health Systems Act, the "first major reform of federal, publicly funded mental health programs" since the 1963 act.

But Mrs. Carter's jubilation was short-lived. Given economic doldrums and the hostage crisis that arose when Iran held U.S. citizens in the U.S. embassy in Tehran, Ronald Reagan defeated her husband, and the Carters returned to Plains. She lamented:

> After four years of hard work and efforts by thousands of people, carefully studying an existing system of care and making changes so it would be responsive and cost-efficient, community-controlled, and accessible to those who so desperately needed it, and after having had the benefit of eighteen months of public scrutiny and careful adjustment—after all this, the funding for our legislation was killed by the philosophy of a new President. It was a bitter loss.[61]

Reagan's Omnibus Budget Reconciliation Act of 1981 proved to be the "death knell" to the Mental Health Systems Act's provisions and to JFK's plan for community care. The money would go to tax cuts, the military, jails, and prisons.

In the 1980s, Jimmy and Rosalynn Carter went on to found the Carter Center on the same hill where General William T. Sherman had watched Atlanta burn. Mrs. Carter has done landmark advocacy from the center's mental health program going on forty years. The Carter Center prescribes three elements for mental health: a good job, a good home, and a good friend. Mrs. Carter also adds decent insurance coverage. She laments the decline of Georgia's mental health system. The missing ingredient, she says, is the will to do the right thing.

Enter the Era of Mass Incarceration

If Ronald Reagan's laissez-faire economics "starved the beast" of New Deal–type public welfare programs, it also fed the monster of prisons and militarization. Beginning in Reagan's administration as a "war on drugs" and escalating under President Bill Clinton, the U.S. prison population grew from 300,000 to its current 2.2 million. This mass incarceration would make prisons and jails, in the words of the National Sheriffs' Association 2014 report, "incomprehensibly . . . the new asylums." This surge in prison population would give the United States the highest rates of incarceration in the world, and higher rates of Black incarceration than South Africa at the height of apartheid. As she traces the hauntingly familiar reconsolidation of white supremacy, civil rights lawyer and prison rights advocate Michelle Alexander in *The New Jim Crow* sounds like W.E.B. Du Bois in Georgia a century before. Decades of austerity budgeting aimed to defeat the Roosevelts' New Deal in favor of an unregulated economy, a slashed social safety net, and an expanded police force in communities where homeless shelters and jails became the new front lines of psychiatric treatment.

The people exiting state hospitals like Georgia's did not, one on one, end up in jails and prisons as part of what Anne Parsons debunks as "a mass exodus . . . from hospitals to streets to prisons." Parsons cites research that "many individuals did return to their communities successfully and received quality mental health and social services." The new psychiatric population emerging in jails and prisons in the 1980s were a different demographic, she argues. At mid-twentieth century, the state hospital population at half a million people "dwarfed the number of prisoners at the time" and consisted of "predominately white and middle aged" people. By the 1980s under Ronald Reagan, the prison population spiked so that prisoners constituted the vast majority of institutionalized people in the United States, and these newly incarcerated were disproportionately African Americans under forty years old. "The over-incarceration of people with psychiatric disabilities in prisons has stemmed in large part from the rapid growth of the criminal legal system itself . . . [due to a] broader shift in governance," including a "war on crime and drugs and the increased policing and surveillance of African American communities." The resulting massive system of U.S. incarceration became "a hallmark of U.S. government" and of U.S. psychiatry. "As the number of people in prisons and jails rose, so too did the number of people with psychiatric disabilities in the criminal legal system."[62] Speeding this growth in incarceration was the conversion of hospital buildings to prisons on state land, a move that "provided the infrastructure that made it easier and more affordable for state governments to build new prisons" in these repurposed buildings.[63]

At Central State Hospital (the institution's fourth name), ten hospital buildings were converted into five maximum-security prisons, giving Georgia in the early 1990s the second largest such conversion rate in the United States. These are the complexes of brick buildings viewed from the road or from the Memorial Cemetery now ringed with silver-bright and razor-sharp barbed wire—and increasingly covered with kudzu as they have first filled up with orange jump-suited and black-skinned prisoners, then emptied out to newer forms of incarceration. Over the last decades of the twentieth century, Baldwin County residents' jobs followed from hospital to prison, both forms of state employment on the state land that had always linked asylum to prison—until these brick prisons also closed down.

The freeing of patients from abysmal state hospitals envisioned by JFK had become an equally dismal process.[64]

The Decade of the Brain

In the 1970s, new technologies of brain imaging via the CT scan, PET, MRI, and fMRI brought the brain and its processes into almost Technicolor view. These new brain images seemed to promise major breakthroughs for psychiatric illnesses. Could new research find major cures waiting in the brain's gray matter and folds? Fed by excitement over the possibilities, the Library of Congress and the National Institutes of Mental Health (or NIMH, the lead federal agency on the research of mental disorders) declared the 1990s "the Decade of the Brain" "to enhance public awareness of the benefits to be derived from brain research . . . appropriate programs, ceremonies, and activities."[65] The assumption of many scientists seemed to be that the "biomedical" models on which DSM-III was founded would reign, and their reign would produce new miracle drugs for those suffering from severe and persistent psychiatric illnesses.

But, as it turned out, these new imaging technologies and the brain research of the decade did not yield these anticipated results.

What it did yield was increasingly convincing research that drug companies' claims for a succession of psychiatric drugs were massively overblown. By 1998, research by Irving Kirsch and his graduate student Guy Sapirstein on antidepressant drugs' results in contrast to the placebos given in drug trials showed that 75 percent of their effect came from placebo. (To clarify, a placebo is basically a "fake pill" or treatment used as a control to highlight the positive or negative effects of the drug under trial. Think: sugar pill.) These conclusions were met by considerable pushback, so Kirsch expanded his team and his research. He filed a Freedom of Information request with the FDA for data on six of the most widely prescribed antidepressants, and when reviewing them his team found that "[only] 18 percent of drug response is due to the pharmacological effects of the medication."[66] What this means is that the medications were only 18 percent more effective than the participant's response to a placebo, a difference, in medical historian Anne Harrington's words, "not readily apparent to a patient or his or her doctor outside an experimental trial setting."[67] Subsequent studies on the placebo effect validated these findings.

A second front was the lack of "biomarkers" between symptoms that DSM checklists provided for a particular drug and the drug's effects in countering them in patients. "Open Letter to DSM-5" discussed in the introduction to this book deplored: "Yet, even after 'the decade of the brain,' not one biological marker ('biomarker') can reliably substantiate a DSM diagnostic category. In addition, empirical studies of etiology are often inconclusive, at best pointing to a diathesis-stress model with multiple (and multifactorial) determinants and correlates." What they found was that a general diagnosis like depression might have various symptomatic expressions. But drug companies could not demonstrate what particular symptom one of their antidepressant drugs might affect—thus the absence of "biomarkers" between a symptom and a drug's effect.

This research made increasingly apparent now, as Harrington writes, that "by the 1980s, a critical mass of clinicians and researchers had aligned their professional interests with the commercial interests of the pharmaceutical industry."[68] Pharmaceutical companies had hired physicians as consultants and spokespeople and placed expensive advertisements in psychiatric journals that, in exchange, often toed the drug company line. In 1997, Big Pharma's profits blossomed even more after the FDA allowed companies to market directly to consumers, ads on television familiar today, as are the voiceovers of dreadful side effects that can occur as family members rollick across the screen. Harrington writes: "The numbers seem to say it all: between 1987 and 2001, the amount of revenue generated by (not so new and not so innovative) psychiatric drugs increased sixfold, twice the rate of prescription drugs overall."[69]

These profits had blossomed *even if* a patient might achieve *similar results* with a *presumably free placebo*. Because of Reagan-era deregulation, these drugs resulting from federally funded research could be patented by companies for lucrative markets.

Anti-psychotic drugs alone net the pharmaceutical industry at least $14.6 [billion] dollars a year. Psycho-pharmaceuticals are the most profitable sector of the industry, which makes it one of the most profitable business sectors in the world. Americans are less than 5% of the world's population, yet they consume 66% of the world's psychological medications.[70]

The European Medicines Agency then stepped in to raise the standards for how drugs had to prove themselves before they could be approved for their market. Steven Hyman, director of the Stanley Center for Psychiatric

Research at MIT and Harvard, explained their response: "'We don't know how to do that.' . . . In essence the EMA called their bluff."[71] As a result, "One after another AstraZeneca, GlaxoSmithKline, and other big companies abandoned the field of psychiatry altogether" and turned to other fields to develop drugs.[72]

Even given these challenges to DSM-5 and the pharmaceutical companies' discredited practices, I would be remiss if I did not make clear that these recent findings should *not* steer readers away from effective psychiatric treatments including effective medications. I would rather locate these treatments among the "ecologies of sanity" that I am positing as our alternatives to psychiatry's "afterlives of slavery." In the twenty-first century, we are left to tease out the "entwined biological, psychological and environmental roots," in Rosalynn Carter's terms, of the intricate connections among the brain's one hundred million nerve cells and the hundreds of trillions of connections between them, mediated by one hundred different chemicals. It's the brain's own complex ecology, and we have learned 95 percent of what we know about it in the last twenty years.[73] And, as in all ecosystems, the best brain research has affirmed the remarkable plasticity of the brain, its adaptability so that "conditions once thought irreversible can be altered."[74]

Mrs. Carter's advice and reassurances from 1999 in *Helping Someone with Mental Illness* still stand. "These illnesses can now be diagnosed, they can be treated, and the overwhelming variety of people who suffer can lead normal lives, living at home, working, and being productive." Her advice is always sensible and humane. If you or someone you love is experiencing "persistent or extreme symptoms" then reach out for help to family members, doctors, clergy, friends, or community organizations to find the right fit for a therapist, which may require "interviewing several before choosing one." Don't give up. If you are prescribed medications by a trusted provider, stay on them until the doctor says to stop and consult with your provider on any side effects. "The new treatments reduce symptoms and restore personal effectiveness—not for all patients, but for many; not every time, but quite often; not always permanently, but for long periods of time."[75]

Mrs. Carter also acknowledges that the use of jails and prisons as treatment centers is a problem of "staggering proportions"—"more than 50 percent of people in jails and prisons have a severe mental illness" and an "estimated 40 percent of people with a serious mental illness will come in contact with the criminal justice system."[76]

The New Abolitionists

By 1998, Lois Curtis had lived most of her life in Georgia's mental institutions, and she had had enough. She put a call in to Atlanta Legal Aid, and Atlanta Legal Aid lawyers, under the leadership of Sue Jamieson, launched the legal battle that went all the way to the U.S. Supreme Court and resulted in the landmark *Olmstead* decision. (Lois was joined by Elaine Wilson as additional plaintiff.) The decision described the two women's circumstances: "L. C. and E. W. are mentally retarded women; L. C. has also been diagnosed with schizophrenia, and E. W., with a personality disorder. Both women were voluntarily admitted to Georgia Regional Hospital at Atlanta (GRH), where they were confined for treatment in a psychiatric unit. Although their treatment professionals eventually concluded that each of the women could be cared for appropriately in a community-based program, the women remained institutionalized at GRH." Curtis and Wilson's lawyers sued the state under Title II of the Americans with Disabilities Act of 1992. It included the "integration regulation" that required a "public entity [to] administer . . . programs . . . in the most integrated setting appropriate to the needs of qualified individuals with disabilities."[77]

The morning of August 21, 1999, Lois Curtis and Elaine Wilson and their lawyers from Atlanta Legal Aid stood on the bottom step of the United States Supreme Court Building on the last leg of a legal journey whose success would legally emancipate disabled people from state hospitals. Lois and Elaine's determination to live in their communities led the U.S. Supreme Court in *Olmstead v. L.C. and E.W.* to find that the segregation of disabled people in state hospitals was a violation of the Americans with Disabilities Act—although not the Fourteenth Amendment, as the lawyers originally argued. Its briefs drew on analogies between disabled Americans and African Americans that referenced Georgia's long history of slavery and segregation. The majority opinion was written by Justice Ruth Bader Ginsburg. Elaine and Lois would gain freedom and large measures of remarkable happiness from their *Olmstead* victory, including a visit by Lois (a folk artist and disability advocate) to Michelle and Barack Obama in the White House.

The *Olmstead* decision was the beginning of the end for the institution that had begun as the Georgia State Lunatic, Idiot, and Epileptic Asylum in 1842, was renamed the Georgia State Sanitarium (1899) and Milledgeville State Hospital (1929), and became today's Central State Hospital (1967).

Psychiatry's Crisis with DSM-5

The number of diagnoses in editions of the DSM was rising, but they were not adding up. In 1952, DSM-I listed 106 forms of mental illness; DSM-II in 1968 listed 182; DSM-III in 1980 listed 285. DSM-IV in 1994 listed 307.[78] These escalating diagnoses could then be mined by drug companies for new disorders to remedy. In 2007, medical author Nancy Andreason reversed course from her 1984 *The Broken Brain*, which had touted the new biomedical revolution, to lament that DSM-III's "checklist approach" had led to loss of "careful clinical evaluation, rich descriptions of patient's conditions" and "the death of phenomenology in the United States"[79]—all characteristics of Kraepelian diagnostics.

The shift in expectations for the Decade of the Brain showed up at the Carter Center in Atlanta. In 2010, at the annual symposium of the Carter Center's Program on Mental Health, Mrs. Carter explained to attendants: "During the 1990s, the Decade of the Brain, advances in research led many of us in the mental health field to believe that medicine would eventually find a 'cure' for the most serious mental illnesses." She continued: "At the same time, some who were struggling with these illnesses began to speak out about a quite different reality, seriously questioning the value of the medical approach."[80] By 2010, National Institute of Mental Health (NIMH) director Tom Insel also voiced grave skepticism: "During the so-called Decade of the Brain, there was neither a marked increase in the rate of recovery from mental illness, nor a detectable decrease in suicide or homelessness—each of which is associated with a full recovery from mental illness."[81] The skeptics' chorus also included Dr. Allen Francis, the editor of DSM-IV, who lamented the lack of biomarkers, whose absence had failed the original "grand ambitions" of the DSM-III editors in 1980.[82]

DSM-5 itself was shaping up to be a major diagnostic crisis, and the new edition was anticipated with some professional dread at the upcoming annual meeting. After the DSM-5 release, the NIMH director Insel shocked the profession when he announced for the leading federal agency doing research on mental disorders, "NIMH will be re-orienting its research away from DSM categories . . . to begin to develop a better system."[83] Steven Hyman, director of the Stanley Center for Psychiatric Research at MIT and Harvard, summarized this debacle. He explained that DSM-III's authors were

> the heroes at the time. . . . They chose a model in which all psychiatric illnesses were represented as categories discontinuous with "normal." [But they were] totally wrong in a way that [they] couldn't have imagined, producing "an absolute scientific nightmare. Many people . . . get five diagnoses, but they don't have five diseases—they have one underlying condition.[84]

It was this situation that led the Humanistic Psychologists to announce their "Open Letter to DSM-5": "We believe that it is time for psychiatry and psychology collaboratively to explore the possibility of developing an alternative approach to the conceptualization of emotional distress. We believe that the risks posed by DSM-5, as outlined below, only highlight the need for a descriptive and empirical approach that is unencumbered by previous deductive and theoretical models."

This seeming collapse of the APA's diagnostic system contributed to a shift in the field toward "behavioral health" and a new appreciation for the peer-based practitioners like Pat Deegan who had originally revolted against their treatments as patients themselves.

In 2016, the Carter Center announced its last symposium, "Widening the Circle of Health and Wellness: The Central Role of Behavioral Health." There, Mrs. Carter lauded a new emphasis in mainstream mental health work on "the concept of recovery . . . that was not even dreamed possible when I began my work on mental health." She uplifted as "the single biggest advance in the last 30 years" the process by which a person comes to the point where they are "defined by other than the illness," in other words, a strength-based approach. She named Pat Deegan and another Georgian, Larry Fricks, as leading practitioners in the field.

Larry Fricks was head of the Georgia Consumer Council that designed the memorial cemetery at Central State Hospital. Fricks, like Deegan, brought a negative experience with his own psychiatric care to help shape the recovery movement. In 1991, he organized the first conference of mental health consumers in Georgia and went on to lead the Office of Consumer Relations and Recovery in the Georgia Division of Mental Health. There, his office created the new mental health position of "peer mental health specialist," who is a person who has experienced mental illness and has been trained to work with patients.[85] Today, Fricks leads the Appalachian Consulting Group, which "trains and consults in health and behavioral health to promote a national workforce of peer specialists who call forth the potential within each individual to self-manage a healthy life with meaning and purpose."[86]

Keynoting at the 2016 Carter Center Symposium was Dr. Paul Summergrad, a professor at the Tufts University School of Medicine and chairman of its Department of Psychiatry. He explained how the relationship between psychiatric symptoms and medical illness has required a rethinking of both behavioral health and integrated care. "We know that many medical disorders can worsen the course of psychiatric care; many psychiatric illnesses can worsen the course of general medical care; and many medical disorders can directly produce psychiatric illness." The emphasis in "holistic care" brought together the primary care center and that of mental health and substance abuse, thus "behavioral health."

Surely, Dr. Goldberger's ghost sat in the back of the Carter Center applauding.

Hidden Shame

The *Olmstead* decision did not end the troubles of Georgia's mental health system. In 2007, a new *Journal-Constitution* exposé, "Hidden Shame: Georgia's New Asylums," documented the ongoing mistreatment of Georgians in its mental health facilities. The newspaper assembled 135 suspicious or wrongful deaths across the state's seven psychiatric hospitals that were still struggling against inadequate funding and the impossibility, given this lack of funding, for community-based care. The ensuing lawsuit closed down the once-gargantuan Central State Hospital that is the subject of this book and required the state to spend $62 million on mental health services.

As Central State Hospital continued to shrink and an able staff worked to bring up its standards of care and treatment, its buildings emptied into other institutional forms of incarceration. These included a new forensic hospital overseen by the Department of Justice and the Riverbend Correctional and Rehabilitation Facility, a privatized prison opened in 2011 and run by the multinational corporation GEO Group Inc. (formerly known as Wackenhut Securities). This GEO hospital on Laying Farm Road (on former Central State Hospital grounds, where in 1950 the hospital bred chickens for meat and eggs) has 1,500 beds. Baldwin County netted three hundred new jobs and fifteen $1,000 scholarships each year. GEO's CEO George Zoley wrote in a letter to the "GEO Family" that the company "financed, developed, and will manage the $80.0 million, 1,500-bed prison on state-owned land pursuant to a 40-year ground lease. This important project marks GEO's entry into the State of Georgia and is expected to generate approximately $28.0 million in annualized revenues for our company."[87]

On the federal side of private prisons in Georgia, in 2016 the U.S. Justice Department decided to end prison-management contracts with private companies, citing GEO and two other prisons—one in Folkston, Georgia—as "inefficient" and "unsafe," with the GEO prisons having "the most incidents per capita." In March 2017, the Trump administration rescinded the order that would have put an end to privately run prisons being run as federal facilities and instead gave a contract to the Folkston, Georgia, GEO prison. "In its first quarter, Geo saw profits rise by 27 percent. [GEO CEO] Zoley said in a conference call that he expects Geo to benefit from the $1 billion in the federal budget resolution earmarked for detention of illegal immigrants." In the Trump administration, GEO is the largest provider of detention services for Immigration and Customs Enforcement, the Federal Bureau of Prisons, and the U.S. Marshals Service.[88]

According to the Southern Center for Human Rights, "Georgia currently has the highest rate in the U.S. of individuals under some form of correctional control—probation, parole, prison or jail. While the national average is 1 out of every 31 people under correctional supervision (prison, jail, probation, parole), Georgia's rate is 1 out of 13 adults."[89]

Prison beds were guaranteed, but medical and psychiatric care for people closer to their homes were not. In 2012, the year after GEO opened its private prison on Laying Farm Road, Georgia's Republican governor Nathan Deal turned down the Affordable Care Act's extension of Medicaid and removed 389,000 poor people in Georgia from extended coverage that would have covered both medical care and mental health services. Southern states provided 4.2 million of the 5.1 million citizens denied such extended coverage (including more benefits for treating mental illnesses).

Today, the largest mental institution in Baldwin County is the Baldwin County Jail. The largest mental institution in the state of Georgia is the Fulton County Jail. And the largest mental institution in the United States, by comparison, is Chicago's Cook County Jail. Baldwin County commissioner Henry Craig, speaking in nearby Macon at a statewide mental health summit, explains: "We have a moral issue. . . . When a person is mentally ill, too often, he goes to jail and the criminal justice system provides the help that the community, the families, the government did not provide. Our judicial and law enforcement know that it's morally wrong. Everyone here probably agrees that it's morally wrong. We need to find a different solution for those that are ill with a mental illness— keyword, ill." Capt. Wesley Lynch of the Whitfield County Sheriff's Office explained how critical issues with mental health are resolved (short term) and the patient is released: "But long-term, this creates a process where many individuals who have difficulty functioning on their own and seem to reoffend, only to be housed in the correctional center instead of mental health systems."[90]

The Atlanta *Journal-Constitution* weighed in on September 21, 2015, with "Georgia's Invisible Epidemic: Poor and Mentally Ill."[91] Nationally, adults with serious mental illness lose twenty-five years of life compared with other people. Nearly one in five adults in Georgia battles mental illness in any given year, and federal data show nearly half a million people with at least one major depressive episode. Overall, 1.4 million adults in Georgia have some form of mental illness, according to the National Survey on Drug Use and Health (2012–13). Georgia ranked near the bottom among state mental health agencies in spending on mental health, spending $59 per capita in 2013, Kaiser Family Foundation data show. This is about half the national average. Georgia also has among the worst ratios of all the states for mental health providers—one mental health professional for every 1,440 people, according to the nonprofit Mental Health of America. In contrast, Massachusetts has one provider for 248 people and is the national leader.

Those people without insurance in Georgia were denied choices that other states allowed, because Georgia's Republican leadership refused to expand Medicaid under the Affordable Care Act when thirty states did so at the ACA's passage. "Instead, then, thousands of people in Georgia remain uninsured and suffer from untreated mental illnesses—such as depression, bipolar disorder or schizophrenia—so severely they can't function in daily life," the AJC explained. From 2009 to 2013, 61 percent of mentally ill Georgia adults received no treatment. As a result of the lack of Medicaid insurance, Georgia hospitals between 2011 and 2015 lost over $150 million caring for uninsured patients with psychiatric disorders, which meant that everyone else in Georgia got higher taxes and higher hospital bills. If the legislature would expand Medicaid, then 233,000 or so Georgians with serious mental illnesses or substance abuse conditions would be insured. On the model of the thirty states that have done so, it would include people with annual incomes of $16,300. Of the estimated 4,800 people in Atlanta's homeless shelters or living on the streets, more than 60 percent have a serious mental illness, substance abuse, or dual diagnosis. Overall, Georgians' access to mental health care is forty-seventh in the United States.[92]

There is one set of people in Georgia getting more adequate treatment—the people targeted in the U.S. Department of Justice's five-year agreement with Georgia after the AJC in 2007 ran a series called "Hidden Shame" about the deaths across Georgia's psychiatric institutions. Under it, "the state has created dozens of new community based services, such as crisis stabilization units and case management teams to help individuals live healthy, productive lives in their own communities," according to the AJC.

But what about the other people in Georgia? Who helps them?

For those forty-six states with records less reprehensible than Georgia's, the lesson here is that this could be you. The race in the United States

Cemetery memorial, Central State Hospital, Milledgeville, Georgia *(Photograph taken by the author)*

today on public mental health is a race to the bottom, and the lower any place sinks, the lower all can fall. Given the Republican Party's continued determination to sack the Affordable Care Act and crash the national insurance markets, we could be in a freefall that will harm everyone.

Atlanta Abolitionists and the Fulton County Jail

If psychiatry is to escape its afterlives of slavery, it will have to help to take apart the current system of mass incarceration and take its own part of the responsibility for the fact that 90 percent of today's psychiatric beds are in jails and prisons. The central question is not whether one's position is anti-psychiatric or not; it is the extent to which an organization or professional takes a stand against the new Shame of the States of mass incarceration of mentally ill people. Many other people around the United States are working to dismantle this prison system in order to transform an afterlife of slavery into a new ecology of sanity. Recent work in Atlanta can provide inspiration and instruction.

Mary Hooks, co-director of Southerners on New Ground (fondly known as SONG), was pissed at the Fulton County commissioners and had come to their meeting to let them know. She and a dozen other SONG members chanted as they came forward in the auditorium, bringing recorded interviews SONG had made of women in the Fulton County Jail. Hooks let the commissioners know: "It's urgent."[93]

We should be able to understand this urgency, given that in this book we have traveled through the permutations of Georgia's penitentiary system.

Today, we encounter this carceral system's resurgence in every community across the United States.

The action at the Fulton County Commission that day was part of SONG's three-year-and-ongoing campaign to end money bail in counties across the South, working along with a national coalition of organizations on ending money bail. "Money bail" or "cash bail" is what people arrested for crimes have to pay in order to get released. Otherwise, they are jailed in "pre-trial detention" until their cases come to court. This practice results in poor people, often with minor charges against them, having to sit in jail for days, weeks, and even months waiting for a court date. They often lose their jobs, homes, and children, only because they have no money to pay the bail that allows their release until their court date or their case is settled. The practice is particularly brutal to women. Given entrenched racism in the United States, these people are disproportionately Black and brown. For the SONG folks, money bail was part of the afterlife of slavery in their community, and they wanted it gone.

Now a suit brought against the Fulton County Jail and its officers by the Georgia Advocacy Office and the Southern Center for Human Rights reveals the shocking extent of abuse, neglect, and gender-based discrimination to which women with negligible charges are subjected today.[94] The conditions that the suit enumerates show the terrible effects that mass incarceration in the United States has had on psychiatric patients. Fulton County is Georgia's most populous county and handles more court cases than any other county in the state.[95] The Union City Jail, built during the Atlanta Olympics, is one of its two annexes. The Fulton County Jail and Mental Health Task Force estimated that between 40 and 70 percent of the people incarcerated in the county's jail system suffer from psychiatric disabilities, "a figure about two to three times the prevalence rate for adults in the United States."[96] Former medical administrator George Herron puts the jail's "prevalence rate" even higher—60 to 80 percent—leading him to characterize the Fulton County Jail as "the new mental health hospital." At any given time, around half of all Fulton County detainees are identified as needing mental health services, making the Fulton County Jail the inheritor of the history of the Georgia Lunatic Asylum as "the largest de facto mental health facility in Georgia."[97]

The suit detailed women lying unresponsive on the floor smeared with food or feces or in their own vomit. Urine pooled on cell floors, some of which were contaminated with overflow from toilets. The combined smell made breathing difficult. Women slept on metal bunks without bedding. Overworked and undertrained officers oversaw two hundred mentally ill women, their cursory interactions through a locked door.

The suit filed by the Georgia Advocacy Office and the Southern Center for Human Rights described the effects of jail conditions on the mental health of the women incarcerated there:

> Prolonged isolation consistently intensifies symptoms of mental illness. Recent tours of the South Fulton Municipal Regional Jail have revealed example after example of the serious psychological harm that isolation inflicts on people subjected to it. . . . The pernicious tendency to isolate and segregate people with psychiatric disabilities is a longstanding and ongoing reality for women accused of crimes in Fulton County, Georgia.[98]

Outrageous to Hooks, the SONGsters, and Atlanta abolitionists, the women in the Fulton County Jail could be held there for minor offenses "for months, a year, or longer, solely because they [were] unable to make the basic decisions needed to resolve their cases." Some are unable to post nominal bonds, while others have been found incompetent to stand trial and are waiting to be admitted to Georgia Regional Hospital–Atlanta or a similar state hospital, the suit said. Unlike the women on the Union City unit, men at the main jail could enter into a therapeutic environment "promptly . . . with full days of structured programming, counseling, and group activities" in order to move through the system. Women, on the other hand, for months at a time after having been arrested for nonviolent, low-level offenses, are "forced to languish in isolation cells for 23 to 24 hours per day while they wait for beds to open at one of the few state-run hospitals."[99] The Georgia Advocacy Office, the Southern Center for

Human Rights, and dedicated activists like those at SONG, the Racial Justice Action Center, and Women on the Rise are determined that such conditions end. This suit is one strategy.

And Atlanta activists are making other progress.

In May 2019, recently elected mayor Keisha Lance Bottoms closed down the Atlanta Detention Center, which once housed up to one thousand people accused of traffic violations and city ordinance violations. The city had ended cash bail, decriminalized marijuana, and terminated the city's contract with the Immigration and Naturalization Service. Consequently, the Atlanta Detention Center population fell to between seventy and one hundred detainees in a facility that cost $32 million per year to run. As Mayor Bottoms considered selling off the jail and giving the money to the police, activists stepped in to demand reinvestment in communities impacted by the jail's twenty-year history and the ongoing effects of white supremacy and institutional racism and misogyny. On May 28, 2019, Mayor Bottoms signed legislation to close the jail and their intent to convert it to a wellness center. She explained, "By repurposing this jail, by reimagining what this space is, we are giving people the opportunity to access tools and resources on the front end so they have the tools for better decision making."[100]

As Mrs. Carter in another context observed, there are adequate financial resources available to fund adequate mental health if we simply invest in the right kinds of programs—the ones that we know work—rather than squandering millions and millions of dollars and lives in jails and prisons.[101]

In Milledgeville in the summer of 2019, the Central State Hospital Authority, responsible for repurposing the two thousand acres of state land to build a new tax base for Baldwin County, soldiers on. Its most recent innovation is to replace the old "Central State Hospital" sign—that for decades greeted visitors driving up the hill to the pecan grove—with a new one that reads "Renascence Park." Behind the new sign stands the Powell Building, five former prisons long taken by over kudzu but still ringed with razor-sharp wire, the memorial cemetery and its guardian angel created by the Georgia Consumers' Council, and the 25,000–30,000 graves of former patients that stretch into the woods. Such a new branding seems sudden and weirdly inappropriate.

But perhaps the new sign fits the pattern of forgetting. After all, two or so years ago at the behest of Georgia's Department of Behavioral Health and Developmental Disabilities (DBHDD), administrators packed up all the material in the old Train Station Museum and stored it first in the Powell Building, and now in the office of a Georgia state college and university administrator, where these documents have become inaccessible. There they sit, boxed, all of the archives and artifacts that were housed for years in the CSH Museum at the Old Train Station: the lobotomy tools, electroshock machines, straitjackets, psychiatric texts, copies of annual reports, clippings of files, the grand piano, and a recording of patients singing the Hallelujah Chorus. The train station will become the new home for the admirable Old Capital Museum, booted out of its place in the old Georgia Legislative Building (from which secession was declared) by its current occupant, a military college. The new Old Capital Museum will have a new exhibit space and a two-hundred-seat theater. It will include exhibits about the history of the hospital but those will not be their primary focus. Nor, apparently, are there plans to make the other archives and artifacts available to scholars and the public.[102]

Such shifts by the Central State Hospital Redevelopment Corporation are probably efforts to amend what its own survey found as the "spiritual and environmental deficits" of their property. But their new sign seems a paltry one if it is to paste over this 170-year history of Georgia's state hospitals, now in psychiatric ruins, when it contains so many stories, so many voices, so necessary for us today.

Acknowledgments

Administrations of Lunacy draws on over a decade of archival work, five fellowships, and multiple residencies and research trips in and out of Georgia. Fellowships include a Mellon Distinguished Professorship at Tulane, a sabbatical semester in Atlanta provided by Connecticut College, an academic year's fellowship at Emory's James Weldon Johnson Institute, an NEH Summer Seminar at the Savannah's Georgia Historical Society, and a semester as Newell Visiting Scholar at Georgia College and State University (GSCU) in Milledgeville. I have worked in the Georgia Archives in Morrow, the Central State Hospital Museum, the Carter Center Library, the Georgia Historical Society in Savannah, the Hargrett collections at the University of Georgia in Athens, MARBL (the Emory library), the Atlanta Historical Society, the National Archives at Atlanta, the Auburn Street Library (Atlanta), the Georgia College and State University rare books and manuscripts, and various county/regional depositories. I have traveled Georgia to learn its terrains (such as Andersonville, New Echota, the Okefenokee Swamp, the Sea Islands). I have interviewed Georgians who were patients, whose families were, or who worked at what became Central State Hospital; or I have had them interject their stories from the front seat of a Savannah cab, from behind me on the street in Athens, or from the Atlanta café's next table. Many Georgians know Central State Hospital intimately, and I have worked to be faithful to their versions of this story. I have published articles in *American Quarterly*, *Southern Quarterly*, and an anthology, *Queer South Rising*. And now, this book.

Notes

EPIGRAPHS

1. T.O. Powell, M.D., "A Sketch of Psychiatry in the Southern States," Presidential Address, fifty-third annual meeting of the American Medico-Psychological Association, Baltimore, MD, May 1897, published in the *American Journal of Insanity* 54 (1897): 51.

2. Joe Ingram quoted in Dr. Peter Cranford, *Milledgeville! But for the Grace of God: The Inside Story of the World's Largest Insane Asylum* (Atlanta: Georgia Consumer Council, 2014), i.

3. Paul Gilroy, "Living Memory: A Meeting with Toni Morrison," in *Small Acts: Thoughts on the Politics of Black Cultures* (London: Serpent's Tail, 1994), 178.

4. Frantz Fanon, "Letter to the Resident Ministry," in *Alienation and Freedom*, ed. Jean Khalfa and Robert J.C. Young, trans. Steven Corcoran (London: Bloomsbury Academic, 2015), 435.

PREFACE

1. Mab Segrest, *Memoir of a Race Traitor* (Cambridge, MA: South End Press, 1994), ix, 4.

2. Michel Servan, *Discours sur l'andministration de la justice aiminelle*, quoted in Michel Foucault, *Psychiatric Power* (New York: Palgrave McMillian, 1974), 2.

3. Carson McCullers, *The Member of the Wedding* (New York: Bantam, 1973), 29.

4. "To the Fat King and Other Head Men of the Lower Creeks," August 7, 1787, Papers of the Continental Congress, 1774–1789, U.S. National Archives microcopy M247, roll 87, frames 349–50. Quoted in Joel Martin, *Sacred Revolt: The Muscogees' Struggle for a New World* (Boston: Beacon Press, 1991), 6–8.

5. Joy Harjo, *American Sunrise* (New York: Norton, 2019), 3.

6. James Trent, *Inventing the Feeble Mind: A History of Mental Retardation in the United States* (Berkeley: University of California Press, 1994), 5.

7. "lunatic," www.thesaurus.com/browse/lunatic?s=t.

8. Anne Harrington, "False Dawns," in *The Mind Fixers: Psychiatry's Troubled Search for the Biology of Mental Illness* (New York: Norton, 2019), 267–70.

INTRODUCTION

1. "Insanity: Mental Illness Among Negroes Exceeds Whites, Overcrowds Already Jammed 'Snake Pits,'" *Ebony* magazine (April 1949): 19–23; Edward Shorter, *A History of Psychiatry: From the Era of the Asylum to the Age of Prozac* (New York: John Wiley & Sons, 1997), 45, 228.

2. "Bedlam," www.google.com/search?q=definition+of+bedlam&oq=Definition +of+Bedlam&aqs=chrome.0.0l6.3372j1j8&sourceid=chrome&ie=UTF-8.

3. Albert Deutsch, *The Shame of the States* (New York: Harcourt, 1948), 90–91.

4. Misty Williams, "Georgia's Invisible Epidemic: Poor and Mentally Ill," Atlanta *Journal-Constitution*, September 21, 2015.

5. Saidiya Hartman, *Lose Your Mother: A Journey Along the Atlantic Slave Route* (New York: Farrar, Straus and Giroux. 2006), 45.

6. Peter Breggin, *Toxic Psychiatry: Why Therapy, Empathy, and Love Must Replace the Drugs, Electroshcock, and Biomedical Theories of the New Psychiatry* (New York: St. Martin's Griffin, 1994); Robert Whitaker, *Mad in America: Bad Science, Bad Medicine, and the Enduring Mistreatment of the Mentally Ill* (New York: Basic Books, 2002); Ron Powers, *No One Cares About Crazy People: The Chaos and Heartbreak of Mental Health in America* (New York: Hachette Books, 2017); D.J. Jaffey, *Insane Consequences: How the Mental Health Industry Fails the Mentally Ill* (Amherst, NY: Prometheus Books, 2017); Allen Frances, *Twilight of American Sanity: A Psychiatrist Analyzes the Age of Trump* (New York: William Morrow, 2017); Ethan Watters, *Crazy Like Us: The Globalization of the American Psyche* (New York: Free Press, 2010); Brandy Lee, *The Dangerous Case of Donald Trump: 27 Psychiatrists and Mental Health Experts Assess a President* (New York: Thomas Dunne Books, 2017).

7. Treatment Advocacy Center and the National Sheriffs' Association Joint Report, "The Treatment of Persons with Mental Illness in Prisons and Jails: A State Survey," April 8, 2014, p. 6.

8. S.R. Kamens, D.N. Elkins, and B.D. Robbins, "Open letter to the DSM-5," *Journal of Humanistic Psychology* 57, no. 6 (2017): 675–87, www.ipetitions.com /petition/dsm5/.

9. Dominique A. Sisti, A. Segal, and E. Emanuel, "Improving Long-term Psychiatric Care: Bring Back the Asylum," *Journal of the American Medical Association* 313, no. 3 (January 20 2015): 243–44.

10. Peter Cranford, "Foreword," in *But for the Grace of God: Milledgeville! The Inside Story of the World's Largest Insane Asylum* (Atlanta: Georgia Consumer Council, 1998), i.

11. Jim Miles, *Weird Georgia: Your Travel Guide to Georgia's Local Legends and Best Kept Secrets* (New York: Sterling Publishing, 2006), 228–31.

12. Richard Nickel Jr., "Central State Hospital, Milledgeville, GA," The Kingston Lounge: Guerilla Preservation and Urban Archealogy: Brooklyn and Beyond, http://kingstonlounge.blogspot.com/2009/09/central-state-hospital-milledgeville -ga.html.

13. Christ McKearney, "Baldwin County's net job losses approaching 3,000 in less than four years," Baldwin Bulletin Online, http://news.mywebpal.com/news_tool_v2 .cfm?show+localnews&pn.

14. Michael Gray, *Hand Me My Travelin' Shoes: In Search of Blind Willie McTell* (Chicago: Chicago Review Press, 2009), 308–35.

15. "Severely Mentally Ill Persons More Likely to be in Jails than Hospitals, State Data Shows," *Business Wire*, May 12, 2010.

16. Michelle Alexander, *The New Jim Crow: Mass Incarceration in the Age of Color Blindness* (New York: The New Press, 2010). Also the organization Critical Resistance has headed up the work of prison abolition for decades, as has Angela Davis. See http:// crwp.live.radicaldesigns.org/ and *The Angela Y. Davis Reader*, edited by Joy James (Malden, MA: Blackwell Publishers, 1998).

17. Frantz Fanon, "Letter to the Resident Ministry," in *Alienation and Freedom*, ed. Jean Khalfa and Robert J.C. Young, trans. Steven Corcoran (London: Bloomsbury Academic, 2015), 435.

18. Wendy Gonaver, *The Peculiar Institution and the Making of Modern Psychiatry* (Chapel Hill: University of North Carolina Press, 2019); Martin Summers, *Madness in the City of Magnificent Institutions: A History of Race and Mental Illness in the Nation's Capital* (Oxford: Oxford University Press, 2019). Peter McCandless, *Moonlight, Magnolias, and Madness: Insanity in South Carolina from the Colonial Period to the Progressive Era* (Chapel Hill: University of North Carolina Press, 1996), raises the question of the importance of race in the South Carolina asylum's history. Jonathan M. Metzl, *The Protest Psychosis: How Schizophrenia Became a Black Disease* (Boston: Beacon Press, 2009), uses the archives of Michigan's Iona State Hospital for the Criminally Insane to trace how during the 1960s schizophrenia morphed from a diagnosis for passive white women to one for rebellious African American men in a period of civil rights protest.

CHAPTER 1

1. Amariah Brigham, *Observations on the Influence of Religion Upon the Health and Physical Welfare of Mankind* (Boston: Marsh, Capen & Lyon, 1835), 275. Reprint by Forgotten Books, Books@www.forgottenbooks.org, 2012.

2. Michel Servan, *Discours sur l'andministration de la justice aiminelle*, quoted in Michel Foucault *Psychiatric Power: Lectures at the Collège de France 1973–1974* (New York: Picador, 1974), 2.

3. *First Published Annual Report of the Resident Physician of the Lunatic, Idiot and Epileptic Asylum of the State of Georgia, to His Excellency, Geo. W. Crawford, Governor; Doctors T.Fort & B.A. White, Trustees. Comprising Its Origins, Progress and Present State; Its Fiscal Concerns and a Detailed Account of Patients Admitted; Their Symptoms, or States of Derangement, Treatment, &c., &c., &c. By David Cooper Resident Physician and Trustee.* Milledgeville, Georgia, 1845. This document hereafter is referenced as 1845 AR.

4. Paul K. Graham, *Admission Register of Central State Hospital, Milledgeville, Georgia, 1842–1861* (Decatur, GA: The Genealogy Company, 2011), 5. This volume contains genealogist Graham's transcriptions of approximately 900 entry ledgers into the Georgia State Lunatic, Idiot, and Epileptic Asylum from ledger volumes and microfiche in the Georgia Archives. Neither Cooper nor Peter Cranford uses actual names, but Graham does. Given that Graham had permission of the Georgia Archives to uses actual names in ledgers, so have I in this book. Here I am working between Graham's ledgers and Cooper's notes. For example, Henderson is #13 for Cooper and thus for Cranford, but eighteenth in the ledger. Cooper omits four patients from his list, so his first thirty-three patients are contained within the first thirty-seven patients in the ledgers, which also provide additional information on these patient deaths, escapes, and releases beyond 1845.

5. James C. Bonner, *Milledgeville: Georgia's Antebellum Capital* (Milledgeville, GA: Old Capital Press, 2007), 30. Originally published by the University of Georgia Press (Athens, GA, 1878). Bonner's history is still the authoritative source on antebellum Milledgeville.

6. Peter Cranford, *But for the Grace of God: Milledgeville! The Inside Story of the World's Largest Insane Asylum* (Atlanta: Georgia Consumer Council, 1998), 18–19.

7. According to Edward Shorter, it was not Pinel but hospital manager Jean-Baptiste Pussin who gave the order, though Pinel was immortalized in Charles Louis Lucien Müller's painting *Philippe Pinel Releasing Lunatics from Their Chains at Bicêtre Asylum in Paris in 1793*," and by Tony Robert-Fleurys *Dr. Philippe Pinel at the Salpetriere, 1795*. See Edward Shorter, *A History of Psychiatry: From the Era of the Asylum to the Age of Prozac* (New York: John Wiley & Sons, 1997), 11.

8. Shorter, 17.

9. 1845 AR, 6.

10. 1845 AR, 6.

11. Roy Porter, *Madness: A Brief History* (Oxford: Oxford University Press, 2002), 10.

12. Henderson's case (13) is 45–48, 1845 AR.

13. Edward Shorter, "Primary Care," in *The Cambridge History of Medicine*, ed. Roy Porter (Cambridge: Cambridge University Press, 2006), 109.

14. 1845 AR, 13, 22–23.

15. 1845 AR, 47–48.

16. Bonner, 3.

17. Bonner, 31.

18. "Dr Thomas Story Kirkbride," Kirkbride Buildings, www.kirkbridebuildings.com /about/kirkbride.html, accessed May 5, 2015. See especially Carla Yanni, *The Architecture of Madness: Insane Asylums in the United States* (Minneapolis: University of Minnesota Press, 2007), chapter 2: "Establishing the Type."

19. 1845 AR.

20. Yanni, 42.

21. 1845 AR, 28.

22. 1845 AR, 27.

23. David Smith is Case 6, 1845 AR, 36–37.

24. Case 10, 1845 AR, 41–42.

25. Case 7, 1845 AR, 37–38.

26. 1845 AR, 46–47.

27. 1845 AR, 46–47.

28. 1845 AR, 33–34.

29. Bonner, 32–33.

30. Lawrence B. Goodheart, *Mad Yankees: The Hartford Retreat for the Insane and Nineteenth Century Psychiatry* (Amherst: University of Massachusetts Press, 2003), 90, 95–97.

31. Goodheart, 92.

32. Quoted in Goodheart, 93, 99. See also, "Brigham, Amariah," The Social Welfare History Project, reprinted from W.O. McClure, "Biographical Sketch of Amariah Brigham, M.D., Late Superintendent of The New York State Lunatic Asylum, Utica, N.Y." (Utica, NY: Curtiss & White Printers, 1858), 110–17. Reproduced at "The Inmates of Willard 1870 to 1900 / A Genealogy Resource," a blog by Linda S. Stuhler, http://inmatesofwillard.com/, accessed April 12, 2015.

33. "Biographical Sketch of Amariah Brigham," 75–76, https://books.google.com /books?id=A0EXAQAAMAAJ&printsec=frontcover&source=gbs_ge_summary _r&cad=0#v=onepage&q&f=false.

34. 1845 AR, 8–9.

35. "Lunatic Asylums in the United States," *American Journal of Insanity* 2 (1845): 165–71.

CHAPTER 2

1. Edward E. Baptist, *The Half Has Never Been Told: Slavery and the Making of American Capitalism* (New York: Basic Books, 2014).

2. *First Published Annual Report of the Resident Physician of the Lunatic, Idiot and Epileptic Asylum of the State of Georgia, to His Excellency, Geo. W. Crawford, Governor; Doctors T.Fort & B.A. White, Trustees. Comprising Its Origins, Progress and Present State; Its Fiscal Concerns and a Detailed Account of Patients Admitted; Their Symptoms, or States of Derangement, Treatment, &c., &c., &c. By David Cooper Resident Physician and Trustee.* Milledgeville, Georgia, 1845, 16–17.

3. 1845 AR, 11–12.

4. 1845 AR, 25.

5. 1845 AR, 13–14.

6. 1845 AR, 7.

7. Thomas Jefferson, *Notes on the State of Virginia: Query XVIII—Manners*, 1781. William Peden, ed. (New York: W.W. Norton, 1982), 163.

8. "Lunatic Asylums of the United States," *American Journal of Insanity* 1 (1844): 256; "Lunatic Asylums of the United States," *American Journal of Insanity* 2 (1845): 160–61.

9. Amariah Brigham, *Observations on the Influence of Religion Upon the Health and Physical Welfare of Mankind* (Boston: Marsh, Capen & Lyon, 1835), 275.

10. Brigham, *Observations*, 301–2, quoted in Lawrence B. Goodheart, *Mad Yankees: The Hartford Retreat for the Insane and Nineteenth Century Psychiatry* (Amherst: University of Massachusetts Press, 2003), 105.

11. Gerald Grob, *The State and the Mentally Ill: A History of Worcester State Hospital in Massachusetts 1830–1920* (Chapel Hill: University of North Carolina Press, 1966), xxi.

12. David Rothman, *The Discovery of the Asylum: Social Order and Disorder in the New Republic* (Boston: Little Brown, 1971), 113; Grob, *State and Mentally Ill*, xii, quotes Samuel Woodward; Norman Dain, *Disordered Minds: The First Century of Eastern State Hospital in Williamsburg Virginia, 1766–1866* (Williamsburg, VA: Colonial Williamsburg Foundation, 1971), 112; Diana Martha Louis, *Colored Insane: Slavery, Asylums and Mental Illness in 19th-Century America* will trace the components of what she terms "pro-slavery psychiatry."

13. Rothman, 113. See Samuel Tuke's "Introduction" to Maximilian Jacobi, *On the Construction and Management of Hospitals for the Insane* (London: John Churchill, 1841), lxiii; Henry Maudsley, *The Pathology of the Mind* (New York: Macmillan, 1879; 1st ed., London, 1867), 127–29, 170–71; Wilhelm Griesinger, *Mental Pathology and Therapeutics* (London, 1867; 1st ed., 1845), 138–39, 157.

14. "Exemption of Cherokee Indians and Africans from Insanity," *American Journal of Insanity* 2 (January 1845): 287–88.

15. Gerald Grob, *Mental Institutions in America: Social Policy to 1875* (New Brunswick, NJ: Transaction Publishers, 2009), 243–44.

16. Grob, *Mental Institutions in America*, 249–51, cites *Massachusetts General Hospital Annual Report* 1836, 4; *Worcester State Lunatic Asylum Hospital Annual Report XXXVII* (1869), 70; *Report of the Superintendent of the Government Hospital for the Insane* (Washington, DC, 1855), 3, 5; *Indiana Hospital for the Insane Annual Report* 1854, 36–37; *Report of the Commission of the Alms House, Bridgewell and Penitentiary, New York City Board of Alderman Doc No 32* (1837), 204.

17. Grob, *Mental Institutions in America*, 244, cites, *Maryland Hospital for the Insane, Annual Report,* 1851, 7–8; *Kentucky Western Lunatic Asylum, Annual Report,* 1865, 14; *Kentucky Eastern Lunatic Asylum, Annual Report XXXIII/XXXIV* (1856/1857), 24; *Virginia Eastern Asylum, Annual Report,* 1846, 4, 1848, 23–29, 1849, 5–6, 17; Dain, 19, 105, 109–13; *Virginia Western Lunatic Asylum, Annual Report,* XVIII (1856) 7–8, 29–31, XXI (1848), 4–5, 32–23, AR, 1867/1868/1869, 6–7.

18. David Gollaher, *Voice for the Mad: The Life of Dorothea Dix* (New York: The Free Press, 1995), 265.

19. Harriet Washington, *Medical Apartheid: The Dark History of Medical Experimentation on Americans from Colonial Times to the Present* (New York: Harlem Moon, 2006), 146. See also Albert Deutsch, "The First U.S. Census of the Insane (1840) and Its Use as a ProSlavery Propaganda," *Bulletin of the History of Medicine* 15 (1944): 469–83; Louis

Dublin, "The Problem of Negro Health as Revealed by Vital Statistics," *Journal of Negro Education* 6 (1937): 266–75; Clayton E. Cramer, "Demographic Data, 1790–1860: A Sourcebook" (2003), at www.claytoncramer.com/.htm.

20. Quoted in Washington, 149–50; see Edward Jarvis, M.D., "Insanity Among the Coloured Population of the Free States," *American Journal of Medical Sciences* 1844, no. 7 (1843): 74–75; "Preliminary Report," *Boston Medical and Surgical Journal* 27 (1843): 126–32, 281–82. See Gerald Grob, *Edward Jarvis and the Medical World of Nineteenth Century America* (Knoxville: University of Tennessee Press, 1978). Grob traces how Jarvis' challenge to the 1840 census data helped lay the foundations for the census to be a source of data and thus policy.

21. *American Journal of Insanity* (1851) quoted by William Ragan Stanton, *The Leopard's Spots: Scientific Attitudes Towards Race in America, 1815–1859* (Chicago: University of Chicago Press, 1960), 65.

22. Grob, *Mental Institutions in America*, 221.

CHAPTER 3

1. Joy Harjo, *American Sunrise* (New York: Norton, 2019), 3.

2. Joel W. Martin, *Sacred Revolt: The Muskogees' Struggle for a New World* (Boston: Beacon Press, 1991), 18.

3. Martin, 24–27.

4. Paul Pressley, *On the Rim of the Caribbean: Colonial Georgia and the British Atlantic World* (Athens: University of Georgia Press, 2013), 19–20.

5. Pressley, 12–17.

6. Quoted in Pressley, 27. Letter from Mr. John Dobell, June 11, 1746, *Colonial Records of the State of Georgia* 25: 72.

7. Pressley, 27, quoting John Reynolds to the Board of Trade, March 27, 1756, in *Colonial Records of the State of Georgia* 27: 113.

8. Philip Morgan, "Lowcountry Georgia and the Early Modern Atlantic World, 1733–ca 1820," in *African American Life in the Georgia Lowcountry: The Atlantic World and the Gullah Geechee*, ed. Philip Morgan (Athens: University of Georgia Press, 2011), 3.

9. Pressley, 33.

10. Pressley, 139–40.

11. Morgan, 26.

12. Pressley, 196–97.

13. Pressley, 197–99.

14. Pressley, 223–25.

15. Pressley, 225–26.

16. Pressley, 227.

17. Morgan, 26.

18. Edward Baptist, *The Half Has Never Been Told: Slavery and the Making of American Capitalism* (New York: Basic Books, 2014), xxi.

19. Peter Wallenstein, *From Slave South to New South: Public Policy in Nineteenth Century Georgia* (Chapel Hill: University of North Carolina Press, 1987), 95

20. Wallenstein, 8–10.

21. Jefferson to Governor John Milledge, November 27, 1802, quoted in Wallenstein, 9.

22. Jim Gigantino, "Land Lottery System," *New Georgia Encyclopedia*, June 8, 2017, accessed December 7, 2018.

23. Wallenstein, 14.

24. Tomlinson Fort Family Papers, 1808–1882, at Emory University Manuscript, Archives, and Rare Book Library, Atlanta, "Biographical Note" http://pid.emory.edu /ark; 25593/8z9jb.

25. Wallenstein, 29.

26. Joy Harjo writes, "There were many trails of tears from the homelands of the Muscogee Creek Nation west, just as there were for the Cherokee, Chickasaw, Choctaw, Seminole and many other tribal nations," ii.

27. Theda Purdue and Michael D. Green, *The Cherokee Nation and the Trail of Tears* (New York: Penguin Books, 2007), xiv.

28. Purdue and Green, 45.

29. Daniel S. Butrick, *The Journal of Rev. Daniel S. Butrick, May 19, 1838–April 1, 1839* (Park Hill, OK: Trail of Tears Association, Oklahoma Chapter, 1998), 6, 10, quoted in Purdue and Green; "Excerpts from the journal of the Reverend Daniel Sabine Butrick," in *Voices from the Trail of Tears*, ed. Vicki Rozema (Winston-Salem, NC: John F. Blair, 2003), 54–61.

30. Chief John Ross to the U.S. Senate and House of Representatives, September 28, 1836, http://historymatters.gmu.edu/d/6598/, accessed on July 12, 2019.

31. Quoted in Baptist, 23.

32. Baptist, 2.

33. Baptist, 1.

34. Baptist, xxvi.

35. Wallenstein, 26–30.

36. "Biographical Note" for Tomlinson Fort Family Papers, 24–30.

37. Wallenstein, 30.

CHAPTER 4

1. Peter Wallenstein, *From Slave South to New South: Public Policy in 19th Century Georgia* (Chapel Hill: University of North Carolina Press, 1987), 95.

2. "Crazy Jane Talks with the Bishop," William Butler Yeats, *The Collected Poems of W.B. Yeats* (New York: Macmillan Company, 1956), 254.

3. "Crazy Jane Talks with the Bishop," Yeats.

4. Case 24, *First Published Annual Report of the Resident Physician of the Lunatic, Idiot and Epileptic Asylum of the State of Georgia, to His Excellency, Geo. W. Crawford, Governor; Doctors T.Fort & B.A. White, Trustees. Comprising Its Origins, Progress and*

Present State; Its Fiscal Concerns and a Detailed Account of Patients Admitted; Their Symptoms, or States of Derangement, Treatment, &c., &c., &c. By David Cooper Resident Physician and Trustee, Milledgeville, Georgia, 1845, 60–61.

5. 1845 AR, 8, case 24, described on 60–61. All quotes are from these pages. Nancy Malone is listed in Paul K. Graham, *Admission Register of Central State Hospital, Milledgeville, Georgia, 1842–1861* (Decatur, GA: The Genealogy Company, 2011), as patient 28.

6. Amariah Brigham, *Observations on the Influence of Religion Upon the Health and Physical Welfare of Mankind* (Boston: Marsh, Capen & Lyon, 1835), 275.

7. 1845 AR, 8.

8. Graham, case #47, 49, 51, 64, 95, 99.

9. Graham, 126, 127, 154–57, 172–73, 99–100.

10. Graham, 9, 13, 16.

11. Peter Cranford, *But for the Grace of God: Milledgeville! The Inside Story of the World's Largest Insane Asylum* (Atlanta: Georgia Consumer Council, 1998), 5.

12. 1845 AR, 22.

13. Worcester, talking about his friend Butler, quoted in "Enemies of Georgia–1831," in *Voices from the Trail of Tears,* ed. Vicki Rozema (Winston-Salem, NC: John F. Blair, 2003), 59.

14. Description of departure: "Letter from Cherokee leader William Shorey Coodey to John Howard Payne on the departure of a land detachment," Washington City, August 13, 1840, in Rozema, 133–34.

15. "Dr Elizur and Ester Butler Missionaries to the Cherokees," Georgia Info, http://georgiainfo.galileo.usg.edu/gahistmarkers/butlerhistmarker.htm, accessed November 10, 2013.

16. John Wade, case 11, 1845 AR, , 42–44; Wade is the fifteenth patient admitted to the GLA.

17. James C. Bonner, *Milledgeville: Georgia's Antebellum Capital* (Milledgeville, GA: Old Capital Press, 2007), 110, 116.

18. Bonner, 112–13.

19. Bonner, 60–63.

20. John Wade, AR 1845, 42–44.

21. 1845 AR, 2.

22. Paul K. Graham, *Admission Register of Central State Hospital Milledgeville, Georgia, 1842–1861* (Decatur, GA: The Genealogy Company, 2011), 2.

CHAPTER 5

1. Georgia Lunatic Asylum Ledgers, Vol. 2, #538; or in Paul K. Graham, *Admission Register of Central State Hospital Milledgeville, Georgia, 1842–1861* (Decatur, GA: The Genealogy Company, 2011), 54. All references to Frances Edwards are from Graham, 54.

2. "Benson L. Edwards," Confederate Soldier in Tennessee, 35th Regiment, Tennessee Infantry (5th Infantry) (1st Mountain Rifle Regiment), Company 3F, Private,

M231 roll 13. National Park Service Civil War Soldiers, 1861–1865 [database online]. B.S. Edwards, Year: 1850; Census Place: Division 15, Cherokee, Georgia; Roll: M432_65; Page: 515A; Image: 232. Frances Edwards, Year: 1850; Census Place: Division 15, Cherokee, Georgia; Roll: M432_65; Page: 515A; Image: 232.

3. F.E. Fodéré, *Traite du delire*, vol. 2, section 6, ch. 3, "Du choix des administrateurs, des medicins, des employes et des servants," 230–31. Quoted in Michel Foucault, *Psychiatric Power: Lectures at the Collège de France 1973–1974* (New York: Picador, 2003), 4.

4. Anna Maria Green Cook, *A History of Baldwin County, Georgia* (Anderson, SC: Hearn Co, 1925; eBook babel.hathitrust.com), 86.

5. Peter Cranford, *But for the Grace of God: Milledgeville! The Inside Story of the World's Largest Insane Asylum* (Atlanta: Georgia Consumer Council, 1998), 25.

6. Philippe Pinel (1745–1826), *A Treatise on Insanity*, trans. B.B. David (New York: Hafner, 1962), Section II: "The Moral Treatment of Insanity," 99. Quoted in Foucault, 2.

7. Foucault, 2; Joseph Michel Antoine Servan (1737–1807), *Discours sur l'administration de la justice criminelle*, delivered by Monsieur Servan (Geneva: 1767), 35.

8. Loren Schweninger, *Families in Crisis in the Old South: Divorce, Slavery, and the Law* (Chapel Hill: University of North Carolina Press, 2012), 48, 51.

9. Schweninger draws his conclusions about antebellum families from his groundbreaking study of a "small but representative group" of divorce, separation, and alimony cases from 211 counties, 15 slave states, and Washington, DC, from "virtually every year" between 1800 and 1860. His research cohort was composed of cases of 610 white women, 123 white men, and 35 free people of color. Eleven of these cases were from Georgia, including six of extreme violence, two of physical abuse, with 73 percent of the cases involving abuse, all by slave owners. Schweninger, 53.

10. Schweninger, 39.

11. Frances Edwards, Year: 1850; Census Place: Division 15, Cherokee, Georgia; Roll M432_65; Page: 515A Image 232. Age given as 25, Birthplace North Carolina, family includes five Edwards and four Beasleys.

12. Cranford, 31.

13. Schweninger, 32–33.

14. Schweninger, 33.

15. Schweninger, 33. See Schweninger, 164, footnote 2, for full listing of court documents.

16. Graham, #202, 19; "Rawdon" is written "Rowdon"—Schweninger gives 1854 as the date of the homicide, but an online edition corrects it to 1848, which matches the GLA notation. Conversation with Loren Schweninger, April 2016.

17. Graham, #512, 51.

18. Graham, all cases, 53.

19. Graham, #714, 81.

20. Benson L. Edwards, Year: 1860; Census Place: District 15, Hamilton, Tennessee; Roll: M653_1253; Page: 140; Family History Library Film: 805253.

21. Schweninger, 46. Schweninger uses these divorce and alimony legal records as a way of understanding more fully the intimate contexts of antebellum white southerners. His research adds to extensive scholarship on the southern culture of violence, which has only recently turned to issues of domestic violence in families for more than what had formerly been "only glimpses into the havoc it wreaked."

22. James C. Bonner, *Milledgeville: Georgia's Antebellum Capital* (Milledgeville, GA: Old Capital Press, 2007), 39–41, 140.

23. Elisabeth Mays, "'The Celebrated Mrs. Cobb,' Mrs. Howell Cobb," *Georgia Historical Quarterly* 24, no. 2 (June 1940): 105, www.jstor.org/stable/40576697.

24. Bonner, 140–42, quotation 140.

25. Bonner, 142–43.

26. Mays, 122–23.

27. Bonner, 143.

28. A.H. Prince to John B. Lamar, Athens, October 12, 1852. MS 1376, B36, f4.

29. Bonner, 144. Quotation from John E. Simpson, *Howell Cobb: The Politics of Ambition* (Chicago: University of Chicago Press, 1973), 19.

30. Conversation with Matthew Davis, executive director, the Old Governor's House, Milledgeville, April 2016.

31. Howell Cobb to his wife, Washington, DC, February 8, 1849, "Howell Cobb Papers," *Georgia Historical Quarterly* 5, no. 2 (June 1921), 29–52. GHQ's collection of Howell's letters continues in 6, no. 2 (June, 1922), 147–73; 6, no. 4 (Dec. 1922), 355–94.

32. R.L. Reid, "Howell Cobb (1815–1868)," *New Georgia Encyclopedia*, September 15, 2014, accessed June 14, 2016. See also Mays, 113–17.

CHAPTER 6

1. Thomas Jefferson, *Notes on the State of Virginia*, William Peden, ed. (New York: W.W. Norton, 1982), 163.

2. W.E.B. Du Bois, *Black Reconstruction in America 1860–1880: Studies in American Negro Life*, ed. A. Meier (New York: Atheneum, 1979), 3.

3. Stephanie McCurry, *Confederate Reckoning: Power and Politics in the Civil War* (Cambridge, MA: Harvard University Press, 2010), 2.

4. William H. Freehling and Craig M. Simpson, *Secession Debated: Georgia's Showdown in 1860* (New York: Oxford, 1992), ix.

5. Freehling and Simpson, "Introduction," in *Secession Debated*, ix–x, quote x.

6. Brown's quotation, Freehling and Simpson, xii.

7. Freehling and Simpson, xviii.; for wording of the preamble, see *Georgia (Weekly Macon) Journal and Messenger*, November 4, 1860.

8. Thomas F. Green. Year: 1840; Census Place: Milledgeville, Baldwin, Georgia; Roll: 37; Page: 48; Image, 102; Family History Library Film: 0007042.

9. Freehling and Simpson, xxi.

10. Freehling and Simpson, xxi.

11. Du Bois, 3, 26.

12. Du Bois, 57.

13. Du Bois, 53.

14. McCurry, 1.

15. Drew Gilpin Faust, *This Republic of Suffering: Death and the American Civil War* (New York: Random House, 2008), xi–xii.

16. Matthew Carr, *Sherman's Ghost: Soldiers, Civilians, and the American Way of War* (New York: The New Press, 2015), 75.

17. Carr, 2–3.

18. Faust, xii.

19. Eric Dean Jr., *Shook Over Hell: Post-Traumatic Stress, Vietnam, and the Civil War* (Cambridge, MA: Harvard University Press, 1997), 204.

20. Dennis W. Brandt, *Pathway to Hell: A Tragedy of the American Civil War* (Lincoln: University of Nebraska Press, 2008), 171–72. See also R. Gregory Lande, *Madness, Malingering, & Malfeasance: The Transformation of Psychiatry and the Law in the Civil War Era* (Washington, DC: Potomac Books, 2003); Michael Adams, *Living Hell: The Dark Side of the Civil War* (Baltimore: Johns Hopkins University Press, 2014), chapter 5, "The Edge of Sanity," 108–32.

21. Albert Deutsch, *A History of Military Psychiatry—a Classic Article on the Civil War, World War I, and World War II* (NP: Whitehead Press, 2011), 367, 377–78.

22. "Reports of American Asylums," *American Journal of Insanity* 19, no. 1 (July 1862): 23.

23. "Reports of American Asylums," *American Journal of Insanity* 19, no. 3 (Jan. 1863): 368–69.

24. Alexander Stephens, "Cornerstone" speech, March 21, 1861, Teaching American History Documents, https://teachingamericanhistory.org/library/document /cornerstone-speech/.

25. Georgia Archives, Central State Hospital Medical Case History Files, 025-12-029, RG 3-2683 (R2 V3), APRIL 24, 1861, pp. 20–21. For future reference: "Case History Files." These records are a continuation of the asylum ledger entries that Graham transcribed and we have cited up until this point.

26. "The Bull Run, or Manassas Campaign," *Confederate Military History*, vol. 3, chapter 7, ed. General Clement A. Evans (Atlanta: Confederate Publishing Company, 1899); see also "The Battle of First Manassas (First Bull Run)," National Park Service, www.nps.gov/mana/learn/historyculture/first-manassas.htm; and Bradley M. Gottfried, "An End to Innocence: The First Battle of Manassas," *Hallowed Ground magazine*, Spring 2011, on Civil War Trust, www.civilwar.org/hallowed-ground-magazine/spring -2011/an-end-to-innocence.html.

27. Carr, 35.

28. Anna Maria Green, *The Journal of a Milledgeville Girl: 1861–1867*, ed. James Bonner (Athens: University of Georgia Press, 1964), 14. I have given Anna Green authorship although Bonner is on the cover and is responsible for "thorough skillful editing [that] made a rather disjoined record into a connected and easily read narrative." This

first volume of Anna's diaries was not published until 1964 after a relative sold it to the University of Georgia Press. The second volume, written after her marriage, "was burned by her daughter, Callie Irvin Cook," because it "contained too many references of an intimate nature ever to be made public" (vii). That the Greens lived in the Georgia Asylum Center Building's upper floor is of particular interest here.

29. Case History, R2V3P35, August 22, 1861.

30. "Brady's Photographs: Pictures of the Dead at Antietam," *New York Times*, October 20, 1962.

31. Anna Marie Green Cook, *History of Baldwin County, Georgia* (Anderson, SC: Hearn Co., 1925), 16. Available in Reprint Edition, 1978.

32. "Reports of American Asylums," *American Journal of Insanity* 19, no. 3: 368–69.

33. Case History, R2V3P97, July 14, 1863.

34. Carr, 15. I found the following chronology useful: "Timeline: Civil War & Reconstruction 1861–1877," GEORGIAINFO: An Online Georgia Almanac, http://georgiainfo.galileo.usg.edu/topics/history/article/civil-war-reconstruction-1861-1877/timeline-civil-war-reconstruction.

35. James C. Bonner, *Milledgeville: Georgia's Antebellum Capital* (Milledgeville, GA: Old Capital Press, 2007), 168.

36. Case History, R2V3P97, July 14, 1863.

37. Case History, R2V3P88, March 3, 1863.

38. Case History, R2V3OO94–95, Spring 1963.

39. Case History, R2V3P57, May 26, 1862.

40. Case History, R2V3P98, August 1, 1863.

41. Cook, 38.

42. McCurry, 315–20.

43. McCurry, 323.

44. McCurry, 325.

45. LeeAnn Whites and Alecia P. Long, "Introduction," in *Occupied Women: Gender, Military Occupation, and the American Civil War* (Baton Rouge: Louisiana State University, 2009), 1.

46. Cook, 14, 21, 58, 28, 65, 82.

47. Peter Cranford, *But for the Grace of God: Milledgeville! The Inside Story of the World's Largest Insane Asylum* (Atlanta: Georgia Consumer Council, 1998), 29.

48. William Tecumseh Sherman, *Memoirs of General W.T. Sherman* (New York: Library of America, 1990), 661.

49. Sherman, 649.

50. Sherman, 654.

51. Sherman, 655–56.

52. Sherman, 662.

53. Sherman, 664.

54. Cook, 60–61.

55. Cook, 60–62.

56. Cranford, 30. See also Bonner, 186–93.

57. *Report of the Trustees, Superintendent and Resident Physician of the Lunatic Asylum of the State of Georgia for the Year 1864–65* (Milledgeville, GA: Boughton, Nisbet, Barnes & Moore, State Printers, 1866), 12–13. The total patient population was 290 on October 2, 1864, and 324 on October 2, 1865.

58. Bonner, 182–98.

59. Cook, 63.

60. James H. Nichols (1834–1897), Find a Grave Memorial 20443581, www .findagrave/memorial/20443581.

61. Bonner, 190.

62. Paul K. Graham, *Admission Register of Central State Hospital Milledgeville, Georgia, 1842–1861* (Decatur, GA: The Genealogy Company, 2011), #638, 70; # 820, 99.

63. Carr, 105.

64. Cook, 63.

65. Cook, 63. See Lisa Tendrich Frank, "Bedrooms as Battlefields: The Role of Gender Politics in Sherman's March," in *Occupied Women: Gender, Military Occupation, and the American Civil War*, ed. LeeAnn Whites and Alecia P. Long (Baton Rouge: Louisiana State University, 2009), 33–48, particularly for the resistance among southern elite women that Sherman's March inspired. See also Lisa Tendrich, *The Civil War: Confederate Women and Union Soldiers During Sherman's March* (Baton Rouge: Louisiana State University Press, 2015).

66. Carr, 15.

67. Dean, 55.

68. Dean, 87.

69. Carr, 83–84.

70. Mrs. Campbell Bryce quoted in Peter McCandless, *Moonlight, Madness, and Magnolias: Insanity in South Carolina from the Colonial to the Progressive Era* (Chapel Hill: University of North Carolina Press, 1996), 217.

71. *Mary Chestnut's Civil War*, ed. C. Vann Woodward (New Haven, CT: Yale University Press, 1981), 676, quoted in McCandless, 217.

72. McCandless, 217–18.

73. Case History. R2V3P141.

74. "Reports of American Asylums," *American Journal of Insanity* 21, no. 3 (Jan. 1865): 426, 427.

75. "Reports of American Asylums," *American Journal of Insanity* 21, no. 3 (Jan. 1865): 567–68.

76. Surgeon General Joseph K. Barnes, "Instructions from the Surgeon General Respecting Insane Soldiers," *American Journal of Insanity* 21, no. 4 (April 1865): 462–65.

77. Deutsch, *Military Psychiatry*, 377.

78. Dean, 37.

79. Bonner 193, 197, 199–200.

80. Graham, #820, 70.

81. Kate Nicholes. Year: 1900; Census Place: Militia District 321, Baldwin, Georgia; Page 18; Enumeration District: 008; FHL microfilm: 1240178.

CHAPTER 7

1. W.E.B. Du Bois, *Black Reconstruction in America 1860–1880: Studies in American Negro Life*, ed. A. Meier (New York: Atheneum, 1979), 30.

2. Saidiya Hartman, *Scenes of Subjection: Terror, Slavery, and Self-Making in Nineteenth Century America* (New York: Oxford University Press, 1997), 7.

3. "Polly," Case History V3P215, September 5, 1867.

4. Paul A. Cimbala, *Under the Guardianship of the Nation: The Freedmen's Bureau and the Reconstruction of Georgia, 1865–1870* (Athens: University of Georgia Press, 1997), 47; and Edmund Drago, "Georgia's First Black Voter Registrars During Reconstruction," *Georgia Historical Quarterly* 78, no. 4 (1994): 778, 787.

5. Carl H. Nightingale, *Segregation: A Global History of Divided Cities* (Chicago: University of Chicago Press, 2012), 2–3.

6. Du Bois, 122, 124.

7. Hartman, 4.

8. Anna McCarly (or McCurly), Case History. V3P212, August 20, 1867. All other details from this source.

9. Hartman, "A Note of Method," *Scenes of Subjection*, 10–11.

10. Paul Gilroy, "Living Memory: A Meeting with Toni Morrison," in *Small Acts: Thoughts on the Politics of Black Cultures* (London: Serpent's Tail, 1994), 178.

11. J.V. DeVanne to Dr. C.F. Greene [*sic*: T.F. Green], Superintendent of the State Lunatic Asylum, June 10, 1867, Office of Staff Officers, Surgeon-in-Chief, LS and Register of LR, Vol 52, September 1865–July 1867, M1903, Roll 26, RG 105, NARA. National Archives and Records Administration, quoted in James Downs, *Sick from Freedom: African American Illness and Suffering During the Civil War and Reconstruction* (Oxford: Oxford University Press, 2012), 150.

12. "Report of the Majority and Minority of the Committee on the Lunatic Asylum," 1866, 7.

13. Alex Lichtenstein, *Twice the Work of Free Labor: The Political Economy of Convict Labor in the New South* (London: Verso, 1996), 27–28; Howell Cobb, Mark Cooper, and John Fitten to Charles Jenkins, "Report of the Committee on the Location of the Penitentiary," November 2, 1866, Box 53, Governor's Incoming Correspondence, Executive Department Papers, GDAH, pp. 4, 7; Principal Keeper, *Report*, 1872–73, p. 21; Principal Keeper, *Report*, 1869, pp. 14–15.

14. James C. Bonner, "The Georgia Penitentiary at Milledgeville," *Georgia Historical Quarterly* 55, no. 3 (Fall 1971): 303–28.

15. Lichtenstein, 29.

16. Lichtenstein, 48, 18–19.

17. Downs, 150–51, quoting J.V. DeVanne to Dr. T.F. Greene, Superintendent of the State Lunatic Asylum, June 10, 1867, Office of Staff Officers, Surgeon-in-Chief, LS and Register of LF, vol. 52, Sept 1865–July 1867, M1903, Roll 26, RG 105, NARA.

18. Downs, 151, quoting J.V. DeVanne to M.F. Barres, June 5, 1867, Augusta GA, LR October 1865–May 1868, Roll 49, M1903, Frame 698.

19. See Case History. V3P212–231, August 20–December 31, 1867.

20. Downs, 149.

21. Downs, 22 (quoting Howard, *Autobiography of Oliver Otis Howard, vol. 2* (New York: Baker and Taylor, 1907), 363–64.

22. Quoted in Downs, 22.

23. Case Histories, Minnie Pulley V3P212, Rachel Luckey V3P213, Poe White V3P214, all August 22, 1867; Jane Campbell V3P214, August 24, 1867.

24. Case Histories, Nathan Grant and Poe White, V3P214, August 22, 1867.

25. Case Histories, Lewis Griffin, V3P218–19 September 14, 1867; Henny Williams V3P222 October 8, 1867.

26. Statistics are taken from "TABLE Showing the Number of Male and Female Pay, Partial Pay and Pauper Patients, Mental Condition, the Date of Reception, their Age at Time of Reception, Date of Discharge, Date of Death, and Disease," from a running tally of patients beginning April 26, 1844, that continued in successive annual reports. This one is from the Annual Report 1867–1868, with 1867 patients listed on pp. 30–36.

27. Christina Sharpe, *In the Wake: On Blackness and Being* (Durham: Duke University Press, 2016), 3, 10, 8, 4.

28. Sharpe, 13–14.

29. Case Histories, Emily Key V3P215 August 27, 1867; Alsey Redding V3P229 September 30, 1867; Rose Harris V3P215 September 5, 1867.

30. Quoted in Carol Anderson, *White Rage: The Unspoken Truth of Our Racial Divide* (New York: Bloomsbury, 2016), 18.

CHAPTER 8

1. Saidiya Hartman, *Scenes of Subjection: Terror, Slavery, and Self-Making in Nineteenth Century America* (New York: Oxford University Press, 1997), 11.

2. M. NourbeSe Philip, *ZONG!* (Hartford, CT: Wesleyan University Press, 2008), 26, quoted in Christina Sharpe, *In the Wake: On Blackness and Being* (Durham, NC: Duke University Press, 2016), 10.

3. Sally Cunnigan, Case History. V3P418. June 10, 1873.

4. This information on lychings from 1867 to 1880 in Georgia comes from a list compiled by historian E.M. Beck at the University of Georgia that complements the list provided by W. Fitzhugh Brundage in the appendix of his book *Lynching in the New South: Georgia and Virginia 1880–1930* (Urbana: University of Illinois Press, 1993), 270–80.

5. Jonathan M. Bryant, "Ku Klux Klan in the Reconstruction Era," *New Georgia Encyclopedia*, May 6, 2017.

6. Lewis, Case History. V3P288. September 22, 1870.

7. Mrs. Eliza Busy, Case History. V3P224-24.

8. Miss Mary E. Bynum, Case History V3P226.

9. James Teat, Case History. V3P228.

10. Testimony of John B. Gordon, Washington, DC, July 27, 1871, *Report of the Joint Select Committee to Inquire into the Condition of Affairs of the Late Insurrectionary States, Made to the Two Houses of Congress, Georgia Volume 6* (Washington: Government Printing Office, 1872), 308, https://archive.org/details/reportofjointsel06unit/page/n6. Reports from Georgia were in Volumes 6 and 7. Thanks to Ashley Kale, who served as my student assistant when I was the Newell Visiting Scholar at Georgia College and State University spring semester of 2015. She compiled the data by county from the Joint Select Committee report and Beck's list of lynchings as it overlaid with African American patients at the GLA from 1870 to 1875.

11. Testimony of George P. Burnett, Washington, DC, July 11, 1871, *Report of the Joint Select Committee*, Vol. 6, 67–68.

12. Edward Pollard, *The Lost Cause: A New Southern History of the War of the Confederates* (New York: E.B. Treat & Co., 1866), NP (last third to last paragraph of the book), https://archive.org/stream/lostcauseanewso01pollgoog#page/n752/mode/2up, 753.

13. Edward Pollard, *The Lost Cause Regained* (New York: G.W. Carleton & Co., 1868), 13–14, https://archive.org/details/lostcauseregain03pollgoog/page/n16.

14. This "race war" concept inspires increasingly violent racist actions today. For example, the war was ongoing on June 17, 2015, when a young white racist, Dylann Roof, opened fire on a Bible study group at Emanuel Church in Charleston, South Carolina, killing nine worshippers, the site picked deliberately for its emancipatory history and his victims' exemplary characters, which he thought would help him succeed in his intent to provoke a war between the races. The March 15, 2019, attack in New Zealand of Muslim worshippers by a white supremacist was also intended to start a race war; the shooter broadcast the slaughter on social media to make the act even more egregiously provocative.

15. "Records of the Assistant Commissioner for the State of Georgia," The Freedmen's Bureau Online: Records of the Bureau of Refugees, Freedmen and Abandoned Lands (National Archives Microfilm Publication M1903, 90 rolls); Records of the Bureau of Refugees, Freedmen and Abandoned Lands, Record Group 105, National Archives, Washington, DC, http://freedmensbureau.com/georgia/gaoutrages2.htm#Athens%201867, accessed on July 13, 2019.

16. "1865–66 Report of Persons Murdered in District of Brunswick, Georgia," Freedmen's Bureau Online, www.bbc.com/news/world-asia-47579243.

17. Sharpe.

18. My gratitude to E.M. Beck, who generously shared with me his unpublished database of lynchings in Georgia between 1867 and 1880. E.M. Beck, "Database of

Lynchings in Georgia, 1867–1880." It lists lynchings in Georgia alphabetized by county and providing citations of newspaper sources and summaries. There are seventy-one incidents, some with multiple victims. Subsequent reference: "Beck's list." My own attempt to understand this history of Georgia Lunatic Asylum patient-inmates in the postbellum years also draws on Beck and Tolnay's 1995 *A Festival of Violence: An Analysis of Southern Lynchings 1882–1930* (Urbana: University of Illinois Press, 1995), and W. Fitzhugh Brundage's 1993 *Lynching in the New South: Georgia and Virginia, 1880–1930*, both of which build on the heroic documentation that formed the basis of international campaigns against lynching in the late nineteenth and early twentieth centuries. Most of these sources begin in the 1880s, making Beck's list from 1867 to 1880 in Georgia immensely helpful to this discussion.

19. Equal Justice Initiative, "Lynching in America: Confronting the Legacy of Racial Terror," 3rd ed. (Montgomery, AL: The Equal Justice Initiative, 2017), https://lynchinginamerica.eji.org/report/, accessed on July 13, 2019.

20. Equal Justice Initiative, "Lynching in America," https://lynchinginamerica.eji.org/report/, accessed on July 13, 2019.

21. Marilee Creelan, "Columbia County," *New Georgia Encyclopedia*, October 31, 2018, accessed July 17, 2019.

22. Beck's list; New York *Herald*, September 9, 1868, p. 7 (GenealogyBank.com); Columbia (SC) *Daily Phoenix*, September 9, 1868 (ChroniclingAmeria.loc.gov); Memphis (TN) *Daily Appeal*, September 17, 1868 (ChroniclingAmrica.loc.gov), Macon *Weekly Telegraph*, September 18, 1868 (Macon Historic Newspapers); Albany, NY, *Daily Albany Argus*, September 28, 1868 (GenealogyBank.com).

23. Paul A. Cimbala, *Under the Guardianship of the Nation: The Freedmen's Bureau and the Reconstruction of Georgia, 1865–1870* (Athens: University of Georgia Press, 1997), 109.

24. Lee W. Fomwalt, "Camilla Massacre," *New Georgia Encyclopedia*, August 1, 2016, accessed May 22, 2017.

25. Jonathan M. Bryant, "Ku Klux Klan in the Reconstruction Era," *New Georgia Encyclopedia*, May 6, 2017, accessed May 9, 2017.

26. Beck's list: Albany (NY) *Evening Journal*, July 28, 1869, p. 2 (GenealogyBank.com); Macon *Weekly Telegraph*, July 30, 1869, p. 4 (GenealogyBank.com); Raleigh (NC) *Weekly North Carolina Standard*, August 4, 1869, p. 3 (ChroniclingAmeria.loc.gov).

27. Beck's list: Columbia (SC) *Daily Phoenix*, December 17, 1869, p. 1 (ChroniclingAmerica.loc.gov); Macon *Weekly Telegraph*, Decemer 21, 1869, p. 6 (GenealogyBank.com).

28. Lucy Lofley, Case History. V4P366. October 24, 1872.

29. According to Beck's list, this incident was covered in the New Orleans *Times* on December 29, 1867, p. 1; the Augusta *Daily Constitutionalist* on December 31, 1867, p. 2; the Memphis *Daily Avalanche* on January 1, 1868, p. 1; and the Harrisburg, PA, *Patriot* on January 21, 1868, p. 5 (all in GenealogyBank.com).

30. Beck's list, covered in the Milledgeville *Federal Union* on November 22, 1870, p. 2; Macon *Weekly Telegraph and Messenger* on November 22, 1870, p. 6 (Georgia Historical Newspapers), and the Sandersonville *Central Georgian* on November 23, 1870, p. 2.

31. Beck's list, covered in the Macon *Telegraph and Messenger* on September 22, 1871, p. 2; Williamsport, PA, *Daily Gazette and Bulletin* on September 23, 1871, p. 1; Columbus *Weekly Enquirer* on September 26, 1871, p. 2; and Galveston, TX, *Daily News* on September 29, 1871, p. 1: from NewspaperArchive.com or GenealogyBank.com.

32. As a result of Georgia's refusal to pass the Fifteenth Amendment, Congress for the second time barred Georgia representatives, and by December 1869 had resumed military rule under General Alfred Terry. January 1870, Gen. Terry expelled the white legislators who had replaced the expelled African Americans. This doubly reconstituted legislative assembly then approved the Fifteenth Amendment, thus again allowing Georgia representation in Congress, and with a white-majority legislature that would bring on white rule.

33. Alex Lichtenstein, *Twice the Work of Free Labor: The Political Economy of Convict Labor in the New South* (London: Verso, 1996), 61.

34. Lichtenstein, 38.

35. Brundage, 105–6.

36. 1868 AR, 8.

37. Eric Dean, Jr., *Shook Over Hell: Post-Traumatic Stress, Vietnam, and the Civil War* (Cambridge, MA: Harvard University Press, 1997), 37.

38. Simon Gikandi, *Slavery and the Culture of Taste* (Princeton, NJ: Princeton University, 2011), x.

39. Jason Silverstein, "I Don't Feel Your Pain," *Slate*, June 23, 2013.

40. Hartman, 14.

CHAPTER 9

1. James C. Bonner, *Milledgeville: Georgia's Antebellum Capital* (Milledgeville, GA: Old Capital Press, 2007), 218.

2. Alex Lichtenstein, *Twice the Work of Free Labor: The Political Economy of Convict Labor in the New South* (London: Verso, 1996), 47.

3. Carl H. Nightingale, *Segregation: A Global History of Divided Cities* (Chicago: University of Chicago Press, 2012), 2–3.

4. Tera Hunter, *To 'Joy My Freedom: Southern Black Women's Lives and Labors After the Civil War* (Cambridge, MA: Harvard University Press, 1997), 48.

5. For uses of "small stories" as archival "micro-narratives" of empire that give particularity and scale to wider national, imperial, and global histories, see Simon Gikandi, *Slavery and the Culture of Taste* (Princeton, NJ: Princeton University Press, 2011), and Linda Colley, *Captives: Britain, Empire and the World* (New York: Anchor, 2004), 12, 17.

6. "A WITLESS WOMAN'S STORY," Atlanta *Constitution* (1881–2001): August 2, 1882, ProQuest Historical Newspapers Atlanta *Constitution* (1868–1939), 7. All quotations are taken from this source.

7. Sue Peyton, Central State Hospital, Medical Case Histories, vol. IV, 367; Georgia Department of Public Health, Milledgeville, GA, 350/19.

8. Craven R. Peyton, 1860 Bibb County, GA, 571: Susan Peyton, age 19 in Craven R. Peyton's household with four Peyton brothers. Year: 1860; Census Place: Vineville, Bibb, Georgia; Roll: M653_111; Page: 571; Family History Library Film: 803111.

9. Craven R. Peyton married Ann M Riddel, July 12, 1857, according to HuntingforBears.com. Georgia Marriages, 1699–1944 [database online]. Provo, UT, USA: Ancestry.com Operations Inc, 2004.

10. For military service, Craven R. Peyton, Roster of Confederate Soldiers of Georgia, 1861–1865, Historical Data Systems, comp. *U.S. Civil War Soldier Records and Profiles, 1861–1865* [database online]. Provo, UT, USA: Ancestry.com Operations Inc, 2009. Confederate Compiled Service Records. Card # 10 in his service record indicates that he died at Palmyra Hospital on March 9, 1863, after being transferred from Chimborazo Hospital, both hospitals in Richmond.

11. Susan Peyton. Year: 1870; Census Place: Subdivision 8, Bibb, Georgia; Roll: M593_136; Page: 614A; Family History Library Film: 545635. She is listed as a domestic servant. John B. Peyton Year: 1870; Census Place: Subdivision 8, Bibb, Georgia; Roll: M593_136; Page: 638B; Family History Library Film: 545635.

12. See *The Roth Home 1902–1993*, which lists its patients, taken from records in the Bibb County Courthouse. (See MGRL-GH from the Macon County library collection, correspondence February 15, 2017.)

13. In an attempt to find out the identity of the doctor who impregnated Sue, I cross-referenced Atlanta city directories with the advertisements for physicians in Macon City Directories for the appropriate years. I did not find any matches.

14. Belle Mitchell. Year: 1880; Census Place: District 1085 Bibb, Georgia; Roll: 134; Family History film: 1254134; Page: 131A; Enumeration District: 012; Image: 0703.

15. 1882 Atlanta City Directory, GA Archives microfilm 290/31, pp. 198, 417.

16. Tera Hunter, *To 'Joy My Freedom: Southern Black Women's Lives and Labors After the Civil War* (Cambridge, MA: Harvard University Press, 1997), 23, 20.

17. Hunter, 57–58.

18. Tera W. Hunter, "Domination and Resistance: The Politics of Wage Household Labor in New South Atlanta," in *Labor History* (1993), 205.

19. Susan Peyton, Central State Hospital Medical Case Histories, vol. 7, 263; Georgia Department of Public Health, Milledgeville, GA; 350/19.

20. Stephen Peters. Year: 1900; Census Place: Atlanta Ward 4, Fulton, Georgia; Roll: 199; Page: 35A; Enumeration District: 0065; FHL microfilm: 1240199. Also living there are Mattie B. [Stafford] Holsey, with her husband, Dr. James H. Holsey. Holsey was the son of a distinguished Methodist bishop. James was educated at Clark University in Atlanta, where he paid his way working as a bricklayer then earned his DDS in dentistry at Howard University in Washington, DC. James and Mattie, married in either 1892 or 1894, in 1900 were in Atlanta living with Mattie's family. Anderson Family Tree database (Ancestry.com: accessed February 28, 2017), "James H. Holsey."

21. Lichtenstein, 60.

22. Sarah Haley, *No Mercy Here: Gender, Punishment, and the Making of Jim Crow Modernity* (Chapel Hill: University of North Carolina Press, 2016), 29–30.

23. Haley, 30.

24. Haley, 21.

CHAPTER 10

1. *Plessy v. Ferguson*, 163 U.S. 537, p. 544.

2. *Health & Place* devoted two issues on asylum geographies, the first on Space, Place, and the Asylum, edited by Deborah C. Park and John P. Radford—see their "Space, Place, and the Asylum: an introduction," *Health & Place* 3 (1997): 71–72; a second in 2000 on Post-asylum Geographies, see Chris Philo, "Post-asylum Geographies: an introduction," *Health & Place* 6 (2000), 135–36.

3. *Report of the Trustees, Superintendent and Resident Physician, Treasurer, Steward, Etc. of the Lunatic Asylum of the State of Georgia from December 1, 1873 to December 1, 1874* (Savannah: J.H. Estill, 1874), 11. Hereafter AR 1874.

4. *Report of the Trustees, Superintendent and Resident Physician, Treasurer, Superintendent, Etc of the Lunatic Asylum of the State of Georgia from December 1, 1872 to December 1, 1873* (Atlanta: W.A. Hemphill, Public Printer, 1873), 12. Hereafter, AR 1873.

5. AR 1874, 11.

6. Peter Cranford, *But for the Grace of God: Milledgeville! The Inside Story of the World's Largest Insane Asylum* (Atlanta: Georgia Consumer Council, 1998), 35–36.

7. See Cranford's account of the investigation, 35–36.

8. Cranford, 35–36.

9. Quoted in Cranford, 36.

10. Anna Marie Green Cook, *History of Baldwin County, Georgia* (Anderson, SC: Hearn Co., 1925), 96–97. Available in Reprint Edition, 1978.

11. *Report of the Trustees, Superintendent and Resident Physician, Treasurer and Steward of the Lunatic Asylum of the State of Georgia from January 1, 1870 to October 1, 1871* (Atlanta: Printed by the Public Printer, 1871), 8. Hereafter AR 1871. The Georgia Archives has digitized annual reports for the years 1864–65, 1867–68, 1870–71, 1872–73, 1873–74, 1878–79, 1885–87, 1892–93, 1896–97.

12. Paul Graham, *Admission Register of Central State Hospital Milledgeville, Georgia, 1842–1861* (Decatur, GA: The Genealogy Company, 2011), #104, 11; #20, 3; #41, 5; 132, 13; #126, 13; #202, 19.

13. *Report of the Trustees and Superintendent and Resident Physician of the Lunatic Asylum of the State of Georgia from December 1, 1874 to December 1, 1875*, 11. Hereafter AR 1875.

14. AR 1875, 10.

15. AR 1870, 24.

16. Numbers taken from AR 1874, 21; AR 1886, 8–9; AR 1897, 10–16.

17. AR 1871, 5.

18. AR 1871, 5, 6, 7.

19. AR 1897, 10–11.

20. Cranford, 38.

21. *Reports of the Trustees and Officers of the Lunatic Asylum of the State of Georgia From December 1, 1878 to September 30, 1879* (Macon, GA: J.W. Burke & Co., Printers and Binders, 1879), 11–12. Hereafter AR 1879.

22. Colony Farm reported on in AR 1903, 9; AR 1900, 27–29.

23. AR 1879, 4, 11, 12, 16, 28.

24. AR 1874, 25.

25. AR 1879, 28.

26. AR 1879, 22.

27. AR 1886, 49, 57.

28. AR 1886, 4.

29. AR 1886, 29.

30. Alex Lichtenstein, *Twice the Work of Free Labor: The Political Economy of Convict Labor in the New South* (London: Verso, 1996), 60, Table 3.1: "Number of Convicts in Georgia Penitentiary, by Race, Selected Years," sourced from the Georgia Principal Keeper's *Reports*. The years for which Lichtenstein provides data do not always match with the Georgia Asylum annual reports to which I have access. In that case, the actual year of convict data is given in the first column, with convict totals marked with an asterisk.

31. AR 1868, 15; AR 1879, 17; AR 1886, 39; AR 1893, 33; AR 1897, 60.

32. Lichtenstein, 60.

33. AR 1871, 5. There is a chart of numbers of "colored" patients in AR 1886, 28, with figures that differ from the actual 1871 report.

34. AR 1886, 15.

35. The data on Georgia convicts come from a chart in Lichtenstein, 60.

36. *Plessy v. Ferguson*.

CHAPTER 11

1. Steve M. Blevins and Michael S. Bronze, "Robert Koch and the 'Golden Age' of Bacteriology," *International Journal of Infectious Diseases*, 14 (2010): e745–47.

2. Blevins and Bronze, e745–47.

3. Blevins and Bronze, e745.

4. Blevins and Bronze, e744–45.

5. Robert Koch, quoted in David McBride, *From TB to AIDS: Epidemics among Urban Blacks since 1900* (Albany: State University of New York Press, 1991), 11.

6. Nancy Tomes, *The Gospel of Germs: Men, Women, and the Microbe in American Life* (Cambridge, MA: Harvard University Press, 1998), 2.

7. Roy Porter, "Medical Science," "Introduction," *The Cambridge History of Medicine*, ed. Roy Porter (Cambridge: Cambridge University Press, 2006), 136–75, 1.

8. Nancy Malone in Paul Graham, *Admission Register of Central State Hospital Milledgeville, Georgia, 1842–1861* (Decatur, GA: The Genealogy Company, 2011), 4, 5 for

quote. The rest are from the first 100 patients in Graham's transcriptions of the early ledgers.

9. See, for example, "Acute diarrhoeal diseases in complex emergencies: CRITICAL STEPS—Decision-making for preparedness and response," World Health Organization Global Task Force on Cholera Control (Geneva, WHO, 2010).

10. Dorothy Roberts, *Fatal Invention: How Science, Politics, and Big Business Recreate Race in the Twenty-First Century* (New York: The New Press, 2011), x, 5.

11. Supt. T.O. Powell, "Special Report on the Increase of Insanity and Its Supposed Causes, Etc., State Lunatic Asylum Near Milledgeville, Georgia, October 1, 1886, to the Honorable Board of Trustees," 19, 12.

12. Powell, 1886, 13.

13. Powell, 1886, 13–14, 15.

14. Catherine de Lange, "How Sickle-Cell Fends Off Malaria," *Life*, May 5, 2011, www.newscientist.com/article/dn20450-how-sickle-cell-carriers-fend-off-malaria/.

15. Powell, 1886, 14.

16. Quoted in Gerald Grob, *Edward Jarvis and the Medical World of Nineteenth-Century America* (Knoxville: University of Tennessee Press, 1978), 72.

17. Powell, 1886, 4–5.

18. Powell, 1886, 6.

19. Edward Shorter, *A History of Psychiatry: From the Era of the Asylum to the Age of Prozac* (New York: John Wiley & Sons, 1997), 53–59.

20. Powell, 1886, 11.

21. Powell, 1886, 8.

22. Powell, 1886, 8.

23. Powell, 1886, 10.

24. Shorter, 93.

25. McBride, 11.

26. Theophilus O. Powell, M.D., "The Increase of Insanity and Tuberculosis in the Southern Negro Since 1860, and Its Alliance, and Some of the Supposed Causes" (Chicago: American Medical Association Press, 1896), 5–6, reprinted from the *Journal of the American Medical Association*, December 5, 1896, and read in the Section on Neurology and Medical Jurisprudence, at the Forty-Seventh Annual Meeting of the American Medical Association, held at Atlanta, GA, May 5–8, 1896.

27. Powell, 1896, 5, 6–7. The entire response from Hopkins is described in this section.

28. Tera Hunter, *To 'Joy My Freedom: Southern Black Women's Lives and Labors After the Civil War* (Cambridge, MA: Harvard University Press, 1997), 191–93.

29. "Sketch of the Hopkins Family of McIntosh County dictated in 1911 by Miss Ida W. Hopkins," Elizabeth F. Hopkins Collection, Hopkins-Gignilliat Family Papers, Georgia Archives microfilm 65/46. These papers are part of the Hopkins Collection at the Thomasville Genealogical, Historical, and Fine Arts Library in Thomasville.

30. Robert Scott Davis, "Andersonville Prison," *New Georgia Encyclopedia*, June 6, 2017, accessed October 25, 2017; Robert Scott Davis, "The Horror," *Andersonville Civil War Prison* (Charleston, SC: The History Press Sesquicentennial Series, 2010). All details from these sources.

31. Testimony of Dr. G.S. Hopkins (*sic*: T.S.), Medical Testimony in "The Trial of Henry Wirz," 376–79, in *Index to the Executive Documents of the House of Representatives of the United States in the Second Session of the Fortieth Congress*, www.loc.gov/rr/frd/Military_Law/pdf/Wirz-trial.pdf.

32. Hopkins, Testimony, 378.

33. John Duffy, *The Sanitarians: A History of Public Health* (Urbana: University of Illinois Press, 1990), 147. For information on Dr. Hopkins's life in Thomasville, see also Mrs. Langdon S. Flowers et al., *Thomasville, Georgia: A Place Apart* (Dallas, TX: Taylor Publishing Co., 1985), 38; and Warren William Rogers, *Thomas County: 1865–1900* (Tallahassee: Florida State University Press, 1973), 439–44.

34. Duffy, 6, 4.

35. Rogers, 441–43.

36. Jan Hebbard and Kaylynn Washnock, "Sites of Wellness, Wilderness and Reinvention" and "Jekyll Island: From Millionaires to the Masses," in "Seeing Georgia: Changing Visions of Tourism in the Modern South," *New Georgia Encyclopedia*, August 18, 2016, accessed September 20, 2017; Rogers, 441; www.jekyllclub.com/.

37. Henry Grady, Atlanta *Constitution*, April 21, 1882.

38. T.S. Hopkins, M.D., *Thomasville: Winter Home for Invalids* (self-published, Thomasville, GA, nd), 6, 4. This source reproduces Hopkins' letter to Rev. S.A. Heilner, pastor of a Methodist Church in Media, PA, reprinted from the *Atlanta Medical Record*, October 1882; an extract from a letter to Dr. Alfred R. Crain, Richfield Springs, New York, July 27, 1884, with similar arguments, and an extract from a "reference hand book of the medical sciences." The Thomasville Board of Trade issued its own version, minus consumption: *The Winter Resort Among the Pines*, no date, but with pictures from 1904, extolling the Country Club of Thomasville and its new golf club.

39. Hopkins, *Thomasville: Winter Home*, 8.

40. Flowers et al., 48.

41. Hunter, *To 'Joy My Freedom*, 201.

42. Powell, 1895, 3.

43. T.O. Powell, M.D., "A Sketch of Psychiatry in the Southern States," Presidential Address, fifty-third annual meeting of the American Medico-Psychological Association, Baltimore, MD, May 1897, published in the *American Journal of Insanity*, 54 (1897): 51.

44. "Edward Cowles (1837–1919)," *American Journal of Psychiatry* 173, no. 10, 967–68.

45. Transactions of the Medical Association of Georgia, 1878–1902 (Powell consistently notes 1867 as his initial year), housed at the Atlanta History Center.

46. AR 1894, 23.

47. *Annual Report of the Trustees of the Georgia Lunatic Asylum for the Fiscal Year from Sept 1, 1896 to September 1, 1897* (Augusta: Chronicle Job Printing, 1897), 20. AR 1897 hereafter.

48. AR 1897, 18, 11.

49. AR 1897, 18, "Table Showing Results of Post-Mortem Examinations from June 20 1896 to Sept 1, 1897" (interspersed with photographs), 32–58.

50. AR 1897, 27.

51. AR 1897, 20, 22, 27.

52. AR 1897, 29.

53. AR 1897, 20.

54. "Emancipation and Insanity in the Negro," *American Journal of Insanity* 53, no. 441 (1897). See J.F. Miller, "The Effects of Emancipation upon the Mental and Physical Health of the Negro of the South," Electronic Edition, Documenting the American South, University of North Carolina, docsouth.unc.edu/nc/miller/miller.html. Published originally in the *North Carolina Medical Journal*.

55. Miller, 5.

CHAPTER 12

1. "Dark Night Blues," Blind Willie McTell, *The Best of Blind Willie McTell*, Audio, 2004.

2. Flannery O'Connor, *The Violent Bear It Away* (New York: Farrar, Straus and Giroux, 2007), 62.

3. AR 1893, 88–97.

4. "Jim Crow Cards" were not playing cards, but hair combs made from repurposed weaving frames.

5. AR 1893, 23.

6. AR 1893, 5–8.

7. AR 1894, 6–7.

8. AR 1894, 12.

9. AR 1897, 9–10.

10. AR 1900, 32.

11. AR 1898, 25–27.

12. Remsen Crawford, "Asylum on Fire: Complete Loss," Atlanta *Constitution*, November 10, 1897, p. 1.

13. "A TERRIBLE SCENE: The Burning of the Northern Ohio Insane Asylum: Six Hundred Lunatics Turned out/Excitement and Terror of the Patients," Cleveland *Herald*, September 25, 1872, reprinted in the Atlanta *Constitution*. There were gruesome deaths in the Ohio fire that did not happen in Georgia.

14. AR 1898, 27.

15. Georgia Department of Public Health, Central State Hospital, Admissions register, vol. 6, pp. 44–45 and 198 (Arnold and Luckie) Georgia Records Group

26-12-29; Fulton County Ordinary Court Minutes Book C, 1876–1882, pp. 642–44 (Arnold, viewed and copied from FamilySearch.org, July 5, 2018); Zack T. Reid, U.S. Bureau of the Census, Population Schedules, 1880 Fulton County, Georgia, p. 307. Viewed and copied from Ancestry.com, July 5, 2018.

16. Augusta University, "MCG Catalogue1893–94 PDF," Medical Department, University of Georgia, Augusta Georgia Session 1983–94, 62nd Annual Announcement, lists both W.H. Doughty, MD (Sr.), and W.H. Doughty, Jr., MD, on page 2, note on Doughty Jr. joining Pathology on p. 4, https://augusta.openrepository.com/handle /10675.2/617587.

17. "Dr. William Henry Doughty, Jr. (1856–1923), Dean, 1910–1923, History of the Medical College of Georgia, 1910–1923," Augusta University, www.augusta.edu /library/greenblatt/history/1822-1828.php.

18. Robert L. Blackly and Judith M. Harrington, *Bones in the Basement: Postmortem Racism in Nineteenth Century Medical Training* (Washington, DC: Smithsonian Press, 1997), flyleaf.

19. Bess Lovejoy, "Meet Grandison Harris, the Grave Robber Enslaved (and then Employed) by the Georgia Medical College," Smithsonian.com, May 6, 2014, 3.

20. AR 1900, 33; "Table Showing Results of Post-Mortem Examinations from September 1, 1807 to Septmber 1, 1898," 34–56; "Table Showing Results of Investigation of Negro Brains," 58–59, summaries of 146 examinations.

21. "Lunatic Pulls Pistol and Fires on Dr. Powell," Atlanta *Constitution*, January 5, 1898, 1.

22. "OSBORN CASE TODAY. The Case of Schrader's Murderer Will Be Called This Morning. INSANITY WILL BE PLEADED. Case Will Be the First One Called and It is Probably That It Will be Tried at Once," Atlanta *Constitution* (1881–1945), November 16, 1896; ProQuest p. 3. Note: the articles use both spellings of Osborne and Osborn.

23. "Dr. Hugh Hagan on Osborn," Atlanta *Constitution* (1881–1945), October 14, 1896; ProQuest., p. 3.

24. "BEN OSBORN GROWS WORSE Schrader's Murderer Has Become Violent in His Cell," Atlanta *Constitution* (1881–1945), October 17, 1896, p. 9; ProQuest.

25. "HIS FAST IS BROKEN. Osborn, Slayer of Schrader, Resumes His Former Eating Manner. HIS FIRST SUNDAY IN JAIL. He Declines the Eggs Because the Shells Had Been Removed. STILL DEMANDS RETURN OF HIS SOUL. Prosecution May Contend that Osborn Killed Schrader Because the Latter Had Him Discharged," Atlanta *Constitution* (1881–1945), October 12, 1896; ProQuest, p. 5.

26. "Lunatic Osborne Writes a Letter," Atlanta *Constitution*, January 6, 1898, Proquest, p. 5.

27. "OSBORNE MAY BE NEAR AUGUSTA: ESCAPED LUNATIC, HEAVILY ARMED, PASSES," Atlanta *Constitution* (1881–1945), January 14, 1898; ProQuest, p. 2.

28. "U.S. Diplomacy and Yellow Journalism, 1895–1898," Office of the Historian, U.S. Department of State, https://history.state.gov/milestones/1866-1898/yellow -journalism, accessed November 8, 2017; "Yellow journalism," *Encyclopaedia Britannica Online*, Encyclopaedia Britannica Inc., 2017. Accessed November 7, 2017.

29. "Nellie Bly," Biography.com, www.biography.com/people/Nellie-bly-9216680, accessed November 8, 2017.

30. James Baldwin, *The First Next Time* (New York: Dial Press, 1963). Thanks to Faulkner scholar Jay Watson for the Faulkner and fire connection.

CHAPTER 13

1. T.O. Powell, "Marriage, Heredity and Its Relations to Insanity and Allied Morbid Conditions" (Atlanta: Franklin Printing and Publishing Company, 1901), 5–6.

2. Patsy Yeager, *Dirt and Desire: Reconstructing Southern Women's Writing 1930–1990* (Chicago: University of Chicago Press, 2000), 13, 15.

3. AR 1893, 22.

4. AR 1893, 76–77. As one measure, $7,288.18 in 1893 is equivalent in purchasing power to about $207,424.03 in 2019, according to the CPI Inflation Calculator, www .in2013dollars.com/us/inflation/1893?amount=7288.18.

5. AR 1893, 17, 20.

6. AR 1893, 3.

7. AR 1893, 118–19.

8. AR 1899, 30.

9. *Annual Report of the Board of Trustees of the Georgia State Sanitarium Near Milledgeville for the Year Ending September 1, 1900* (Augusta: Chronicle Printing Company, 1900), 6.

10. AR 1900, photos on pages 60 and 78, hogs on 39, an African American man standing beside a hanging carcass of a hog on 103, its title "Hog Raised at Sanitarium," and a severe picture of the rebuilt colored building, 32.

11. Talitha L. LeFlouria, *Chained in Silence: Women and Convict Labor in the New South* (Chapel Hill: University of North Carolina Press, 2015); Sarah Haley, *No Mercy Here: Gender, Punishment, and the Making of Jim Crow Modernity* (Chapel Hill: University of North Carolina Press, 2016); see LeFlouria, 147, for opening of the Georgia Prison Farm.

12. See Lichtenstein's chart, Alex Lichtenstein, *Twice the Work of Free Labor: The Political Economy of Convict Labor in the New South* (London: Verso, 1996), 60.

13. Haley, 3.

14. Haley, 4.

15. Powell, "Marriage, Heredity and Its Relations," 1–2. Read before the Georgia Medical Association, April 1901.

16. Powell, "Marriage, Heredity and Its Relations," 9.

17. Powell, "Marriage, Heredity and Its Relations," 5.

18. Edward Black, *War Against the Weak: Eugenics and America's Campaign to Create a Master Race* (Washington, DC: Dialogue Press, 2012), 64.

19. Black, 43.

20. "Report of Trustee Nisbet," AR 1900, 32–38.

21. AR 1900, 33.

22. Marjoria O'Rorke, *Haven on the Hill: A History of North Carolina's Dorothea Dix Hospital* (Raleigh, NC: Office of Archives and History, 2010), 23–24, 16.

23. AR 1900, 33–34.

24. AR 1900, 34.

25. AR 1900, 34.

26. *Plessy v. Ferguson*, Oyez, www.oyez.org/cases/1850-1900/163us537, accessed July 22, 2019.

27. AR 1900, 35.

28. LeFlouria, 142–43.

29. AR 1900, 36–38.

30. AR 1900, 36–38.

31. AR 1900, 36.

32. THE MANLY PORTABLE CONVICT CAR, printed for Manly Jail Works, Dalton, GA, in 1915. See Friends of Central State Hospital Facebook page.

33. Peter Cranford, *But for the Grace of God: Milledgeville! The Inside Story of the World's Largest Insane Asylum* (Atlanta: Georgia Consumer Council, 1998).

34. "Insanity: Mental Illness Among Negroes Exceeds Whites, Overcrowds Already Jammed 'Snake Pits,'" *Ebony* (April 1949): 19–23.

CHAPTER 14

1. Cedric J. Robinson, *Forgeries of Memory & Meaning: Blacks & the Regimes of Race in American Film and Theater Before World War II* (Chapel Hill: University of North Carolina, 2007), 3–4.

2. Paul Gilroy, *The Black Atlantic: Modernity and Double Consciousness* (Cambridge, MA: Harvard University Press, 1993), 38. For more on Gilroy's influence, see Lucy Evans, "The Black Atlantic: Exploring Gilroy's Legacy," *Atlantic Studies*, 6: 2, 255–68.

3. Names in these case histories are changed to protect their families' privacy and as a requirement of my access to these materials. But I have been able to use the names to gain more information of who they were through census and other records. Archival citations are accurate except for names. (The names of patients I have used from ledgers are accurate.)

4. Gilroy, 36.

5. "Stork Hardly," Central State Hospital Medical Case Records, February 1909–November 1926, Public Health Central State Hospital, RG-SG-26-12-048,

Vol. 2193, April to August 1912, 144–52; pp. 148, 145. Hereafter, "Hardly," with page. All names from these case histories are pseudonyms.

6. "Hardly," 147.

7. "Hardly," 145.

8. "Hardly," 145.

9. "Hardly," 146.

10. "Hardly," 149.

11. "Hardly," 147.

12. Robinson, 82–83, 92–93.

13. Sigmund Freud, "First Lecture," *Five Lectures on Psycho-Analysis* (NP: BN Publishing, 2008), 3.

14. Peter Cranford, *But for the Grace of God: Milledgeville! The Inside Story of the World's Largest Insane Asylum* (Atlanta: Georgia Consumer Council, 1998), 58.

15. Cranford, 59, 75.

16. "Conditions at Sanitarium as Reported by Commission," Atlanta *Constitution*, ProQuest Historical Newspapers, Atlanta *Constitution* 1868–1945, August 2, 1909, Cs. Retrieved January 31, 2010.

17. *Sixty-Seventh Annual Report of the Board of Trustees of the Georgia State Sanitarium for the Year Ending December 31, 1910* (Atlanta: Lester Book & Stationary Co. Printers, 1911), 6, 7, 13, 17.

18. Edward Shorter, *A History of Psychiatry: From the Era of the Asylum to the Age of Prozac* (New York: John Wiley & Sons, 1997), 100.

19. Shorter, 106.

20. Michael Shepherd, "Two Faces of Emil Kraepelin," *British Journal of Psychiatry* 167, no 2 (1995): 114, 178.

21. Emil Kraepelin, Verbrechen als soziale Krankheit. Monatschrift K/S, 258–65, quoted in Shepherd, 179.

22. Shorter, 109–12.

23. *Forty-Fifth Annual Report for the Georgia Lunatic Asylum for the Year Ending 1888*, 15.

24. *Sixty-Sixth Annual Report of the Board of Trustees of the Georgia State Sanitarium for the Year Ending December 31, 1909*, 50; *Sixty-Seventh Annual Report*, 30–39.

25. For various answers see Case History. VI-2193 026-12-048, pp. 85–98, 106, 145, 215.

26. W.E.B. Du Bois, *The Souls of Black Folk* (Oxford: Oxford University Press, 2008), 54. Also quoted in Sarah Haley, *No Mercy Here: Gender, Punishment, and the Making of Jim Crow Modernity* (Chapel Hill: University of North Carolina Press, 2016), 13; Whitney Battle-Baptiste and Britt Rusert, ed., *W.E.B. Du Bois's Data Portraits Visualizing Black America: The Color Line at the Turn of the Twentieth Century* (New York: Princeton Architectural Press, 2018), the Georgia plates, 1–36.

27. See "Measuring America: The Decennial Censuses from 1790 to 2000" (Washington, DC: U.S. Department of Commerce Economics and Statistics

Administration, April 2002), 47–48, www.census.gov/prod/2002pubs/pol02-ma.pdf, accessed July 26, 2019; it includes census forms and instructions to census workers by decade from 1790, from which race explanations are taken.

28. "Table 2: Insane Enumerated in Hospitals on January 1, 1910, Classified by Race, Nativity, Parentage, and Sex, by Division and States," in *Insane and Feeble-Minded in Institutions 1910* (Washington, DC: Government Printing Office, 1914), 22–23. Numbers in the last column are from the 1910 census cited below.

29. Historical Census Browser, State Level Results for 1910, University of Virginia, Geospatial and Statistical Data Center (2004), http://mapserver.lib .virginia.edu/collections/stats/histcensus/index.html, accessed on July 8, 2013. Nationally, the overall percentage of African Americans institutionalized to total institutionalized was 6.9 percent, whereas in the South it was 29.44 percent. Only Washington, DC (with 648 individuals or 22.4 percent) and Maryland, a borderline and slave state (with 413 or 12.8 percent), had anywhere near equivalent percentages of African American insane patients as the states of the former Confederacy. In comparison, New York, with a much larger population than Georgia, had 701 institutionalized African Americans while Georgia had 979, and overall New York had the most institutionalized insane in the nation, at 31,280 patients. The states with significant Native American populations were South Dakota, with 60 out of the 166 national total of hospitalized insane Indians; and Oklahoma with 32 Indian patients in an institution. In 1903 in Canton, North Dakota, the federal government opened the only insane asylum for Native Americans, known colloquially as the Hiawatha Asylum. The national total of "other colored" patients was 491, among which New York had 33, Texas 29, and California 288—presumably Chinese, Japanese, and Mexican.

30. Edward A. Hartfield, "Segregation," *New Georgia Encyclopedia*, August 17, 2017, accessed April 3, 2018.

31. Robinson, 92.

32. Lillian Smith, *Killers of the Dream*, with a new introduction by Margaret Rose Gladney (New York: WW Norton, 1994), 96.

33. Edwin Black, *War Against the Weak: Eugenics and America's Campaign to Create a Master Race* (Washington, DC: Dialogue Press, 2012), 36–37.

34. Black, 38.

35. Charles Davenport, *Heredity in Relation to Eugenics* (New York: Henry Holt, 1911), 271; Davenport, "Report of Committee on Eugenics," *Report of the American Breeders Association,* 1909: 6:91, 92 quoted in Black, 45.

36. Black, 70–73.

37. Madison Grant, *The Passing of the Great Race or The Racial Basis of European History* (New York: Charles Scribner's Sons, 1916), vii.

38. Manuscripts and Rare Books Library (MARBL), Emory University, Leo Frank Collection, #674, Box 1, "The Ballad of Mary Phagan," stanza 4, Folder 18, Item 2.

39. MARBL Emory University, Leo Frank Collection, #674, Box 1, Folder 1, "Sentence Commutation Hearing Transcript, 1915," 30.

40. MARBL, "Sentence Commutation Hearing Transcript, 1915," 11.

41. AR 1910, "Other Constitutional Disorders and Inferiorities," 37.

42. *Sixty-eighth Annual Report of the Board of Trustees of the Georgia State Sanitarium for the Year Ending December 31, 1911* (Savannah: The Morning News, 1911), 47.

43. Steve Oney, *And the Dead Shall Rise: The Murder of Mary Phagan and the Lynching of Leo Frank* (New York: Vintage, 2003), 72–79, 242–43.

44. Oney, 513–28, 520; See also Oney's "A Hole in the Heart of Georgia," *The Bitter Southerner*, bittersoutherner.com/from-the-southern-perspective/miscellany/a-hole-in-the-heart-of-georgia-state-prison-farm-demolition.

45. Clayton Hampton, OIT- Data Management, "History of the Death Penalty in Georgia: Executions by Year, 1924–2019," 1, 4–7.

46. Quoted in Oney, *And the Dead Shall Rise*, 575.

47. Robinson, 108.

48. Robinson, 107–8.

49. John Hope Franklin, "The Birth of a Nation: Propaganda as History," *Massachusetts Review*, 20, no. 3 (Autumn 1979): quotes on p. 430.

50. Robinson, 103, 108.

51. Simmons quoted in Oney, 607.

52. Robinson, 103.

53. Edward J. Larson, *Sex, Race, and Science: Eugenics in the Deep South* (Baltimore: Johns Hopkins Press, 1995), 45.

54. R.C. Smith [R.C. Swint], "Some Facts Concerning the Etiology of Insanity Based on a Study of the Admissions to the Georgia State Sanitarium during the year 1912," *Journal of the Medical Association of Georgia* 3 (1913): 148, quoted in Larson, 45–46.

55. C.E. Williams, "Care and Treatment of the Patients at the State Hospital for the Insane," *Journal of South Carolina Medical Association* 12 (1916): 119, quoted in Larson, 46.

56. Thos. H. Haines, "Preventative Medicine as Applied to Mental Deficiency in Mississippi," *Transactions of MSMA* (1919): 138, as quoted in Larson, 63.

57. W.B. Hardman, "The Medical Gospel of the Twentieth Century, " *Journal of Medical Association of Georgia* 4 (1914): 72–73.

58. See *Georgia Commission on Feeblemindedness, Report* (Atlanta: Byrd, 1919). It was reprinted as "Mental Defect in a Southern State," *Mental Hygiene* 3 (1919): 527–65; and in *GA House Journal* (1919 Reg. Sess.), 203–64. See Larson, 68–71. See also Stephen Michael Smith, "Eugenic Sterilization in 20th Century Georgia: From Progressive Utilitarianism to Individual Rights" (2010), Electronic Theses & Dissertations, 594, https://digitalcommons.georgiasouthern.edu/etd/594.

CHAPTER 15

1. Saidiya Hartman, *Scenes of Subjection: Terror, Slavery, and Self-Making in Nineteenth Century America* (New York: Oxford University Press, 1997), 8.

2. Central State Hospital Medical Case Records February 1909–November 1926, Public Health Central State Hospital, RG-SG-S 26-12-048, Vol 1-2193 (April 1909–August 1912), Georgia Archives. "Abraham Lincoln Jones" is pp. 85–99.

3. Jones, Case History, "Mental Examination May 12, 1910," quotes pp. 85–86.

4. Jones, Case History, "Intake Form," April 28, 1910. NP.

5. Jones, Case History, 85.

6. Jones, Case History, "Mental Summary Sheet," 97.

7. Jones, Case History, "Mental Examination," 93–94.

8. Jones, Case History, 88.

9. Jones, Case History, 88–89.

10. Jones, Case History, 88–89.

11. Jones, Case History, 90.

12. Jones, Case History, 91–92.

13. Jones, Case History, 89.

14. Emil Kraepelin and A. Ross Diefendorf, *Clinical Psychiatry: A Textbook for Students and Physicians*, abstracted and adapted by Diefendorf from the seventh German edition of Kraepelin's *Lehrbuch Der Psychiatrie* (New York: Macmillan Company, 1912), 5, 55.

15. Jones, Case History, 89–90.

16. "Define Signifying," Ask/Define, https://signifying.askdefine.com/.

17. Michel Foucault, *Psychiatric Power: Lectures at the Collège de France 1973–1974* (New York: Picador, 2003), 27.

18. Jean-Francois Lyotard, *The Postmodern Condition: A Report on Knowledge* (Manchester, U.K.: Manchester University Press, 1984), 89 n25, n34; quoted in Susan Stryker, "(De)Subjugated Knowledges: An Introduction to Transgender Studies," in *The Transgender Studies Read*, ed. Susan Stryker and Stephen Whittle (New York: Routledge, 2006), 11.

19. Jones, Case History, "Autopsy No. 584," NP.

20. Peter Cranford, *But for the Grace of God: Milledgeville! The Inside Story of the World's Largest Insane Asylum* (Atlanta: Georgia Consumer Council, 1998), 59.

21. "Cures Against Syphilis Through History," www.academia.dk/Blog/syphilis/.

22. Cranford, 63.

23. Kumaravel Rajakumar, *Southern Medical Journal* 93, no. 3 (2000), posted March 10, 2000 on www.Medscape.com/viewerarticle/410909; retrieved January 11, 2010.

24. See "Society proceedings, conference on pellagra," *Journal of the American Medical Association* 1909: 53, 1659–70; see also E.W. Etheridge, *The Butterfly Caste: A Social History of Pellagra in the South* (Westport, CT: Greenwood Publishing Co., 1972), and

Alan M. Kraut, *Goldberger's War: The Life and Work of a Public Health Crusader* (New York: Hill and Wang, 2003). See also Charles S. Bryan, *Asylum Doctor: James Woods Babcock and the Red Plague of Pellagra* (Columbia: University of South Carolina Press, 2014).

25. The description of the dining hall is from Etheridge, 72–73, 74. This is still the best book on the Public Health Service pellagra campaign. Also see Kraut, *Goldberger's War*.

26. Cranford, 57.

27. Cranford, 65.

28. Goldberger, "The Prevention of Pellagra. A Test of Diet Among Institutional Inmates," *Public Health Report* 30, no. 43 (October 22, 1915): 35.

29. Joseph Goldberger, "The Etiology of Pellagra. The Significance of Certain Epidemiological Observations with Respect Thereto," *Public Health Report* 29, no. 26 (June 26, 1914), 1683–86. In *Goldberger on Pellagra*, ed. Milton Terris (Baton Rouge: Louisiana State University Press, 1864), 20–21; well-to-do also noted, 29.

30. Goldberger, 1915, 29.

31. Etheridge, 63.

32. Goldberger, 1915, 35–36.

33. Goldberger, 1915, 37.

34. Goldberger, 1915, 37.

35. Goldberger, 1915, 43.

36. Joseph Goldberger to Mary Farr Goldberger, June 20, 1915, Jackson, MS. Folder 17, January to July 1915, in the Joseph Goldberger Papers, #1641, Southern Historical Collection, the Wilson Library, University of North Carolina at Chapel Hill.

37. Goldberger, 1915, 43.

38. Emil Kraepelin, "Psychiatrische Randbemerkungen zur Zeitgeschichte," *Suddeutsche Monatshefte*, 16, no. 2 (1919): 176–79, quoted in Eric J. Engstrom, "Emil Kraepelin: Psychiatry and Public Affairs in Wilhelmine Germany," *History of Psychiatry*, 2, no. 6 (1991): 130.

39. Edgar Sydenstricker, "The Prevalence of Pellagra. Its Possible Relation to the Rise in Cost of Food," *Goldberger on Pellagra*, 121–23; reprinted from *Public Health Report* 30, no. 43 (October 22, 1915), 3132–48.

40. Joseph Goldberger, G.A. Wheeler, Edgar Sydenstricker, "A Study of the Relation of Diet to Pellagra Incidence in Seven Textile-Mill Communities of South Carolina in 1916," in *Goldberger on Pellagra*, 128; reprinted from *Public Health Report*, 35, no. 12, March 19, 1920), 648–713.

41. Harry M. Marks, "Epidemiologists Explain Pellagra: Gender, Race, and Political Economy in the Work of Edgar Sydenstricker," *Journal of the History of Medicine and Allied Sciences* 58, no. 1 (January 2003): 35, 46.

42. Marks, 35.

43. Emil Kraepelin, 1922, "Psychiatric Observations on Contemporary Issues," quoted in Michael Shepherd, "Two Faces of Emil Kraepelin," *British Journal of Psychiatry* 167 (1995): 181.

CHAPTER 16

1. Molly McCully Brown, "The Central Virginia Training Center (Formerly Known as the Virginia State Colony for Epileptics and Feeblemided," in *The Virginia State Colony for Epileptics and Feebleminded: Poems* (New York: Persea Books, 2017), 4. https://poetry.lib.uidaho.edu/category/molly-mccully-brown/.

2. "Dora Williams" (pseudonym), Central State Hospital Medical Case Records, February 1909–November 1926, Public Health Central State Hospital, RG-SG-26-12-048, Vol. 2193, April to August 1912, 135. All information comes either from this page or from the Intake Form.

3. Steve Silberman, *Neurotribes: The Legacy of Autism and the Future of NeuroDiversity* (New York: Penguin, 2015).

4. James Trent, *Inventing the Feeble Mind: A History of Mental Retardation in the United States* (Berkeley: University of California Press, 1994), 5.

5. Madison Grant, *The Passing of the Great Race or The Racial Basis of European History* (New York: Charles Scribner's Sons, 1916).

6. Williams, Case History, 135.

7. Georgia State Department of Public Welfare, *Georgia's Fight Against Dependency and Delinquency*, 1, quoted in Stephen Noll, *Feeble-Minded in Our Midst: Institutions for the Mentally Retarded in the South, 1900–1940* (Chapel Hill: University of North Carolina Press, 1995), 5.

8. Mamie Bonner, Central State Hospital Medical Case Histories Vol 27, p. 259, #22, 731. Those census records put her age at thirty-seven in 1912. One of the records probably misnumbered her age.

9. "Kindergarten Aids Unfortunate Children at State Sanitarium/Inmate in State Sanitarium Starts Special Class for Feeble Minded Children. Authorities Want to Make Kindergarten Permanent," Atlanta *Constitution*, June 25, 1916; ProQuest Historical Newspapers Atlanta *Constitution* (1868–1945), p. B8.

10. Stephen Noll and James Trent, eds., *Mental Retardation in America: An Historical Reader* (New York: New York University Press, 2004), 1–2.

11. William B. Fish, "A Thesis on Idiocy," in Noll and Trent, 37.

12. *Olmstead v. L.C.*, 527 U.S. 581 (1999).

13. Noll, 30.

14. Henry H. Goddard, *The Kallikak Family: A Study in the Heredity of Feeble-Mindedness* (Vineland, NJ: 1913), 53, quoted in Edwin Black, *War Against the Weak: Eugenics and America's Campaign to Create a Master Race* (Washington, DC: Dialogue Press, 2012), 76.

15. Noll, 29. See Henry H. Goddard, "Four Hundred Feeble-Minded Children Classified by the Binet Method," 29, for coining of "moron" for ages seven to twelve. See also "Report on the Committee on Classification of the Feeble-Minded" and "The New Classification (Tentative) of the Feeble Minded" in Noll and Trent.

16. Noll, 3.

17. Black, 75.

18. Noll, 30–31.

19. Quoted in Black, 78.

20. Quoted in Black, 123, from E. Carlton MacDowell, "Charles Benedict Davenport, 1866–1944. A Study of Conflicting Influences," BIOS XVII, no. 1: 30. LYRICS: https://meetmythamerica.wordpress.com/2014/07/28/the-new-mount-sinai/.

21. Noll, 32–33; Lippmann in Clarence Karier, *Shaping the American Educational State, 1900 to the Present* (New York: Free Press, 1974), 282–316.

22. Quoted in Noll, 40, FN 63.

23. Quoted in Noll, 40, FN 63.

24. Quoted in Black, 102, "Where to Begin," San Francisco *Daily News*, October 14, 1915.

25. Noll, 128.

26. Georgia State Department for Public Welfare, Georgia's Progress in Social Welfare, p. 53, quoted in Noll, 141.

27. Annual Report of the Georgia Training School for Mental Defectives, 1939, quoted in Noll 134, 136.

28. Adam Cohen, *Imbeciles: The Supreme Court, American Eugenics, and the Sterilization of Carrie Buck* (New York: Penguin, 2016), 15–35; see Black, 108–17, for Carrie Buck's story.

29. Black, 109; see also J. David Smith and K. Ray Nelson, *The Sterilization of Carrie Buck* (Far Hills, NJ: New Horizon Press, 1989), 17–18.

30. Cohen, 24–25; see also Black, 113.

31. Black, 113.

32. Black's language, 114.

33. Quoted in Black 114–15; see also Letter, A.S. Priddy to J.S. DeJarnette, November 1, 1924: Carrie Buck File, Central Virginia Training Center Archives.

34. Black, 117.

35. Quoted in Cohen, 222. See "Holmes," Cohen, 251–82.

36. See Black, 119–20, and Cohen, 225. Herbert Spencer, *Principles of Biology* (London: Williams and Norgate, 1864), Vol. 1, p. 444. Available as e-book from books.google.com.

37. "Syllabus," *Giles v. Harris*, 189 U.S. 475 (1903) No. 493, Submitted February 24, 1903, Decided April 27, 1903, 189 U.S. 475, 189.

38. *Giles v. Harris*, 189.

39. *Giles v. Harris*, 189.

40. Harlan's dissent, *Giles v. Harris*, 189.

41. Angela Davis, *Women, Race, and Class* (New York: Vintage, 1983), 210–13, quotes 210 and 213.

42. Lotrop Stoddard, *The Rising Tide of Color Against White World-Supremacy* (New York: Charles Scribner's Sons, 1921). See Davis, 214.

43. Davis, 214.

44. *Buck v. Bell* 274 US 200 (1927) No. 292, Argued April 22, 1927, Decided May 2, 1927. Page 274 US 208.

45. Black, 122, 123.

46. Davis, 217, 218, 219.

47. Cohen, 297.

CHAPTER 17

1. "Mary Roberts," Central State Hospital Medical Case Records Feb. 1909–Nov. 1926, Public Health Central State Hospital, RG-SG-S 26-12-048, Vol 1-2193 (April 1909–August 1912), Georgia Archives. The case for "Mary Roberts" (a pseudonym) is pages 245–57, this section 245, 248.

2. Mary Roberts, Case History, 250.

3. Mary Roberts, Case History, 250, 254.

4. Mary Roberts, Case History, 251.

5. Mary Roberts, Case History, 250–51.

6. Mary Roberts, Case History, 245–46, 248, 249, 252–53.

7. Roberts is a pseudonym. Using her real name on Ancestry, I obtained information about her family. Year: 1900; Census Place: Millwood, War, Georgia; Roll T623_227; Page: 5B. I have not used the names of her children or her mother for purposes of confidentiality.

8. Mary Roberts, Case History, 247–49.

9. Mary Roberts, Case History, 248, 249.

10. Mary Roberts, Case History, 249, 253.

11. CH, 255; for information on speech acts, see John L. Austin, *How to Do Things with Words* (Oxford: Oxford University Press, 1970); John R. Searles, *Speech Acts: An Essay in the Philosophy of Language* (Cambridge, MA: Cambridge University Press, 1969).

12. Emil Kraepelin and A. Ross Diefendorf, *Clinical Psychiatry: A Textbook for Students and Physicians*, 381–82.

13. Kraepelin and Diefendorf, *Clinical Psychiatry*, 304, 384, 386, 388, 389, 390–93, 395, 400, 409.

14. Mary Roberts, "Diagnosis," Case History, 254.

15. Mary Roberts, Case History, 256–57.

16. Mary A.H. Gay, *Life in Dixie During the War*, ed. J.H. Segars (Macon, GA: Mercer University Press, 2001); originally published 1882.

17. For a fuller treatment of O'Connor and the Milledgeville State Hospital, see my "The Milledgeville Asylum and the Georgia Surreal," *Southern Quarterly* (Spring 2011): 114–50.

18. Alice Walker, "In Search of Our Mothers' Gardens," in *In Search of Our Mothers' Gardens: Womanist Prose*, by Alice Walker (New York: Harcourt, 1983), 232, 233.

19. Edward Shorter, *A History of Psychiatry: From the Era of the Asylum to the Age of Prozac* (New York: John Wiley & Sons, 1997), 107.

20. Harriet Washington, *Medical Apartheid: The Dark History of Medical Experimentation on Americans from Colonial Times to the Present* (New York: Harlem Moon, 2006), 48.

21. Erskine Clarke, *Dwelling Place: A Plantation Epic* (New Haven, CT: Yale University Press, 2005), 160–61.

22. Quoted in Savannah Unit Georgia Writers' Project, Work Projects Administration, *Drums and Shadows: Survival Studies Among the Georgia Coastal Negroes* (Athens: University of Georgia Press, 1940; reprint 1986), 154.

23. Althea Sumpter, "Geechee and Gullah Culture," *New Georgia Encyclopedia*, August 21, 2013, accessed October 23, 2013.

24. Kraepelin and Diefendorf, 419–22.

25. "About Zora Neale Hurston," http://zoranealehurston.com/about/, April 30, 2018.

26. Dr. E.M. Green, "Manic-Depressive Psychosis in the Negro," *American Journal of Insanity* 72 (April 1916): 619–20, 621.

27. Green, 626.

28. www.cartercenter.org/health/mental_health/symposium/archived-webcast-presentations.html.

29. Michael Shepherd, "Two Faces of Emil Kraepelin," *British Journal of Psychiatry* (1995) 167: 180. In 2015, Doctors Rael D. Strous, Annette A. Opler, and Louis A. Opler (variously from the Beer Yaakov Mental Health Center in Tel Aviv, the PANSS Institute in New York, and the Clinical Psychology Doctoral Program at Long Island University) would assess the meaning of Kraepelin's contribution to Nazi extermination in a letter to the *American Journal of Psychiatry* in response to an article "Emil Kraepelin: Icon and Reality." The earlier article's authors Engstrom and Kendler examined Kraepelin's resurgence "in the last third of the 20th century [when he] . . . became an icon of post-psychoanalytic medical-model psychiatry in the United States . . . his name synonymous with a proto-biological, antipsychological, brain-based, and hard-nosed nosologic approach to psychiatry."

30. Ann Cvetkovich, "Depression Is Ordinary: Public Feelings and Saidiya Hartman's *Lose Your Mother*," *Feminist Theory* 13, no. 2: 131–46.

31. Edward Beardsley, *A History of Neglect: Health Care for Blacks and Mill Workers in the Twentieth Century South* (Knoxville: University of Tennessee, 1987), 15–16.

32. Frazier quoted in Beardsley, 137.

33. Beardsley, 163–65.

34. Linda Villarosa, "Why Black Mothers and Babies Are in a Life-or-Death Crisis: The answer to the disparity in death rates has everything to do with the lived experience of being a black woman in America," *The New York Times Magazine*, April 11, 2018.

35. Villarosa, 6.

36. Michael Haynes, "Fertility and Mortality in the United States." E.H. Net Encyclopedia, edited by Robert Whaples. March 19, 2008. http://eh.net/encyclopedia/fertility-and-mortality-in-the-united-states, accessed on 7/9/2019.

37. Maternal Mortality Weekly Report (MMWR): Achievements in Public Health 1900–1999: Healthier Mothers and Babies October 1, 1999 48(38); 849–858 www.cdc.gov/mmwr/preview/mmwrhtml/mm4838a2.htm, accessed on 7/9/2019.

38. OECD (2019), Infant mortality rates (indicator). doi: 10.1787/83dea506-en https://data.oecd.org/healthstat/infant-mortality-rates.htm, accessed on 7/9/2019.

39. United Health Foundation (2019) "America's Health Rankings" 2018 Annual Report www.americashealthrankings.org/learn/reports/2018-annual-report/findings -international-comparison, accessed on 7/9/2019.

40. Villarosa, 6–7.

41. Villarosa, 8.

42. Arline Geronimus, "The weathering hypothesis and the health of African-American women and infants: evidence and speculations," *Ethnicity and Disease* 2, no.3 (1992): 207–21.

43. *The Language You Cry In*, dir. and prod. Alvaro Toepke and Angel Serrano, writ. Alvaro Toepke ([Sierra Leone]: Inko Producciones, 1998), video.

44. The first line is from Erskine Clark's description of the ring shout, and is a kind of supplication for the day the angels come to lift them up and away. The second line is a quote from a Georgia Writers Project interview. African American critics like Saidiya Hartman have critiqued these interviews and their transcriptions of the speech of the Black people being interviewed, but have also appreciated having the material. I would translate these sentences into "standard English," although to me it has much less power than the expressive forms provided in the text: "All of a sudden they get together and start to move around in a range. Round they go faster and faster. Then one by one they rise up and take wing and fly like a bird."

EPILOGUE

1. "The Souls of White Folk," in *Darkwater: Voices from Within the Veil* (New York: Harcourt, Brace and Company, 1920), available from the Internet Archive https:// medium.com/religion-bites/the-souls-of-white-folk-by-w-e-b-du-bois -354f91ca08ef, page 15.

2. Ethan Watters, *Crazy Like Us: The Globalization of the American Psyche* (New York: Free Press, 2010), 2.

3. Watters, 3.

4. Watters, 3.

5. W.E.Burghardt Du Bois, "The Souls of White Folk," *Independent*, vol. LXIX (August 18, 1910), 342.

6. Quoted in William Anderson, *The Wild Man From Sugar Creek: The Political Career of Eugene Talmadge* (Baton Rouge: LSU Press, 1975), 120.

7. Thomas Borstelmann, *The Cold War and the Color Line: American Race Relations in the Global Arena* (Cambridge, MA: Harvard University Press, 2001), 27–28.

8. Supt. R.C. Swint, "Report to Honorable Board of Control, State Eleemosynary Institutions", April 10, 1933, pp. 1, 2, 5.

9. Supt. John W. Oden to Dr. C.J. Wellborn, Director, Division of Institutions State Department of Public Welfare, July 1, 1933, 14.

10. Lamar Q Ball, "350 Will Be Sent to Fulton County by Milledgeville," *Atlanta Constitution*, May 7, 1939, p. 1.

11. Ball, "350 Will Be . . ."

12. Lamar Q. Ball, "Fulton Commission Refuses 2 Returned by Milledgeville," Atlanta *Constitution*, May 16, 1939, 1.

13. "Insane Patients May Be Swapped," Atlanta *Constitution*, July 14, 1939, page 5.

14. Stephen Michael Smith. "Eugenic Sterilization in 20th Century Georgia: From Progressive Utilitarianism to Individual Rights." A thesis submitted to the Graduate Faculty of Georgia Southern University in Partial Fulfillment of the Requirements for the Degree of Master of Arts, Statesboro, Georgia 2010, abstract.

15. Hugh Gregory Gallagher, *By Trust Betrayed: Patients, Physicians, and the License to Kill in the Third Reich* (Arlington, VA: Vandaere Press, 1995), 85.

16. Gallagher, 86–87.

17. Doctors Rael D. Stroud, Annette A. Opler, and Louis A. Opler (variously from the Beer Yaakov Mental Health Center in Tel Aviv, the PANSS Institute in New York, and the Clinical Psychology Doctoral Program at Long Island University) wrote in response to an article "Emil Kraepelin: Icon and Reality." Its authors, Eric J. Engstrom and Kenneth Kendler, examined Kraepelin's resurgence "in the last third of the 20th century [when he] . . . became an icon of post-psychoanalytic medical-model psychiatry in the United States . . . his name synonymous with a proto-biological, antipsychological, brain-based, and hard-nosed nosologic approach to psychiatry." Eric J. Engstrom, Kenneth Kendler, "Emil Kraepelin: Icon and Reality," *American Journal of Psychiatry* 172, no. 12 (December 2015): 1190–196, quoted on p. 1190. Rael D. Stroud, Annette A. Opler, and Louis A. Opler, "A Focus on Kraepelin's Clinical Research Methodology," *American Journal of Psychiatry* 173, no. 3 (March 2016): 300–301. Kendler and Engstrom answered in the same issue, 301–2.

18. Supt. L.P. Longino, Milledgeville State Hospital, August 5, 1942, 4.

19. Supt. W.H. Yarbrough, Milledgeville State Hospital, AR July 1, 1946, 1, 3; AR June 30, 1947, 1, 3; AR June 30, 1948, 4.

20. Peter Cranford, *But for the Grace of God: Milledgeville! The Inside Story of the World's Largest Insane Asylum* (Atlanta: Georgia Consumer Council, 1998), 87.

21. Alex Sareyan, *The Turning Point: How Men of Conscience Brought About Major Change in the Care of America's Mentally Ill* (Washington, DC: American Psychiatric Press, 1994).

22. Jack El-Hai, *The Lobotomist: A Maverick Medical Genius and His Tragic Quest to Rid the World of Mental Illness* (New York: Wiley, 2007).

23. Letter from Dr. T.G. Peacock, Superintendent, Milledgeville State Hospital, to T.B. Peacock, MD. Chairman and Secretary of the State Board of Eugenics, Alan Kemper, Director, State Welfare Dept, and T.F. Sellers, M.D. Director, State Health

Department, June 14, 1950. Provided by Amy D'Unger from redacted records of the Georgia Eugenics Commission housed at the Georgia Archives.

24. Stephen Michael Smith, "Eugenic Sterilization in 20th Century Georgia: From Progressive Utilitarianism to Individual Rights" (2010). Electronic Theses and Dissertations. 594. https://digitalcommons.georgiasouthern.edu/etd/594.

25. *One Hundred Seventh Annual Report of the Milledgeville State Hospital at Milledgeville, Georgia for the Year Ending June 30, 1950.* Hereafter "1950 AR."

26. 1950 AR, 128.

27. 1950 AR, 133.

28. 1950 AR, 126.

29. 1950 AR, 123.

30. 1950 AR, 143–44.

31. "Injuries and Accident Causes in the Slaughtering and Meat-Packing Industry, 1943," Bulletin No. 855 of the United States Bureau of Labor Statistics, 6; reprinted in the *Monthly Labor Review*, November–December 1945. https://fraser.stlouisfed.org /files/docs/publications/bls/bls_0855_1946.pdf.

32. "Injuries and Accident Causes," 13.

33. Michael Lebwohl, "A Call to Action: Psychological Harm in Slaughterhouse Workers," *Yale Global Health Review*, January 25, 2016: 1, 2. https://yaleglobalhealth review.com/2016/01/25/a-call-to-action-psychological-harm-in-slaughterhouse -workers/.

34. Lebwohl, 4.

35. James C. Bonner, *Milledgeville: Georgia's Antebellum Capital* (Milledgeville, GA: Old Capital Press, 2007), 123.

36. E.g., total income for 1950 $7,263,966, and medical expenses $1,484,416.

37. 1950 AR, 133.

38. Albert Deutsch, *The Shame of the States* (New York: Harcourt, 1948), 39.

39. Robert Whitaker, *Mad in America: Bad Science, Bad Medicine, and the Enduring Mistreatment of the Mentally Ill* (New York: Basic Books, 2002). See pages 141–47.

40. Whitaker, 145.

41. Whitaker, 155.

42. Whitaker, 149.

43. President John F. Kennedy, News Conference, March 6, 1963. YouTube. www .youtube.com/watch?v=4yhSzjmNjjI.

44. See "Community Mental Health Act," National Council for Behavioral Health, www.thenationalcouncil.org/about/national-mental-health-association/overview /community-mental-health-act/.

45. "Unapproved Drugs Given Mental Cases," Atlanta *Constitution*, March 5, 1959.

46. "Alcohol, Drug History Is Found in 25 Pct. of State Hospital Doctors; Physicians Seen Under Influence," Atlanta *Constitution*, March 6, 1959.

47. "Milledgeville Data Is 'Must' Reading," Atlanta *Constitution*, April 27, 1959.

48. "MAG Gives Full Okay to Report; Rejects Attempt to Black Press," Atlanta *Constitution*, May 21, 1959; "Dr. Gibson, 7 Others Quit Staff," Atlanta *Constitution*, nd.

49. Biographical note, "S. Ernest Vandiver Papers," University of Georgia Special Collections, Russell Library, University of Georgia, Athens, http://russelldoc.galib.uga.edu/russell/view?docId=ead/RBRL186SEV-ead.xml.

50. Harold Paulk Kenderson, *Ernest Vandiver: Governor of Georgia* (Athens: University of Georgia, 2000), 180–81.

51. *Wyatt v. Stickney*, 325 F.Supp. 781 (M.D. Ala. 1971), https://disabilityjustice.org/wyatt-v-stickney/.

52. See, for example, Jack Drescher, "Out of DSM: Depathologizing Homosexuality," *Behavioral Science* 5, no.4 (December 2015): 565–75. Published online December 4, 2015, doi: 10.3390/bs5040565.

53. "Introduction," *Madness Network News Reader* (San Francisco: Glide Publications, 1974), 11.

54. Pat Deegan, "Recovery as a Journey of the Heart," *Psychiatric Rehabilitation Journal* 19, no. 3 (1965): 96–97, http://dx.doi.org/10.1037/h0101301.

55. Jimmy Carter, *An Hour Before Daylight: Memoirs of a Rural Boyhood* (New York: Simon and Schuster, 2001), 143.

56. For an insider's account of how Carter's political ambitions played out, see Peter G. Bourne, *Jimmy Carter: A Comprehensive Biography from Plains to Postpresidency* (New York: Scribner, 1997); for discussion on mental health, see pp. 134, 208, 260, 378–79. An MD and member of the Emory faculty, Bourne worked with Mrs. Carter on her mental health initiative then served as assistant to the president in the White House and then as assistant secretary-general at the United Nations.

57. Rosalynn Carter, *First Lady from Plains* (New York: Fawcett, 1984), 91.

58. R. Carter, 92.

59. R. Carter, 258.

60. R. Carter, 259.

61. R. Carter, 265.

62. Anne E. Parsons, *From Asylum to Prison: Deinstitutionalization and the Rise of Mass Incarceration After 1945* (Chapel Hill: University of North Carolina Press, 2018), 4–5.

63. Parsons, 9.

64. "transinstitutionalization," A Dictionary of Sociology, Encyclopedia.com. (August 31, 2019), www.encyclopedia.com/social-sciences/dictionaries-thesauruses-pictures-and-press-releases/transinstitutionalization.

65. "Project on the Decade of the Brain," https://www.loc.gov/loc/brain/.

66. Irving Kirsch et al., "Emperor's New Drugs: An Analysis of Antidepressants Medication Data Submitted to the U.S. Food and Drug Administration," *Prevention and Treatment* 5, no 1 (July 2002), doi.org/10.1037/1522-3736.5.1.523a. Also, Irving Kirsch, "Antidepressants and Placebo Effect," *Zeitschrift für Psychologie* 222, no. 3 (2014): 128–34.

67. Anne Harrington, "False Dawns," in *The Mind Fixers: Psychiatry's Troubled Search for the Biology of Mental Illness* (New York: Norton, 2019), 264.

68. Harrington, 250.

69. Harrington, 252.

70. Harriet Fraud, "Profiting from Mental Health," *The Guardian*, March 11, 2011.

71. Steven Hyman to Harrington, May 2, 2018, quoted in Harrington, 266.

72. Harrington, 266.

73. Rosalynn Carter with Susan K. Golant, *Helping Someone with Mental Illness* (New York: Three Rivers Press, 1999), 121.

74. Rosalynn Carter with Susan K. Golant and Kathryn E. Cade, *Within Our Reach: Ending the Mental Health Crisis* (New York: Rodale, 2010), 141.

75. R. Carter, *Helping*, 127.

76. R. Carter, *Within Our Reach*, 100.

77. 28 CFR § 35.130(d), www.law.cornell.edu/supct/html/98-536.ZS.html.

78. Harrington, 267.

79. Nancy Andreasen, "DSM and the Death of Phenomenology in America: An Example of Unintended Consequences," *Schizophrenia Bulletin* 33, no. 1 (January 1, 2007): 108–12, doi.org/10.1093/scgbyk.sbl054; Harrington, 268.

80. Rosalynn Carter, "Opening Remarks at 'Widening the Circle of Health and Wellness,'" Carter Center 2016 Symposium, November 17–18, 2016, www.cartercenter .org/health/mental_health/symposium/index.html.

81. Tom Insel, "Understanding Mental Disorders as Circuit Disorders," National Institute of Mental Health, 2010, quoted in Harrington, 267.

82. Allen Frances, "Whither DSM-V?" *British Journal of Psychiatry* 195, no. 5 (November 1, 2009): 391–92, esp. 391. Allen J. Frances, "DSM 5 Is Guide Not Bible— Ignore Its Ten Worst Changes" (blogpost), *Psychology Today*, December 2, 2012. Frances went on to write *Saving Normal: An Insider's Revolt against Out-of-Control Psychiatric Diagnosis, DSM-5, Big Pharma, and the Medicalization of Ordinary Life* (New York: William Morrow, 2014); and *Twilight of American Sanity: A Psychiatrist Analyzes the Age of Trump* (New York: William Morrow, 2017).

83. Tom Insel, "Transforming Diagnosis," *NIMH Director's blog Posts from 2013* (blog), April 29, 2013.

84. Hyman quoted in Harrington from personal interview, November 24, 2010.

85. R. Carter, *Within Our Reach*, 152, 153.

86. Larry Fricks, Appalachian Consulting Group, Cleveland, Georgia, http:// acgpeersupport.com/contact/.

87. Chairman's Letter, "The GEO Group Opens Riverbend Facility in Milledgeville, Georgia," Quarter 1, 201, www.geogroup.com/userfiles/18137ea6-ca5a-4b0d-a6d4 -1ec7f72204f6.pdf.

88. Marcia Heroux Pounds, "Geo Awarded Two Federal Contracts Worth $664 Million," *Sun Sentinel*, May 26, 2017, www.sun-sentinel.com/business/fl-bz-geo-federal -prison-renewals-20170526-story.html.

89. "Private Prisons," Southern Center for Human Rights, www.schr.org/our-work /prisons-jails/private-prisons.

90. Taylor Hembree, "Mental Health Crisis: Georgia Ranks 47th in Mental Health Care Access," *Union Recorder*, June 4, 2019.

91. "Georgia's Invisible Epidemic: Poor and Mentally Ill.," Atlanta *Journal-Constitution*, September 21, 2015.

92. "Georgia's Invisible Epidemic."

93. Bill Rankin, "Lawsuit: Conditions Horrific for Women at the South Fulton County Jail," Atlanta *Journal-Constitution*, April 10, 2019.

94. *Georgia Advocacy Office et al. v. Jackson et al.* (1:19-CV-01634), filed April 10, 2019.

95. *Georgia Advocacy Office et al. v. Jackson*, 15. Each year between 2012 and 2016, approximately 32,000 people are booked into the Fulton County jail system, which averaged 2,800 people per day from 2005 to 2014.

96. Fulton County Justice and Mental Health Task Force, Final Report 29 (2017).

97. Super. Ct of Fulton City, Accountability Courts—Behavioral Health Treatment Court, available at www.fultoncourt.org/accountabilityacc-bhte.php, last visited March 10, 2019.

98. *Georgia Advocacy Office et al.*, 4.

99. *Georgia Advocacy Office et al.*, 6.

100. David Huddleston, "Atlanta's mayor signs legislation to shut down city's jail, plans to repurpose it," WSB-TV2, May 28, 2019, 6:53 p.m, www.wsbtv.com/news/local /atlanta/atlanta-mayor-to-sign-legislation-shutting-down-city-s-jail/952983263.

101. R. Carter, *Within Our Reach*, 121.

102. Email communication, Johnny Grant, Georgia College and State University, July 16–18, 2019.

Index

About the Author

Mab Segrest is professor emeritus of gender and women's studies at Connecticut College and the author of *Memoir of a Race Traitor* (The New Press). A longtime activist in social justice movements and a past fellow at the National Humanities Center, she lives in Durham, North Carolina.

Publishing in the Public Interest

Thank you for reading this book published by The New Press. The New Press is a nonprofit, public-interest publisher. New Press books and authors play a crucial role in sparking conversations about the key political and social issues of our day.

We hope you enjoyed this book and that you will stay in touch with The New Press. Here are a few ways to stay up to date with our books, events, and the issues we cover:

- Sign up at www.thenewpress.com/subscribe to receive updates on New Press authors and issues and to be notified about local events
- Like us on Facebook: www.facebook.com/newpressbooks
- Follow us on Twitter: www.twitter.com/thenewpress

Please consider buying New Press books for yourself; for friends and family; or to donate to schools, libraries, community centers, prison libraries, and other organizations involved with the issues our authors write about.

The New Press is a 501(c)(3) nonprofit organization. You can also support our work with a tax-deductible gift by visiting www.thenewpress.com/donate.